D1606377

THE RELIGION OF
CHINA

MAX WEBER

THE RELIGION OF CHINA

CONFUCIANISM AND TAOISM

TRANSLATED AND EDITED BY HANS H. GERTH

WITH AN INTRODUCTION BY C. K. YANG

THE FREE PRESS
A Division of Macmillan Publishing Co., Inc.
New York

Collier Macmillan Publishers
London

CONTENTS

Prefatory Note   ix
Introduction by C. K. Yang   xiii

PART ONE—SOCIOLOGICAL FOUNDATIONS

I. *City, Prince and God*   3

  1. On Chinese Money   3
  2. City and Guild   13
  3. Princely Administration and the Conception of Deity:
     A Comparison with the Middle East   20
  4. The Charismatic and Pontifical Position of the Central
     Monarch   30

II. *The Feudal and Prebendal State*   33

  1. The Hereditary Charismatic Nature of Feudalism   33
  2. The Restoration of the Unified Bureaucratic State   42
  3. Central Government and Local Officialdom   47
  4. Public Charges: the Corvée-State and the Tax-State   50
  5. Officialdom and Tax Collection by Quota Levies   55

III. *Administration and Rural Structure*   63

  1. Feudal and Fiscal Organization   64
  2. Army Organization and Wang An-shih's Attempt at
     Reform   75
  3. The Fiscal Protection of Peasants and Its Results for
     Rural Society   79

IV. *Self-Government, Law, and Capitalism*   84

  1. Absence of Capitalist Relationships   84
  2. The Sib Association   86

» v «

PAGE

3. Organization of the Sib — 88
4. Self-Government of the Chinese Village — 91
5. Sib Fetters of the Economy — 95
6. The Patrimonial Structure of Law — 100

PART TWO—ORTHODOXY

V. *The Literati* — 107

1. Confucius — 113
2. The Development of the Examination System — 115
3. The Typological Position of Confucian Education — 119
4. The Status-Honor of the Literati — 129
5. The Gentleman Ideal — 131
6. The Prestige of Officialdom — 133
7. Views on Economic Policy — 136
8. Sultanism and the Eunuchs as Political Opponents of the Literati — 138

VI. *The Confucian Life Orientation* — 142

1. Bureaucracy and Hierocracy — 142
2. Absence of Natural Law and Formal Logic of Legal Thought — 147
3. Absence of Natural Sciences — 150
4. The Nature of Confucianism — 152
5. Freedom from Metaphysics and Innerworldly Nature of Confucianism — 155
6. The Central Concept of Propriety — 156
7. Piety — 157
8. The Confucian Attitude Toward the Economy and Confucianism's Rejection of the Professional Expert — 159
9. The Gentleman Ideal — 161
10. The Significance of the Classics — 163
11. Historical Development of Orthodoxy — 165
12. The "Pathos" of Early Confucianism — 167
13. The Pacifist Character of Confucianism — 169

PART THREE—TAOISM

VII. *Orthodoxy and Heterodoxy* — 173

1. Doctrine and Ritual in China — 173
2. Anchoretism and Lao-tzu — 178
3. Tao and Mysticism — 179
4. The Practical Consequences of Mysticism — 180

PAGE

5. The Contrast Between the Orthodox and Heterodox
   Schools   181
6. Taoist Macrobiotics   191
7. The Taoist Hierocracy   192
8. The General Position of Buddhism in China   195
9. The Systematic Rationalization of Magic   196
10. The Ethic of Taoism   204
11. The Traditionalist Character of Chinese Orthodox and
    Heterodox Ethics   205
12. Sects and the Persecution of Heresies in China   213
13. The T'ai P'ing Rebellion   219
14. The Result of the Development   224

VIII. *Conclusions: Confucianism and Puritanism*   226

Notes   250

Glossary and Index   298

PREFATORY NOTE

THE PUBLICATION of Max Weber's *Confucianism and Taoism* now makes available to the English reader the entire first volume of Weber's *Collected Essays in the Sociology of Religion*, a work which Professor A. D. Nock has evaluated as "not merely work of great ability, but of genius."[1]

Talcott Parsons has published *The Protestant Ethic and the Spirit of Capitalism* (London, 1930), the essay which sets forth Weber's basic thesis. It has given rise to an entire literature.[2] The essay volume *From Max Weber*, edited by H. H. Gerth and C. Wright Mills, Oxford Press (New York, 1946) includes the companion piece, "The Protestant Sects and the Spirit of Capitalism" and the introductory essay to the present volume. For contextual reasons we took the liberty of substituting the title "The Social Psychology of the World Religions" for the original heading "The Economic Ethic of the World Religions, Comparative Essays in the Sociology of Religion, Introduction." We have named this volume *The Religion of China* in order to avoid the isms. The last essay, "Zwischenbetrachtung," of the German volume, leading over to the study of *Hinduism and Buddhism*, has been published in the aforementioned essays *From Max Weber*.

1. Talcott Parsons, *The Structure of Social Action* (New York and London, 1937), pp. 500 f., footnote 1.
2. Cf. Hans Gerth and Hedwig Ide Gerth, "Bibliography on Max Weber," *Social Research*, vol. 16, no. 1 (March 1949) pp. 70-89.

For our principles of translating Weber we refer the reader to the Preface of the essays. We feel encouraged by Professor Baumgarten who evaluates the English editions to be "in part more readable" than the original text.[*] We hope that the present volume will not fall short of this mark. Possibly we have felt freer than before to drop what in literal translation would seem to be superfluous and redundant words making for overwritten prose in English.

Despite our aim to transpose Weber's thought from one language into another the frequent use of the term sib instead of clan might give the text the flavor of a "translation." By now Baden Powell's usage of the term clan for Far Eastern kinship groups seems to be common usage. A. M. Henderson and Talcott Parsons have honored it in their translation of Weber's *Theory of Social and Economic Organization* (New York, 1947). In spite of the precedent and with great hesitancy we have felt obliged to use the term sib rather than clan for *Sippe* as Weber rejected the "Irish term clan as ambiguous" and used the term sib in a technical sense for "gentile charismatically outstanding agnatic descendants of charismatic chieftains."[4] As the term sib has not become obsolete as yet in sociological literature and Joseph K. Folsom has used it in his *The Family and Democratic Society* (New York, 1943) we prefer it to clan at the risk of deviating from common usage.

Weber was no sinologist and published his study of China without the benefit of a sinologist's revision of his text. As he was no pedant he freely used transliterations from the Chinese as found in English, French, German and Russian romanizations. Naturally this presented some difficulties to us. I am grateful to my sinologically trained colleague, Professor M. L. Barnett, for going over the galley proofs and checking the romanizations of

3. Eduard Baumgarten, "Versuch über die menschlichen Gesellschaften und das Gewissen," *Studium Generale*, vol. 3, no. 10 (September 1950), p. 547.

4. Max Weber, *The Hindu Social System*, tr. by Hans Gerth and Don Martindale, University of Minnesota Sociology Club Bulletin, no. 1 (1950) p. 66. (German text: p. 56, footnote 1.)

Chinese names and phrases. Some fine points were kindly settled by Professor Y. T. Wang.

First draft translations of several chapters have been revised some years ago by Messrs. Joseph Bensman and Bernard Green-blatt. I am grateful for their valuable assistance. Special thanks are due to Dr. Patricke Johns Heine for her careful reading of the manuscript and numerous stylistic improvements. Dr. Hedwig Ide Gerth has rendered valuable assistance throughout.

I am grateful to Professor C. Wright Mills and the publishers, Oxford University Press, New York, for their kind permission to reprint the chapter "The Chinese Literati" of the essay volume *From Max Weber*.

HANS GERTH

Madison, Wisconsin
Spring 1951

INTRODUCTION

Max Weber's *The Religion of China, Confucianism and Taoism,* represents the lone example of systematic characterization of Chinese society and its dominant value system by a great Western intellect of the modern age. Though half of a century of rapid social science development has elapsed since its original publication, the book remains an extremely stimulating work in comparative study of complex social systems and a source of provocative ideas for the study of Chinese society and its pattern of socioeconomic development. In addition, the volume constitutes a part of Weber's enormous scheme of empirical studies which contributed to the establishment of the behavioral trend in the social sciences,[1] and demonstrated the fruitfulness of the comparative approach for testing the validity of sociological hypotheses. Bold indeed was Weber's spirit when we consider the overwhelming complexity of his extensive cross-cultural studies, and his genius becomes apparent if we view the general soundness of his analysis of traditional Chinese society and its dominant values against the background of paucity of scientific field data on China available at the time, a point to which we shall return.

For the general nonprofessional reader, the comprehension of this book may pose some problems. It is the purpose of this introduction to offer some assistance in this direction as far as I understand it, keeping in mind that more than one interpretation is possible with a work of such theoretical complexity and empirical extensiveness as Weber's. Fortunately, there is guidance from such forerunners as Talcott Parsons, Reinhard Bendix, Hans Gerth and others who introduced Max Weber's works into the English-speaking world, and it is important to consult their translations and interpretations. Critical evaluation of the book, while occasionally undertaken, is not the main purpose of this introduction, and this applies especially to the accuracy of the empirical data used, a point for which Weber can hardly be held responsible because of the general shortage of precise information on China in the Western languages at the time.

[1] Talcott Parsons, *The Structure of Social Action,* 2d ed., Free Press of Glencoe, New York, 1961, p. B, hereafter to be cited as *Structure.*

Should a general reader find certain parts of this book hard to follow, it may attributable to several reasons. Partly it may stem from the style of Weber's original writing which even Reinhard Bendix thought to contain "not only long, involved sentences but qualifying phrases and digression." In addition, Bendix cautioned, "[Weber's style] tends to bury the main points of the argument in a jungle of statements that require detailed analysis, or in long analyses of special topics that are not clearly related to either the preceding or the ensuing materials."[2] We may add that Weber's digressions sometimes took the form of sudden shift of time setting in discussions of historical developments. In this connection, the reader is deeply indebted to Hans Gerth whose insight and art of translation have indeed made the present English version " 'in part more readable' than the original text."[3]

1. Wider Thematic Context of the Book

One way which may help us follow Weber's theme in this book is to keep constantly in mind two points: First, Weber's major objective in this volume was to demonstrate that China's failure to develop rational bourgeois capitalism was owing mainly to the absence of a particular kind of religious ethic as the needed motivating force. Second, this study was intended as a support for his major theme that rational bourgeois capitalism developed in Europe because of the unique presence of the ascetic Protestant ethic as the moving spirit. Hence *The Religion of China* cannot be properly understood apart from the wider context of Weber's intellectual endeavors, especially regarding his theory of religious values as independent voluntaristic influences on the nature of socioeconomic development.

Max Weber (1864-1920) lived in a period when the industrial revolution was a fresh, rampaging force which wrought profound changes in the life of Europe and carried the Western civilization to the summit of world power, wealth, and prestige, and it was a period when one of the greatest polemics was on the question of causation of this mighty revolution and the destiny of human society under its inexorable controlling influence. Marxian historical materialism was a dominant theme offering not only an explanation for the origin of this revolution but also a law of its development and decay. It is to be expected that this central issue of an age, the rise of rational bourgeois capitalism and its social, economic, and political implications, did not escape the brilliant

[2] Reinhard Bendix, *Max Weber, An Intellectual Portrait,* Anchor Books, Doubleday & Company, Inc., Garden City, New York, 1962, pp. 6 and xxi, hereafter cited as *Max Weber.*

[3] See Gerth's Prefatory Note, p. x, in the present volume.

searching mind of Weber, who was deeply interested in political as well
as economic issues.[4]

Trained in law and economics, Weber's early work dealt with European economic and legal history and contemporaneous German economic problems.[5] When he investigated the depletion of farm laborers
in east Elbian Germany, he noted that the laborers left the farms not
so much for economic advantage in the Marxian sense as for gaining
freedom from subservience to the arbitrary landlords and for status
improvement. The report made clear Weber's emphasis on the ideal
interest of freedom, instead of materialistic interest, as a motivating influence on the movement of the farm laborers. ". . . Man and so also
the farm laborers do not live 'by bread alone.' "[6]

Some years later, when he wrote his essays that constituted the
famous volume *The Protestant Ethic and The Spirit of Capitalism*,[7]
Weber moved into the center of the issue of the causation of rational
bourgeois capitalism, and offered a forceful alternative interpretation
to the one-sided Marxian materialism: ideas and ideals, instead of
always being reflections of materialistic conditions, can be independent,
voluntaristic forces in initiating socioeconomic change. As *The Religion
of China* volume was intended as a part of the substantiation for this
thesis, it is necessary to review briefly the leading arguments as set forth
in the *Protestant Ethic*.[8]

Weber noted that in the sixteenth and seventeenth centuries, the
period preceding the large-scale development of rational bourgeois capitalism, there was a strong moral climate of Protestant ethic, the nature
of which was very favorable to the development of the "spirit of capitalism," a spirit or a "state of mind" designed to fit the functional
characteristics of the capitalistic economy.[9] Rational bourgeois or industrial capitalism is distinguished from other forms of capitalism by these
leading features: 1. Capitalistic enterprise holds profit-making as its
sole end; profit is the criterion of its success or survival. 2. Profit is pur-

[4] *From Max Weber, Essays in Sociology*, tr. by Hans Gerth and C. Wright
Mills, Galaxy Books, Oxford University Press, Fairlawn, New Jersey, 1958,
pp. 46–50, hereafter cited as *Essays*.
[5] Bendix, *Max Weber*, chapters I and II.
[6] *Verhältnisse der Landarbeiter*, quoted in *ibid.*, p. 23.
[7] Charles Scribner's Sons, New York, 1958, tr. by Talcott Parsons, hereafter
cited as *Protestant Ethic*.
[8] The most useful summary of the *Protestant Ethic* for this purpose is provided by its translator, Talcott Parsons, in his *Structure*, pp. 516–33.
[9] *Protestant Ethic*, pp. 91 ff.; Talcott Parsons, *Structure*, p. 517; Bendix,
Max Weber, pp. 56 ff.

sued by rationality, continuity, moral restraint. 3. The basic labor force is a legally free wage-earning class separated from ownership of means of production. 4. Free labor is rationally organized under bureaucracy, the most efficient pattern of organizing large numbers of people for performing common impersonal functions. 5. It involves modern technical features such as production technology and technical means of exchange and distribution, and the price mechanism in a competitive market.[10]

Associated with these characteristics of the capitalistic economy is a set of values and attitudes that constitutes the "spirit of capitalism" with these leading features: 1. Activities of money acquisition are treated as an end, not as a means to some other end, nor an evil. 2. Gain is pursued without limit as set by either the needs of a standard of living or a traditional sense of contentment. 3. No sacred character is attached to the means and traditional modes of operation; these are subject to alteration and improvement. 4. Hard work is regarded as a duty and a moral obligation. 5. There is an emphasis on discipline and control, on "systematic, continuous rational honest work in the service of economic acquisition."[11]

Among influential Protestant doctrines on the eve of major develop· ment of capitalism, Calvinism was chosen by Weber as an example of the ascetic branches containing traits bearing close affinity to the spirit of capitalism. Calvinism rested on the foundation of predeterminism: the world, its order of things, and the state of grace of every man in it, was created and predetermined solely by God's absolute power which could not "owe anything to [man's] own cooperation or . . . be connected with achievements or qualities of [man's] own faith and will."[12] Furthermore, God stood with "such terrifying majesty that He transcended all human entreaty and comprehension. Before this God, man stood alone."[13] No one, not even the priests or church, could help him; from the "secret places of his heart" he was directly related to God. Man in this situation could only be God's obedient instrument to do His will, to labor for the building of the Kingdom of God on Earth by following a calling.

These Calvinist teachings had implications for practical life highly congruent to the characteristics of capitalistic economy and the spirit of capitalism. The unbridgeable hiatus between God and man turned away any thought of mystical contemplation to achieve union with the

[10] Parsons, *Structure*, pp. 503–507; and Weber, *The Theory of Social and Economic Organization*, tr. by A. M. Henderson and Talcott Parsons, Free Press of Glencoe, Illinois, 1947, pp. 278–79, hereafter cited as *Theory*.

[11] *Protestant Ethic*, pp. 54–67; Bendix, *Max Weber*, pp. 51–55.

[12] *Protestant Ethic*, pp. 99–118; Parsons, *Structure*, pp. 516–33.

[13] Bendix, *Max Weber*, p. 59.

divine, and the injunction to serve God's will on this Earth firmly committed him to an active, ascetic, this-worldly course of action. The world and the order of things in it as God's creation ruled against magic, and encouraged rational understanding of the world as a way to know God. Serving God's will in active asceticism deemphasized indulging in ritualism which could breed passive traditionalism. Calvinist attitude toward economic labor was particularly important for its affinity to the spirit of capitalism. Unceasing work in a calling was first enjoined for each man as a sign of true faith and self-confidence that oneself was among God's chosen. Later, good work and success were interpreted as a sign of grace and salvation, and riches were "commended insofar as they resulted from the performance of duty. Man should not refuse to accept God's gifts and to be His steward: 'You may labor to be rich for God, though not for the flesh and sin.' "[14] The fear of indulging in things of the flesh would discourage luxury consumption and would generate "ascetic compulsion to save."[15]

The Calvinist doctrine did not condone the easy absolution of sin such as in the "Catholic cycle of sin, repentance, atonement, release, followed by renewed sin."[16] The moral conduct of the average man was thus deprived of its planless and unsystematic character. In addition, at least two other Calvinist features tended to produce personality traits which would meet requirements of the bureaucratic organization in modern capitalism. Calvinist commitment of the individual to labor in his workaday life for an impersonal end would cultivate an impersonal attitude toward duties of an office. And the inner isolation of the individual from his fellowmen, including the closest of kin, fostered an individualism which would facilitate rational organization of labor in a competitive setting.[17]

In his *Protestant Ethic*, Weber tried to establish the Protestant ethic as an independent causal factor in the development of modern capitalism by the following steps.[18] First, he demonstrated statistically a higher concentration of Protestants than Catholics in ownership and leadership of capitalistic enterprises and in fields of higher educational training for science, technology, and business. Secondly, by analytic description, he demonstrated the close affinity and mutual congruence between the characteristics of the Protestant ethic and the spirit of capitalism; here,

[14] Baxter's *Christian Directory in Protestant Ethic,* quoted in Bendix, *Max Weber*, p. 62.
[15] *Protestant Ethic*, p. 172.
[16] *Ibid.*, pp. 117–18.
[17] Parsons, *Structure*, pp. 525–26.
[18] *Ibid.*, pp. 511–12.

the large number of points of congruence between the two complex systems of values indicated a strong probability of functional relationship beyond chance coincidence. This assumption was further strengthened by the time sequence in which the Protestant ethic preceded the general development of both the spirit of capitalism and the actual capitalistic structure. Thirdly, Weber traced the transition process in which the Protestant writings gradually developed a position of sanctioning unlimited acquisitive activities provided they were righteous. Beyond these steps of proof in the *Protestant Ethic,* Weber undertook

an ambitious series of comparative studies all directed to the question, why did modern rational bourgeois capitalism appear as a dominant phenomenon *only* in the modern West? What are the differentiating factors that account for its failure to appear in other cultures? The comparative study is couched mainly in terms of the Marxian dichotomy of "material" and "ideal" factors. The general upshot is the thesis that at the relevant stages in the development of cultures the material conditions in China, India, Judea compared favorably, from the point of view of capitalistic-bureaucratic potentialities, with those of our own medieval and early modern times, while in each culture the "economic ethic" of the dominant religious tradition concerned was directly antagonistic to such a development. On the other hand, in Protestantism (to a less extent in Christianity as a whole) the economic ethic was directly favorable. This conclusion confirms the functional relationship between Protestantism and capitalism.[19]

The series of comparative studies Parsons referred to were the three volumes of "Economic Ethics of the World Religions" ("Die Wirtschaftsethik der Weltreligionen," *Gesammelte Aufsatze zur Religionssoziologie*) which included studies of Confucianism and Taoism, Hinduism and Buddhism, and ancient Judaism.

2. Characteristics of Chinese Social Structure

In this volume of *Confucianism and Taoism,* renamed *The Religion of China* by Gerth to avoid the isms, Weber continued from his theme in the *Protestant Ethic* by trying to contrast the distinguishing features of traditional Chinese society, Confucianism and Taoism, with the characteristics of the capitalistic economy and the spirit of capitalism. In reading this volume, the general reader may be puzzled if he guides himself too strictly by the translation title, *The Religion of China,* for the book deals with much more than religion. In fact, of the 249 pages

[19] *Ibid*, pp. 512–13.

of translated text, 141 pages, or better than half of the total, were devoted chiefly to characterizing various aspects of Chinese society and their contrast with analogous parts in the Western and other societies, and religion was taken up only in occasional sections. It is not until well into the second half of the volume that we see consistent concentration on the subject of religious ideas and values. Moreover, Weber treated Confucianism more as an ethical doctrine than as a theistic religion because of its lack of metaphysical foundations, in spite of its toleration of magic. It may help the general reader to follow Weber's theme better if the volume is treated as a study of Chinese social structure, ethical values, and religion with special relevance to their propensity toward development of rational bourgeois capitalism.

The lengthy treatment on the characteristics of Chinese social structure (chapters I to IV) was apparently designed to give due consideration to the "material" factors before assigning primary importance to the "ideal" factor in the failure of rational bourgeois capitalism to appear in China. In the following pages, there is no intention adequately to summarize the contents of the volume; rather, the purpose is to facilitate clarification of Weber's main theme of argument, so far as I understand it, and to bring up to date certain issues involved in the light of recent knowledge in the study of Chinese society.

The three parts into which the book is divided show a clear logical unity in Weber's argument. In Part I, Weber examined the economic, political, and social aspects of Chinese society, and presented a mixture of structural or "material" characteristics, some of which were favorable, and some unfavorable to the development of capitalism; in other words, comparison of "material" conditions yielded no decisive distinction between Chinese and Western societies in terms of propensity for capitalistic development. In Part II, Weber presented a decisive contrast between Confucian values and the ascetic Protestant ethic in the sense that the former lacked the dynamic motivation which the latter had for capitalistic development. Part III contains Weber's characterization of Taoism as a system of negative and conservative values incapable of developing a dynamic social orientation toward capitalism. Weber thus located the decisive differentiating element in the passive and traditionalist character in Confucian and Taoist values, explaining why capitalism developed in the West but not in China.

But the arrangement of materials in each part and each chapter lacks similar logical clarity. Weber was not interested in making any systematic presentation of Chinese social structure and its value system; instead, his main purpose was to contrast these factors with analogous components in Western society. The difficulty arises where he provided no explicit rationale for his selection and arrangement of the points for comparison. His main points of argument often became obfuscated, and this is especially so with Part I, in which he dealt with the characteristics of Chinese social structure under the title, "sociological foundations."

To follow his own order of arrangement in Part I, Weber chose five major concrete factors in the Chinese social system as characterizing features having relevance to the functional requirements of modern capitalism: monetary system, cities and guilds, the patrimonial state, kinship organization, and law. If we regard structural factors as a category, we perhaps could add to them Weber's discussion on literati as a status group in the first chapter of Part II.

Weber started the discussion with the subjects of monetary system and cities, probably because these two factors were most intimately related to the breeding of the capitalistic economy in Western history. Then, he turned to two distinguishing features of Chinese society, the patrimonial state and the kinship organization, the two poles on the scale of institutional structure in terms of size. The subject of law followed, perhaps because its characteristic is affected by the nature of both the state and the kinship system. Many other subjects, especially historical development of institutions, were interspersed between the foregoing major points.

Weber began the study with the subject of money, as he fully recognized the vital role of money in his economic sociology: money extends the area of economic exchange, facilitates the acquisition and accumulation of wealth, and provides a common denominator of economic value to measure the relative economic significance of heterogeneous goods and services, thus making it possible to determine profit or loss in budget operations.[20] Owing to the importance of these functions of money, China's historical failure to establish an effective monetary system was a sign of lack of capitalistic development and an obstacle to any significant large-scale rational capitalistic development. But Weber did point out the increased silver supply since the eighteenth century as a possible stimulant to capitalistic development which, however, did not take place.

The cities gave birth to Western capitalism, but failed to perform the same function in China, because Chinese cities lacked political and military autonomy and the organizational unity to act as a corporate body, autonomy and unity that guaranteed the financial and legal grounds for rational development of Western bourgeois capitalistic en-

[20] Max Weber, the *Theory,* pp. 173–90, 280–308.

terprises.[21] Weber recognized the central importance of guilds in the socioeconomic structure of Chinese cities, and he regarded the organizational autonomy of the guilds as a favorable factor for the development of capitalism. But he thought the absence of legal guarantee for guild privileges had compelled the guilds to develop intensive functional self-sufficiency, and discouraged development of formal legal foundations for "a free and cooperatively regulated organization of industry and commerce, such as known in the Occident."[22]

Weber certainly had ample theoretical and historical justification for emphasizing money and the cities as strategic factors affecting the propensity of a society toward capitalistic development. Limited recent studies on Chinese urban communities seem to support Weber's thesis that the Chinese urban community could not function as a corporate unit, although recent sources[23] indicate the presence of certain kinds of government guarantees for guild monopolies and privileges as against Weber's assertions. Since Weber's time, research on traditional Chinese urban community and economy has been disappointingly scarce, and there is as yet insufficient reliable information systematically to evaluate Weber's amazingly incisive observations from the extremely scanty materials he had to work with. It was not until the mid-1950's that we saw some systematic effort made by scholars in Communist China to study traditional Chinese urban economy and the development of "capitalism."[24] Some significant data have been published on the traditional merchant class and the nature of handicrafts and commercial firms; important facts that Weber did not have an opportunity to examine.

Weber ascribed the cities' lack of politicomilitary autonomy to the early unification of the Chinese empire which brought centralization of civil and military administration under a national bureaucracy.[25] After the elimination of feudalism, the individual city's resources were too limited to win autonomy from the monolithic politicomilitary power of a unified, extensive empire. The socioeconomic implications of the centralized imperial state thus became a significant problem for the study

[21] *The Religion of China*, pp. 13, 15, 16, 20. (References are to pages in present edition.)
[22] *Ibid.*, p. 20, also pp. 17, 63.
[23] See, for example, Meng Yuan-lao, *Tungching Meng Hua Lu* (Reminiscence of the Luxuries in the Eastern Capital), Sung period, reprinted by the Commercial Press, Hong Kong, 1961, chapters 2, 3, and 4.
[24] See for example, Fu-Yi-ling, *Ming Tai Kiangnan Shi-min Ching-chi Shih-tán* (Exploration on the Bourgeois Economy in the Yangtzu Region During the Ming Period), Jen Min Publishers, Shanghai, 1957.
[25] *The Religion of China*, pp. 20–26.

of China's propensity toward capitalistic development. Weber analyzed these implications by examining the imperial state from several vantage points: general significance, the state's relationship to religion, central-local relationship and the patrimonial bureaucracy, agrarian policy and rural administration.

The unity and peace of the imperial state had both favorable and unfavorable general implications for the development of capitalism. Among the favorable ones was the obvious freedom of movement of goods and population over a territory as extensive as Europe and with no political restriction. The unfavorable implications included the elimination of the political autonomy of cities, autonomy that could have provided stimulation and compatible conditions for capitalistic enterprises. The substitution of peace and unity for rivalry and conflict between feudal states also meant the removal of competitive pressure for rationalization measures to improve the bureaucratic and economic organization needed by national interests and for survival.[26] In addition, without wars between the states, there was no more occasion for war loans and war commissions, factors which led to the development of political capitalism in the West.[27]

There were many supportive influences for the establishment and maintenance of peace and unity of the imperial state which had relevance for capitalistic development. One was the early development of cultural unity among the Chinese feudal states. But a more important one was the assumption of religious functions by the emperor and his officialdom.[28] This eliminated the role of a powerful priesthood which might have challenged the secular power, and threatened the internal unity of the imperial state. The emphasis on peace, order, and tranquillity was the cause for consistently purging ecstatic expressions and emotional upheaval from official cults. Popular religion, deprived of any official status, was oriented toward pluralism[29] which had a divisive influence and a crippling effect on the ability of popular religion to challenge the unified power of the state. This yielded a situation in which there was neither a priesthood nor an independent religious force strong enough to introduce radical innovations into the socioeconomic order as required by capitalistic development.

But peace and unity did not imply intensive centralized administration throughout the extensive empire. Much of Chinese history was given to incessant struggles between the central power and local in-

[26] *Ibid.*, pp. 33–47, 61–62.
[27] *Ibid.*, p. 103.
[28] *Ibid.*, pp. 20–32.
[29] *Ibid.*, pp. 20–47, *passim.*

terests.[30] The patrimonial bureaucracy and ancient organization that had characterized the Chinese imperial state failed thoroughly to resolve the conflict and effectively to rationalize administration on both the central and local levels of government.

The bureaucracy recruited its members from the literati by examinations, hence bureaucratic status was based neither on birth nor on supernatural consideration or divine grace. This universalistic feature was conducive to bureaucratic rationalization. Other features such as the triannual system of shift of official posts, the prohibition of holding office in one's home province, and the full removability of the official by central command served to detach the bureaucrat from developing permanent local interests detrimental to the central power.

But these centralization measures had adverse effects: they weakened the relation between formal bureaucratic rule and local life,[31] and prevented rationalization of local administration by the central authority. The tax quota system allowed the official to meet administrative expenses, and to make a profit from official revenues and unofficial fees and "gifts," so long as the quota was handed over. There was no strict separation between public and private income.[32] Consequently, "the empire resembled a confederation of satrapies under a pontifical head,"[33] frustrating central attempts at unifying and rationalizing local administration. The rational effectiveness of the bureaucracy was further reduced by the Confucian rejection of specialization as an appropriate quality of the educated gentleman.[34] The ranking members of the bureaucracy were generalists, and specialized tasks were relegated to the clerical staff, according to Weber.[35] These characteristics of the bureaucracy, together with the farflung territory of the empire without modern transportation and communication,[36] reduced formal central administration at the local level to a minimum, often to nonexistence. One economic implication in this situation is the weakness of the formal sociopolitical order on the local level as a legal foundation for the development of capitalistic enterprises.

[30] *Ibid.*, Chapter II, sections 1–3.
[31] *Ibid.*, pp. 48–50.
[32] *Ibid.*, pp. 48, 56–62, 64–75.
[33] *Ibid.*, p. 48.
[34] *Ibid.*, pp. 159–60.
[35] See my somewhat different interpretation on this characteristic of the Chinese bureaucracy in "Some Characteristics of Chinese Bureaucratic Behavior," *Confucianism in Action*, ed. by David S. Nivison and Arthur F. Wright, Stanford University Press, Stanford, California, 1959, pp. 134–64.
[36] *Ibid.*, p. 47.

Weber contributed richly to the characterization of the Chinese bureaucracy and the literati in various parts of this book and in his other writings.[37] Since then, quite a literature has arisen on the subject of Chinese bureaucracy and the literati[38] as a vital factor affecting the nature of Chinese society, and this recent research lent support to most of Weber's observations and assumptions. Particularly sharp and accurate is Weber's interpretation of the central bureaucracy's devices for detaching officials from forming firm alliance and collusion with local interests. These devices resulted in the isolation of the authorized official from effective direct handling of local affairs, and enhanced the strategic importance of the unofficial secretaries, aides, and clerical staff who mediated between the official and the population.[39]

This failure of the central formal administration to reach directly down to the local population is now largely verified in a recent splendid study of Chinese local government by T'ung-Tsu Ch'u.[40] Ch'u produced a clear, empirical picture showing that Chinese traditional local government at the prefect and county levels was jointly administered by the formal bureaucratic organization of a very limited number of central appointees, and by a much larger informal organization made up mainly of the magistrate's personal employees who dealt directly with local problems in ways that often overstepped the formal rules prescribed by the bureaucracy. The centrally appointed official found it extremely difficult, often impossible, to penetrate through the tight control by local interests, or to alter their rules of operation by imposing formal regulations. This agrees essentially with the way Weber analyzed the situation.

Weber's analysis of the history of Chinese agrarian policy and rural administration seems to be based on very inadequate sources of information, and his arrangement of the data appears confusing in terms of both logical connection and time sequence. His main source on Wang An-shih's "state socialist" reform in the eleventh century was apparently

[37] See for example, "Bureaucracy," in *Essays*, pp. 226 ff.

[38] Examples: Edward A. Kracke, *Civil Service in Early Sung China*, Harvard University Press, Cambridge, Massachusetts, 1953; Hsiao-t'ung Fei, *China's Gentry*, University of Chicago Press, Chicago, Illinois, 1953; Chung-li Chang, *The Chinese Gentry*, University of Washington Press, Seattle, Washington, 1955, and his *The Income of Chinese Gentry*, University of Washington Press, 1962; P. T. Ho, *The Ladder of Success in Imperial China*, Columbia University Press, New York, 1962; Robert M. Marsh, *The Mandarins*, Free Press of Glencoe, New York, 1961; S. N. Eisenstadt, *The Political Systems of Empires*, Free Press of Glencoe, 1963.

[39] *The Religion of China*, pp. 48–50.

[40] T'ung-tsu Ch'u, *Local Government in China under the Ching*, Harvard University Press, Cambridge, Massachusetts, 1962.

limited to A. J. Iwanoff's early Russian study on the subject.[41] Many new studies have since been made on the political order of the rural community and on Wang An-shih's reforms,[42] tracing out a much clearer picture than Weber's of such organizations as the ever-normal granary or the collective responsibility system (*pao chia* or, in Weber's term, liability associations), which characterized China's rural sociopolitical order. But on the issue of historical land reforms and their effect on the pattern of agricultural production, Weber brought forth a challenging interpretation, in spite of his handicap of limited data.

The radical label of Communism often leads us to think that the Chinese Communist land reform in the early 1950's was something unique in the seemingly conservative history of Chinese agricultural policy. But Weber presented the essential fact that Chinese history was partly characterized by recurrent agrarian crises and concomitant remedial attempts such as land redistribution, limitation of land ownership, and obligatory cultivation for owners of land (compare Sun Yat-sen's modern "land to the tillers" policy).[43]

Though neglected in Western literature, historical land reforms received considerable attention in Chinese literature in recent decades.[44] But scholars concerned with this issue, Chinese and Western alike, interpreted the historical measures in the light of humanitarianism, egalitarianism, and the stabilization of rural economic and political order. Weber alone put forth the idea that the succession of many land reforms in the past two thousand years contributed to the partitioning of the land into innumerable farms of microscopic size which came to be a characteristic feature of Chinese rural economy.[45] For Weber, this interpretation has relevance for the absence of capitalistic development in China: "The various attempts at land reform by the state led to . . .

[41] A. J. Iwanoff, *Wang-An-Schi i jevo reformy*, St. Petersburg, 1906.

[42] Examples: Henry R. Williamson, *Wang An-Shih*, A. Probsthain, London, 1935; James T. C. Liu, *Reform in Sung China*, Harvard University Press, Cambridge, Massachusetts, 1959.

[43] *The Religion of China*, pp. 79–83.

[44] See, for example, Chen, Teng-yuan, *Chung-kuo T'u-ti Chi'tu* (Chinese land system), Commercial Press, Shanghai, 1932.

[45] Weber was aware of the complex causes that led to the small size of the Chinese farms in addition to the effects from land reforms. For instance, he mentioned population increase and continuous subdivision of the land among many descendants in inheritance in which primogeniture had long been eliminated. See *The Religion of China*, pp. 46, 54–55. For small farm size as a characteristic of Chinese rural economy, see my *A Chinese Village in Early Communist Transition*, Technology Press, Cambridge, Massachusetts, 1959, Chapter IV; see also Hans Gerth's note 30, p. 274 of this book.

the absence of rational and large-scale agricultural enterprise. . . . Technological improvements were almost ruled out by the extensive partitioning of land; tradition held sway despite a developed money economy."[46]

The Chinese kinship system, like the imperial state, posed many obstacles to rational entrepreneurial development.[47] An important pattern of wealth acquisition was through family investment in helping a scholarly member to obtain an education, and later a bureaucratic office, in order to practice internal "booty capitalism." This form of familial investment would not lead to development of "rational economic corporate enterprises." The extensive kinship organization performed so many functions to meet the individual's social and economic needs that it discouraged individualism and independence.[48] The extensive development of family auxiliary industries such as textile impeded the development of such production in the form of independent industries. The strong solidarity of the kinship organization and the effective power of the elders, together with the self-governing status of the village, confined effective formal administrative authority mainly within the city walls, thus depriving capitalism of the law and order necessary for trading over a wide territory. Kinship protection for the individual against any outside discrimination or grievance also would hinder work discipline and the free market selection of labor required by large modern enterprises. Consequently, "large private capitalist factories can scarcely be traced historically."[49]

The familistic aspect of Chinese society is one field that has received considerable scholastic treatment since Weber's time,[50] and recent findings do not, in general principle, contradict Weber's interpretation of the implications of the Chinese kinship system as an inhibiting influence against capitalistic development. But there is the problem of appropriate community setting in Weber's data. Much of the kinship phenomena in Weber's discussion occurred in the rural village, while

[46] *The Religion of China,* pp. 79 and 83.

[47] *Ibid.,* pp. 86–97.

[48] This concurs with many Chinese scholars' opinions; see, for example, Mai, Hui-t'ing, *Chung-kuo Chia-t'ing Wen-t'i* (Chinese family problem), Chunghua Publishers, Shanghai, 1930.

[49] *Ibid.,* p. 97

[50] Examples: Hsien-chin Hu, *The Common Descent Group in China and Its Functions,* Viking Fund, New York, 1948; Morton H. Fried, *Fabric of Chinese Society,* Frederick A. Praeger, Inc., New York, 1953; Olga Lang, *Chinese Family and Society,* Oxford University Press, Fairlawn, New Jersey, 1946; Yao-Hua Lin, *The Golden Wing,* American Institute of Pacific Relations, New York, 1948; C. K. Yang, *The Chinese Family in the Communist Revolution,* Technology Press, M.I.T., Cambridge, Massachusetts, 1959.

the likely community for capitalistic development would be the city, where the kinship organization assumed a different role. In the urban setting, we do not know whether kinship relations would pose similar obstacles to capitalistic development as Weber had assumed. It is unfortunate that there is not much accurate data on the characteristics and functions of the Chinese family in urban centers to offer an answer to this question. As to whether there were large private capitalist factories in Chinese history, recent research seem to indicate that at least in several lines of traditional industries, such as silk textile and chinaware, the size and complexity of organization of enterprises were considerable.[51] But even now data on this problem are still too limited for reliable evaluation of Weber's interpretation.

Among factors of Chinese social structure, substantive ethical law that dominated in traditional China was a clearly negative influence on capitalistic development. Modern capital investment requires rational and calculable law and legal procedure to function. But formal law which embodies rationality and calculability did not flourish in the Chinese patrimonial state where any formal rule and fixed procedure tended to restrict the patrimonial power and prerogatives. Chinese statutes were "codified ethical rather than legal norms."[52] This observation by Weber is fully verified by the findings of T'ung-tsu Ch'u, who demonstrated the overwhelming importance of ethical, ritualistic norms in the formulation of Chinese law.[53] Substantive ethical law served well the patrimonial rulers' political expedience or ethical goals. But substantive ethical law could not develop precise forms and procedure. Formal law did not have a favorable environment to develop in traditional China partly also because of the dominance of highly particularistic influence of the kinship organization and the absence of professional jurists as a strategic group vitally interested in the formalization of the law, for administration and justice were combined in the power of the officialdom.

Although Weber saw in China many unfavorable conditions for the development of capitalism, he also presented many favorable factors such as the absence of status restriction by birth, free migration and settlement outside of one's home community, free choice of occupations, absence of compulsory schooling and military service, and absence of

[51] See, for example, *Chung-kuo shou-kung-yeh shih tzu-liao* (Sources of Chinese Handicraft Industries), ed. Peng Tse- and others, San Lien Publishing Company, Peking, 1957, especially volumes I and II.

[52] *The Religion of China*, p. 102; also Bendix, *Max Weber*, pp. 398–99.

[53] T'ung-tsu Ch'u, *Law and Society in Traditional China*, Mouton, The Hague, Netherlands, 1961.

legal restraint on usury or trade. "From a purely economic point of view, a genuine bourgeois industrial capitalism might have developed. . . ."[54] The failure of capitalism to appear in China was basically owing to the lack of a "particular mentality" such as that of ascetic Protestantism.

3. Confucian Traditionalism as Decisive Inhibiting Factor

After analyzing the structural features of Chinese society as material conditions affecting capitalistic development, Weber proceeded to Part II of his work to characterize the "mentality" or the "ideal" factor that could have caused the failure of capitalism to appear in China. This means essentially an examination of Confucianism as the dominant value system and of the literati group as its carriers. To Weber, the effective orientation of a value system can be understood best in terms of the material and ideal interests of its social carriers as guiding influence for social action. Characterization of the literati thus became a necessary step for understanding the orientation of Confucianism.[55]

The literati are characterized first of all by their preeminence as China's undisputed ruling stratum for the past two millennia. They were distinct from the literati in other cultures by their vested interest in bureaucratic office, their high social prestige, their nonhereditary status, their system of qualification through literary classical education, their origin in secular feudal nobility but not in any priesthood. In this light, the literati were a group rooted in secular interests, entrenched in political power and social prestige, and highly cultured in literary classical education. Departing from Weber's original contents, we may interpret that these characteristics could lead the Chinese literati toward an intense interest in this-worldly orientation, in structure and maintenance of order, in orthodoxy and traditionalism instead of renovation and change, in the literary and conservative contents of classical education, and their aversion to subject matters of economic production. Their general inclination toward order and traditionalism is reflected in the qualities of the "gentleman ideal," which includes the ability to cite classical quotations in conversation, a pure literary intellectuality, meticulous observance of rules of piety, constant self-control for proper adjustment to situations and contempt for militarism.[56] These leading interests of the literati seem highly compatible with the "Confucian life orientation."

There have been considerable studies on the social position and characteristics of the Chinese literary elite in recent decades. For example, H. G. Creel, in his splendid book *The Birth of China*, has revealed

[54] *The Religion of China*, p. 100.
[55] *Ibid.*, pp. 107 ff.
[56] *Ibid.*, pp. 123–26, 131–33.

the sociopolitical setting that accompanied the rise of the literary elite, thus answering Weber's puzzle about the literati's origin.[57] We now know much more about the development of the examination system. Under the general designation "gentry" (those literati who had passed at least the lowest grade of examination), a host of studies have appeared to reveal the degree of class mobility made possible by the examinations.[58]

But these "gentry" studies largely substantiated Weber's position, and they were made from a rather static viewpoint—the functional position of the gentry in the traditional social structure. Not even the most perceptive "gentry" study by Hsiao-t'ung Fei[59] took up Weber's dynamic problem: the implication of the position and characteristics of the literati for the pattern of Chinese socioeconomic development. In this respect, Weber's account may appear empirically crude today, but the problem he posed and the approach he used remain a fresh challenge to those interested in the cross-cultural study of the patterns of socioeconomic development.

Weber's characterization of the literati was a preparatory step to the main theme of his book: the traditionalist nature of Confucianism (and Taoism) precluded such radical renovation as the development of rational bourgeois capitalism. The heart of the Confucian (and Taoist) doctrines was the *tao*, the immutable order of harmony, tranquillity, and equilibrium underlying the universe and human society. The Confucian orientation for man lay in making rational adjustment to the eternal cosmic and social order. This Confucian acceptance of the world "as given"* contrasts with the Puritan rejection of it on God's command. For Weber, "Confucian rationalism meant rational adjustment to the world; Puritan rationalism meant rational mastery of the world."[60] This is Weber's fundamental position in accounting for the failure of the Confucian ethic to initiate any drastic change of the socioeconomic order toward capitalism. Other aspects of Confucianism converge on this central position.

Confucianism had no metaphysical foundation; its basic interest was this-worldly; it had a cosmogony which, however, developed largely into magical theodicy devoted to this-worldly matters.[61] There was no serious

[57] *Ibid.*, p. 110.

[58] *Ibid.*, p. 46.

[59] See his "Peasantry and Gentry" in *American Journal of Sociology*, LII, No. 1, July, 1946, pp. 1–17.

*This acceptance of the "given" was Weber's characterization of the Confucian course of action. Weber's position finds support from the empirical pattern of Confucian behavior, but it may be questioned on theoretical grounds, as will be discussed later.

[60] *The Religion of China*, p. 248.

[61] *Ibid.*, pp. 155 ff.

concern for the world beyond. Confucian notions of the cosmic and social order contained a "radical world-optimism": the perfectability of man and his social world by human effort.[62] Man's duty lay in pious conformity to the requirements of cosmic and social harmony as set by tradition, and in the cultivation of a "harmoniously balanced personality" which would represent a microcosm. A watchful self-control should be exercised to reduce tension and to repress the irrational passions aroused in ecstatic and orgiastic acts which might destroy harmony and poise. This would bring long life, health, wealth and a good name after death, the ultimate objectives for the Confucian this-worldly struggle, in Weber's analysis.

In this "best of all possible worlds," there was neither the burdensome idea of original sin, nor the compulsion to fulfill God's ethical demands upon a sinful world as a condition for salvation. In contrast to Puritanism, "all transcendental anchorage of ethics, all tension between the imperatives of a supra-mundane God and a creatural world, all orientation toward a goal in the beyond, and all conception of radical evil, were absent."[63] Unlike the Puritan, the Confucian lacked the emotional tension to drive him to remake the world according to God's ethical imperatives. And because the Puritan could "live *in* the world and yet not be *of* it,"[64] he could develop rational aptitudes for remolding the world. But the Confucian lived *in* the world as a well adjusted part *of* it, so his objectivity and rationality were severely restricted by the tyrannical influence of traditionalism. There was neither inducement nor sanction to rebel against the established social order or even to upset its equilibrium. Orgiastic and ecstatic elements, which might disturb the harmony of the social order or generate deviational tendencies, were thoroughly expurgated from the classics by Confucius, and were suppressed from popular religiosity by rulers.[65] "Not reaching beyond this world," the Confucian had "no leverage for influencing conduct through inner forces freed of tradition and convention."[66]

Confucian affirmation of the world and adjustment to it implied sanctification of tradition and toleration of popular magical religion.[67] Both tradition and magic were obstacles to the rational development of capitalistic enterprise. On the other hand, Puritanism rejected the sanctity of tradition, and carried out radical elimination of magic from the

[62] *Ibid.*, pp. 212, 227–28, 235.
[63] *Ibid.*, p. 228.
[64] *Ibid.*, p. 247.
[65] *Ibid.*, pp. 113–14.
[66] *Ibid.*, pp. 235–36.
[67] *Ibid.*, p. 229; Parsons, *Structure*, p. 549.

world. Said Parsons, "...everywhere traditionalism is the rule in the earlier stages of a given social development. It is so powerful that it requires forces of exceptional strength to break through it even appreciably, and only when that has happened are certain kinds of social development, like that of rational bourgeois capitalism, possible. Not only did the Confucian ethic . . . fail to do this; on the contrary it provided a direct and powerful sanction of the traditional order."[68] In the West, these "forces of exceptional strength" were supplied from the Puritan enthusiasm for salvation through rationally and ethically mastering the given world of wicked creatures and irrationality. But Confucianism accepted the given world and needed no ethical salvation from it or rational transformation of it.[69] Instead, the supreme demand upon the individual was to adapt to it.

The structural core of this "given world" in the Confucian sense was the so-called "five cardinal relations": relations between sovereign and subject, parents and children, brothers, husband and wife, and friends. The central ethical obligation within these relations was piety. Weber characterized these personal relations and their resemblances as "organic relations" and as "organically given," accepted by the Confucian as an intrinsic part of the given social order. But beyond this order of personalism lay the "impersonal community" toward which the sense of piety or the devotion of ethical reciprocity would not apply. This ethical boundary set up a "community of blood" in contrast to the Puritan "community of faith" where a common ethical way of life was extended beyond kinship and personalism to cover business dealings with everyone.[70] This is essentially the contrast between particularism and universalism in the Parsonian pattern variables. There is obvious consequence to the pattern of economic development whether mutual confidence based on ethical obligations is to be confined to small circles of kinship and personal relations or to be extended universally to all parties of business dealing. In addition, the ethic of piety and "personalist principle" was a barrier to impersonal rationalization and to the development of the attitude of "impersonal matter-of-factness," because it tended to tie the individual to concrete persons instead of to objective functional tasks.[71]

Several further points in Weber's analysis of Confucianism require some consideration. One is the "central concept of propriety" and its implications for the socioeconomic order.[72] The Confucian ethic required

[68] Parsons, *ibid.*
[69] *The Religion of China,* p. 240.
[70] *Ibid.,* pp. 209, 236–37.
[71] *Ibid.,* pp. 236–37.
[72] *Ibid.,* pp. 156–57, 233–34.

an educated person to control every act of his life conduct according to *li* or traditionalized normative rules governing the correct behavior in every significant social situation. This was to fit the individual into the cosmic and social order and to repress passions that might disturb its equilibrium and harmony. The requirement of propriety is thus a vital part of the basic Confucian theme of adaptation to the given world.

Weber offered an interpretation of the Confucian emphasis on propriety. In this view, the innumerable propriety rules governing one's entire life were each a discrete norm unconnected to the others, and the ceremonial conduct guided by these rules was largely external acts divested of genuine emotional content. These two qualities of ceremonial behavior together deprived the Chinese of a dynamic inward core of "unified personality" based on a central value position which served as an autonomous motivating force for the Puritan in his confrontation with the world.[73] Propriety held the Confucian to the traditionalist course.

Weber's interpretation seems to receive confirmation from a familiar present-day theme: David Riesman's tradition-directed type versus the inner-directed type of personality, or his shame culture versus guilt culture. But we may raise one point here: Chinese sources suggest that propriety norms were based on a set of generalized and unified ethical principles, and acts of propriety retained a definite emotional foundation in spite of the required self-control over passions. Acts of propriety were neither discrete and unorganized nor devoid of emotional content, and there was a unified structure in the Confucian ethical principles that form the motivating core of the Confucian personality. Careful study on these points may lead to interpretations on propriety somewhat different from Weber's. Nevertheless, there is as yet no systematic conceptual study on the vital subject of *li* or propriety norms soundly to challenge Weber's interpretation.

Another point of considerable significance is the Confucian rejection of professional specialization because of the fundamental Confucian position that, "a cultured man is not a tool." In his adjustment to the world, the Confucian was an end unto himself, not a means to some functional purpose.[74] The gentleman was the all-rounded generalist or universalist, rejecting as lowly the position of an expert, especially in the pursuit of profit. This Confucian position blocked specialization in bureaucratic functions and in rational development of economic enterprises. This is in sharp contrast to the Puritan position of regarding a specialized calling as a means of serving God's design in transforming a creaturally wicked world.

[73] *Ibid.*, pp. 232, 235.
[74] *Ibid.*, pp. 160, 246.

We cannot question Weber's position that Confucian rejection of specialization was an obstacle to rationalized development in bureaucratic organization and economic enterprise. There is, however, room for thought on Weber's interpretation of the rejection of professional specialization as a consequence of the Confucian position that the gentleman was "not a tool" but an end unto himself. There was clear Confucian recognition of the individual's functional position in the scheme of division of labor,[75] and the educated man was consistently admonished on the responsibility of being a means to the duties of an office, to the missions from the superior, and to the moral responsibility to humanity. The gentleman was "an end unto himself" only in the sense that he was responsible to himself alone for the course he took in fulfilling the Confucian ethical mission.[76] Thus, the Confucian aversion to specialization, especially specialization in economic production for profit, might not have stemmed from the gentleman's refusal to being a means to an end in general. Instead, it might be a consequence of the differential evaluation of various types of labor and functional positions in terms of Confucian ethical criteria as well as the vested interests of the literati as a status group.

In accounting for the absence of capitalistic development in China, the lack of "ethical prophecy" as an innovating influence must be added to the inhibiting factors already mentioned. On this point, Weber merely mentioned that "the Chinese soul has never been revolutionized by a prophet,"[77] and that this was owing to the absence of tension between "nature and deity" and to the lack of ethical demands raised by a supramundane God in opposition to tradition and convention.[78] The dynamic significance of prophecy to socioeconomic development was not treated in this volume but in other works, especially in his *Ancient Judaism* and sociology of law.[79] Weber felt that "material" situations, established and traditionalized, could compel the individual to behave in a normalized

[75] See how Mencius justified the specialized administrative function of the ruler of a state as a basic reason for his being unable simultaneously to take up the occupation of economic production. *The Works of Mencius*, tr. by James Legge, Oxford University Press, London, England, Book III, Chapter IV, reprinted by the International Publication Society, Shanghai, 1947.
[76] See my *Religion in Chinese Society*, University of California Press, Berkeley, California, 1961, Chapter X.
[77] *The Religion of China*, p. 142.
[78] *Ibid.*, pp. 229–30.
[79] Bendix, *Max Weber*, pp. 264–65; *Max Weber on Law in Economy and Society*, University of Harvard Press, Cambridge, Massachusetts, 1954, pp. 20 ff.; *Protestant Ethic*, pp. 54–55; *Essays*, pp. 62–64, 284–86 *passim;* Parsons, *Structure*, pp. 510, 567–75.

pattern, but could not explain the rise of new situations and behavior. It was ethical prophecy that initiated new ideas, broke through the inertia of convention, and set up new ethical norms for a different pattern of conduct. In this light, the absence of prophecy was compatible with Confucian traditionalism and its ethic of adaptation to the given world without basic innovation. Weber's assumption that prophecy was not a feature of Confucianism can hardly be questioned. But a remaining problem was the presence of emissary or ethical prophecy in Chinese popular religion, especially in eclectic sectarianism, for prophecy often played a prominent role in sectarian movements during historical crises and dynastic change.[80]

4. Lack of Innovating Impetus from Taoist Heterodoxy

The third and last part of Weber's empirical study of the case of China was an examination of heterodoxy as represented by Taoism. For two millennia, Taoism as the leading heterodoxy existed in a heretic status under the official dominance of the Confucian orthodoxy. If the Confucian orthodoxy failed to lend impetus to capitalistic development, Weber's problem was to find out whether such heterodoxy as Taoism could have been "the source of a methodical way of life different from the official orientation"[81] and could have initiated a trend toward capitalism.

One difficulty in this problem is the drastic difference between Taoism as a philosophy and Taoism as a religion, and the frequently obscure relationship between the two. Weber did not consistently differentiate between these two aspects of Taoism, thus causing certain confusion in his treatment. Nevertheless, Weber's general position is discernible: although Taoism had certain features favoring innovation, its otherworldly orientation and its traditionalist qualities led to the same social consequence as that which stemmed from Confucianism.

Certain features of Taoism tended to detach the individual from the influence of the world, including its conventions. Taoist mysticism enjoined the maintenance of "one's goodness and humility by leading an incognito existence in the world," or by living away in the mountains and woods as an anchoret. "This constitutes the mystic's specifically

[80] See my *Religion in Chinese Society*, University of California Press, Berkeley, California, 1961, Chapter IX. Such a case as the prophecy by the White Lotus sect, containing ethical imperatives from the sectarian god Buddha Maitreya, clearly belongs to the emissary or ethical category. In fact, few of the militant sects had passive exemplary prophecy, in contrast to Weber's assumption. See *Essay*, pp. 284–86.

[81] *The Religion of China*, p. 174.

broken relationship with the world."[82] Taoism sought enlightenment in
the ultimate principle of the cosmic order, and regarded as obstacle to
this attainment such Confucian trappings as worldly knowledge, literary
learning, propriety and self-control; the road to illumination was to "let
things and men go as they can."[83] The Taoist principle of inaction and
simplicity led to rejection of the centralized bureaucratic state in favor
of the small, isolated, self-sufficient, primitivist community as most conducive to man's well-being. Contrary to Confucianism, Taoist sectarians
retained orgiastic and ecstatic elements which could liberate the individual from the fetters of convention, and lead him into realms of new
ideas. These features of Taoism tended to devaluate the given world
and to minimize the control of the individual by the complex social order
of the civilized society. They favored the development of creativity and
individuality, and this could lead to social innovation. But historically
Taoism performed no such revolutionary function for the social order,
and this was attributable to the overriding effect of negative Taoist
tendencies.

Since Taoist contemplative mysticism sought illumination and magical power for the individual, it had no enthusiasm for transforming the
world. Taoist cultivation of magic turned the world into a weird, irrational realm of spirits and demons; the a-literate character of Taoism
and the unalterable procedure of magical formulas rendered even
stronger support to traditionalism than that given by Confucianism. "The
magic stereotyping of technology and economics . . . precluded the advent of indigenous modern enterprises. . . ."[84]

Like Confucianism, Taoism assumed a "cosmos of internally harmonic order of nature and society."[85] There was a total absence of
tension toward the world which was assumed to harbor no intrinsic
ethical deficiency or evil. To the religious Taoist, the world seemed to
be a wonderful place for enjoying life, not an object for struggle and
transformation. Two of the leading Taoist magical goals, the potion of
immortality and the alchemy of converting base metal into gold, expressed complete satisfaction with the given world, hence the longing
for a limitless life and limitless gold with which to enjoy it. As a con-
sequnce, Taoism failed to alter the traditionalist course of Confucianism.

On this point, Joseph Needham would perhaps point to the long
centuries of Confucian condemnation of Taoism to heresy as an explanation for such failure. In his recent enormous project on the study of

[82] *Ibid.,* p. 182.
[83] *Ibid.,* p. 188.
[84] *Ibid.,* pp. 199–200.
[85] *Ibid.,* p. 200.

Chinese science and civilization, Needham revealed an impressive list of Taoist contributions to science and technology.[86] He differed drastically from Weber in the Taoist meaning of the *tao:* "The Tao is the Order of Nature, which brought all things into existence and governs their every action, not so much by force as by a kind of natural curvature in space and time. . . . The sage is to imitate the Tao, which works unseen and does not dominate. By yielding, by not imposing his preconceptions on Nature, he will be able to observe and understand, and so to govern and control."[87] But the long and unrelenting domination of Confucian traditionalism had choked off any Taoist potentiality for innovation. Needham's work is among the few recent studies which contained new interpretations of the inadequately explored but vital subject of Taoism.

5. Some Evaluative Comments

Let us recall Weber's basic assumption: Ascetic Protestantism was a major impetus for the development of rational bourgeois capitalism in the West, and the absence of similar dominant religious values caused the failure of capitalism to appear in China. As we have seen in the long discussion above, Weber tried to prove his thesis on the Chinese case by three steps: (1.) Chinese social structure on the "material" conditions contained a mixture of elements both favorable and unfavorable to capitalistic economy and the spirit of capitalism. Thus, the structural characteristics could not be a decisive factor in China's failure to develop capitalism. (2.) Confucianism, the dominant system of ultimate values, was consistently traditionalistic, enjoining adaptation to the given world and not the transformation of it.   (3.) Taoism, the leading heterodoxy, was unable to alter the Confucian traditionalist trend because of its otherworldly mysticism and its own magical tradition. The consequence was that Confucian traditionalism was left in its dominant position which, together with the literati's lack of interest in economic production enterprises, inhibited socioeconomic innovation in the direction of Western capitalism.

Although critical evaluation of this book is not the purpose of this introduction, it may nevertheless be asked for general interest whether Weber has supplied a satisfactory answer to the momentous question: Why did China fail to develop industrial capitalism despite her long history and cultural achievement? A review of the above arguments shows that Weber has firmly established at least two points in this book:

[86] Joseph Needham, *Science and Civilization in China,* Cambridge University Press, London, 1956, Vol. II, pp. 34–164.
[87] *Ibid.,* p. 37.

the strongly traditionalist nature of Confucianism as a dominant system of ultimate values, and the congruence of this nature with the general traditionalist characteristic of Chinese society. The traditionalist quality of both Confucianism and Chinese society is a plainly observable fact, and Weber could have built an even stronger case along this line if today's data on China had been available to him. Operating with his "ideal type" construction as a typical course of action issuing from a central value position, the expected types of action from Confucianism corresponded broadly with the actual nature of Chinese society. The Confucian inhibiting effect on capitalistic development was demonstrated partly by contrasting traditionalist qualities of Confucianism with rational characteristics of the capitalistic economy and the spirit of capitalism, rational characteristics which found compatibility in the Protestant ethic. To Weber, no rational capitalism could ever be born of a traditionalist system of ultimate values dominant in a traditionalist social order.

Weber's position can be challenged by a different theoretical interpretation of the nature of Confucianism. In confrontation with the world, Confucianism (and Taoism) kept harking back to the ideal qualities of the *tao* (governing principle of the cosmic and social order) and the "golden past" when the *tao* was thought to be in perfect operation. This meant that the given world was at ethical variance with the *tao* and the "golden past." Public indictment and personal criticism against the sociopolitical order that abounded in the Chinese literature of every age expressed no acceptance of the world "as given." What became accepted by the Confucian was the world *as interpreted* by the Confucian orthodoxy. Meanwhile, the concrete form and qualities of the *tao* and the "golden past" were subject to interpretations by authoritative men of knowledge (witness Mencius' imputation of democratic qualities into the legendary kings Yao and Shun), just as God's will was variously interpreted by the Hebrew prophets.

Confucian rationalism and asceticism stemmed from this tension or variance between the *tao* and worldly realities, especially during historical crises when mass suffering reigned. For the Chinese culture in which theistic religion early lost political dominance, secular men of knowledge played the role of prophets in advancing propositions for controlling or remolding the world in conformity to the various interpretations of ideal or ethical demands by the *tao*, such as history witnessed in the "100 schools" of philosophy during the late feudal period. Thus, in Confucianism and in the general Chinese moral tradition, there was pressure for transforming the given world in conformity to ideals which were often disguised under the label of the *tao* or the "golden past." The *tao* was an abstract concept, not the concrete form, of cosmic and social order.

But this possible argument may be only academic. In historical reality, it was traditionalism, not the innovating potentiality from the ideal of the *tao* and the "golden past," which became established as the dominant orientation for Confucianism and Chinese society. For Weber, what mattered was this historical traditionalist reality which exerted inhibiting influence on capitalistic development. Weber advanced many sharp observations on the indecisive role of social structural features in China's failure to develop capitalism. But insufficient scientific information on Chinese social structure does not permit adequate evaluation of Weber's work in this respect. Particularly lacking is information on the traditional Chinese urban community, the likely spawning ground for capitalistic development. Weber often mixed rural with urban features in his characterization of Chinese social structure, and thus failed to characterize the realistic life of a definite type (either rural or urban) of community life. We are still quite ignorant about such phenomena as the role of kinship system in the urban economy, the relative power position of the merchant and artisan groups with particular reference to the political elite, the value system of these urban groups and their relation to Confucianism, and the role of science and technology. In Weber's days, information on these vital problems was even more limited than what little is available at the present.

It may be relevant to try to see what types of sources Weber had to work with. Generally speaking, standard texts of Chinese classics and most of the basic historical references available today in Western languages were already available to Weber in his days. James Legge had translated most of the basic classics by then, and the encyclopedic historical reference, *Yüch'uan T'ung Chien Kang Mu,* was rendered into French by Delamarre and published in Paris by 1865. In basic classics and historical references, Weber was not at any great disadvantage as compared with Western sinologists today. These sources contained basic information on the nature of traditional Chinese values essential to Weber's analysis. But in another category of material, namely field observations and primary and secondary sources of contemporary China, Weber had extremely few reports from trained scientists. He had access to the translated copies of the *Peking Gazette,* the "newspaper" of Peking's officialdom, an excellent source of information. He used the *Journal of the Peking Royal Society* containing occasional fine papers from sinologists like E. de Chavannes. But for the most part, he had to rely on writings from missionaries, travelers, and Western diplomatic officials, the vast majority of whom had neither training in the social sciences nor the necessary objectivity for reliable observation and analysis. Often, Weber's only source of information on intimate Chinese personal and social life had to come from such missionary observers as A. H. Smith (*Village Life in China,* for example). Deficiency in this category of data might have seriously hampered him in his work, especially in analyzing Chinese social structure, and caused many of the inaccuracies of factual details found throughout the text of this volume.

But Weber tried to use his sources with good discrimination. For religious life he had to make extensive use of the writings from the embittered Dutch missionary, J. J. M. de Groot, but he did not hesitate to label as a "temperamental pamphlet" de Groot's two-volume *magnum opus, Sectarianism and Religious Persecution in China* (Amsterdam, 1903).[88] But reliance on this type of material sometimes misled him into empirical inaccuracies such as the assumption of absence of predeterminism on an individual basis in China.[89] Correction for such assumptions as this might have affected Weber's interpretation on certain characteristics of Confucianism and Taoism.

But, data handicap notwithstanding, Weber everywhere exhibited startling insight into facts. Speaking of the absence of the concept of original sin among the Chinese, Weber stated: ". . . an educated Chinese would simply refuse to be continually burdened with 'sin.' Incidentally, the concept of 'sin' is usually felt as rather shocking and lacking in dignity by genteel intellectuals everywhere."[90] Only a mind with extremely sensitive imagination and empathy could have made this observation, especially without having been in the field in China. Weber's statement almost amounted to reporting an actual scene: A young and proud Chinese college boy was traveling on a steamer along the China coast in 1933. He was leaning on the railing on the deck and gazing at the sunset when an American Baptist missionary picked him for a likely object of conversion by walking up to him and suddenly declaring, "Young man, you are full of sin, you need to repent." The young man was surprised with shock, and yelled back in rage: "I come of reputable ancestry, I have a good conscience, and I have always been strict about my moral responsibilities and conduct. How is it that I am full of sin? Maybe you are full of sin, but I am not." The wrathful verbal combat that ensued showed clearly that the missionary, despite his years in China, did not have the insight Weber had about the absence of the

[88] *The Religion of China,* p. 293, note 42.
[89] *Ibid.,* pp. 206–208; for widespread individual predeterminism, see my *Religion in Chinese Society,* University of California Press, Berkeley, California, 1961, pp. 247–74, *passim.*
[90] *Religion of China,* p. 228.

concept of sin in Chinese metaphysics. This and many similar indications of Weber's extraordinary intellectual acuteness mitigated much of his data disadvantages and contributed to the soundness of most of his interpretations on significant phenomena in this volume.

6. Relevance to Current Interests

Although written half a century ago, this book still has full relevance to present-day scientific study of Chinese society and to comparative sociology of religions. We have pointed out earlier that in this book Weber had gone far beyond the subject of Chinese religion in the narrow sense to explore extensively into a wide range of subject matter bearing on the problem of ultimate values and capitalism. From this viewpoint, we find this book more richly endowed with vital ideas and hypotheses on the structure and value system of traditional Chinese society than any other volume available today. Many important problems on the structure and function of Chinese society were here brought up for the first time by Weber, and some of them remain largely unexplored even now.

An example is the problem of the typology of law in relation to the nature of Chinese social structure. Weber posed the hypothesis of the dominance of substantive ethical law in China and the absence of formal law either as an institution in the statutes or as an idea in traditional systems of thought. Up till now there has been no testing of Weber's hypothesis or the advance of other significant theoretical formulation on the abstract nature of law in traditional China, a subject so intimately related to the scientific understanding of Chinese society. Even T'ung-tsu Ch'u's work, cited above, did not develop the subject of Chinese law from the theoretical viewpoint of typology.

Weber confined himself to traditional China. He did not deal with the transitional process of Chinese society during the Republican period (1911-1949), nor did he attempt to project the course of change including the emergence of the Chinese Communist revolution. But his insightful interpretations of the characteristics of the traditional society supplied valuable suggestions on the directions of change likely to take place. An interesting point in this sense is his observation on the collective "appropriation" of privileges by Chinese bureaucratic officialdom as a whole. This collective pattern of vested interest turned the entire officialdom against any reform or change which was viewed likely to damage established privileges. Consequently, "only military conquest of the country, or successful military or religious revolution could shatter the firm structure of prebendary interests, thus creating completely new power distributions and in turn new economic conditions. Any attempt at internal innovation, however, was wrecked by the aforementioned obstacles."[91]

Weber's remarks were directed at the reform attempts during the time of the Empress Dowager at the end of the last century. But his words could well be regarded as a scientific prediction of the course of events in the Republican period leading up to the Communist revolution in 1949. Collective vested interest of the officialdom doomed all Republican reforms to failure. An official in the Republican government joined the Chinese Communist cause in the 1930's because, he said, "so long as the traditional officialdom kept its power status, any piecemeal reform effort is bound to be ruined by the collective opposition and collusion of the officials. The only way to build a new social and political order is by total revolution which will wipe out the power status of the traditional officialdom as a whole."[92] What resemblance between Weber's statement and the view of a perceptive Chinese Communist!

On the study of socioeconomic development in Communist China, one can draw help from Weber's work in at least two ways. First, Weber's list of characteristics of Chinese social structure and dominant values relevant to capitalistic development could serve as points of departure for studying the present possible directions of change, now that the Chinese Communists have drastically removed many of these inhibiting characteristics. Weber's problem of development of rational bourgeois capitalism is of course different from the Communist problem of socialist industrialization. But the two share such vital common grounds as emphasis on technological and organizational rationality and the development of modern bureaucratic administration.

Secondly, inasmuch as Chinese and Western brands of Communism share important common features in socioeconomic structure, Weber's work in other volumes on socialism and Marxism could suggest valuable orientations. Weber, for instance, viewed socialism as merely extension of bureaucracy from the political to the economic field, thus vastly expanding the power of the state and its bureaucracy.[93] This view has particular relevance to Chinese Communism because of the long historical development of political bureaucracy and frequent government intervention in economic activities.

As we have pointed out at the beginning, Weber intended this volume to be the first of a series of comparative studies of religions in the civilizations of China, India, the Middle East and Europe. Thus, the significance of this volume is not confined to China, but extends to the

[91] *Ibid.*, p. 61.
[92] From personal interview notes with a Communist cadre in Peking, 1951.
[93] *Essays*, pp. 48–50; Parsons, *Theory*, p. 37 and Chapter II *passim*.

general field of comparative sociology of religion. In his series of studies, however, Weber made no attempt to produce a general, systematic "sociology of religion." Instead, his purpose was specifically oriented toward "a comparative study of the ethics of other religions in respects relevant to the spirit of capitalism and the ethics of ascetic Protestant-ism."[94] Following this orientation, Weber produced from his compara-tive studies a set of typological concepts of religions and religious ele-ments very useful for the study of socioeconomic change in general and capitalistic development in particular.

It is impractical here to try to present Weber's entire range of typological concepts as developed in his extensive comparative series. As far as this volume is concerned, its typological concepts were already implied in the contrasting characteristics between Confucianism and ascetic Protestantism. At the risk of repetition, a few examples will illustrate the nature of these typological concepts and their usefulness to the general field of comparative sociology of religion.

A basic point of departure in Weber's comparative studies was the ethical discrepancy between religious values and the given world. De-veloping from this orientation, religions may be classified according to their rejection or acceptance of the world; the presence or absence of tension toward the world; the impulse to transform the world, to adapt to it or to escape from it. In terms of the course of religious salvation, religious behavior may be oriented toward controlling the world (asceticism) or toward devaluating it and cultivating an attitude of indifference to it (mysticism). Asceticism and mysticism are each further subdivided into this-worldly and otherworldly types.

In this light, Confucianism supplied an empirical case of this-worldly asceticism aimed at controlling the conduct of oneself and others for the purpose of adaptation to the given world. This is in contrast to the Puritan type of otherworldly asceticism seeking salvation in the world beyond. In terms of magical influence, Confucianism represents a type of rationalist ethic which tolerated magic and its traditionalist effects, in contrast to the puritan type which radically eliminated magic as unholy, thus liberating rationality from magical influence.

Weber's typological concepts as just illustrated have significance for general comparative study of religions. They can serve, for instance, as hypothetical criteria to explore the propensity of a religion or a system of ultimate values toward socioeconomic change, particularly in the direction of rational capitalistic development. In this sense, Weber's typological concepts have greater significance for dynamic study of

[94] Parsons, *Structure*, p. 540.

socioeconomic development involving religion than the contributions from many others in the field of comparative religion.

For example, Durkheim's dichotomy of sacred and profane and his concept of collective representation in religious symbolism are oriented more toward understanding the function of religion in the structure of a social system rather than toward understanding the dynamic disposition of a religion toward the socioeconomic order. This is particularly clear when we compare Durkheim's *"sacré"* with Weber's dynamic concept of "charisma" in the context of religious prophecy. A similar difference applies to the comparison of Weber's typological concepts with Malinowski's concept of magic which emphasized its supportive function to institutionalized patterns of social action. In addition, both Durkheim and Malinowski concentrated mainly on primitive societies in contrast to Weber's bold approach of systematically comparing the dominant complex religious systems in all four great civilizations of the world: the European, the Middle Eastern, the Indian and the Chinese.

In this light, this volume on Chinese religion has significance for the general field of comparative sociology of religion in the sense that it supplied an empirical case for Weber's generalized typological concepts, and that these concepts were dynamically oriented toward the study of socioeconomic change. Hence, it stands as a rich source of challenging ideas and conceptual formulations for the student of comparative religion confronting a world in the throes of revolutionary transformation.

C. K. YANG
University of Pittsburgh

September, 1963

PART I
SOCIOLOGICAL FOUNDATIONS

CHAPTER I

CITY, PRINCE AND GOD[1]

1. On Chinese Money

I̲N SHARP contrast with Japan, China was already a country of large walled cities in times prehistoric by our conception. Only cities had a canonized local patron with a cult and the prince was primarily lord of a city. Even in the official documents of large constitutive states the term for "state" remained "your capital" or "my humble city." And even in the last third of the 19th century the definite subjection of the *Miao* (1872) was accomplished by a compulsory synoecism, a collective settling in cities, just as in ancient Rome until the 3rd century. In effect the taxation policy of the Chinese administration strongly favored the urban residents at the expense of the open country.[2] From early times China was the scene of an inland trade indispensable for providing the needs of large areas. Nevertheless, because of the preponderance of agrarian production, money economy was, until modern times, scarcely as well developed as it was in Ptolemaic Egypt. Sufficient indication of this is to be found in the monetary system—in any case partially to be understood as a product of disintegration—with the exchange rate between copper currency and silver bullion (the coinage of which was in the hands of the guilds) continually fluctuating from time to time and from place to place.[8]

Chinese currency[4] combines extremely archaic features with apparently modern elements. The sign for "wealth" still retains the old meaning of "mussel" (*pei*). It appears that as late as 1578 tributes in *shell* money still issued from Yunnan (a mining province!). There is still a character for "coins" which means "tortoise shell."⁵ *Pu pe* (silk money) is said to have existed under the Chous, and payment of taxes in silk is found in many varying periods. Pearls, precious stones, and tin are cited alongside these as old bearers of monetary function, and even the usurper Wang Mang (after 7 A.D.) tried in vain to set up a monetary scale in which tortoise shells and sea shells functioned alongside gold, silver and copper as means of payment. Conversely, but from an admittedly unreliable account, the rationalistic unifier of the Empire, Shih Huang Ti, had only "round" coins cast from copper and gold (*i* and *ch'ien*), forbidding all other media of exchange or payment—again without success. Silver seems to have become important as a currency metal only in late times (under Wu Ti, end of 2nd century B.C.) and as a tax on the Southern provinces, only in 1035 A.D. This was doubtless attributable to technical factors: the gold was of the panning type and copper was originally obtained by a relatively easy technical process. But silver could be obtained only by full-scale mining and the mining as well as the coining techniques of the Chinese remained on a completely primitive level. The coins, allegedly made as early as the 12th century B.C. (but probably actually only in the 9th) and first inscribed about 200 B.C., were cast rather than stamped. Hence they could be very easily imitated. Also their intrinsic content varied greatly, much more so than European coins up to the 17th century (e.g., English crowns varied up to 10%). Eighteen pieces of the same issue in the 11th century ranged in weight, according to Biot's finding, from 2.7 grams to 4.08 grams; 6 pieces of 620 A.D. issue ranged from 2.5 to 4.39 grams copper. For this reason alone they were neither unambiguous nor utilizable standards for trade. From time to time the gold reserves were suddenly augmented by Tatar booty gold, only rapidly to decline again. Therefore, gold and silver early became very scarce, silver in spite of the fact that it would have been worthwhile to operate the mines by existing techniques.⁶ Copper remained the currency of everyday trade. The far greater expansion of precious metals in the Occident was well known to the annalists, especially of the Han period. In fact the many large annual silk caravans which were supplied by tributes in kind brought occidental gold into the country, as evidenced by Roman coins that have been found. This of course ceased with the end of the Roman Empire, and only in the period of the Mongol Empire was the currency situation improved.

Trade with the West reached a turning point in the period after the opening of the Mexican-Peruvian silver mines, for their yield flowed in considerable portion to China in exchange for silk, porcelain, and tea. The depreciation of silver in relation to gold is evidenced in the following ratios:

1368	4:1		1840	18:1
1574	8:1		1850	14:1
1635	10:1		1882	18:1
1737	20:1			

But the rising valuation of silver which came in the wake of increasing needs for silver money nonetheless caused the price of copper to decline relative to silver. Mining and minting were regalia of political authority; even the nine semi-legendary departments mentioned in the *Chou Li* include the master of the mint. The mines were operated partly under public management with corvée[7] and partly by private operators, but the government monopolized the purchase of the yield. The discrepancy between price and costs is sufficient explanation for the very low output.

The high costs of transporting the copper to the mint in Peking —which sold everything in excess of state coinage needs—considerably increased the cost of minting. These costs were tremendous in themselves. In the 8th century (752 according to Ma Tuan-lin) each of the 99 existing minting plants reportedly produced about 3,330 *min* (1000 pieces each) in copper coins annually. Each required 30 laborers for this, and utilized 21,200 *chin* (550 grams each) of copper, 3700 *chin* of lead, and 500 of tin. The cost of manufacturing 1000 pieces amounted to 750 pieces, i.e., 75 percent. To this must be added an exorbitant minting profit claimed by the monopolized mint,[8] nominally 25 percent. The constant battle which was waged through all the centuries against the fabulously profitable counterfeiting was made hopeless by this alone. The mining districts were threatened by enemy invasion. It was not uncommon for the government to buy copper for coinage from foreign countries (e.g., Japan) or to confiscate private copper holdings in order to assure fulfillment of the large coinage requirements. From time to time regalia and public operation were extended to practically all metal mines. The silver mines paid a very considerable royalty to the Kwangtung mandarins involved. (In Kwangtung in mid-19th century, these royalties amounted from 20 to 33⅓ percent; or in combination with lead, 55 percent.) Such revenue was the chief source of income for these mandarins in return for a lump payment made to the government. The gold mines, located mainly in Yunnan Province, like all others were allotted in small fields to mining master craftsmen for small-scale operation, and each paid up to 40 percent royalties according to output. As late as the 17th century the mines were reported as poorly exploited from a technical standpoint. The reason, apart from the difficulties created by the geomancers[9] (see Chapter VII, 9), was the general traditionalism inherent in the political, economic and ideological structure of China. This traditionalism repeatedly caused the miscarriage of all serious monetary reform. Regarding the debasement of coinage, it is further mentioned at a very early date in the Annals (Chuang Wang and Ch'u) that the imposition of debased coinage failed. We are told of the great disturbance of trade when, under Emperor Ching Ti, gold coinage was debased for the first time—but by no means the last.

Obviously, the basic evil was the fluctuation of monetary metal.[10] The North, the defense area against the barbarians of the steppes, suffered much more from this than the South, which as the seat of trade was always better provided with means of circulation. The financing of every war forced monetary reforms, and copper coins were converted to the manufacture of arms (comparable to the use of nickel coins in Germany during World War I). With the restoration of peace the country was flooded with copper since the "demobilized" soldiers freely used army property. Any political unrest could close the mines. The shortage or surplus of coinage is reported to have resulted in price fluctuations which are amazing even when we allow for probable exaggeration. Again and again numerous private counterfeiting mints emerged, undoubtedly tolerated by the officials. The various satrapies also regularly defied the state monopoly. Desperate because it failed in each and every attempt to enforce the monopoly, the government repeatedly allowed the private citizen to mint money according to set standards. It was done first under Wen Ti (175 B.C.) and naturally resulted in complete monetary muddle. To be sure after this first experiment Wu Ti promptly succeeded in restoring the mining monopoly. He abolished the private mints and by improving the minting technique (hard-rimmed coins) the prestige of state coins was raised. But the necessity of financing warfare against the Hsiung Nu (the Huns) —at all times contributive to monetary muddle—resulted in issuing credit currency of white deer skin. Moreover, the ease with which his silver coins could be imitated eventually condemned this attempt to failure.

Probably as a result of political unrest, the shortage of minting metal under Yuan Ti (about 40 B.C.) was as great as ever.[11] Following this the usurper Wang Mang vainly experimented with coinage scales of 28 different types of coins. Since then no governmental restoration of gold and silver coinage seems to have been recorded, but in any case it had occurred only occasionally. Following the banks' example,[12] the government first issued means of exchange in 807,[13] a practice which flourished especially under the Mongols. At first, in the manner of the banks, the issue was based on metal, but later this was less and less so. The memory of the debasement of coinage and the depreciation of the assignats has since firmly established bank currency. Bank currency used silver bar deposits as the base for means of exchange in wholesale trade, calculating in tael units. Despite the very low prices of copper currency, the latter meant a tremendous increase in minting costs and besides was a cumbersome form of money for trade. Thus it was a hindrance to the development of the money economy since the charges for money transport were high.

Originally a string filed with 1000 copper coins (*ch'ien*) was equivalent to 1 and later to ½ an ounce of silver. The fluctuations of available amounts of copper also remained very important in peace time because of the industrial and artistic uses of copper (Buddha statues) which tangibly affected prices and taxes. The wide variations of the mint price and its influence on the price level have thus regularly doomed to failure the attempts at establishing a unified budget on the basis of pure or approximately pure money taxes. Repeatedly it was necessary to fall back (at least in part) on taxation in kind with its natural stereotyping ramifications for the economy.[14]

Besides direct defense requirements and other budgetary considerations, the central authorities were primarily concerned with price policy in money matters. Inflationary tendencies, such as decontrol of coinage for the sake of stimulating the production of copper money, alternated with counter-inflationary measures, such as closure of part of the mints.[15] Above all, currency considerations played a role in the prohibition and control of foreign trade. This was because loss of money was feared if imports were free and a deluge of foreign money feared if exports were free.[16] To be sure, the persecution of the Buddhists and Taoists was essentially determined by religious policy, but monetary reasons of state were often co-determining factors. Stimulated by monastic art, the Buddha statues, vases and paraments and the conversion of coinage to artistic uses repeatedly endangered the currency. The melting of coinage en masse led to a great shortage of money and the hoarding of copper, as well as to price declines which ended in a barter economy.[17] The state systematically looted the monasteries, imposed tariffs on copper goods,[18] and finally[19] attempted to monopolize the manufacturing of bronze and copper goods. Later this state monopoly was extended to all metal goods in order to bring private dilution of coinage under control. Both measures failed in the long run. The accumulation of land was prohibited (to be discussed below), a prohibition which was enforced with varying efficiency by officials who repeatedly accumulated considerable sums of copper in their own hands. During periods of money shortage high taxes were levied on monied wealth. Maximal money holdings were defined[20] with increasing frequency for reasons of price policy and budgetary considerations. The situation was not improved by recurrent attempts to change to iron money which was used for a time along with copper. The official petition mentioned in the time of Schitong (tenth century) demanded that profits from coinage be renounced and the utilization of metal decontrolled in order to avoid monopoly prices on metal goods and the concomitant stimulus given to its industrial utilization. This was not carried out.

Paper money was dealt with similarly. The bank issues at first were obviously of the quality of those certificates by means of which wholesale trade usually guards itself against currency muddle. Later they became essentially a means of exchange for facilitating interlocal remittances. These bank issues provoked imitation. The technical prerequisite was the emergence of the paper industry, imported since the 2nd century A.D., and a suitable process of printing wood cuts,[21] especially relief cuts rather than the earlier intaglio process. Early in the ninth century the state began to remove the profitable exchange opportunities from the traders' hands. At first the principle of an exchange fund of ¼ to ⅓ was taken over. Note issues based on a fiscal monopoly of bank deposits are also to be found later. Naturally this was not all. The notes, which were first reproduced from wood cuts and then from copper engravings, were quickly worn because of the poor quality of paper. Because of the shortage of coinage metal in war the notes became illegible with increased use. This led to the reduction of coins to the smallest denominations, the repudiation of the illegible paper slips, and the levying of a charge for printing new money for old.[22]

Above all, it led to the elimination of the metal reserve,[23] or at least it made it more difficult to exchange paper money as the place of exchange shifted to the interior.[24] At first withdrawal of currency from circulation was spaced over a short period but this was later extended from 22 to 25 years.[25] Mostly new notes, often of lower denomination,[26] were issued for old ones, which were turned in. Repeatedly authorities refused to accept the old notes for all tax payments. These measures discredited paper money again and again. Naturally the frequent orders to effect every large payment in defined quotas of paper money,[27] or the occasional prohibition of payment in metal did not check this.

The repeated withdrawal of all paper money from circulation led to deflation and lower prices. Recurrent attempts to increase the means of circulation in a planned manner failed because the temptation of all-out inflation, for budgetary reasons, always promptly arose. Under normal conditions the ratio of note circulation to coinage roughly remained that of 18th century England (1 to 10 or even less). Inflation was brought about by war and by loss of mining districts to the barbarians. Though less relevant, the use of metal for industrial, or rather, artistic purposes was also conducive to inflation at times when great wealth was accumulated and the monastic foundations of Buddhism were built. The aftermath of war always led to bankruptcy of the currency, reminiscent of the assignats of the French revolution. The Mongol rulers (Kublai Khan) had tried to issue graded metal certificates (?), a measure which Marco Polo, as is known, greatly admired,[28] but this led to a tremendous inflation. As early as 1288 the currency was devalued by 80 percent; then the great influx of silver brought it back into circulation. Thereupon an attempt was made to establish exchange rates between gold, silver and copper (gold to silver 10, actually 10, 25:1. An ounce of silver equalled 2005 ch'ien, hence copper was devalued by 50 percent). Private possession of gold and silver bars was forbidden and precious metal was only to be coverage for the certificates. The precious metal and copper industries were taken over by the state and no coins were minted. Actually this led to a pure paper currency. With the fall of the dynasty it was abolished.

The Ming resumed orderly minting. That gold and silver were

allegedly valued in the ratio of 4 to 1 is a characteristic example of the instability of the price ratios of precious metals. Soon the Ming prohibited gold and silver (in 1375), and then copper money (in 1450), because the paper money which was circulated at the same time was devalued. Therewith, paper currency seemed to be definitely established. Yet 1489 is the last year for which the annalists mention paper money. The 16th century witnessed great efforts to coin copper but these efforts also failed.

In the 16th century conditions became tolerable with the influx of European silver through direct trade. By the end of the 16th century the silver standard (bullion—actually bank) was adopted in wholesale trade. Copper coinage was resumed and the copper-silver ratio changed considerably at the expense of copper.[29] Paper money of all sorts remained completely suppressed after it was prohibited by the Mings in 1620, a prohibition honored by the Manchus. The slow but considerable increase of the metal reserve is expressed in the increasing pecuniary structure of state budgetary accounts. The issue of paper money by the state during the second T'ai P'ing rebellion ended in a devaluation and repudiation similar to that of the assignats.

Yet the circulation of silver bullion caused great difficulties. It had to be weighed each time, and it was considered legitimate for provincial bankers to recover their higher costs by using scales other than those used in the port cities. The grain of silver had to be tested by silversmiths. Because of the great proportionate increase in silver payments the central government demanded a certificate stating the place of origin and the examining board of each silver bar. The silver was molded in the form of a shoe and differed in grain by regions.

Obviously these conditions necessarily led to bank currency. In wholesale places the bankers' guilds, whose bills of exchange were honored everywhere, sponsored guild organization and enforced payment of all commercial debts in bank money. To be sure, during the 19th century there were recommendations that the state introduce paper currency (memorial of 1831).[30] The arguments remained exactly those of the beginning of the 17th century and the Middle Ages: namely, the industrial use of copper was said to endanger monetary circulation and therewith price policies. Although bank money was said to surrender currency control to the traders, paper currency was not introduced then. The salaries of the officials—the most powerful interest group— were substantially paid in silver. Because their income opportunities depended on trade, broad strata of officials shared the interest of the traders in opposing the interference of the Peking government in currency matters. In any case, all provincial officials were unanimously against any strengthening of central finance, above all, against financial control by the central government.

The mass of the petty bourgeois and small holders was little or not at all interested in changing existing conditions. This was so despite, and partly because of, the great decline in the purchasing power of copper, a decline which had been gradual through the centuries. Here the technicalities of Chinese bank credit and exchange may be left aside. We would only like to mention that the tael, the standard unit of account, circulated in three main but also some minor forms. Moreover, the grain of the bars carrying a banker's stamp and moulded in the form of a shoe was quite unreliable. For quite some time the state had no longer enforced a tariff on copper coins. In the interior the copper standard was the only effective one, but the silver hoard, and especially the rate of its growth since 1516, was quite significant.

We now face two peculiar facts. 1. The strong increase of wealth in precious metals had unmistakably led to a stronger development of the money economy, especially in state finance. This, however, did not accompany a shattering of traditionalism, but rather its distinct increase. Capitalist phenomena, as far as can be seen, were not effected to any tangible extent. 2. The enormous growth of population, to be discussed below, was neither stimulated by, nor did it stimulate, capitalist development. Rather it was, to say the least, associated with a stationary form of economy.

2. City and Guild

DURING Antiquity in the Occident the cities, and during the Middle Ages, the cities, the papal curia, and the emerging states were vehicles of financial rationalization, of money economy and of politically oriented capitalism. But, in China, we have seen that the monasteries were even regarded as detrimental to the retention of a metal standard. In China, there were no cities like Florence which could have created a standard coin and guided the state in monetary policies. And the state, as shown, not only failed in its currency policy but also in its attempt to establish the money economy.

The valuation of temples and of many other prebends[31] primarily as payment in kind was characteristic until recent times. Thus, the Chinese city, despite all analogies differed decisively from that of the Occident. The Chinese character for city means "fortress," as was also true for occidental antiquity and the Middle Ages. In Antiquity, the Chinese city was a princely residence[32] and until modern times primarily remained the residence of the viceroy and other dignitaries. In such cities as those of Antiquity and, let us say, the Moscow of the period of serfdom, it was primarily rent that was spent. This was partly ground rent, partly income from office prebends, and other income that was either directly or indirectly politically determined. Of course the cities were the usual locus of trade and crafts, the latter to a noticeably lesser degree than in the occidental Middle Ages. The village, too, had the right to open markets under the protection of the village temple but no urban market monopoly was guaranteed by state privilege.[33]

In contrast to the Occident, the cities in China and throughout the Orient lacked political autonomy. The oriental city was not a "polis" in the sense of Antiquity, and it knew nothing of the "city law" of the Middle Ages, for it was not a "commune" with political privileges of its own. Nor was there a citizenry in the sense of a self-equipped military estate such as existed in occidental Antiquity. No military oath-bound communities like the

Compagna Communis of Genoa or other *coniurationes* ever sprang up to fight or ally themselves with feudal lords of the city in order to attain autonomy. No forces emerged like the consuls, councils, or political associations of merchant and craft guilds such as the *Mercanza* which were based upon the military independence of the city district.[34] Revolts of the urban populace which forced the officials to flee into the citadel have always been the order of the day. But they always aimed at removing a concrete official or a concrete decree, especially a new tax, never at gaining a charter which might, at least in a relative way, guarantee the freedom of the city. This was hardly possible along occidental lines because the fetters of the sib were never shattered. The new citizen, above all the newly rich one, retained his relations to the native place of his sib, its ancestral land and temple. Hence all ritually and personally important relations with the native village were maintained. This was rather comparable to the way in which a member of the Russian peasantry retained his birthright within his *mir,* with all ensuing rights and obligations, even though he had his permanent occupation in the city as factory worker, journey man, merchant, manufacturer or writer.

In the Occident the Zeus Erkeios of the Attic citizen, and since Cleisthenes his demos, or the *Hantgemal* of the Saxon, were residues of similar conditions.[35] But the city was a "community"— in Antiquity a religious association, in the Middle Ages a *coniuratio* (oath-bound fraternity). Of this China knows only preliminary stages, not realization. The Chinese city god was only a local tutelary deity, not the god of an association, and as a rule he was a canonized urban mandarin.[36]

In China, this was due to the absence of the oath-bound political association formed by an armed citizenry. Craft and merchant guilds, city leagues, and even in some instances a "city guild," externally similar to the English *gilda mercatoria,* have existed in China until now. Indeed, the imperial officials had to reckon with the various urban associations and actually these associations extensively controlled the economic life of the city. In fact they did so with greater intensity than the imperial administration, and in many ways this control was firmer than that of the average occidental association. In some respects the condition of Chinese cities is suggestive of English cities at the time of the *firma burgi* or of the Tudors. Yet the obvious and significant difference is that the English city, even at that time had the "charter" which guaranteed its "liberties." In China nothing of the kind could be found.[37] In sharp contrast with the Occident, but in harmony with Indian conditions, the city as an imperial fortress actually had fewer formal guarantees of self-government[38] than the village. Legally the city consisted of "village districts" under particular *tipao* (elders). Often it belonged to several lower (*hsien*), in some cases even to several superior (*fu*) districts under separate governmental departments[39]—quite an advantage to thieves. Unlike the village, the city could not legally make contracts, either economic or political ones. It could not file law suits and in general it could not function as a corporate body. The actual occasional rule of a powerful merchant guild over a city, to be found in India and in other parts of the world, was no substitute.

This can be explained in terms of the different origins of the occidental and oriental city. The polis of Antiquity originated as an overseas trading city, however strong its base in landlordism, but China was predominantly an inland area. Nautically considered, the range of operations of Chinese junks was occasionally quite extensive and nautical technology (eclimeter and compass[40])was highly developed. Nevertheless, oversea trade in relation to the land mass of the interior was of minor significance. Moreover, for centuries China had renounced seapower, the indispensable basis of export trade. Finally, for the sake of preserving tradition, China, as is well known, had confined foreign contact to a single port, namely Canton, and to a small number of licensed firms, specifically thirteen. The result was not accidental. Even the imperial canal, as every map and every preserved report shows, was actually built for the sole purpose of avoiding the transport of rice from South to North by sea because of the hazards of piracy and especially because of typhoons. Even recent official reports state that the losses of the treasury through sea transport warrant the tremendous costs for reconstructing the canal.

On the other hand, the characteristic inland city of the occidental Middle Ages, like the Chinese and the Middle Eastern city, was usually founded by princes and feudal lords in order to gain money rents and taxes. Yet at an early date the European city turned into a highly privileged association with fixed rights. These could be and were extended in a planned manner because at the time the lord of the city lacked the technical means to administer the city. Moreover, the city represented a military association which could successfully close the city gates to an army of knights. In contrast, the great Middle Eastern cities, such as Babylon, at an early time were completely at the mercy of the royal bureaucracy because of canal construction and administration. The same held for the Chinese city despite the paucity of Chinese central administration. The prosperity of the Chinese city did not primarily depend upon the citizens' enterprising spirit in economic and political ventures but rather upon the imperial administration, especially the administration of the rivers. (Just as in Egypt the sign of "government" is the Pharaoh holding the lash in his hand, so the Chinese character identifies "governing" (*chih*) with the handling of a stick. In the old terminology this is identified with the "regulation of waters." The concept of "law" (*fa*) however, means "the release of water.")[41]

Our occidental bureaucracy is of recent origin and in part has been learned from the experiences of the autonomous city states. The imperial bureaucracy of China is very ancient. The Chinese city was predominantly a product of rational administration, as its very form indicated. First, there was the stockade or wall. Then the population, which was often insufficiently centered, was brought together within the walled area, possibly by coercion.[42] As in Egypt, a change of dynasty also meant a change of the capital or at least its name. The residence of Peking eventually became permanent but until recent times it was only in a limited way a place of trade and industrial exports.

The paucity of imperial administration actually meant that the

Chinese in town and country "governed themselves." Like the sibs
in rural areas, the occupational associations in the city held sovereign sway over the way of life of their members. This they did
at the side of the sibs as well as over those who did not belong
to any sib, or at least not to any old and strong one. With the
exception of the Indian castes and their different forms, nowhere
was the individual so unconditionally dependent upon craft and
merchant guild (which were not differentiated terminologically)
as in China.[43] Although in a few instances there were monopolistic
guilds and though these were not officially recognized, the guilds
had often in reality appropriated absolute jurisdiction over their
members. Formally this seemed to be especially true of the Hwei-
kwan guilds of officials and merchants who derived from other
provinces. These guilds may be compared to the German Hansa.
They had definitely emerged by the 14th, but perhaps even by
the eighth century, in order to protect these groups against the
hostility of the local merchants. That, anyway, is occasionally
stated in the preambles to the statutes. Membership was required
and whoever wished to engage in business had to join at the risk
of his life. The guilds owned club houses and levied taxes proportionate to the official's salary or the merchant's turnover. They
punished any member who appealed in court against another
member. They provided tombs in a special cemetery as a substitute for native soil. They bore the trial costs of their members
suing outsiders and, were there conflict with local authorities,
they managed the appeals to central authorities. Of course, they
provided the requisite *douceurs*. In 1809, they protested the local
prohibition of rice exports. Besides non-native officials and merchants there were also non-native artisans enrolled in the guilds—
needle makers from Kiangsu and Taichow living in Wenchow.
The goldbeater's guild of Wenchow consisted exclusively of people from Ningpo. These organizations are residues of tribal craft
organizations and the ethnic specialization of crafts. This is evidenced by the goldbeater's guild which denied membership and
the imparting of its art to a native. In all these cases the absolute
authority of the guild was a natural response to the always pre-

carious situation of the guild members in an ethnically strange environment. It was identical to the strict though far less rigorous discipline of the Hansa in London and Novgorod. The local craft and merchant guilds (*kung so*), however, also held almost absolute sway over their members through expulsion, boycott, and lynch justice. In the 19th century a guild member was bitten to death for infraction of the rule defining the maximum number of apprentices!

The guild controlled all economic matters relating to its members: weights and measures, or currency made by stamping silver bars, as practiced, e.g., by the great guild of Newchwang which also provided for street maintenance. Credit affairs of the members were controlled especially by the *hui-kuan* guilds (Hansa leagues) whose monopolistic practices stipulated the terms of delivery, storage, payment, insurance and interest rates. Thus, the opium guild at Wuchow determined when opium could be brought to market; the bankers' guilds in Ningpo, Shanghai and elsewhere determined the interest rates; the tea guild in Shanghai the rates of storage and insurance. The guilds repressed feigned or otherwise illegal transactions. They provided for the orderly compensation of creditors in case of business transfer, e.g., the druggists' guilds of Wenchow did this. The bankers' guilds regulated the monetary exchange rates. The guilds gave advances on goods in storage, as, for instance, the opium guild did because of the aforementioned regulation of the selling season.

As regards artisans, it is important to note that the guilds regulated and restricted the number of apprentices. They even excluded family members. Occasionally the guilds secured craft secrets.[44]

A few guilds had at their disposal a fortune amounting to millions and often this was invested in joint landholdings. They taxed their members and from new members they raised initiation fees. They provided for bail and for the burial of impoverished members. They also financed theaters. Charity organization and common religious worship, however, were less developed than might be supposed by European analogy. If initiation fees were occasionally paid to a deity (temple treasury) this arrangement (originally) served as security against seizure by political authorities. Only poor guilds, being unable to afford a club house of their own, would regularly use a temple as a meeting hall. The theater featured secular plays, not "mysteria" as in the West. The religious fraternities (*hui*) developed only slight religious interests.

The majority of the occupational associations were open to all who engaged in a particular trade and usually membership was obligatory. There were numerous survivals of ancient sib and tribal crafts. Actually they represented hereditary monopolies or even hereditary secret arts.[45] But there were also monopolistic merchant guilds which were established by fiscal interests or by the anti-foreign policy of the state. We may mention especially the Co-hong guild in Canton. Until the peace of Nanking its thirteen firms monopolized all foreign trade. It was one of the few guilds based on official privilege granted by the government.

During the Middle Ages the Chinese administration repeatedly sought to shift to liturgical ways of providing for public needs. It seems justifiable to infer that the transition from inter-ethnic specialization of migrating itinerant sib and tribal crafts to resident handicraft, with free admission to apprenticeship for some crafts, has been consummated in stages. Possibly this transition was enforced from above by means of compulsory trade associations which in turn were regimented for government commissions. Consequently, a broad section of industry remained essentially organized as sib and tribal crafts. Under the Han, manifold industrial pursuits were still strict family secrets. The art of producing Foochow lacquer, for instance, died out during the T'ai P'ing rebellion because the sib who kept the secret had been eradicated. Generally, there was no urban monopolization of industry. The local division of labor between town and country which we refer to as "city economy" had developed as it had elsewhere, and individual policy measures of the city economy can be found. In the occidental Middle Ages these were the guilds which, once in power, actually sought to execute the "policy of a city economy." In China, despite many beginnings, this sort of systematic city policy has never fully matured. To be sure, Chinese public authorities have repeatedly reverted to liturgical controls, but they failed to create a system of guild privileges comparable to that of the West during the Middle Ages. The very absence of these legal guarantees led the occupational associations of China to the road of relentless and incomparable self help. In China, this also accounted for the absence of fixed, publicly recognized, formal and reliable legal foundations for a free and cooperatively regulated organization of industry and commerce, such as is known in the Occident. These were the legal foundations beneficial to the development of petty capitalism in occidental medieval artisan crafts but in China they were absent because the cities and guilds had no politico-military power of their own. This in turn is explained by the early development of bureaucratic organization in the army (officer corps) and civil administration.

3. Princely Administration and the Conception of Deity: A Comparison with the Middle East

IN CHINA, as in Egypt, the need to control the rivers was prerequisite to a rational economy. This need was decisive for the inception of central authority and its patrimonial officialdom, which has existed throughout Chinese history. Distinct proof of this is the resolution of an alleged cartel of the feudal princes which Mencius mentions and which is ascribed to the seventh century B.C. Irrigation was already developed at the time when the art of writing emerged and perhaps the latter was connected with the administrative needs of the former.[46] In contrast to Egypt and Mesopotamia, however, at least in Northern China, the nucleus of the empire, priority was given to dike construction against floods or canal construction for inland water transport, especially transport of forage. Canal construction for irrigation purposes was secondary. In Mesopotamia the latter was a prerequisite to the cultivation of the desert area. The river administrators and the "police" formed the nucleus of the pre-literary and purely patrimonial bureaucracy. The police are mentioned in early documents as forming a class below the "productive" estates but above the "eunuchs" and "carriers."

It may be asked to what extent these conditions were consequential not only as they unquestionably were for politics, but also for religion. The god of the Middle East was fashioned on the model of the king. To the Mesopotamian and Egyptian subject who hardly knew rain, weal and woe, and above all, the harvest depended upon the activities of the king and his administration. The king directly "created" the harvest. The case was somewhat similar, though by no means as compelling, in some parts of Southern China where the regulation of water was of paramount significance. Irrigation led to the direct transition from hoe culture to gardening. However, in Northern China, natural events, especially rainfall, loomed much larger despite the considerable development of irrigation. In the Middle East the old centralized bureaucratic administration undoubtedly promoted the concept of the supreme deity as a King of Heavens who had "created" man and the world from nothing. Now, as supramundane ethical ruler, he demands each creature to do his duty. Only in the Middle East has this idea of God retained the upper hand with such forcefulness. It must be added at once that this fact cannot be deduced solely from economic conditions. In the Middle East the Heavenly King also rose to the highest position of power and finally—though only with Deutero Isaiah in exile—to an absolutely supramundane supremacy. In Palestine, in contrast to the desert regions, rain and sunshine, the sources of fertility, were sent by the grace of this God. Jehovah expressly expostulated with the Israelites about this. Obviously factors other than economic factors, namely foreign political ones, played a part in these contrasting conceptions of deity. This requires further elaboration.

The contrast between the Middle and Far Eastern conception of deity was by no means always as sharp. On the one hand, Chinese antiquity knew a dual god of the peasantry (*She-chi*) for every local association; it represented a fusion of the spirit of fertile soil (*She*) and the spirit of harvest (*Chi*). This God had already assumed the character of a deity meting out ethical sanctions. On the other hand, the temples of ancestral spirits (*Chung-miao*) were objects of worship. These spirits together (*She-chi chung-miao*) were the main object of the local rural cults. As the tutelary spirit of the local community it was probably first conceived naturalistically as a semi-material magical force or substance. Its position roughly corresponded to that of the local deity in Western Asia but at an early time the latter was essentially more personalized. With the increase of princely power the spirit of the ploughland became the spirit of the princely territory. As is usually the case, when a stratum of noble heroes developed in China, then too a personal God of Heavens originated who roughly corresponded to the Hellenic Zeus. The founder of the Chou dynasty worshipped as a dualist unit this God of Heavens together with the local spirit. Originally imperial power was like a feudal suzerainty over the princes. Thus, sacrificial rites to Heaven became the monopoly of the emperor who was considered the "Son" of Heaven. The princes made sacrifices to the spirits of the land and to the ancestors; the heads of households made sacrifices to the ancestral spirits of their kinship group. As usual, the character of the spirits was tinged with animist-naturalist notions. This was especially true of the Spirit of Heaven (*Shang Ti*) who could be conceived either as the Heaven itself or as King of Heaven. Then the Chinese spirits, especially the mighty and universal ones, increasingly assumed an impersonal character.[47] This was exactly in reverse to the Middle Eastern situation where the personal supramundane creator and royal ruler of the world was raised above the animist semi-personal spirits and the local deity.

For a long time the concept of deity among Chinese philosophers remained very contradictory. For Wang Ch'ung, God was not conceived anthropomorphically but He nevertheless had a "body," apparently a sort of fluid substance. The same philosopher, on the other hand, argued a denial of immortality by pointing to the complete "formlessness" of God and to this the human spirit—similar to the Israelite *"ruach"*—returned after life.

A similar conception has been expressed in inscriptions. But the impersonal nature of the supreme supramundane powers was more and more emphasized. In Confucian philosophy the idea of a personal god had been upheld during the eleventh century but vanished in the twelfth century. This was due to the influence of the materialist, Chu Fu-tzu, whom Emperor K'ang Hsi, the author of the "Sacred Edict," still regarded as an authority. That this development toward an impersonal conception of deity[48] was not consummated without permanent residues of the personalist conception will be discussed later. But in the official cult the impersonal conception gained the upper hand.

In the Semitic Orient, too, the fertile land, the land with natural water, was the "land of Baal" and at the same time his residence. The Baal of the peasant's land, in the sense of harvest-yielding soil, also became the local deity of the political association of the homeland. But here this land was considered the "property" of the god; "heaven" was not conceived in the Chinese manner as impersonal and yet animated, that is to say, as a heaven which might compete with a lord of heaven. The Israelite Yahwe was originally a mountain deity of storms and natural catastrophes. In war he made his approach through clouds and thunderstorms in order to render aid to the heroes. He was the federal deity of the conquering oath-bound confederacy which had been placed under his protection by means of a covenant mediated by priests. Hence foreign affairs permanently remained his desmesne and the concern of the greatest among his prophets, who were political publicists in times when the mighty Mesopotamian robber states were tremendously feared. The final shaping of his image was determined by this circumstance. Foreign affairs set the stage for his deeds, namely, for the peripeties of war and the destiny of nations. Therefore, he was and remained first of all a God of the extraordinary, that is, of the destiny of his people in war. But his people could not create a world empire of their own and remained a small state in the midst of world powers to which they finally succumbed. Thus Jehovah could only become a "world God" as a supramundane ruler of destiny. Even his own chosen people were accorded mere creatural significance; once blessed they might also be rejected depending on their merit.

In contrast, the Chinese Empire, in historical times, became an increasingly pacified world empire despite its war campaigns. To be sure, Chinese culture originated under the banner of pure militarism. Originally the *shih* is the "hero," later the official. The "hall of studies" *(Pi-yung kung)* where, according to ritual, the emperor in person interpreted the classics seems orginally to have been a "bachelor house" (ἀνδρεῖον) such as prevailed among almost all warrior and hunting peoples. There the fraternity of young warriors were garrisoned by age group away from family life. After having proven themselves they were armed and initiated through the "capping" ceremony which is still preserved. The extent to which the typical system of age groups was elaborated remains open to question. Etymology seems to suggest that women originally managed tillage alone, but never participated in non-domestic rites. Obviously the bachelor house was that of the (charismatic) warrior chieftain where diplomatic transactions (such as the surrender of enemies) were consummated, where weapons were stored, and trophies (cut-off ears) were deposited. Here the league of young warriors practiced rhythmic, that is disciplined archery, which allowed the prince to choose his followers and officials by their merits (hence the ceremonial significance of archery until recent times). It is possible that ancestral spirits also gave advice there. If all this is true, the reports concerning original matrilineal descent accords with it. "Matriarchy," as far as can be ascertained, seems primarily and regularly to have resulted from the father's military estrangement from family life.[49] All this was very remote in historical time.

Use of the horse in individual hero combat—in China as well as the world over—led to the disintegration of the bachelor house of foot soldiers. The horse was first used as a draft animal for the war chariot and was instrumental in the ascendancy of hero combat. The highly trained individual hero, equipped with costly arms, stepped forward. This "Homeric" age of China was also very remote in historical time. In China, as in Egypt and Mesopotamia, the technique of knightly combat apparently never led to an individualist social order as strong as that of Homeric Hellas or the occidental Middle Ages.

We assume that the main counter-weight was the dependence on river regulation and therewith an autonomous bureaucratic management by the prince. As in India, the individual districts were obliged to furnish war chariots and armored men. Hence there was no personal contract like that of the occidental feudal association. The army of knights rested on the obligation of the districts to furnish warriors according to census registration. The "noble man," *chün tzu* (gentleman) of Confucius was originally the knight trained in arms. But the static pressures of economic life never allowed the war gods to ascend to Olympian heights. The Chinese emperor executed the rite of ploughing; having become the patron saint of the ploughman, he was no longer a knightly prince. The purely chthonian mythologies[50] were never of paramount significance. With the rule of the literati the increasingly pacifist turn of ideologies was natural and vice versa.

Since the abolition of feudalism the Spirit of Heaven, like the Egyptian deities, has been conceived as a sort of ideal court of appeal against the office holders of this earth, from the emperor right down to the lowest official. In China, this bureaucratic concept produced a special fear of the curse of the oppressed and the poor. This also happened in Egypt and—less explicitly—in Mesopotamia. (For the impact of this fear on their Israelite neighbors see "*Das antike Judentum*," Tübingen, 1921.) It is characteristic of the bureaucratic and at the same time pacifist mentality of the Chinese that this idea—a quasi-superstitious Magna Charta—was the only available and gravely feared weapon the subjects could use against the privileged, the officials, and the rich.

In China, the period of genuine people's wars in any case belongs to remote times. To be sure, the bureaucratic state signified no break with the warlike epoch of China. It led its armies to Indo-China and central Turkistan. The early literary-documentary sources give special praise to the warrior hero. However, in historical times, according to the official view, only once was a victorious general proclaimed emperor by the army (Wang Mang about the time of the birth of Christ). Actually of course, this has happened more often; but it occurred through the ritually required forms, or by ritually recognized conquest, or as rebellion against a ritually incorrect emperor. In the period between the eighth and the third centuries B.C., which was decisive for the formation of intellectual culture, the empire was a very loose association of dominions. The latter formally recognized the suzerainty of the politically impotent emperor but were permanently embattled in struggle for the position of *major domo*.

The fact that the imperial lord paramount was simultaneously and primarily high priest demarcated the Chinese from the occidental Holy Roman Empire. This important state of affairs may be traced to pre-historic times and was comparable to the position which the occidental pope had claimed in the manner of Boniface VIII.[51] Its indispensable function determined its preservation. In the role of high priest the emperor was an essential element of cultural cohesion among the individual states which always varied in size and power. An at least formal homogeneity of ritual cemented this cohesion. In China, as in the occidental Middle Ages, religious unity determined the ritually free interstate mobility of the noble families. The noble statesman was ritually free to transfer his services from one prince to another.

The unification of the empire, which proceeded with only minor interruptions from the third century B.C. onward represented the internal pacification of the empire, at least in principle. No longer was there legitimate opportunity for internal warfare. The defense against and the subjection of the barbarians became simply a governmental police duty. Thus, in China, the God of Heaven could not assume the form of a hero-God who revealed himself in the irrational destiny of his people through its foreign relations, or who was worshipped in war, victory, defeat, exile and nostalgia. Disregarding the Mongol invasion, such irrational fate was no longer of paramount importance in China after the construction of the Great Wall. When quiet religious speculation was being developed such events were too remote to be seized upon. They were not constantly visualized as ordained menaces, or as ordeals which had been mastered, or as problems governing man's very existence. Above all, such matters of fate were not the business of the common people. Successful usurpation of the throne or successful invasion simply meant a different tax receiver, not an altered social order. (Thus, Otto Francke much emphasizes the fact that the Manchu rule was not experienced as "foreign domination." But this does not hold for periods of revolutionary agitation, as highlighted by the manifestoes of the T'ai P'ing.)

Thus, the unshaken order of internal political and social life, with thousands of years behind it, was placed under divine tutelage and then considered as the revelation of the divine. The Israelite God also took note of internal social relationships; for he used misfortune in war as the occasion to punish his people for having broken the old order of the confederacy which he had instituted. These offenses were, however, only one among many sins, the most important of which was idolatry. For the heavenly powers of China, however, the ancient social order was the one and only one. Heaven reigned as guardian of its permanence and undisturbed sanctity, and as the seat of tranquility guaranteed by the rule of reasonable norms—not as the fountainhead of irrational, feared, or hoped for peripeties of fate. Such peripeties implied unrest and disorder, and were specifically regarded as demonic in origin. Tranquility and internal order could best be guaranteed by a power which, impersonal in nature, was specifically above mundane affairs. Such a power had to steer clear of passion, above all, "wrath"—the most important attribute of Yahwe.

These political foundations of Chinese life also favored the triumph of those elements of animist belief which inhered in all magic evolving toward the cult. In the West this development had been broken by the ascent of hero-gods and eventually by the faith of plebeian strata in a personal and ethical God of world redemption. In China, the genuine chthonian cults along with their typical orgies were also eliminated, by the aristocracy of knights and later by the literati.[52]

Dances are not to be found—the old war dance had vanished—

nor are sexual, musical, or other forms of toxic orgies found. There
are scarcely even survivals of such. Only a single act of ritual
seems to have assumed a "sacramental" character, and it was
quite non-orgiastic. The God of Heaven was also trimphant here.
Following Ssu-ma Ch'ien's biography of Confucius, the philosophers argued that the gods of the mountains and rivulets rule
the world because rain comes from the mountains. But the God
of Heaven was victorious as the God of heavenly order, not
heavenly hosts. It was a turn of religion which was specifically
Chinese; for other reasons and in a different form, it had also
remained dominant in India. Here the timeless and irrevocable
attained religious supremacy. This was brought about by joining an inviolate and uniform magical ritual to the calendar. The
ritual compelled the spirits; the calendar was indispensable for
a people of peasants. Thus, the laws of nature and of rites were
fused into the unity of *Tao*.[53] Not a supramundane lord creator,
but a supra-divine, impersonal, forever indentical and eternal
existence was felt to be the ultimate and supreme. This was to
sanction the validity of eternal order and its timeless existence.
The impersonal power of Heaven did not "speak" to man. It
revealed itself in the regimen on earth, in the firm order of nature
and tradition which were part of the cosmic order, and, as elsewhere, it revealed itself in what occurred to man. The welfare of
the subjects documented heavenly contentment and the correct
functioning of the order. All bad events were symptomatic of
disturbance in the providential harmony of heaven and earth
through magical forces. This optimistic conception of cosmic
harmony is fundamental for China and has gradually evolved
from the primitive belief in spirits. Here as elsewhere, there was
originally a dualism[54] of good (useful) and evil (harmful)
spirits, of the "*shen*" and the "*kuei*," which animated the whole
universe and expressed themselves in natural events as well as in
man's conduct and condition. Man's "soul," too, was believed
to be composed of the heaven-derived *shen* and the earthly *kuei*
substance which separated again after death. This corresponds
to the widely diffused assumption of a plurality of animating

forces. The doctrine held in common by all schools of philosophy summarized the "good" spirits as the (heavenly and masculine) *Yang* principle, the "evil" ones as the (earthly and feminine) *Yin* principle, explaining the origin of the world from their fusion. Both principles were, like heaven and earth, external. Here, as almost everywhere else, this consistent dualism was optimistically attenuated and supported by identifying the redeeming magical charisma of sorcerers and heroes with the *shen* spirits who originated in the benign heavenly power, the *Yang*. The charismatically qualified man obviously had power over the evil demons (the *kuei*), and the heavenly power was also certainly the good and supreme leader of the social cosmos. The *shen* spirits and their functions had to be supported in man and in the world.[55] To this end the demonic *kuei* spirits had to be kept at rest so that the heavenly protected order would function correctly. For, the demons could do no harm unless suffered by Heaven to do it.

The gods and spirits were powerful beings. No single God, no apotheosized hero or spirit, however powerful, was "omniscient" or "omnipotent." The Confucian's sober wisdom of life concerning the misfortunes of the pious was simply that "God's will is often unsteady." All superhuman beings were stronger than man but were far below the impersonal supreme power of Heaven, and also below the imperial pontifex who was in Heaven's good graces. Accordingly, only these and similar impersonal powers could be considered as objects of worship by the supra-individual community and such powers were conceived as determining its destiny.[56] But the spirits, who could be magically influenced, might also determine the individual's fate.

With these spirits one was on a footing of primitive mutuality: so and so many ritual acts brought so and so many benefits. If a tutelary spirit proved insufficiently strong to protect a man, in spite of all sacrifices and virtues, he had to be substituted, for only the spirit who proved to be truly powerful was worthy of worship. Actually such shifts occurred frequently. Moreover, the emperor granted recognition to proven deities as objects of worship; he bestowed title and rank[57] upon them and occasionally demoted them again. Only proven charisma legitimatized a spirit. To be sure, the emperor was responsible for misfortune, but misfortune also disgraced the God who, through oracles drawn by lot or other imperatives, was responsible for the failure of a venture. As late as 1455 an emperor publicly gave verbal lashing to the spirit of the Tasi mountain. In similar cases worship and sacrifice were withheld from the spirits. Among the great emperors the "rationalist" unifier of the empire, Shih Huang Ti, according to Ssu-ma Ch'ien's biography, had a mountain deforested in order to punish a renitent spirit for obstructing access to the mountain.

4. The Charismatic and Pontifical Position of the Central Monarch

IN KEEPING with the principle of charismatic authority, the emperor, of course, fared similarly. The whole construction, after all, issued from this political habituation. The emperor had to prove his charismatic authority, which had been tempered by hereditary successorship. Charisma was always an extraordinary force (maga, orenda) and was revealed in sorcery and heroism. The charismatic qualification of the novice was tested by trials in magical asceticism, or, given different ideas, it was acquired in the form of a "new soul." But originally the charismatic quality could be lost; the hero or magician could be "forsaken" by his spirit or God. Charisma seemed to be guaranteed only so long as it was confirmed by recurrent miracles and heroic feats. In any case, the magician or hero must not expose himself and his following to obvious failure. Originally, heroic strength was considered quite as much a magical quality as "magical force" in the narrower sense, for instance rainmaking, magical healing or extraordinary craftsmanship.[58] For cultural evolution the decisive question was whether or not the military charisma of the warlord and the pacifist charisma of the (usually meteorological) sorcerer were united in the same hand. If they lay in the hand of the war lord—the case of Caesaro-papism—the question was: What charismatic source served as the basis for the evolution of princely power?

In China, as discussed above, some fundamental prehistoric events, themselves probably co-determined by the great significance of river regulation,[59] caused imperial authority to emerge from magical charisma. Secular and spiritual authority were combined in one hand, the spiritual strongly predominating. To be sure, the emperor had to prove his magical charisma through military success or at least he had to avoid striking failures. Above all, he had to secure good weather for harvest and guarantee the peaceful internal order of the realm. However the personal qualities which were necessary to the charismatic image of the emperor were turned into ritualism and then into ethics by the ritualists and philosophers.

The emperor had to conduct himself according to the ethical imperatives of the old classical scriptures. Thus, the Chinese monarch remained primarily a pontifex; he was the old rainmaker of magical religion[60] translated into ethics. Since the ethically rationalized "Heaven" guarded eternal order, the charisma of the monarch depended on his virtues.[61] Like all genuinely charismatic rulers he was a monarch by divine right, and not in the comfortable manner of modern sovereigns who, by the grace of God, claim to be responsible to Him only for their blunders. The latter are de facto irresponsible, but the Chinese emperor ruled in the old genuine sense of charismatic authority. He had to prove himself as the "Son of Heaven" and as the lord approved by Heaven insofar as the people fared well under him. If he failed, he simply lacked charisma. Thus, if the rivers broke the dikes, or if rain did not fall despite the sacrifices made, it was evidence—such was expressly taught—that the emperor did not have the charismatic qualities demanded by Heaven. In such cases the emperor did public penitence for his sins, as happened even in recent times. The Annals record similar public confession of sins even by the princes of feudal times[62] and the custom continued to exist. As late as 1832 rain soon followed the public confession of the emperor.[63] If this was of no avail the emperor had to expect abdication; in the past, it probably meant self-sacrifice. Like other officials he was open to official reprimand by the censors.[64] Moreover, were a monarch to offend the ancient and established social order theoretically his charisma would forsake him, for the social order was part of the cosmos and its impersonal norm and harmony surpassed all deities. Were the monarch, for instance, to change the absolutely divine natural law of ancestral piety it would be judged that charisma had abandoned him, that he had fallen prey to demonic forces. And theory, after all, was not quite irrelevant. Having become a private person the monarch could be killed,[65] though naturally not everyone was authorized to do this. Rather it lay within the jurisdiction of the great officials, in much the same way as Calvin ascribed the right of resistance to the estates [66]

Officialdom, the pillar of public order and the state, was held to partake of charisma too.[67] Like the monarch it was also considered a sanctified institution although until now the individual official could be *ad nutum amovibel*. The official's qualification was also charismatically determined. All unrest and disorder in his bailiwick—whether social or cosmic-meteorological in nature—demonstrated that the official was not in the grace of the spirits. Without questioning the reasons, the official had to retire from office.

This position of officialdom had evolved since prehistoric times. The old semi-legendary sacred order of the Chou dynasty, as transmitted in the *Chou Li*, had already arrived at the point of primitive patriarchialism, initiating its transition to feudalism.

CHAPTER II

THE FEUDAL AND PREBEN-
DAL STATE

1. The Hereditary Charismatic
Nature of Feudalism

I N CHINA, as far as one can judge, political feudalism was not primarily connected with landlordism in the occidental sense. Both emerged from the "state organization of the *gentes*," as in India, when the chieftains' sibs escaped the ancient fetters of the bachelor house and its derivatives. The sib, which according to a documentary note originally furnished the war chariots, was basic to the ancient status structure. The actual political constitution was clearly delineated at the threshold of recorded history. It directly continued the primeval administrative structure common to all conquering empires including even the great nineteenth century Negro empires.

Outlying areas ruled by tributory princes were increasingly affiliated with the "middle realm," i.e., the "inner" territory surrounding the royal residence. This territory, as if under domestic authority, was directly administered by the victorious ruler and his officials, personal clients, and lower nobles. The emperor of the "middle realm" interfered with the administration of tributory princes only if this were practicable and necessary for maintaining his power and, related thereto, safeguarding his interest in tributes. His intervention naturally became more sporadic and less intense the further removed the tributory prince was from the area of domestic control.

Some of the political problems were: Were the rulers of out-lying areas removable in practice or were they hereditary dynas-tic rulers? Could the subjects make practical use of their right of appeal to the emperor, a right acknowledged in the theory of the *Chou Li,* and if so, how often? Did such appeals lead to interfer-ences by the imperial administration? Were the co-ordinate or subordinate officials of the princes, as theory had it, actually de-pendent upon the emperor's officials and appointed and removed by them? Hence, could the central administration of the three great and the three little councils *(kung* and *ku)* actually extend beyond the domestic authority? And were the armed forces of the outlying states actually at the disposition of the lord-paramount? Such problems were always solved by unstable provisions, result-ing in political feudalization.

In China this took the same course that we shall find most consistently in India. There, only the sibs of already ruling politi-cal overlords and their followings claimed and were considered for subordinate positions—from the tributory prince down to the court or provincial official. In this the emperor's sib had prece-dence, but also the sibs of princes who had submitted in good time were left in partial or full possession of their power. There was often a reluctance to deprive chieftains' families of all their lands because of the powerful ancestral spirits of charismatic sibs.[1] The feudal and prebendal opportunities were determined by sib charisma and this in turn partially explains the strong posi-tion of the ancestral spirits. Finally there were the sibs of all those who had distinguished themselves as heroes and trustees. In any case, for a long time charisma was no longer attached strictly to the individual but to his sib, a typical phenomenon as we shall find in our discussion of India. Status was not created by the feudal fief nor by receiving fief as a vassal through free com-mendation and investiture. Rather, at least in principle, the re-verse obtained. One qualified for an office fief of a certain rank as a member of a noble family with a customary rank.

During the Chinese Middle Ages we find posts of ministers and even of some ambassadors firmly vested in the hands of certain families. Confucius, too, was a genteel man because he stemmed from a ruling family. These "great families," as they appear in later inscriptions, were the charismatic sibs whose position was financed largely through political incomes and hereditary landed wealth. Of course, the contrast to the Occident, while in some respects only relative, was of no small significance. In the Occident the hereditary nature of the fiefs was a mere consequence of historical development. The fief-holders were differentiated by status into those who had and had not received judicial prerogatives; the *beneficia* were differentiated by type of service; and finally, the knights were segregated from the other estates, even from the urban patriciate. All this was consummated in a society firmly structured through appropriation of land and the fixed distribution of all sorts of profit opportunities.

Often the hereditary charismatic position of the early Medieval German "dynasties"—at the time quite hypothetical dynasties—seems to approximate Chinese conditions. In the essential areas of Western feudalism, however, reversal of traditional rank orders, conquest, and migration greatly loosened the firm sib structure. Besides, defense needs required the enrollment of every able man trained as a knight so that any man living as a knight was perforce admitted to knightly status. Hereditary charisma and the eventual proof of nobility were later developments.

In China, during historical times the hereditary charisma of the sib was, at least theoretically, always primary, though there were always successful parvenus. A dictum in the *Shu Ching* reads: "A family is esteemed for its age, an object for its newness." The hereditary nature of the fief itself was not decisive, as in the Occident it came to be, but was rather considered a gross abuse. However, it was decisive that the claim to a certain fief was based on the hereditary rank of the sib. It may well be legendary that the Chou dynasty established the five degrees of nobility and then introduced the principled distribution of fiefs according to noble rank. But it is quite credible that the high vassals of the time (*chu hou*, the princes) were exclusively selected from the descendants of the ancient rulers.[2]

This corresponds to early Japanese conditions and was typical of the "state of the gentes." According to the Annals, after the downfall of the Han dynasty, the Wei moved their capital to Loyang and had the aristocracy follow suit. The aristocracy consisted of their own and other old hereditary, charismatic sibs who originally, of course, were families of tribal chieftains. Even at that time they were descendants of feudal and prebendal office-holders; and they distributed rank (and therewith the claim to prebends) according to ancestral office, a principle identical with that of the Roman nobility and the Russian *mjestnieshestvo*.[3] Similarly, during the Period of the Warring States, the highest offices were firmly vested in the hands of certain sibs of high, hereditary charismatic rank.[4] A true court nobility emerged only during the time of Shih Huang Ti (beginning 221 B.C.) and was concomitant with the downfall of Feudalism. The award of rank is first mentioned in the Annals at that time.[5] Also financial needs for the first time compelled the sale of offices, and hence the selection of officials according to monied wealth. Hereditary charisma disintegrated despite the maintenance of rank differences in principle. As late as 1399, even the degradation to a plebeian level *(min)* is mentioned,[6] however under very different conditions and a totally different sense. It then meant that the graduate literati, exempt from corvée or being caned, could be degraded to servitude. During feudal times, an order of fiefs corresponded to rank gradation by hereditary charisma. After the abolition of subinfeudation, an order of prebends corresponded to the shift toward bureaucratic administration. The prebends were soon firmly classified under the Ch'in; the Han followed their example by classifying them into 16 classes of money and rice rents.[7] This meant the complete abolition of feudalism.

The transition was represented by the division of offices[8] into two different ranks, namely, *kuan nei hou,* i.e., land prebends and *lieh hou,* i.e., rent prebends, which depended upon the taxes of certain localities. The old, purely feudal fiefs were succeeded by land prebends. In practice these entailed broad prerogatives over the peasants. They continued to exist until the army of

knights was replaced by the princely and later the imperial standing army of disciplined and drafted peasants. Hence, despite
internal differences, there was a broad, external similarity between ancient Chinese and occidental feudalism.

In China, as elsewhere, men who did not bear arms because of
economic or educational disqualification were thereby deprived
of political rights. It is certain that this held even in pre-feudal
times. The prince of the period of the Chou allegedly consulted
the "people," i.e., the armed sibs, before giving a verdict of capital
punishment and before going to war, and the latter was compatible with the prevailing draft system. Presumably, with the advent
of the war chariot the old army system was shattered and only
then did hereditary, charismatic "feudalism" emerge and spread
to political offices.

The aforementioned *Chou Li*,[9] the oldest preserved document
concerning administrative organization, portrays a very schematic
state organization[10] under the rational leadership of officials. It
was based upon bureaucratically controlled irrigation, special
crop cultivation (silk), draft registers for the army, statistics, and
magazines. Its actual existence, however, seems problematical
since, according to the Annals, this administrative rationalization
was produced only through the competition of the feudal Warring
States.[11] Yet it is possible that a patriarchal epoch like that of the
Old Kingdom of Egypt preceded the feudal period,[12] for in both
cases the irrigation and construction bureaucracy was undoubtedly ancient and grew out of the royal clientele. From the beginning its existence tempered the feudal character of the Epoch of
the Warring States and repeatedly steered the thinking of the
literati to the tracks of administrative technology and bureaucratic utilitarianism. In any case, political feudalism held sway
for more than half a millennium.

The ninth to the third century B.C. represented a period of
well-nigh independent feudal states. The Annals portray rather
clearly the conditions of this feudal age, briefly touched upon
above.[13] The emperor was lord-paramount, before whom the vassals descended from their chariots. In the final analysis political

property "rights" could be deduced solely from infeudation by the emperor who received gifts from the princely vassals. These voluntary gifts increasingly weakened the emperor and brought him into an awkward dependency. He awarded degrees of princely rank; the sub-vassals had no direct contact with him. This principle was of great political significance for the *fu jung* (sub vassals) and is best explained by the fact that many originally independent political vassals later emerged as tributory princes. Except for obligatory military contributions, the gifts of the vassals, even those to the emperor, were considered voluntary and the emperor was obliged to compensate them in turn.[14]

That fiefs originated through the award of a castle for guardianship has often been reported of the feudal state of Ch'in. In theory, the fiefs were to be renewed by the heir, and the emperor was entitled to freely determine the qualified heir. According to the Annals, were the father's and the emperor's designation of the heir to conflict the emperor gave way. The knightly fiefs may well have varied in size. According to a note in the Annals,[15] a fief was to comprise 10 to 50,000 *mou* (1 *mou* at 5.26 *Ar* hence 526 to 2,630 *ha*) with 100 to 500 people. In other places the provision of one war chariot per thousand persons[16] is considered normal. Another count (594 B.C.) considers four settlements of undefined size[17] as equivalent to 144 warriors. Later counts, again, stipulate certain deliveries of war chariots, armored men, horses, and provisions (cattle), usually in return for very large units of land.[18] The whole manner in which taxes, forced labor, and recruits were subsequently allocated obviously continued these feudal traditions. In the older period they also proceeded to levy chariots and knights, later to raise recruits for the army, laborers for corvées, taxes in kind, and finally money taxes, as we shall show below.

There were joint fiefs, and hence joint heirs under a leading elder. By ritual the younger sons ranked lower than the oldest. No longer were they considered "vassals" but officials (office nobles), and they made sacrifices at side altars instead of the great ancestral family altar.[19] In the imperial house primogeniture and designation of a successor from among sons and relatives by the ruler or by the highest officials also obtained. Occasionally, by-passing the oldest son or the son of the chief wife in favor of a younger son or the son of a concubine caused the vassals to rebel against the emperor. Later, up to the last phase of the monarchy and for ritual reasons connected with ancestral sacrifice, the rule was that a successor be chosen from an age group younger than that of the dead ruler. Thus, during the last decades of the monarchy minors succeeded one another and as a result a relative (Prince Kung) or the Empress dowager ruled. Politically, the feudal prerogatives of the overlord were reduced to zero because only the border vassals, the overlords of frontier provinces, engaged in warfare and represented military power. Probably for this reason, too, the emperors gradually became mere pacifist hierarchs.

The emperor, as supreme pontifex, had ritual privileges which entitled him alone to offer the highest sacrifices. Warfare of a vassal against the emperor was theoretically a ritual offense and a possible source of magical evils, but this did not preclude occasional warfare against the emperor. Just as the Bishop in the Roman Empire claimed the chair in church councils so the Chinese emperor or his legate claimed the chair in the princely assemblies; this is repeatedly mentioned in the Annals. At the time when great individual vassals were powerful *major-domos* (lord protectors) this claim was disregarded—in literary theory, a ritual offense. Such princely councils met repeatedly. One of them in 650 B.C., e.g., opposed disinheritance of the true heir, opposed hereditary offices and the accumulation of offices, capital punishment of high officials, "crooked" politics, and prohibitions of grain resale; but piety, honor to old age and recognition of merit were upheld.

The unity of the empire found practical expression less in those occasional princely assemblies than in cultural homogeneity. As in the occidental Middle Ages cultural unity was represented by three factors: first, the homogeneous status-mores of chivalry; second, religious or ritual unity; and third, the homogeneity of the literati.

In point of ritual and status, the forms of homogeneity among chariot-fighting, chivalrous vassals and castled fief-holders were similar to the Occident. Just as "barbarians" and "heathens" were identified in the latter, so in China, a lack of ritual correctitude was considered a mark of the barbarian or semi-barbarian. When at a far later time the prince of Ch'in made mistakes in offering sacrifices he was considered a semi-barbarian. Warfare against a ritually incorrect prince was considered meritorious work. In later times every one of the numerous conquering Tatar dynasties of China was considered "legitimate" by the depositories of ritualist tradition when they correctly adjusted to the rules of ritual and thus to the authority of the literati caste. The demands of "international law," addressed to the conduct of princes in at least theoretical expression of cultural unity, originated partly in ritual, partly in the status groups of the knights.

There was an attempt to have the princely assembly agree upon a "peace of the land." Theoretically, were a neighboring prince in mourning, or in need, or especially were he beset by famine, warfare was condemned as ritually incorrect. In the case of famine it was a stipulated duty to give brotherly aid in distress in order to please the spirits. He who wronged his feudal superior or fought for an unjust cause gained a place neither in Heaven nor in the ancestral temple.[20] To announce the time and place of battle was considered a chivalrous obligation. Somehow the fight had to be settled and, since the battle was an ordeal, it was necessary to know the victor and the defeated.[21]

In practice, princely politics appeared instead to be a relentless struggle between great and small vassals. The sub-vassals sought every opportunity to gain independence. With single-mindedness the great princes awaited the opportunity to fall upon their neighbors so that the whole epoch, to judge from the Annals, was an age of unspeakably bloody wars. Yet the theory was not without significance and was a rather important expression of cultural unity. The representatives of this unity were the literati, i.e., the scriptural scholars whose services the princes utilized in rationalizing their administrations for power purposes just as the Indian princes used the Brahmans and occidental princes the Christian clerics.

Even the odes of the seventh century sing the praises of warriors in preference to sages and literati. The proud, ancient Chinese stoicism and the complete rejection of interest in the "beyond" was a legacy of this militaristic epoch. In the year 753, however, there is mentioned the appointment of an official court annalist who was also court astronomer in the state of Ch'in. The "books" of the princes, i.e., books of Rites and Annals (collections of precedents), came to be considered booty and the literati obviously gained significance.[22] They kept the accounts and conducted the diplomatic correspondence of the princes. Of the latter, the Annals have preserved numerous examples, perhaps edited as paradigms. They usually indicated rather Machiavellian means for overwhelming neighboring princes by war and diplomacy. They forged alliances and prepared for war, primarily through rational organization of the army, stockpiling, and taxation policy. Here the literati obviously qualified as budgetary experts of the princes.[23] The princes sought to influence one another in the choice of literati, and to entice them from their rivals. The literati in turn corresponded among themselves, changed their employment, and often led a sort of migratory existence.[24] They went from court to court just like the occidental clerics and secular intellectuals of the later Middle Ages and, like the latter, considered themselves homogeneous strata.

Competition of the Warring States for political power caused the princes to initiate rational economic policies.[25] The literati executed them. Shang Yang, a representative of the literati, is regarded as the creator of rational internal administration; another, Wei Yang founded the rational state army system which was later to surpass all others. In China, as in the Occident, a large population and especially the wealth of the prince and his subjects were political objectives which also served as means to power.[26] As in the Occident, the princes and their literati, i.e., ritualist advisers, first had to struggle against the stubborn resistance of their sub-vassals who threatened them with a fate identical to the one which they had prepared for their own feudal overlords. Princely cartels against subinfeudation were formed and the literati established principles according to which inheritance of office was ritually offensive and neglect of official duty incurred magical harm (early death).[27] This characterizes the way in which bureaucratic ad-ministration displaced the administration of vassals, and hence the charismatically qualified great families.

The corresponding transformation in the military sphere was effected when the princes established body guards,[28] equipped and provisioned armies under officers with concomitant taxation and stock-piling policy instead of raising levies of vassals. Throughout the Annals the status antagonism between the com-mon people and the great charismatically qualified sibs is pre-supposed. With war chariots and retinue the latter followed the prince into the field. There were fixed statutes regulating dress.[29] The great families sought to secure their position through mar-riage policies,[30] and even under the rational administration of Shang Yang in the state of Ch'in such status barriers were retained. The nobles were always distinguished from the people and it is apparent that "the people" referred not to the serfs but to free plebeian sibs who were simply excluded from the feudal hier-archy, from knightly combat, and from chivalrous education. It was found that the people took political positions different from the nobles.[31] Nevertheless, as we shall demonstrate later, the situation of the mass of peasantry was precarious and it was only when the patrimonial state developed that the princes allied themselves with the underprivileged strata against the nobility.

2. The Restoration of the Unified Bureaucratic State

STRUGGLE reduced the number of Warring States to an ever smaller circle of rationally administered, unified states. Finally, in the year 221, after the nominal dynasty and all other vassals were displaced, the prince of Ch'in as first Emperor succeeded in incorporating all China into the "Middle Realm." That is to say, he placed it as the patrimonium of the ruler under his own bureaucratic administration. A true "autocracy" displaced the theocratic feudal order by removing the old feudal crown council and substituting two grand viziers in the manner of the *praefecti praetorio*. Then military and civil governors were separated (as they were in late Roman institutions) and both placed under princely supervisory officials (as in Persia), such officials later becoming the travelling censors *(missi dominici)*.

With this a strictly bureaucratic order developed which was open to all and which promoted according to merit and favor. A financial factor operated alongside the universally effective and natural alliance of the autocratic ruler and the plebeian strata in opposition to the status dignitaries and in favor of "democratization" of officialdom. As mentioned above, it was not accidental that the Annals ascribed the earliest sale of office to the first Emperor, Shih Huang Ti. This practice necessarily brought well-to-do plebeians into state prebends. The struggle against feudalism, however, was one of principle. Any transfer of political authority was prohibited, even within the sib of the Emperor, but the status structure remained unaffected.[32]

Ascent opportunities for officials of lowly birth increased when a fixed hierarchy of offices was established, preliminary steps to which had been taken in the Warring States. But until the new imperial authority, aided by plebeian forces, had triumphed over feudal powers, men of plebeian descent could become politically influential only within the literati class and then only under special conditions. Since the beginning of the administrative rationalization the Annals of the Warring States have contained examples of princely trustees who were poor and of common descent and who owed their position solely to their knowledge.[33] The literati by virtue of their ability and mastery of the rites claimed preference for supreme offices even above the princely next of kin,[34] a claim contested by the vassals. Thus, the literati usually found themselves in unofficial positions rather like ministers without portfolio or, if you will, in the role of father-confessor to the prince.

The feudal nobility, as in the Occident, opposed the admission of strangers to offices which they tried to monopolize—hence the struggle between literati and nobility. During the early years of Shih Huang Ti's rule and before the unification of the empire, we find in the year 237 a report of the expulsion of foreign-born literati (and traders). The prince's interest in power, however, led him to revoke this measure[35] and henceforth his first minister was a *literatus* who referred to himself as a parvenu of lowly birth. After the unification of the empire, it is revealed in inscriptions[36] that the rational anti-traditionalist absolutism of the autocrat was also forcefully turned against this socially influential aristocracy of education, i.e., the literati.

It was said, "The Emperor is more than Antiquity,"[37] meaning that the past was not to rule the present and its interpreters were not to dominate the monarch. If we may trust tradition it describes a tremendous catastrophe. The Emperor tried to destroy the whole of classical literature and the estate of the literati by burning the sacred books and allegedly burying alive 460 literati. Therewith, pure absolutism was ushered in; it was a rule based upon personal favorites regardless of descent or education. It was signalized by the nomination of a eunuch for grand master of the household[38] and instructor for the second son. After the Emperor's death, the eunuch and the parvenu literati brought the second son to the throne in opposition to the oldest son supported by the army commander.

The favoritism of purely oriental sultanism, with its combination of status-levelling and absolute autocracy, seemed to descend upon China. It was a system which the aristocracy of the cultured literati were to fight with varying success for centuries throughout the Middle Ages.

The Emperor, in order to express the claim to his position, abolished for free commoners the anciently used name of "the people" *(min)* and replaced it with the name of *ch'in shou,* "blackheads" or "subjects." The colossal increase in forced labor[39] for imperial constructions required—as in the Empire of the Pharaohs—the relentless and unlimited control over labor forces and over the tax resources of the land.[40] On the other hand, the omnipotent palace eunuch[41] of Shih Huang Ti's successor is expressly reported to have recommended that the ruler ally himself with "the people" and distribute offices without regard to station or education. Now is the time for the sabre to rule, not fine manners. This advice is in perfect agreement with typical oriental patrimonialism. However, the emperor fought against the magicians' attempt[42] to make him "invisible" under the pretext of raising his prestige. That would have meant interning him like the Dalai Lama and placing the administration entirely in the hands of officials. Rather he reserved "autocratic rule" in the proper sense for himself.

Against this harsh sultanism a violent reaction came simultaneously from the old families, the literati, the army (embittered over construction services) and peasant sibs (overburdened by army draft, corvées and taxes). The leaders were men of lowly descent: Ch'en She, the leader of the army revolt, was a worker [a peasant, Ed.] Liu Pang, the leader of the peasants and founder of the Han dynasty, was the field-watchman of a village. The nucleus of his power was a league of his sib and other peasant sibs. It was not one from the genteel strata but a parvenu who conquered. He brought about the fall of the dynasty and placed in power the new dynasty which reunited the realm after its separate states had fallen asunder. In the end, however, success fell to the literati whose rational administrative and economic policies were again decisive in restoring imperial authority. Also they were technically superior to the administration of favorites and eunuchs, who were constantly opposed, and, above all, they had on their side the tremendous prestige associated with knowledge of precedent, ritual, and scripture—at that time something of a secret art.

Shih Huang Ti had created or at least sought to establish unified systems of script, measurement, and weight, as well as unified

laws and rules of administrative procedure. He boastfully ac-
credited to himself the abolition of warfare[43] and the foundation
of peace and internal order all of which he attained by "working
day and night."[44] Not all aspects of external unity were preserved.
Most important, however, was the abolition of the feudal system
and the establishment of a régime of officials who qualified
through personal merit. These patrimonialist innovations were
retained with the restoration of the Han dynasty and ultimately
only the literati profited by them even though they had cursed
them as outrages to the old theocratic order.

Feudal relapses occurred at a much later time. Under Emperor
Wu Ti and his favorite Chu-fu Yen during Ssu-ma Ch'ien's epoch
(second century B.C.) the newly established feudalism had to be
overthrown when it re-emerged in the office fiefs of imperial
princes. First imperial resident-ministers were dispatched to
supervise the vassals' courts. Then, in 127 B.C., in order to weaken
the vassals, partitioning the fiefs among the heirs was ordered.
Finally, under Wu Ti, court offices, hitherto claimed by nobles,
were granted to men of lowly birth (among them a former swine-
herd). The nobles violently opposed this measure, but in 124 B.C.
the literati succeeded in having the high offices reserved for
themselves. We shall show below how the Confucian literati
fought the anti-literati Taoists who were averse to popular education and whose magical interest allied them first to the aristocrats
and later to the eunuchs. This struggle was decisive for the
structure of Chinese politics and culture, but was not definitely
settled at the time. Strong feudal residues survived in the status-
ethic of Confucianism. One may infer to Confucius covert and
self-explanatory belief in classical education (he had that education) as the decisive prerequisite for entering the ruling status-
group. As a rule, educational attainment should *de facto* be restricted to the ruling stratum of the traditional "old families."
Thus, for the educated Confucian the term *chün tzu*, princely
man, originally meant "hero." Even for Confucius it was equivalent to the "educated" man and it was derived from the period of
the ruling estates when the hereditary charismatic sibs qualified

for political power. Yet one could not completely withhold recognition of the new principle of "enlightened" patrimonialism which stipulated that personal merit and merit alone should qualify a man for office, including that of the ruler. To be sure, this principle made extremely slow headway and suffered continuous relapse even on a theoretical level. Its practical significance will be discussed below. Feudal elements in the social order gradually receded and patrimonialism became the structural form fundamental to the Confucian spirit. In the Annals antagonism between the Confucians and the vassals is distinctly revealed in the latter's hatred and scorn for the scholars wandering from court to court.[45]

3. Central Government and Local Officialdom

LIKE all farflung patrimonial states with undeveloped techniques of communication the scope of administrative centralization characteristically remained very limited. After the bureaucratic state had been established the contrast and rank differences continued to exist between internal and external officials, i.e., employees of the old imperial patrimonium and provincial officials. Moreover, when successive attempts at centralization failed, patronage privileges—except for some supreme provincial offices—together with almost the entire system of finance were relegated to the provinces. Fresh struggles surrounded this question throughout the great periods of financial reform. Like other reformers Wang Anshih (11th century) demanded effective financial unification, the transfer of all tax income minus costs of collection, and an imperial budget. The tremendous transportation difficulties and the interests of provincial officials always watered this wine. Unless the ruler was exceptionally energetic the officials usually understated the taxable area and the number of taxpayers by about 40 percent as is shown by the figures of published registrations.[46] The local and provincial costs, of course, had to be deducted so that a very unpredictable tax-income remained to the central authorities. In the end they capitulated: from the 18th century

to modern times the governors, just like Persian satraps, transferred tribute normally fixed in lump sums and in theory only did
this vary according to central need. Of this later.

The regulation of taxes by quota had universal ramifications for
the power of the provincial governors. They nominated and presented for appointment to central authorities most of the district
officials. They executed the appointments but the small number
of authorized officials[47] leads one to conclude that they were
hardly able personally to administer their gigantic bailiwicks.
Considering the all-encompassing duties of Chinese officials one
must conclude that a district the size of a Prussian county, administered by one official, could not be adequately administered even
by hundreds. The empire resembled a confederation of satrapies
under a pontifical head. Formal authority was exclusively in the
hands of the high provincial officials. After the unification of the
empire and for the sake of their personal authority the emperors
ingenuously employed characteristic patrimonialist means. There
were short office terms, formally of three years, after which the
official was to be removed to a different province.[48] Employment
of an official in his home province was prohibited and likewise
the employment of relatives in the same bailiwick. There was a
thorough spy system in the form of so-called censors. Actually all
of these measures failed to establish a precise and unified administration for reasons to be discussed presently. In the central and
collegiate bodies the president of one *yamen* was subordinated
as a member of other collegiate bodies to the presidents of other
yamens. This principle handicapped administrative precision
without contributing essentially to unity. In dealing with the
provinces personal authority fared even worse. Except under
occasionally strong rulers the local administrative districts deducted their expenses from tax-collections and falsified land registrations. If there were financially "passive" provinces as places
for garrisons and magazines a complicated system provided the
transfer of yields from surplus provinces. For the rest there were
only the traditional appropriations and an unreliable budget both
at the central offices and in the provinces.

The central authorities did not have clear insight into provincial finances, the results of which we shall show below. Until recently the provincial governors concluded treaties with foreign powers since the central government was not sufficiently organized to do so. As we shall show, almost all important administrative measures which the provincial governors formally issued were actually issued by their unofficial subordinates. Until recently, subordinate authorities commonly considered the decrees of the central government as ethical and authoritative proposals or desires rather than orders. This agreed with the pontifical and charismatic nature of Imperial authority. Besides, as can be seen at a glance, these were essentially criticisms of administrative procedure rather than orders. To be sure, the individual official was removable at any time but this did not benefit the central authorities. For the central authorities the official was prevented from becoming independently powerful in the manner of the feudal vassal by prohibiting employment in his home province and prescribing his tri-annual shift, if not to another province, at least to another office. These measures contributed to the external unity of the empire but its price was the failure of the authorized official to strike roots in his bailiwick.

The mandarin, accompanied by a whole flock of sib members, friends, and personal clients assumed office in an unknown province. Usually he did not understand its dialect and from the beginning was dependent upon an interpreter's services. Furthermore, not knowing provincial law, which was based upon precedent, he could only incur danger by infraction of its sacred traditions. Thus, he was entirely dependent upon the instructions of an unofficial adviser, a native man of literary education who was thoroughly familiar with local customs. He was a sort of father-confessor; the official treated him with respect, often with devotion, and called him his "teacher." Further, the official was dependent upon unofficial assistants whom he had to pay from his own pocket. Whereas his official state-paid staff had to be born outside the province, his unofficial assistants were chosen from a number of qualified candidates born in the province. It was necessary to rely upon such men not yet appointed to office but familiar with persons and local affairs, since the official lacked orientation of his own. Finally, when assuming the governorship of a new province, he relied upon the chief of the usual provincial departments who had acquired knowledge about the subject matter and the locale.⁴⁹ After all, the latter preceded him through several years of familiarity with local conditions. Obviously this resulted in actual power being vested in the hands of the unofficial, native subordinates. And the higher the rank of the authorized official the less was he able to correct and control their management. Thus the local and central government officials were not sufficiently informed about local conditions to facilitate consistent and rational intervention.

The emergence of feudal status and thus the emancipation of officials from central authority was prevented under Chinese patrimonialism by world-famous and highly efficient means. These means were the introduction of examinations and appointment to office on the basis of educational rather than birth and rank qualifications. This was of decisive significance for Chinese administration and culture and will be discussed below. But given the conditions, no mechanism could have functioned precisely in the hands of the central authorities. When we later discuss the education of officials we shall show further blockages resulting from the status honor of officialdom, the intimate nature of which was in part religiously determined. In China, as in the Occident, the patrimonial bureaucracy was the firmly growing nucleus to which the formation of the great state was bound. In both cases collegiate authorities and "departments" typically emerged, but the spirit of bureaucratic work differed widely in the East and in the West as will be shown below.

4. Public Charges: the Corvée-State and the Tax-State

FROM the standpoint of sociological determinants, the spirit of Chinese bureaucracy was connected with the system of public charges as this developed with the vacillating money economy. As usual the chieftain or prince (*kung t'ien,* corresponding to the Homeric *tenemor*) originally received a land allotment which was jointly cultivated by the people. The universal corvée originated in the "well system"—the state field being in the centre surrounded by eight square fields—and found additional support in the compelling need for waterworks. Land-use joined to river administration suggested the ever-emergent idea of imperial regality and is still terminologically retained (as in England). However, like the Egyptian Pharaoh, the Chinese emperor could scarcely prevent the distinction between leased desmesnes and taxed private lands. According to their apparent terminological traces, the taxes developed partly from customary gifts, partly from obligatory tributes of subject populations and partly from the claim to regalities. Public land, obligatory tax, and forced labor were permanently co-existent and variously interrelated. Which predominated depended partly on the scope of the budgetary economy—very unstable for reasons of currency as we have shown—partly upon the extent of pacification, and partly on the reliability of the bureaucratic machine.

According to the legend, the "holy" (legendary) Emperor Yü controlled the incoming tide and regulated the construction of canals and Shih Huang Ti, the first Emperor to rule with a pure bureaucracy, was considered the greatest builder of canals, roads, fortifications, and especially the Great Wall (which he actually brought only to partial completion). Such legend graphically expresses the origin of the patrimonial bureaucracy in the control of the incoming tide and canal construction. The monarch's power is derived from the servitude of his subjects, as indispensable for flood control as it was in Egypt and the Middle East. The legend also describes how the unified empire developed from a growing interest in unified flood control over wider areas, an interest connected with the political need to secure the culture-area against nomadic invasions.

Besides irrigation, the buildings served fiscal, military, and provisioning needs. Thus the famous Grand Canal from the Yangtze

to the Huang Ho was used to transport rice tributes from the South
to the new capital of the Mongol Khans (Peking).[50] According to
official report, at one time 50,000 forced laborers worked on a river
dike but building work was piecemeal and extended through
many centuries. Even Mencius considered the corvée rather than
the tax as the truly ideal method of meeting public requirements.
After divination had designated the proper place for a new capital
the Chinese king resettled his subjects despite resistance, just as
was done in the Middle East. Penal deportees and impressed soldiers stood guard over dikes and sluices and provided part of the
labor force for construction and clearing. Step by step the labor
forces of the army reclaimed desert soil in the border provinces of
the West.[51] Mournful complaints about the terrible burden of this
monotonous fate, particularly the labor on the Great Wall, are to
be found in the poems preserved. The service was often almost
life-time, wives missed their husbands and it seemed better not
to rear sons.[52] Classical doctrine had to oppose emphatically the
wasteful expenditure of corvées by the prince for private construction purposes in the Egyptian manner. In China, such waste
also accompanied the development of bureaucratically organized
public works. Once the system of forced labor disintegrated the
desert began to advance into the areas of Central Asia and the
dearly-won soil is completely covered by sand today.[53] Besides,
the political strength of the empire gave out. The Annals bewail
the negligent cultivation by the peasants on the royal estates. Only
exceptional personalities could centrally organize and direct the
state based on serfdom.

The corvée remained the classical way of meeting state requirements. As means of financing public needs, the relationship between taxes in kind (corvée) and money taxes (for commissions)
is indicated in a seventeenth century discussion before the Emperor of the best system for making certain repairs on the Grand
Canal. It was decided that the work should be commissioned for
money payment since the repairs would otherwise require ten
years time.[54] Repeated attempts were made to relieve the civilian
populace by regimenting the peace-time army for corvées. Thus,

until 1471 under the Ming, it was prescribed that half of the grain for the capital should be transported by the army and half of it by the civilian population. In 1471, it was ordered that the army alone should ship the grain.[55]

Even in early times there were taxes besides army levies, corvées and liturgies. Apparently the corvée on royal land, in particular, was abolished very early in the state of Ch'in (during the sixth century B.C.); later, in the third century B.C., its ruler was to become the first Emperor of the whole realm.

Of course, taxes existed much earlier. As usual, the imperial requirements were levied in kind and distributed among certain regions[56] and residues of this system survived until recently. The system of taxes in kind was intimately connected with the establishment of the patrimonial army and officialdom. As usual, both were provisioned from imperial magazines and fixed prebends-in-kind developed. At times, however, the state money economy also advanced, as the documents indicate at least for the Han Dynasty around the beginning of our chronology.[57] Alongside the increasing general drift toward money economy there continued to exist, until recently, sporadic servitude (especially for construction purposes, courier and transportation services), fees, taxes in kind as well as in money, and a princely *oikos* economy for certain luxury demands of the court.[58]

This shift toward money taxes pertained also and especially to the land tax, until recently the most important tax. We do not intend to trace its interesting history in detail here,[59] but shall discuss necessary points in connection with the agrarian system. Here it may suffice to state that the tax system in China, though occasionally more differentiated, increasingly tended toward a unified tax just as in the patrimonial states of the Occident; it was done by changing all other levies into surtaxes on the land tax.

This resulted from the fact that wealth not invested in land remained "invisible" to the extensive imperial administration and could not be reached by its taxation technique. That invisible wealth tends to evaporate perhaps partly determined the endeavors to meet as many state requirements as possible through means typical of subsistence economy, i.e., by corvées and liturgies. Probably in addition to this, currency conditions were primarily and truly decisive. There are two developmental tendencies of the land tax which generally affect all extensively administered patrimonial states. First, there is a tendency to commute the land tax into a money tax, a tendency which spreads to all other charges, especially to forced labor and other liturgies. Second, there is a tendency to change the land tax into a lump sum tax and ultimately into a fixed tribute collected from the provinces according to fixed quota. We have already touched upon this highly important process.

The pacification of the empire under the Manchu dynasty allowed the court to renounce movable income and led to the famous edict of 1713, praised as a source of the renewed flowering of China in the 18th century. In intent this edict transmuted the land tax of the provinces into fixed charges, as we shall discuss presently. Besides the land tax, the *gabelle,* mine taxes, and, finally, the customs contributed to the income of the central administration. The amount transferable to Peking became, *de facto,* traditionally fixed just as it was for the central administration. Only the wars with the European powers and the financial emergency following the T'ai P'ing rebellion (1850-1864) pushed the *li kin* customs of Sir Robert Hart's splendid administration into the foreground of the imperial finances.

With quota-regulation of taxes and subsequent pacification of the empire, the population increased tremendously. Further ramifications were the expendability and elimination of servitude and the controls of occupational choice, of the compulsory passport and other barriers to free mobility, of house ownership and control of production. According to the registration figures, which in part are highly questionable, the population of China apparently fluctuated widely but at the beginning of the Manchu dynasty the population was not much larger than under Shih Huang Ti almost 1900 years earlier. In any case, for centuries, the alleged population figure had fluctuated between 50 and 60 million people, but from the middle of the 17th century until the end of the

19th century, this figure rose to some 350 to 400 million people.[60] Proverbial Chinese acquisitiveness developed on both a small and large scale and considerable fortunes were accumulated. The following phenomena must appear the most striking of the epoch: despite the astounding population increase and the material welfare of the population, Chinese intellectual life remained completely static, and despite seemingly favorable conditions modern capitalist developments simply did not appear.

The once considerable export trade of China did not revive and there was only passive trade in a single port (Canton) which was open to Europeans but strictly controlled. Popular endeavor, such as might have been nourished by internal capitalist interests, did not arise to shatter this barrier. All evidence points to the contrary, for in the European sense, "progressivism," generally speaking, emerged neither in the field of technology, nor economy, nor administration. Finally, the financial strength of the empire could not apparently withstand the serious pressures necessitated by requirements of foreign policy. It is our central problem to explain all these striking phenomena in view of the unusual population growth which, despite all criticism, cannot be doubted.

Both economic and intellectual factors were at work. The former, which we shall discuss first, pertained to the state economy and were therefore political in nature. The political-economic like the "intellectual" factors at work resulted from the peculiarity of the leading stratum of China, the estate of officials and candidates for office, the mandarins. First we shall discuss the material situation of the latter.

5. Officialdom and Tax Collection by Quota Levies

AS SHOWN above, the Chinese official originally depended on prebends in kind from royal magazines, but later on money salaries were permanently substituted. Thus the government formally gave salaries to its officials, but only a fraction of the forces actually engaged in administration were so paid. Often the salaries formed but a small, indeed an insignificant part of their income. The official could neither have lived on his salary, nor have covered the administrative costs which it was his official obligation to cover. What actually happened was this. The official, like a feudal lord or satrap, was responsible to the central government (the sub-official to the provincial government) for the delivery of certain amounts. In turn, he financed most of his administrative expenditures from fees and tax-income and retained a surplus. Though not recognized *de jure,* it was *de facto* the case and was among the lasting consequences of the tax-quota system.

The so-called fixation of the land tax in the year 1713 was actually the crown's financial and political capitulation to the office prebendaries. In reality, the charges on land were by no means transmuted into a fixed ground rent (as for instance in England). Instead the central administration fixed the amount of tax yield to be credited to the district and provincial officials. That was the sum from which the crown demanded a quota as its tribute. In effect, the central government had merely fixed taxes on the prebends of these satraps for an indefinite time. This meaning is clearly revealed in an otherwise nonsensical formulation of the measure: a number of provincial districts were liable to taxation while other districts were completely exempted. Periodic population censuses actually listed the districts in that manner. Naturally, it did not mean that a corresponding number of inhabitants were tax exempt but merely that officials counted them as tax exempt. As early as 1735, the emperors ceased to distinguish between the two categories in census enumerations since it served no purpose.

It was thoroughly in keeping with the nature of patrimonialism to have considered the official's income from administering a district as his prebend, from which his private income was not really separated.[61] The office prebendaries felt the strongest reservations about raising the land tax or any other tax as a lump sum from the taxpayer. It cannot really be held that the imperial administration seriously intended to fix taxes in such a manner. In keeping with patrimonial principle, the official not only had to finance the civil and legal requirements of his district administration from this income but in addition his administrative staff. Experts estimated a staff varying from 30 to 300 even for the smallest administrative unit *(hsien)* and frequently these men were recruited from the scum of the populace. As we have seen, the official, a stranger in the province, was hardly in a position to administer without such a staff. His personal and administrative expenditures were not separated. Thus, the central administration did not know the actual gross income of the individual provinces and districts, the provincial governors did not know the prefects' income, etc.

On the other hand, the taxpayers maintained a principled resistance to any payments not fixed by tradition. That we shall see, and also why, within broad limits, they could very successfully do so. Their resistance to the continuous endeavors to raise surtaxes was precarious, and it depended essentially upon the power constellation. Apart from this, officials had two means of increasing the income. First, they could raise a surtax of at least 10 percent to cover the cost of tax collection. Second, a similar surtax could be levied for untimely payments, whether the arrears were caused willingly or unwillingly by the debtor or (often enough) intentionally by the official. Furthermore, the taxes in kind were changed into money taxes; then the money taxes were changed into silver, next into copper, and again into silver, all of this at changing rates the determination of which was reserved to the tax collector himself. For this reason influential men always preferred, and successfully insisted on, payment in kind.

It should not be overlooked that by patrimonial standards every official act had to be paid in "gifts," for there was no legal schedule of fees. The gross income of the official, including extra profits, was first used to defray the material office costs and the cost of administrative duties. The state expenditure on internal administration was a minute fraction of the total expenditure. Moreover, superior officials drew their incomes from the gross income of the lowest-rung official who was directly at the source of the taxes. He had to transfer to his superior the often rather small amount which represented his obligation in the traditional tax register. Upon assuming office, and on regularly recurrent occasions, he had to make the largest possible "gifts" in order to secure the good will of the superior so decisive for his own fate.[62] In addition, he had to provide ample tips for the superior's unofficial advisers and sub-officials inasmuch as they could influence his fate. This extended to the doorman should he wish to be received for a conference, and it continued upward to the palace eunuch who exacted tribute even from the highest officials. From the land tax alone, experts estimated a one to four ratio between the officially announced and the actual tax income.[63]

In 1712-13, the central government and the provincial officials compromised on tax repartition. In terms of money economy this compromise was roughly comparable to the fixation of feudal obligations in the subsistence economy of the Occident. There were, however, differences. First, in China, as in all specifically patrimonial states, prebends not fiefs were at stake. There were tributes in kind and especially in money from both fee and tax prebendaries upon whose administrative services the central authorities typically depended. It was not a question of the military services of self-equipped knights upon whom the prince depended. There was a second significant difference. In the Occident, prebends, both fee and tax prebends, were also known. At first this was true only of church territory, but later the patrimonial state was similarly modelled. However, the prebend was either for life (except in the case of formal removal) or it was hereditarily appropriated like the fief. Frequently it could even be transferred by purchase. The fees, customs, and taxes supporting the prebends were fixed by privilege or custom.

In China, as we have shown, it was precisely the authorized official who could be freely removed and transferred. Moreover, after short periods he had to move from one office to another. Partly (and mainly) this helped the central authorities to retain power, but partly it gave opportunity to other candidates, as is occasionally indicated.[64] Officialdom as a whole was secure in its enjoyment of tremendous income from prebends, but the position of the individual official was very precarious. Acquiring office was very costly (study, purchase, gifts, and "fees") and the official, often having plunged himself into debt, was compelled to make the most of his short term of office. In the absence of fixed taxes and guarantees he could do this. Indeed, it went without saying that the office existed for the making of a fortune, which was objectionable only if done to excess, as numerous rescripts reveal. According to the *Peking Gazette* of March 23, 1882, a Canton official in a few months had accumulated 100,000 taels in excess of the usual amount (sic!). A hired scribe in Fukien was able to purchase the prefecture in Kiangsu. Customs officials had annual incomes of 100 to 150,000 taels.

There were, however, other broader ramifications of this situation. First, the power-position of the central government was most effectively guaranteed by the system of transferring individual officials. Because of continuous regrouping and changing opportunity, each official competed with every other for prebends. Each was prevented from reconciling personal and inter-personal interests, and the relation of each to his superiors was very precarious. The whole authoritarian and internalized bondage of Chinese officialdom was connected with this. To be sure, there were "parties" among the officials. They grouped themselves by common regional descent or, connected with this, by the traditional character of the schools where they had been educated. Recently the "conservative" school of the northern provinces was opposed by the "progressive" school of the central provinces and the "radical" school of the Cantonese. Imperial edicts even at that time spoke of the antagonism between those following the educational method of the Sung and those following that of the Han in one and the same *yamen*. However, no regional particularism such as to endanger the unity of the empire could develop on this basis for, by principle, the officials had to be strangers to the province and were continuously moved about. Besides the authorities were careful to mix adherents of rival schools and regional groupings within the same bailiwick and office rank. Separatism had quite different bases, as we shall discuss presently. The official paid for his weakness in relation to superiors in being the dependent victim of his inferiors. An even more important result of this prebendal structure was its extreme administrative and politico-economic traditionalism. While originating in a special ethos this traditionalism also had a highly "rational" basis.

Any intervention in the traditional economy and administration impinged upon the unforeseeable and innumerable interests of the dominant stratum in its fees and prebends. Since any official could once be removed to a less remunerative post, officialdom stood together as one man and obstructed as strongly as the tax payer every attempt to change the system of fee, custom, or tax payments. In the Occident the permanent appropriation of fees and profit opportunities made the interests involved abundantly clear. That was the case with payment of customs, convoys, tolls, and rights of way, or of storage and road passage. As a rule, definite interest groups had the opportunity to organize and to remove obstructions to communication by force, compromise, or privilege. In China, however, this was out of the question. Profit opportunities were not individually appropriated by the highest and dominant stratum of officialdom; rather, they were appropriated by the whole estate of removable officials. It was the latter who collectively opposed intervention and persecuted with deadly hatred any rational ideologist who called for "reform." Only violent revolution from above or below could have changed this. In general, any innovation endangered either the present or future interest of each official in his fees—whether this meant substituting the much cheaper transport of tributes by ocean steamer for barge traffic through the Imperial Canal, changing traditional ways of collecting customs or of transporting persons, or settling petitions and trials. In going over the series of reforms projected by the Emperor in the year 1898, one can realize that even partially executing them would have produced tremendous reverses in income. Then one can estimate the complete hopelessness of reform because of the vast material interests opposing it, and because there were no disinterested executive organs independent of these interest groups.

The particularism of the provinces, primarily financial particularism, originated in this traditionalism. It arose because any administrative centralization seriously jeopardized the prebends of the provincial official and his unofficial retinue. Indeed, it was this that prevented the central administrative rationalization of the empire as well as a unified economic policy.

It is important to recognize in principle that, contrary to our expectations, the pure patrimonial state organizations in the Orient did not follow an otherwise almost universal destiny. For rather than weakening traditionalism, the money economy, in effect, strengthened it. This was because the money economy, associated with prebends, created special profit opportunities for the dominant stratum. Generally it reenforced their rentier mentality[65] and rendered paramount their interest in preserving those economic conditions so decisive for their own profit from prebends. With every advance of the money economy in Egypt, the Islamite states, and China, we observe the concomitant and increasing prebendalization of state income. There are short intermediary periods for the appropriation of prebends to be completed, but, in general, that phenomenon presents itself which we usually evaluate as "ossification" (Erstarrung).

A general result of oriental patrimonialism with its pecuniary prebends was that, typically, only military conquest of the country, or successful military or religious revolutions could shatter the firm structure of prebendary interests, thus creating completely new power distributions and in turn new economic conditions. Any attempt at internal innovation, however, was wrecked by the aforementioned obstacles. Modern Europe, as noted, is a great historical exception to this because, above all, pacification of a unified empire was lacking. We may recall that, in the Warring States, the very stratum of state prebendaries who blocked administrative rationalization in the world empire were once its most powerful promoters. Then, the stimulus was gone. Just as competition for markets compelled the rationalization of private enterprise, so competition for political power compelled the rationalization of state economy and economic policy both in the

Occident and in the China of the Warring States. In the private economy, cartellization weakens rational calculation which is the soul of capitalism; among states, power monopoly prostrates rational management in administration, finance, and economic policy. The impulse toward rationalization which existed while the Warring States were in competition was no longer contained in the world empire. But this was not all. In China during the Period of the Warring States the scope of administrative and economic rationalization was much more limited than in the Occident. In addition to the aforementioned differences, in the Occident, there were strong and independent forces. With these princely power could ally itself in order to shatter traditional fetters; or, under very special conditions, these forces could use their own military power to throw off the bonds of patrimonial power. This was the case in the five great revolutions which decided the destiny of the Occident: the Italian revolution of the 12th and 13th centuries, the Netherland revolution of the 16th century, the English revolution of the 17th century, and the American and French revolutions of the 18th century. We may ask: were there no comparable forces in China?

CHAPTER III

ADMINISTRATION AND
RURAL STRUCTURE

THE intense acquisitiveness of the Chinese has undoubtedly been highly developed for a long time. This drive and the unscrupulous competitiveness toward sib outsiders were incomparably strong among the Chinese. The only possible exceptions to it were the monopolistic guilds of the wholesale and especially the overseas-traders. Ethically, their acquisitiveness was strongly tempered for reasons of business.

Industry and capacity for work among the Chinese have always been considered unsurpassed. The merchant guilds, as we have seen, were more powerful than in other countries and their autonomy was practically unlimited. By European conceptions the tremendous growth of the Chinese population since the early 18th century and the constant increase of precious metals would lead one to expect favorable opportunities for capitalist development. Again we return to our initial problem. Although we have adduced some reasons for the fact that capitalism did not emerge we have no satisfactory answer as yet.

The following features of Chinese development stand in sharp contrast to the Occident: The epoch beginning with the eighteenth century was characterized by a tremendously increasing population—not, as in England, by a relatively decreasing rural one. In the countryside there were typically more and smaller holdings of peasants rather than the large scale agricultural enterprises to be found, for example, in Eastern Germany. Finally, and in connection with this, the cattle population was negligible. Cattle were rarely slaughtered (practically only for sacrificial purposes); milk consumption was absent; and "eating meat" was equivalent to being genteel, since it indicated the privilege of the official to share meat at sacrificial feasts. How did all this come about?

1. Feudal and Fiscal Organization

BECAUSE the sources available to the non-sinologist are limited, we cannot possibly describe the development of Chinese agriculture.[1] In our context we need consider it only insofar as problems of agrarian policy reveal the nature of Chinese state organization. For it will be seen at a glance that military and financial reform determined fundamental changes in the rural economy. Hence, the history of Chinese agriculture displays a monotonous to and fro between alternate, equally possible principles of taxation. The resultant ways of dealing with rural property have been quite unrelated to internal "evolution" ever since the breakdown of feudalism.

In feudal times the peasants were undoubtedly serfs of the feudal lords to whom they owed taxes and labor. This was true, if not for all, at least for most of the peasants. At the time of Shih Huang Ti they apparently still retained some ability to bear arms. Even had this not been the case, manorial serfdom under a feudal lord in the Western sense should not necessarily be assumed. Rather political subjection to princely power was determined by river control in the manner of Egypt and the Middle East.

Conditions called *chien ping* in the Annals were usually sharply fought by the government. Under these conditions the peasants, because of the threat of war and insecurity or because of overindebtedness through taxes and loans, crowded around the seats of the propertied and commended themselves as clients (*t'ien k'e*). The government sought to secure direct tax payment from the peasants in order to prevent the rise of a politically dangerous caste of landlords. Yet, under the Han dynasty, landlords are at least sometimes expressly reported[2] to have paid the taxes of their *coloni*. The military "usurper" Wang Mang, like the military monarch Shih Huang Ti, sought to destroy the position of the landlords by introducing imperial land regalia. Apparently he failed.

We know nothing of the initial extent of a manorial economy like that of the Occident. In any case, such a manorial economy—should its existence be demonstrated—would probably not have to be considered typical. Even less need it be regarded the result of feudalism, for the legal provisions do not allow us to ascertain whether manors of the occidental type could be based upon them. Nor do the sources available to the non-sinologist permit us to ascertain the nature of the agrarian community. It remains doubtful whether, and how, the village community was connected with the feudal system. That is usually the case,[3] but it is also possible that the community was fiscal in origin, as has often happened elsewhere.

For instance, under the T'ang dynasty in 624 A.D., the peasants were organized into small administrative districts *(hsiang)* for purposes of taxation. In these districts the peasants were guaranteed certain allotments which were perhaps received from public land. These facts are beyond doubt, since Japan has borrowed the institution. Retirement from the *hsiang* and land sale in this case was permissible, but purchase into another tax collectivity was required. Certainly the associations of landlords did not end with this merely relative closure.

The very radical regrouping of population into joint liability associations of tax payers, serfs, and draftees indicates that the duty of tilling the soil in the fiscal interest of the state was always considered primary. The corresponding "right" to the land was derivative.

Apparently this did not result in a communal village economy which would correspond to Germanic, Russian, or Indian conditions. The existence of village commons *(Allmende)* in the Western sense can only be inferred from occasional hints and as part of the remote past. The imperial tax rescripts define not the village but the family as the taxable unit. This included those from 15 to 56 years who were its working members *(ting)*. They were organized by rescript into artificial liability associations, at the latest during the 11th century and probably much earlier. We shall show below that the village nevertheless represented an association which was largely self-governing. Considering the sharp fiscal interventions it is not at all self-evident that a different association, which was perhaps originally confined to noble families,[4] could have comprised, since remote times, the entire rural population in good standing. The association was not destroyed by these fiscal measures.

The unbroken and continued existence of the cohesive sib and the pre-eminent position of its head, can be ascertained through thousands of years. Ancient landlordism in China may well have originated in this. As we noted above, military service and presumably all public charges were originally allocated to the sib. From numerous analogies and subsequent changes, we may infer that the head of the sib was held responsible for the allocation of taxes and labor. After private property had been instituted, i.e., after the land or its use had been formally appropriated by individual families, the head of the sib is reported to have occasionally been replaced by the wealthiest landlord (according to tradition in 1055). Thus the "old man" who had been entrusted with the allocation of land taxes, and who had thereby gained an opportunity for accumulating wealth, became a landlord. His impoverished sib members became his serfs. This change has numerous and well-known parallels. Besides, this "privilege" of the wealthy was not experienced as such but rather as a liturgy. That was intended, and some sought to evade the burden by means of fictitious land sales and family divisions. The non-sinologist cannot judge whether a stratum of serfs without sib affiliation existed alongside the sib members who, as usual, constituted an upper stratum and claimed a monopoly in land and slave holdings. In China, too, the right to own slaves was an exclusive privilege of high status groups. The existence of serfs has been ascertained and originally most of the peasants were probably serfs. During the 4th century B.C. only the *kuan* families who qualified for office were allowed to own serfs. The serfs did not pay *k'o* (land tax) nor did they render *yü* (forced labor). Obviously, unless they had acquired tax immunity, their lords paid their taxes. According to the Annals individual families owned "up to forty" serfs. This permits us to conclude that the estates of wealthy landlords were, at that time, modest in size. Slavery has always existed in China, but apparently it was economically important only when moneyed wealth was being accumulated in trade and state commissions. Thus, slavery took the form of debt slavery and peonage, as we shall discuss below.

Decisive changes in the rural economy apparently always emanated from the government. They were connected with the regulation of taxes and military service. The "First Emperor," Shih Huang Ti, reportedly effected a general disarmament of the country. This measure was undoubtedly primarily directed against the armed forces of the feudal lords, radically suppressed by the Emperor. But the course of the rebellion which brought about the fall of the dynasty makes it apparent that, until then, broad strata of peasants were armed (just as in Germany before the disarmament which followed the Peasant War). The founder of the Han dynasty and other rebels were peasants and relied, at least in part, upon the military support of their sibs.

At the same time "private property" was instituted—a process which has since recurred in China. The institution of private property meant that land was distributed among peasant families (among which ones can hardly be ascertained); that the peasant owners were freed from the existing taxes (which ones?); and that new state burdens were directly imposed upon them. These state burdens were partly in the form of taxes, partly forced labor, and partly a draft for the emperor's patrimonial army. Decisive for later developments was the relative degree to which the government was concerned with defense, the corvée, or the peasant's tax-paying ability. It was important whether there were more taxes in kind or in money, and related to this, whether the army was composed of regimented subjects or of mercenaries. Finally, what technical means were used by the administration to enforce these obligations[5] was of decisive import.

These component factors have all changed, and the antagonisms between literati schools—which have pervaded the entire Chinese literature—were largely centered in the technical problems of administration. With the threatening storm of the Mongols at the beginning of the 11th century A.D., these antagonisms became acute. A central problem for all social reformers of the time—as for the Gracchi—was how to maintain or establish an adequate army to face the barbarians of the Northwest, and whether to raise the necessary means by money payment or payment in kind.

The typical and by no means peculiarly Chinese way of securing the various contributions from the peasants was to form compulsory and joint liability associations (of five to ten families) and tax classes of land owners, graded by holdings (for instance into five classes). The attempt was made to maintain and raise the number of taxable peasants in order to prevent the accumulation of property and the development of uncultivated or extensively farmed lands. Moreover, repeated attempts were made to define maximal holdings, to link the right to own land to effective cultivation, to open up land for settlement, and to redistribute land on the basis of an average land allotment per working peasant—roughly comparable to the Russian "nadyel."

The Chinese tax administration faced considerable difficulty in this as in all land registration, since its measuring technique was very poor. The only truly scientific and "geometrical" work[6] was borrowed from the Hindus and indicates techniques of measurement short of trigonometry. The measurement of the individual acres hardly equalled the ancient Germanic or even the truly primitive technique of the Roman *agrimensores*. Astounding errors in measurement—comparable to the Medieval bankers' miscalculations—apparently were commonplace. Obviously the unit of measurement, the Chinese "foot," differed from province to province despite Shih Huang Ti's reforms. The imperial foot

SEMINARY CO-OP BOOKSTORE
5757 S. UNIVERSITY AVE.
CHICAGO, IL 60637
773-752-4381

---- CUSTOMER NAME & ADDRESS ----
SUSAN GAUNT
PIERCE 309
FAC EX   ,   00009

CLERK   : 35
REGISTER   : 28
RECEIPT # : 9102203149
DATE   : 04/23/00
TIME   : 1:44 PM

 ISBN/SPCN   PRICE   QUANTITY   AMOUNT
 0029344506   19.95   1   19.95
 PT RELIGION OF CHINA

                  SUB TOTAL   19.95
            DISCOUNT OF 10.0%   1.99
         DISCOUNTED SUB TOTAL   17.96
  SALES TAX ON 17.96 @ 8.750   1.57
                GRAND TOTAL   19.53
             PAID WITH CASH   20.00
                CHANGE RECVD   .47

We hope you are happy with your purchase
Returns of stocked items within 30 days

SEMINARY CO-OP BOOKSTORE
5757 S. UNIVERSITY AVE.
CHICAGO, IL 60637
773-752-4381

----- CUSTOMER NAME & ADDRESS -----
SUSAN BAUNT
PIERCE 309
REGISTER: 28
RECEIPT # 9102203143
DATE   : 04/23/00
TIME   : 1:44 PM

ISBN/SPCN	PRICE	QUANTITY	AMOUNT
0029344506	19.95	1	19.95
OF RELIGION OF CHINA			

SUB TOTAL	19.95
DISCOUNT OF 10.0%	1.99
DISCOUNTED SUB TOTAL	17.96
SALES TAX ON 17.96 @ 8.750	1.57
GRAND TOTAL	19.53
PAID WITH CASH	20.00
CHANGE RECVD	.47

We hope you are happy with your purchase
Returns of stocked items within 30 days

(equal to 320 mm.) was usually the largest, but the unit varied by 255, 306, 315, 318 to 328 mm.

The basic unit of land measurement was the *mou*, in theory, a long strip of land which was at first 100, later 240 times 1 *pu* and equivalent sometimes to 5, sometimes 6 feet. In the latter case, if a foot of 306 mm. were the base, the strip equalled 5.62 *ar*. There were 100 *mou* to a *ch'ing*, equivalent to 5.62 *ha*. Under the Han 12 *mou* were considered necessary for the individual—in Russian terms, the "soul nadyel." Each *mou* produced 1½ *shih* of rice. The earliest note implies that before Wen Wang's rule (12th century B.C.), 50 *mou* (then 3.24 *ar*) were calculated *per capita*, 5 *mou* of which (i.e., 1/10) were cultivated for the treasury as *kung hsien t'ien* (royal land). Hence, a holding of 2.916 *ha* was considered the normal *per capita* holding. This note, however, is wholly un-reliable.[7]

For a thousand years or longer, not land units but families were normally counted as the unit and, as noted above, the classifica-tion was perhaps by *ting*, i.e., number of working members.[8] But the soil was crudely classified as "black" or "red," most probably as irrigated or nonirrigated land, and this resulted in two tax classes. Or, classification was by the extent of fallow: 1. land with-out fallow, hence irrigated land; 2. the three field system; 3. pas-ture *(Feldgraswirtschaftsland)*.

The oldest available notices calculated the normal family claim at 100 *mou* (5.62 *ha*) for the first soil category; 200 *mou* (11.24 *ha*) for the second; 300 *mou* (16.86 *ha*) for the third. This would correspond to a single tax per family not per unit of land. Occa-sionally the differences by age composition and size led to the idea of placing large families on good soil and small ones on poor soil. It is of course very doubtful to what extent this was realized. To be sure, resettlement of the population has always been consid-ered an easy way to equalize standards of living, the corvée, and the ability to pay taxes. The entire regular tax assessment could, however, hardly have been based on this possibility. At times the families were differentiated by their ownership or non-ownership of draft animals (5th century A.D.). But this system of personal taxation (*tsu* system) constantly alternated with variations of the pure land tax (*tu* systems).

On the one hand, there was a tax quota on yields (*Natural-quotensteuer*) such as was proposed by the minister Shang Yang for the state of Ch'in (360 B.C.). This quota was considerable, allegedly from ⅙ to ½ of the produce, and it bespeaks the impotence of the peasant before strong princely prerogatives. According to the Annals, despite the size of taxes, land cultivation prospered because the peasant was personally interested in it. Later we find regularly lower tax quotas (from 1/10 to 1/15 of the yield).

On the other hand, taxes in kind were fixed according to soil quality, as was the case under Shang Ti (78 B.C.) and apparently also during the 4th century A.D. Both times taxes were based on a rather crude soil classification.

Finally, we meet with money taxes, as, for example, in 766 A.D. when 15 *ch'ien* were charged per *mou*. Unsatisfactory harvest yields in 780 necessitated taxes in kind and the tax collectors' estimates of their cash value led to endless abuses. But authorities repeatedly turned to these experiments after having failed to establish a money economy. Obviously such attempts were made in order to establish an efficient army, i.e., an army of mercenaries. The form of taxation changed when under the usurper Heu tung, taxes in kind were "sold back" to the taxable subjects. One can imagine the result! While the Sung dynasty sought to establish one in 960 A.D., the absence of a reliable bureaucracy of tax collectors was most important. Pao Chi's memorial of 987 painted in somber colors the mass flight of the tax payers and Wang An-shih's attempted registration of land (1072 A.D.) under Emperor Shen Tsung could not be executed. By the end of this régime estimates had not been made of some 70 percent of the land. The budget of 1077[9] showed that money income had increased over income in kind but it was still a far cry from pecuniary accounting. The paper money of the 13th century and the debasement of coinage under Shang Ti (1st century A.D.) again caused collapse and reversion to taxation in kind. Only under the Ming do we find a considerable amount of silver along with a large receipt of grain and a moderate amount of silk.

Pacification under the Manchus—partly a result of the Mongols being domesticated by Buddhism—together with the tax quotas of 1712-13 caused a tax decrease. During the first half of the 19th century the tax was fixed at a moderate one tenth of the produce. The last vestiges of "duty to the land" and control of cultivation were thus eliminated. Imperial edicts of recent decades have forbidden holding liable for taxes the heads of groupings of ten.[10]

In the two thousand years following Shih Huang Ti, obligatory tillage has not been mere theory. Occasionally it has been tangible reality for all *"ting,"* that is for all able-bodied workers subject to the corvée. The same was true for the sib communities and their sub-groups of ten who were jointly responsible for the corvée and for tax payments. Quite real also was the fixed maximum size of land holdings and the right of resettlement. Since taxes and corvées were charged to families,[11] fiscal authorities favored and even compelled the division of families in order to maximize the number of taxable units. This became usual because it was extremely difficult to establish systematic land measurement. Family division may have considerably influenced the emergence of the small holding which was typically Chinese, but from a social point of view this influence was limited.

While all this handicapped the rise of large units of production, *de facto* it promoted cohesion among the old landowning peasant sibs who claimed usufruct rights when the emperor claimed land regalia. The sibs[12] were actually the cadres of the tax liability associations.[13] Attempted equalization of property—in the sense of the *Nadjel* principle—failed because the administration lacked efficient means of enforcement. The "state socialist" experiments of the 11th century as well as those of some later rulers were solely motivated by fiscal considerations. They obviously left an intense aversion toward each and every interference by central authorities. In this the local prebendaries of office agreed with other strata of the population. For instance, during the 10th century the central government demanded that it have at its disposal not fixed amounts but all surpluses of corvées and taxes above the local requirements, but this was enforced only temporarily and by unusually energetic emperors. The measure thus gradually fell into abeyance and, as mentioned, was finally abandoned under the Manchu.

Some aspects of this agrarian and fiscal policy may be emphasized in order to round out the picture.

Silk cultivation for the court and export trade and "wet," i.e., irrigated, rice cultivation occupied a special place in the agrarian economy. Silk was an ancient element of garden culture and of domestic industry. According to the Annals, during the 5th century A.D., the cultivation of silk and fruit was imposed on the peasants' households according to land allotments.

The land allotment may be considered the actual or at least the original basis of the so-called "well system." Among Chinese authors the well system enjoyed quasi-classical status as a genuinely national system of land distribution.[14] The basic unit consisted of a square field divided into nine parts by tripartitioning the sides. The centre part had to be cultivated by the eight surrounding holders for the state, possibly for the landlord. The universal diffusion of the system is inconceivable for, apart from intrinsic improbabilities, it would contradict the data of the Annals concerning the history of land ownership. The abolition of the well system under the Ch'in dynasty in the 4th century A.D. is probably identical with the substitution of taxes for the general system of the "king's field," and for the admittedly unsuccessful "restoration of the well system." It has been confirmed that the well system was localized. While undoubtedly it was essential for the irrigation of rice fields, it has only occasionally been transferred to ploughland and, in any case, it was not the historically basic institution of rural China that has sometimes been assumed. It was simply a form of the old *kung-t'ien* principle (royal land) occasionally applied to wet rice culture.

While agrarian institutions have changed, the imperial grants and enfeoffed estates have occupied a special legal position. Usually they were renewed for life if qualified descendants assumed the obligations. Evidently they were partly prebends intended to provide sustenance for the trusted warrior, perhaps for his retirement at the age of sixty as in the case of the Japanese *inkyo*. These military fiefs, graded by class of warrior, appeared especially after the 1st century A.D. and from the 7th to the 9th century; they played their role up to the time of the Ming dynasty. Only the Manchu allowed them to fall into abeyance, or rather, replaced them by their banner fiefs. Similarly, at varying times, land grants were made to officials in lieu of payment in kind, especially with the decline of the magazine system which had been its basis. These were partly small plebeian fiefs and were charged with liturgies of all sorts: corvées for water regulation, bridge and road construction like the *lex agraria* of Antiquity (111 B.C.) and of the Middle Ages. In China, such properties were re-established as late as the 18th century.[15]

After the so-called introduction of "private property" by Shih Huang Ti, the most varied changes in land distribution can be observed. Periods of great internal unrest have always known the rise of large landlordism. It was the result of voluntary commendation and the subjection and preemption of impoverished and defenseless peasants. The idea of defining maximal holdings naturally tied the peasant again to the clod, or rather to the joint liability association. Formally these interventions were determined simply by fiscal and corvée interests. Thus, after some earlier beginnings, the Eastern Chin dynasty during the 4th century proclaimed a public land monopoly. The reports reveal that the decisive intention was to facilitate general regulation of the corvée.

In the warring kingdoms of the 3rd century the idea emerged of equal "soul" shares for all those from 15-60 years of age, with annual redistribution of land. At that time the rather crude system of combining the land tax with a head tax for every *t'ing* soul—at first simply from every holding—had led to quite unsatisfactory results.

In 485 A.D., and again under the T'ang during the 7th century, there appeared in various "social policies" (in theory!) the idea of providing separate houses for the aged, for war veterans, and similar groups. Thus, hereditary and transferable holdings, like the "commons acreage" in Badenia or properties determined by rank, could be variously combined. In 624, the state of T'ang permitted basic holdings of a certain size to be hereditary and granted additional land according to size of family. Grain levies and corvées were based on the established tax unit; sometimes these were cumulative, sometimes alternate.

At the beginning of the 11th century the land holdings were classified by rank and, in case of land scarcity, resettlement was permitted. At the time much land was available for settlement in the north and this accounts for the at least temporary possibility of executing the policy. In case of resettlement or of available surplus land over and above the norm, free land sales were permitted if the sib had refused its preemption. Otherwise free sales were permitted only were there "genuine need," such as lack of funds to meet burial expenses. Actually land was soon quite freely transferred, and thus the attempt to establish equality in land holdings miscarried. This became especially the case when the new tax system of 780 caused the administration to lose interest in the subject's ability to render military and other compulsory services.

All of these measures, as noted, were connected with fiscal and military requirements. Once the administration failed in its policy of protecting the peasants by equalizing land holdings, it only intervened in the accumulation of tenancy rents. The prohibition of corvées for private benefit, especially messenger service and the compulsory supply of relays, had, however, to be repeatedly emphasized during the 10th century. The corvée-exempt officials exploited this opportunity for enriching themselves with land. Therefore, in 1022 maximal landholdings were set for officials and, according to the Annals, landownership was unusually precarious because of such interferences. Moreover, liturgical charges on land strongly discouraged land improvement.

The "liturgy state" was always threatened by financial and

military failure. These difficulties stimulated the many attempts at land reform. The famous edict of Wang An-shi in the 11th century, primarily oriented toward military finance, provides an example. Let us consider the reform in its setting.

2. Army Organization and Wang An-shih's Attempt at Reform

THROUGH disarmament, as he repeatedly announced in his edicts, Emperor Shih Huang Ti sought permanent pacification of the country. Tradition maintains that the officials collected weapons in the 36 districts formed for that purpose and that the weapons were melted into bells. The frontier fortifications, however, had to be manned. Therefore, the population was regimented for service—theoretically for one year—at border settlements and for work on imperial construction. Thus, the establishment of the unified empire was accompanied by a tremendous increase in construction work by the civilian population. Yet civil wars were chronic, for the army remained essentially a professional army of praetorian guards. Under the Han dynasty, therefore, the attempt was made to replace, or at least supplement, the professional army by conscription. Everyone 23 years of age was to serve for one year in the standing army (*wei shih*) and then for two years in the militia (*chai huang shih*). Exercises in archery, riding, and charioteering were planned for men up to 55. The annual corvée was to last one month; hiring of substitutes was permissible.

To what extent these plans to organize a gigantic military force were ever realized is questionable. In any case, during the 6th century A.D. the corvée was heavy. Officially, one worker per family was annually called to serve after the harvest for one to three decades. Added to this were manoeuvres and frontier service in the Far West. Because the latter rent families asunder for years, it was especially bewailed in Chinese poetry. During the land "reform" of the T'ang, servitude was extended upward and might last five decades for tax exempt persons. It has been alleged that, on occasion, over a million men were drafted for construction work on the great rivers. There was, officially, a universal draft for the militia, but this evidently remained a dead letter and prevented the development of a technically efficient army. Under the Sung dynasty there was a standing guard as well as two local troop formations and militias, but after being unified, they disintegrated. At that time the recruits for the "guards" were impressed and, at least in some provinces, were branded as they were in the Middle East in 1042. The nucleus of the army, as all available reports show, was composed exclusively of mercenaries whose reliability, always doubtful, depended mainly on regular pay.

In 1049, the chronic financial emergency required a reduction of the army at a time when the barbarians of the North West threatened to raid the empire. Wang An-shih then tried to introduce rational reform as a means of raising an adequate and efficient national army. His attempted reform has been called "state socialism." The term is properly applicable only in the narrow if not quite identical sense in which it has been used for the monopolistic banking and grain storage policy of the Ptolemies, although the latter was based on a highly developed money economy.

Actually[16] the central authorities sought to plan the subsidization and regulation of grain production, and to monopolize and systematically organize grain sales by substituting money taxes for servitudes and taxes in kind (the *ch'ien-shui-fa* system). Thus it was hoped that money taxes could be raised in order to establish a large, disciplined, and trained national army which would be ready unconditionally to serve the Emperor. Theoretically one of every two adults was subject to the draft. Census registration was introduced and the system of groups of ten (*pao chia fa*) was renewed. The groups were headed by elected elders who were to deliver reprimands and take turns at night watches. Moreover, arms (bows) were to be distributed by the state to draftees who were assigned to the local militia. The state was also to purchase horses and place them at the disposal of drafted horsemen who were held responsible for them. The horsemen were subject to annual review and possibly entitled to premium pay.

Formerly, the state magazines were supplied through levies in kind and liturgically administered by the propertied. This was ruinous to them and led to every conceivable squeeze-play. Now the magazines were to be managed by paid officials and their pecuniary operation was systematically to implement the development of the money economy. The administration distributed grain seed on credit (*ch'ing miao*, i.e., "green seeds"), and other credit in kind or in money, at 20 percent interest. Landed property was to be revalued and reclassified. Land tax, corvée (*mo-chi*), and per capita allotment were to be determined by classes. Money payment was to be substituted for corvée and laborers were to be hired by means of money taxes.

Apart from the introduction of money taxes, the monopoly of the grain trade was the central point of reform proposals, which were subsequently often renewed. The government was to buy grain cheaply at harvest time, store it, and distribute credit from these stores. Moreover, the government was expected to make speculative profits. An administrative body of expert officials, especially trained jurists, was supposed to implement the reform, which included the drafting and presentation of annual budgets by all local authorities. In this way, a central and unified administration of finance was to be facilitated.

Wang An-shih's Confucian opponents criticized 1. the militarist nature of the system; 2. the arming of the people, which they thought might provoke rebellion and endanger the official authorities; 3. the elimination of trade, which would jeopardize the tax capacity; 4. and above all, the Emperor's grain usury, the seed credits at interest,[17] and the experiments in money taxation.

Wang An-shih's reforms failed completely in the decisive point of army organization. From analogy it may be said that this was undoubtedly due to the absence of an indispensable staff, and due to the fact that the country's economic organization made the prompt collection of money taxes impossible. The canonization of Wang An-shih and the sacrifices inaugurated after his death in 1086 were revoked in the 12th century. By the end of the 11th century the bulk of the army was again comprised of mercenaries. The literati knew how to sabotage the establishment of expert officialdom for their prebendal interests were at stake, and these interests were the decisive force in the whole struggle for and against the reform. The empresses, whose eunuchs saw their power jeopardized by such a new order, opposed the reform from the beginning.[18]

While Wang An-shih's reform failed at that decisive point, it apparently left deep traces on the Chinese system of "self-government." Through the rationalization of the much-mentioned groups of ten and a hundred a structure was preserved the influence of which is felt to this day.

Later governments repeatedly interfered with land distribution. During the struggle against the Mongols, in 1263, the government raised funds by expropriating all landholdings in excess of 100 *mou* for government bonds. In later periods occasional confiscations led to great increases of state property. When the Ming dynasty rose to power in Chekiang one fifteenth of the land was supposedly private property.

The system of state magazines *per se (ts'un shu)* was old[19] and quite important even before Wang An-shih's plans. Since the 15th century it has acquired its permanent form of operation: grain purchases in fall and winter and sales in spring and summer increasingly served as measures of price control and as a basis for maintaining internal peace. Originally, the government purchased not voluntary but forced deliveries. The quota requirements on the harvest, which were credited as tax payment, normally oscillated around one-half of the yield. The tax rates fluctuated widely between $\frac{1}{15}$ and $\frac{1}{10}$ of the yield; as noted, a very low quota was the normal tax rate under the Han Emperors. Additional servitude, however, has to be taken into consideration and it would be pointless to make a detailed analysis of tax rates since they do not represent the actual tax burdens.

3. The Fiscal Protection of
Peasants and Its Results
for Rural Society

THE various attempts at land reform by the state led to two results: the absence of rational and large scale agricultural enterprise, and the intensely suspicious aversion of the entire peasantry toward any governmental interference in landownership and land utilization. The laissez-faire theories of many Chinese cameralists enjoyed increasing popularity among the rural population. Of course, political measures for the control of consumption and dearth were necessarily retained. For the rest, only the policy of governmental protection of the peasants found support with the people, since this worked against capitalist accumulation, i.e., the conversion into landed wealth of profits from office holding, tax farming, and trade. This mood alone made possible the legislation —we have discussed it in part—which cut deeply into the property of the wealthy. It originated in the struggle of the autocratic government against the vassals and the noble sibs who, originally, were alone fully qualified for military service. Later, legislation repeatedly opposed the capitalistic resurgence of landlordism.

As shown above, the type of interference changed greatly. The Annals report for the state of Ch'in[20] (from which the "First Emperor" Shih Huang Ti set out) that during Hsiao Kung's reign (361-338) the scholar Wei Yang, his minister, taught him as the "highest wisdom" the art of "how to become master of his vassals." Land distribution and reform of the tax system stood in the foreground, directed particularly toward the substitution of the general land tax for the tillage corvée. The measures entailed family registration, the compulsory division of family communes, tax premiums for forming a family, corvée exemption for intensive production, and the renunciation of private revenge. They were typical means for fighting the rise and establishment of landlordism; likewise they indicate how population policy was typically bound to fiscal policy. As we have noticed, legislation wavered. The government alternately freed the peasants or handed them over to the landlords by restricting their mobility and permitting their commendation into servitude. On the whole, the tendency to protect the peasantry prevailed.

Under the Wei dynasty in 485 A.D. the government, obviously for populationist reasons, permitted the sale of surplus land. The injunction against traffic in land and, especially in 653 A.D., the injunction forbidding land purchases by the wealthy were designed to protect the peasantry. This was likewise the aim of the injunction against land sales and the enjoinder (in 1205 A.D.) to stay on the land as the buyer's bondsman.[21] The latter two provisions certainly allow us to infer that alienable private property in land existed at the time of the reform legislation and even long before, according to other reports. The aim of such provisions was to forestall developments which have frequently occurred elsewhere, particularly in the early Hellenic polis. In Athens, e.g., moneyed wealth, accumulated in trade or in politics, sought investment opportunities in land. This was done by buying out the indebted peasants and exploiting them as indebted serfs, tenants, or bondsmen on the small holdings which had been bought up.

Enough of these monotonous repetitions which are not intended as a depiction of "economic history." So far, the decisive data on prices, wages, etc., are absent. From the above, the precarious nature of landownership is apparent through long centuries, that is, for one and one half thousand years. The largely irrational conditions of landownership were due to fiscal policies which alternated between arbitrary intervention and complete laissez-faire. The literati rejected legal codification with the characteristic argument that the people would be contemptuous of the ruling classes if they knew their rights. Under such conditions, maintaining the sib as an association for self-help was the only way out.

The contemporary Chinese law of real property, therefore, contains traces of the earliest structure along with apparently modern features.[22] Land transfer by mere transfer of documents has been greatly facilitated through general land registration, and the requirement—continually faltering in the face of popular obstruction—of a fee and seal *(shou ch'i)* for every document of sale.

Similarly, the possession of titles of purchase, copies of the land register, and receipts for tax payment have come to be considered property certificates. Every document of sale *(mai ch'i)* contains the clause that the property is sold "in consequence of a real need for money and for a legitimate purpose." Today this clause is an empty formula. In connection, however, with the aforementioned explicit provision of 485 A.D., we may certainly conclude that originally sales were permitted only in cases of "real need." While nowadays there is a purely formal preemption right of relatives accompanying this measure, in former days this right was undoubtedly obligatory. Moreover, such usage is confirmed by the fact that even today it is an "abuse" to demand, in distress, that the buyer, and under certain conditions his descendants, make one or several later payments as "charity"[23] or *tan ch'i ("billet de géminance")*.[24]

In China, as in the ancient occidental polis, the typical land buyer was the creditor and man of moneyed wealth. However, originally, landownership was tied to the sib by right of retraction. The truly national form of alienation, therefore, was not the unconditional and permanent sale but rather the sale with reservation of the right to re-purchase *(hsiao mai)*—a universally diffused emergency transaction—or else the hereditary lease. For the *t'ien mien,* the owner of the surface was obviously the hereditary tenant in contrast to the *t'ien ti,* the landowner. The *anti-cresis (t'ien tang)* usually applied to rural properties; the mortgage, *ti ya,* only to urban real estate.

All other aspects of agrarian institutions point in the same direction. For instance, the old sib, bound to the land, struggled against the moneyed power of land buyers, and the patrimonial authorities intervened as moderators out of essentially fiscal interests. The official terminology of the *Shih Ching* and the Annals of the Han dynasty—like Roman law—distinguish only private and public property, public tenants on royal land and tax payers on private land (people's land *mien ti*). The indivisible and inalienable ancestral land (for tombs and ancestral sacrifices) remained family property.[25] The oldest son of the chief wife and his descendants succeeded as testators. After the victory of patrimonialism, however, the estate, including the land, became legally subject to real division among all children. Provisions of the testator were considered mere ethical obligations, like "entailed estates" in the proper sense of the term. Ultimately, the forms of tenancy were share cropping, rents in kind, and money rents.

The tenant could secure himself against the owner's notice by giving bail. The usual tenancy contracts indicate[26] that the tenant was thought of as *colonus* in the sense of the ancient and South European tenant farmer of a small holding. Along with the right, he assumed the obligation to till the land and, as a rule, the lessee remained indebted to the lessor. A big landlord who exploited his scattered holdings by leasing them was the typical lessor. Landlordism of sib communities was especially frequent. Such sibs inherited and acquired numerous small scattered holdings, the documents pertaining to which they preserved and registered[27] in special files and inventory books. The land register listed the holdings under a special common name,[28] as if designating a common firm for all holdings.[29] It was the same name which was posted on a tablet in the family hall. Through its elder the family ruled the *coloni* with the tone and patriarchical manner of the ancient or South European landlord or the English squire. As usual, the great old families and the wealthy parvenus of trade and politics firmly preserved their wealth and hereditary position in familial communities. Clearly, this form was the economic substitute for the privileged status position of the old nobility which patrimonialism had shattered.

Landlordism, quite extensive in some places, unfortunately cannot be statistically evaluated.[30] Only part of it has a long history and, in any case, it largely consisted of scattered holdings. Nevertheless; landlordism has existed until now and presumably was even more extensive in former days. Associated with it was the typical *colonus* of the patrimonial state. The landlord's power was strongly curbed by two peculiarly Chinese circumstances: the power of the sib (to be discussed presently), and the impotence and extensiveness of the civil and legal administration. If a ruthless landlord wished to use his power he had slight chance of seeing his legal claim promptly enforced unless he had personal connections or could purchase administrative coercion by way of costly bribes. But when the state official attempted to squeeze ground rent out of the tenant for the landlord he had to be as considerate as if he were squeezing taxes for himself. For all social unrest was considered symptomatic of magical evil which might cost the local official his office if it bestirred the central authorities. Some highly characteristic usages of landlords show that this situation precluded the intensive exploitation of the *coloni.* The intensive work[31] and the economic superiority of the small holder were patently expressed in immense land values[32] and the relatively low interest rate for agricultural credit.[33] Technological improvements were almost ruled out by the extensive partitioning of land; tradition held sway despite a developed money economy.

The equalitarian levelling tendency corresponded to patrimonial bureaucratization. Agricultural production based on intensive rice cultivation remained almost entirely in the hands of small peasants, and industrial production in the hands of the artisan.

In the long run the hereditary partitioning of land greatly democratized landownership, although in individual cases the process was slowed down by joint inheritance. A holding of a few acres was regarded as sizeable. A holding of less than two and one half acres (15 *mou* = 85 *ar*) was considered sufficient to provide sustenance for five persons even without gardening.

The feudal elements of the social order were, at least legally, divested of their status position. Even recent official reports always mention rural "notables" as the socially dominant stratum. But this rural "gentry" of village notables did not have a state-guaranteed position vis-à-vis the lower strata. By law, the patrimonial bureaucratic machine stood directly over the petty burgher and small peasant. The feudal stratum which mediated during the occidental Middle Ages was non-existent *de jure* and *de facto*. Only recent times and European influence have brought about capitalist conditions in their typically occidental form. Why?

CHAPTER IV

SELF-GOVERNMENT, LAW,
AND CAPITALISM

1. Absence of Capitalist Relationships

DURING the Period of the Warring Kingdoms and their contest for political power, there was a capitalism of money-lenders and purveyors which was politically determined and apparently very significant. High rates of profit seem to have been the rule. In China, as in other patrimonial states, this type of capitalism was customary. In addition to transactions which were politically determined, mining and trade are mentioned as sources for the accumulation of wealth. Multimillionaires (on a copper standard) are said to have existed under the Han dynasty. When China was politically unified into a world empire like the unified *orbis terrarum* of Imperial Rome, the result was an obvious retrogression of this capitalism, essentially linked to competition between states. On the other hand, the development of pure market capitalism, seeking free trading opportunities, was only rudimentary. Within industry the merchant obviously was in a position superior to the technician. This applied also to the cooperative forms of enterprise to be discussed shortly. The predominance of the merchant is clearly shown in the way profit was usually distributed within associations. Often inter-local industries also yielded considerable speculative gains. Even during the first century B.C., the old and classical esteem for the truly sacred vocation of agriculture did not prevent that profit opportunities were judged to be greater in industry and greatest in trade. (From Talmudic references, it may be inferred that a similar development occurred in the Middle East.)

Such forms of capitalist pursuits, however, were not a point of departure for modern capitalism. To this very day, the institutions characteristically developed by the flourishing burghers of the Medieval cities are either entirely lacking in China or they typically display a different physiognomy. The legal forms and societal foundations for capitalist "enterprise" were absent in the Chinese economy. There was no rational depersonalization of business comparable to its unmistakable beginnings in the commercial law of the Italian cities. In early Chinese history a point of departure for the possible development of personal credit was the joint liability of the sib. This survived in tax law and in the law of political crime but developed no further. To be sure, among the propertied strata, there were associations of heirs organized as household partnerships for the joint pursuit of profit. Such associations played a role like that of the family associations from which our occidental "trading company" later emerged (at least in Italy). In China, however, the economic meaning was characteristically different. As is usual with patrimonial states, he who was formally an official, and actually a tax farmer, had the best opportunities to accumulate wealth. For example, the "hoppo," i.e., the supervisor and holder of the customs at Canton, was famous for his exploitation of tremendous profit opportunities. The income of his first year, 200,000 taels, went for the purchase of his office; that of the second for "gifts"; and that of the third and last year, the "hoppo" kept for himself (according to the account of the North China Herald).

Retired officials invested their fortunes, more or less legally acquired, in landholdings. The sons, in order to preserve their wealth and influence, remained in hereditary partnership as co-heirs and, in turn, raised the means enabling some members of the family to study. Since these members had the opportunity of entering remunerative offices, they, in turn, were usually expected to enrich the co-heirs and provide sib members with public offices.

Thus, through political accumulation of property, there had developed a stratum of land magnates who leased lots. This (albeit unstable) patriciate bore neither a feudal nor a bourgeois stamp, but speculated in opportunities for the purely political exploitation of office. As is characteristic of patrimonial states, the accumulation of wealth, and especially landed wealth, was not primarily a matter of rational profit-making. In addition to trade, a system of internal booty capitalism prevailed which also led to the investment of money in land. For, as noted above, the officials made their fortunes by jobbing tax premiums, that is, by arbitrarily defining the exchange rate of the currency in which the tax obligations had to be calculated. Examination degrees also constituted a claim to the feed from this trough. Accordingly, the examinations were always distributed anew among the provinces, though it was exceptional to restrict them to a fixed quota. Thus, cessation of examinations in a district was a most effective economic sanction for the ranking families concerned. It is clear that this sort of acquisitive familial community pointed in a direction opposite to the development of rational economic corporate enterprises. Above all, this community was held together by rigid kinship bonds. This brings us to the discussion of the significance of the sib associations.

2. The Sib Association

THE sib, which in the occidental Middle Ages was practically extinct, in China was completely preserved in the administration of the smallest political units as well as in the operation of economic associations. Moreover, the sib developed to an extent unknown elsewhere—even in India. The patrimonial rule from above clashed with the sibs' strong counterbalance from below. To the present day, a considerable proportion of all politically dangerous "secret societies" has consisted of sibs.[1] The villages were often named after the sib[2] which was exclusively or predominantly represented in the village. At times the village societies were confederations of sibs. The old boundary marks indicate that the land was not allotted to individuals but to sibs. The cohesiveness of the sibs was important in maintaining this condition.

The village head—often a salaried man—was elected from the sib most powerful numerically. "Elders" of the sib stood beside him and claimed the right to depose him. The individual sib, with which we must deal first, claimed the right to impose sanctions on its members and enforced this claim, however little modern public authorities officially recognized it. Only domestic authority and the jurisdiction of the imperial sib over its members were officially recognized.

The cohesion of the sib undoubtedly rested wholly upon the ancestor cult. The sib withstood the ruthless encroachments of the patrimonial administration, its mechanically constructed liability associations, its resettlements, its land repartitions, and the classification of the population in terms of *ting*, i.e., employable *individuals*. The ancestor cult was the only folk-cult that was not managed by the Caesaro-papist government and its officials. Rather, the head of the household, as the house priest, managed it with the assistance of the family. Undoubtedly it was a classical and ancient folk-cult. Even in the "long house" of archaic militarist times, ancestral spirits seem to have played a role. We may mention in passing that the existence of the "long house" hardly seems consistent with true totemism. This suggests the probability that the long house, the most ancient form of organization, can be deduced from the routinization of hereditary charisma of the prince and his war following.[3] However that may be, in historical times the most fundamental belief of the Chinese people has been to ascribe power to ancestral spirits, not exclusively but predominantly to the spirits of one's own ancestors.[4] Ritual and literature testify to belief in the ancestral spirits and to their role as mediators of, the descendant's wishes before the Spirit or God of Heaven.[5] Furthermore, it was believed absolutely necessary to satisfy the spirits and to win their favor by sacrifices. The ancestral spirits of the emperors were of almost equal rank with the following of the Heavenly Spirit.[6] A Chinese without male descendants, indeed, had to resort to adoption and, if he failed to do so, the family undertook a posthumous and fictitious adoption on his behalf.[7] This was done less in his interest than in their own concern to be at rest with his spirit. The social consequences of these all-pervasive ideas are evident in the enormous support gained by patriarchal power[8] and in the reinforcement of sib cohesion. In Egypt, not the ancestral cult but the cult of the dead dominated everything, and there sib-cohesion was broken under the influence of bureaucratization and fiscalism just as it was broken later in Mesopotamia. In China, the influence of the sib was maintained and grew to equal the prerogatives of the overlord.

3. Organization of the Sib

IN PRINCIPLE, to this very day, every sib has its ancestral hall in the village.[9] In addition to paraments of the cult, the temple often contained a tablet with the "moral codes" recognized by the sib, for the sib had the unquestionable right to lay down the law for its members—a right which operated not only *praeter legem* but, under certain conditions and even in questions of ritual, *contra legem*.[10] The sib faced the outside world with solidarity. Although joint liability did not exist outside of criminal law, nevertheless the sib was accustomed to settle the debts of its members whenever possible. With the elder presiding in the chair, the sib not only meted out lashes and ordered excommunication (meaning civil death) but, like the Russian *Mir,* also decreed punitive exile. The frequently intense need for consumer loans was essentially met by the sib which morally bound its propertied members to give succour. To be sure, a sufficient number of kotows also secured a loan to an outsider, for no one dared draw the wrath of the desperate man's spirit upon himself should he commit suicide.[11] Nobody seems to have voluntarily repaid loans, least of all when the debtor knew he had a strong sib behind him. Nevertheless, only the sib was, by rule, clearly obliged to aid the needy and to give credit assistance.

If need be, the sib conducted feuds against outsiders.[12] Here, where personal interest and personal ties were at stake, the relentless bravery of the Chinese contrasted most glaringly with the much vaunted "cowardice" of the governmental army which, after all, consisted of impressed recruits or mercenaries. Where necessary, again, the sib provided medicaments, doctors, and burial services; it cared for the aged and widows, and above all, it provided schools.

The sib owned property, especially landed property (ancestral land, *shih t'ien*),[13] and prosperous sibs often owned extensive lands in trust. The sib utilized this land by leasing it out (usually for three years, by auction), but alienation of such land was permissible only with the consent of three-fourths of the sib. The yield was distributed among the heads of the households. The typical method of this distribution was to give all men and all widows one unit each; then from the age of fifty-nine on, two units; sixty-nine on, three units.

Within the sib a combination of hereditary-charismatic, and democratic principles prevailed. All married men had equal franchise; unmarried men had only the right to be heard in council; women were excluded from the sib councils altogether as well as from the right of inheritance (they had only dowry rights). The executive committee consisted of the elders, each representing a separate lineage within the sib. The elders were, however, annually elected by a vote of all sib members. The functions of the elders were to collect revenues, utilize possessions and distribute income, and most important of all, attend to the ancestral sacrifices, the ancestral halls, and schools. The retiring elders nominated candidates for election according to seniority; in case the office was declined, the next eldest was presented.

Up to the present, it was common to acquire land jointly through purchase or lease and to distribute it among the heads of the households. Mandarins, merchants, or others who definitely moved off the land received compensation and an abstract from the family book as a record. They remained subject to the jurisdiction of the sib and could repurchase their claim. Where the old conditions remained dominant, hereditary land seldom passed into the hands of strangers.

Because of the home spinning, weaving, and tailoring of the women, and especially because the women also marketed their products,[14] an independent textile industry could emerge only on a modest scale. Head and foot gear were also home-made. The sib association strongly supported the self-sufficiency of the households, thereby delimiting market developments. Socially the sib meant everything for its members—for those living far from home and especially for those living in the city.[15] This is apparent and important for the following reasons:

First, the sib was the ceremonial unit necessary for those festivities most important to the individual (especially the semi-annual ancestor festivals). It was also the topical unit for the family history which the housefathers had to write.

Second, hitherto it was considered proper for the sib to lend capital at low interest rates to apprentices and to wage-earning artisans without resources, thus enabling them to become "self employed" artisans.

Third, as already noted, the sib elders elected young men who were qualified for study and provided for their expenses incurred by preparatory studies, examination, and purchase of office.

As generally indicated above, the "city" was, therefore never the "hometown" but typically "a place away from home" for the majority of its inhabitants. The alien character of the city was further sharpened by the above-mentioned absence of the organized self-government found in the village. Without undue exaggeration, it may be said that Chinese administrative history is replete with instances of the imperial administration endeavoring to assert itself beyond the city districts. In this, apart from compromises over tax levies, the imperial administration succeeded only for short periods of time; given the territorial scope of the administration it could not do so permanently. The extensiveness of administration, i.e., the small number of actual officials per administrative unit, resulted from the state of finances and that, in turn, determined the financial returns.

The official imperial administration remained, in fact, an administration of urban districts and sub-districts. Here, if it was amenable to merchant and craft guilds, the administration operated effectively for it did not encounter the intense kinship ties of the sibs as it did outside. Beyond the city walls the effectiveness of administrative authority became narrowly circumscribed. For in addition to the power of the sibs, great in itself, the administration also confronted the organized self-government of the village. There were also numerous peasants living in the cities and, since the latter were merely urban settlements of farmers, there remained only a technical administrative difference between city and village. A "city" was the seat of the mandarin and was not self-governing; a "village" was a self-governing settlement without a mandarin!

4. Self-Government of the Chinese Village

IN CHINA, village settlement[16] was based upon the need for security which the extensive administration of the empire, lacking any notion of "police," was unable to meet. Originally, and often even today, the villages were fortified. Not only were they protected by palisades, like the ancient cities, but they were also frequently surrounded by walls. The village employed salaried watchmen, thus relieving its members of alternate turns of guard duty.

Occasionally numbering many thousands of residents, the villages differed from the "cities"[17] simply in that they took care of this function through their own organization. The village temple served as a central agency as Chinese law and the peasant's way of thinking naturally involved no concept of "corporation." In the modern period the village temple[18] has usually been dedicated to any one of the popular deities, to General *Kuan Ti* (God of War), *Po Ti* (God of Trade), *Wen Ch'ang* (God of Schools), *Lang Wang* (God of Rain), to *T'u Ti* (a non-classical God who had to be notified in case of death to assure the deceased person's *"conduite"* in the beyond); and to others. The specific dedication of the temple appears to have been regarded rather indifferently. As in classical antiquity of the Occident, the "religious" significance of the temple[19] was confined to a few ritual manipulations and occasional prayers of individuals. For the rest, the significance of the temple lay in its secular social and legal practices.

Like the ancestral hall the temple held property, especially real property,[20] and frequently also money which it loaned at rates that were not consistently low.[21] The pecuniary fund stemmed primarily from traditional market-fees. As is the case almost everywhere in the world, the market stands had always been under the protection of the local god. Like the ancestral land, temple land was leased, preferably to unpropertied villagers. Similarly, the collection of rents from this source and all revenues of the temple in general were annually allotted to tax farmers. The profits remaining after deduction of expenses were distributed.

The administrative positions of the temple seem to have been mainly occupied and financed by a liturgy of the housefathers of the village. They took turns from house to house and for this purpose the village was divided into districts of 100 to 500 inhabitants. Alongside these administrators were the "notables" of the village, the elders of the sibs, and the literati who received nominal remuneration. The political administration discouraged the legalization of corporations or their agents and recognized the notables as the sole represenatives of the village. The notables in turn, however, acted in the name of the "temple" and the "temple" concluded contracts for the village through them.

The "temple" had jurisdiction over petty causes and very often usurped jurisdiction over causes of all sorts. The government intervened only where interests of state were concerned. The temple court, not the court authorities of the state, enjoyed the confidence of the people. The "temple" took care of the roads, canals, defense, safety; it rotated obligatory guard-duty which, in actuality, was mostly bought off. The temple took charge of defense against robbers or neighboring villages, and provided schools, doctors, medicaments, and burials insofar as the sibs could not or would not do so. The temple contained the armory of the village. The village legally and actually was capable of acting as a corporate body through the temple—an impossibility for the "city." Actually, not the city but the village was the armed association capable of defending the interests of those in its orbit.

The government has not always taken a laissez-faire stand toward this unofficial self-government, as was the case during the last period of the old régime. Under the Han Emperors, for instance, the government sought to abandon the pure patrimonial absolutism of Shih Huang Ti by methodically calling on the village elders to assume local government offices *(san lao)*. They sought thus to regulate and to legalize the primeval village autonomy.[22] The village chief *(shou shih jen)* was to be elected and confirmed and the landowners were to guarantee his good conduct, but only occasionally did this actually happen. The government again and again ignored the village as a unit, purely fiscal interest repeatedly coming to the fore. Wang An-shih, especially, rationalized the system from this point of view, as has been mentioned in another connection.

Even today every ten families constitute a *"pao"* formally under a headman, every hundred families constitute a *"chia"* under a *"pao chia"* who usually is called *"ti pao."* At every house in village and city a placard has to be posted, and where tradition is alive, is actually posted which states the house number, the *chia,* the *pai,* the owner, the name of the family head, the nativity of the family (its denizenship), which lists the family members, the tenants and their occupations, absent family members (if so for how long?), the rent and tax liability, the number of rooms used and sublet.

The *pao chia* was officially responsible for the policing and surveillance of criminals and secret societies. The duties of Imperial religious police were not the least of his responsibilities. This agent *(ti pao)* was meant to constitute the link between self-government and public authorities. Where and when the system functioned well he would usually spend some time at the *hsien* magistrate's office to impart information. In modern times, however, all this has become quite formal; frequently—according to Chinese authors apparently as a rule—the *ti pao's* office has simply changed into an unclassical, hence less preferred government position.

The forces which the state had to take practically into account were the sib elders behind the village administration who might function as a sort of vehme and, in conflict, might be dangerous.

For all this peasant life in a Chinese village should by no means be imagined as a harmonious, patriarchal idyll. The individual peasant was frequently threatened by feuds outside the village. Moreover, the power of the sib and the administration of the village temple all too frequently failed to protect efficiently property, especially that of the wealthy. The solvent peasants (*lao shih* as they were called) were typically at the mercy of the arbitrary *kuang kun* or the *kulaki* (fists), as one would say in Russian peasant terminology. But they were not exposed to the domination of the "village bourgeoisie," of usurers and their interested affiliates, as were the *kulaki* in Russia. Against these, the Chinese peasant would easily have found human and divine assistance. Rather, the peasant was exposed to the non-propertied villagers[23] organized by the *kuang kun,* thus the *bjednata,* the "village poor" in the terminology of Bolshevism which, in this respect, might be attractive in China. Against this organization every individual and even groups of large owners were often completely unprotected and powerless.[24] And if, during the last centuries, larger estates in China have been exceptional, the above circumstances have contributed. Their paucity has been due to a sort of ethical and naïve peasant Bolshevism strongly tempered by the power of the sibs and to the absence of state sanctions guaranteeing property.

Below the level of the *hsien* district, which after all was about the size of an English county, there were only those governing agents who were, officially, honorific office holders and, actually, often *kulaki*. But very frequently committees functioned along-side the official administration of the districts right up to the level of the province. Officially the committees were appointed or "delegated" authority for a three-year term and were subject to recall at any time. Actually, they held their positions through recognized or usurped charisma and they "gave advice"[25] to the officials. We shall not be concerned here with the structure of these bodies.

5. Sib Fetters of the Economy

IT WAS necessary to reach agreement with this body, a firmly cohesive stratum of village notables, whenever any change what-soever was to be introduced, for instance raising the traditional taxes. Otherwise the state official was just as certain of meeting stubborn resistance as were the landlord, lessor, employer, and in general any "superior" outside of the sib. The sib stood as one man in support of any member who felt discriminated against[26] and the joint resistance of the sib, naturally, was incomparably more efficacious than a strike by a freely formed trade union in the Occident. In this fact alone, "work discipline" and the free market selection of labor which have characterized modern large enterprise have been thwarted in China. And this has been true of all rational administration along occidental lines. The strongest counterweight to officials educated in literature was a-literate old age *per se*. No matter how many examinations the official had passed, he had to obey unconditionally the completely unedu-cated sib elder in the traditionally fixed affairs of the sib.

In practical terms, a considerable measure of usurped and con-ceded self-government faced the patrimonial bureaucracy. On the one hand, there were the sibs and on the other hand, the organizations of the village poor. The rationalism of the bureauc-racy was confronted with a resolute and traditionalistic power which, on the whole and in the long run, was stronger because it operated continuously and was supported by the most intimate personal associations. Moreover, any innovation could call forth magic evils. Above all, fiscal innovations were suspect and met with sharp resistance. No peasant would have chanced upon the idea of "disinterested" motives and in this he was quite similar to the Russian peasants in Tolstoy's *Resurrection*. Besides, the influence of the sib elders was mostly decisive for the acceptance or rejection of religious innovations, which is of special concern to us. Naturally, and almost without exception, their weight tipped the balance in favor of tradition, especially when they sniffed a threat to ancestral piety. This tremendous power of the strictly patriarchical sib was, in truth, the carrier of the much discussed "democracy" of China, which had nothing whatsoever in common with "modern" democracy. It was rather the expression first, of the abolition of feudal estates, second, of the extensiveness of patrimonial bureaucratic administration, and third, of the unbroken vigor and omnipotence of the patriarchical sibs.

Economic organizations which went beyond the scope of the individual establishment rested almost wholly upon actual or imitated personal sib relationships. First we wish to consider the community of the *tsung-tsu*. This sib organization owned, in addition to the ancestral temple and the school building, sib houses for provisions and implements for the processing of rice, for the preparation of conserves, for weaving, and other domestic industries. Possibly a manager was employed. Apart from that, the *tsung-tsu* supported its members in need through mutual aid and free or cheap credit. Thus, it amounted to a sib and cumulative household community which had been expanded into a producers' cooperative.

On the other hand, in the cities there were, besides the shops of individual artisans, specific entrepreneurial communities. Small-capitalist in nature, these were organized as communal workshops with an intensive division of manual labor. Furthermore, technical and commercial management were often specialized and profits were distributed partly according to capital shares and partly according to special commercial or technical services. Similar arrangements have been known in Hellenistic antiquity and the Islamic Middle Ages. It seems that such establishments in China were found especially to facilitate joint sustaining of the slack period in seasonal industries and, of course, to facilitate credit and the specialization of productive work.

These ways of establishing large economic units had, in their social aspects, a specifically democratic character. They protected the individual against the danger of proletarization and capitalist subjection. From a purely economic point of view, however, such domination could creep in through high investments by absentee capitalists and through the superior power and higher profit shares enjoyed by employed sales managers. The putting-out system, however, which introduced capitalist domination in the West, was apparently confined until the present to the various forms of purely factual dependence of the artisan on the merchant. Only in individual trades did it advance to the level of domestic work with interspersed shops for finishing work and a central sales bureau. At present the putting-out system has developed on a significant scale in trades working for distant markets. As we have seen, it may well have been decisive that there was extremely little opportunity of coercing the services of dependent workers and getting them to deliver on time in prescribed quantity and quality. Apparently, large private capitalist factories can scarcely be traced historically. Probably no factories producing mass consumer's goods existed since there was no steady market for them. Except for silk which could be marketed, the textile industry could hardly compete with the domestic industry even in distant places. Long-distance trade, however, was monopolized by the silk caravans of the imperial *oikos*. Metal industry, because of the low productivity of the mines, could develop only on a modest scale. This handicap resulted from the general conditions which we have discussed in part above and which will receive consideration in the passage below. In the processing of tea there are pictorial representations of large plants with specialization of labor. They are comparable to ancient Egyptian pictures. The state manufacturing establishments normally produced luxury goods, as in Islamic Egypt. The expansion of the state metal industry, for reasons of currency valuation, was only transitory.

The guilds, discussed above, regulated apprenticeship, but there is no mention of journeymen associations. Only in individual cases did the workers combine against the masters in a strike; otherwise they had scarcely begun to develop into a class of their own, for reasons similar to those in Russia thirty years ago. As far as is known the workers were members of the guilds with equal rights. More precisely, that the guild did not generally practice monopolistic exclusion of apprentices was in harmony with the handicraft nature of the trade which was not even petty capitalist. Similarly, the liturgical closure of occupations repeatedly emerged and for a time was apparently carried through. This might have led to caste formation, but never did. The Annals specifically mention an attempt of this nature which was made toward the end of the sixth century and ended in failure. A residue of magically "unclean" tribes and occupations had survived. Usually[27] nine kinds of degraded "castes" were distinguished: certain kinds of slaves, descendants of certain slaves and *coloni*, beggars, descendants of former insurgents, descendants of immigrant barbarians (guest tribes), musicians and performers participating in family ceremonies, actors and jugglers as in the Middle Ages. As in India, patronage of the unclean occupations was of three types: fixed, hereditary, and alienable. Connubium, commensalism, and eligibility for degrees was denied. By imperial decree, however, those who left an unclean occupation could legally rehabilitate themselves by court action (for instance such decrees were made for some of these castes as late as 1894). Slavery originated after the wars of conquest through surrender or sale by parents, or as a form of punishment by the government. As in the Occident, the freed man had to be obedient to his patron and was unable to acquire examination degrees. During their period of service contract laborers *(ku kung)* had to be obedient to their masters and were denied commensalism with them. The *coloni* and land laborers, formerly helots of the ruling stratum, did not belong to this category.

Whatever has survived of such caste-like phenomena is only a pitiful residue of the former status structure. Its principal consequence was that the privileged estates were exempted from corvée and corporal punishment (i.e., "the literati" and the "great families." The term "the hundred families," meaning the "empire," signified this latter stratum). Instead, corvée and corporal punishment were transmuted into money fines and detention, and degradation to "plebeian" status was possible. At an early time, and for fiscal reasons, the old status structure based upon hereditary charisma was punctured by recurrent classifications solely according to property.

Until recent times in China (for the past the outsider has no certain evidence),[28] club associations flourished *(hui)* alongside the sibs, the merchant and craftguilds. The club thrived in all spheres of life, especially in credit relations.[29] Details of this development shall not concern us here. In modern times, in equalitarian China just as in democratic America, the successful man has striven to legitimize himself socially by joining a highly esteemed club. Similarly in China, a guild membership card was affixed to the shop to guarantee quality products to buyers, or there was a corresponding announcement of the business principle of fixed prices, "one price," "truly one price."[30] In contrast to the Puritans, however, strict adherence to the principle was not guaranteed. These phenomena resulted from the extensiveness of the patrimonial bureaucracy and the absence of a legally guaranteed status structure.

In the modern period, apart from a titular nobility, no status differentiation by birth has existed among the Chinese. This leaves aside the strict separation of the families registered in the Manchu army, the expression of a foreign rule which has existed since the seventeenth century. As early as the eighteenth century the "bourgeois" strata had succeeded in loosening the fetters of the police state. In the nineteenth century there was free residential mobility which had obviously existed for a long time.

Official edicts, however, did not recognize this. Freedom to settle and acquire land in a community other than one's native community had been imposed by taxation authorities, just as in the Occident. Since 1794, membership in a new community has been attained by acquiring real estate and paying taxes for twenty years, thereby forfeiting membership in one's native community.[31] For a long time there has been free choice of occupations, despite the Sacred Edict of 1671 which recommended adherence to one's occupation. In the modern period we find neither compulsory passport, schooling, nor military service. There are neither laws restraining usury nor any similar legal restrictions to trade. Though this state of affairs would seem to be very favorable to the free development of profitable, bourgeois enterprise, a bourgeois stratum of occidental character has failed to develop. As we noted, not even those forms of capitalist enterprise which were known in the Occident during the Middle Ages have fully matured. Again there is the old question that, from a purely economic point of view, a genuine bourgeois, industrial capitalism might have developed from the petty capitalist beginnings we have mentioned above. A number of reasons—mostly related to the structure of the state—can be seen for the fact that capitalism failed to develop.

6. The Patrimonial Structure of Law

IN THE patrimonial state, the typical ramifications of administration and judiciary created a realm of unshakable sacred tradition alongside a realm of prerogative and favoritism. Especially sensitive to these political factors, industrial capitalism was impeded by them in its development. Rational and calculable administration and law enforcement, necessary for industrial development, did not exist. Be it China, India, or Islam, in general, wherever rational enactment and adjudication of law had not triumphed, the *dictum* was: Prerogatives have precedence over common law. (*Willkür bricht Landrecht*). However, this dictum could not benefit the development of capitalist legal institutions as it had done in the occidental Middle Ages. On the one hand, the cities lacked corporate political autonomy and on the other, decisive legal institutions, fixed and guaranteed by privilege, did not exist. Yet it was exactly by aid of these combined principles that all the legal schemata appropriate to capitalism were created in the occidental Middle Ages.

To a large extent the law was no longer a norm valid from the remote past and justice was no longer "found" by magical means alone. For imperial administration of the occidental Middle Ages enacted statutes *en masse,* and the legal provisions were distinguished, at least technically, by their relatively brief and business-like form. Criminal law, as J. F. Kohler has emphasized, knew a considerable sublimation of legal facts and took motives into consideration.

This contrasted to the patriarchical instructions and admonitions of the Buddhist monarchs of India whose ethical and administrative decrees resembled some of the Chinese statutes. The Chinese statutes were also systematically collected in the *Ta Ch'ing Lü Li.* But there were few and only indirectly pertinent legal acts covering subject matter most important for commerce in our sense. No "fundamental freedoms of the individual" were guaranteed. In one case among the Warring States (the state of Ch'en, 563 A.D.), the rationalism of the literati officials found expression in a codification of the laws engraved on metal plates. But according to the Annals,[32] when the question was discussed among the stratum of literati a minister of the state of Ch'in successfully objected: "If the people can read, they will despise their superiors." The charismatic prestige of the educated patrimonial bureaucracy seemed endangered and these power interests never again allowed such an idea to emerge.

Though formally under separate secretaries for taxation and for justice, administration and law were not actually separated. The mandarin official, in patrimonial fashion, hired domestic servants at his own expense for both police work and minor office duties. The basically anti-formalist and patriarchical character of mandarin administration is unmistakable—offensive deportment was punished even without specific provisions. Most significant was the intrinsic character of adjudication. Patrimonialism, being ethically oriented, always sought substantive justice rather than formal law. Hence, in spite of the traditionalism, there was no official collection of precedents because legal formalism was rejected and, above all, because there was no central court as in England. The local "shepherd" of the official knew the precedents. In following tried models, as advised, the judicial procedure of the Chinese official corresponded externally to the use of "*similia*" among our junior judges. What is impotence in the latter case was extreme virtue in China.

For the most part, the administrative edicts of the Emperor were couched in the pedagogical form peculiar to papal bulls of the Middle Ages but without a similarly precise legal content. The best known statutes codified ethical rather than legal norms and excelled in literary erudition. For example even the second last Emperor announced in the *Peking Gazette* that the decree of a remote ancestor had been found and would be published in the near future as a code of conduct. Insofar as it was oriented to orthodoxy the whole imperial administration was controlled by an essentially theocratic board of literati. This was the oft-mentioned "Academy" (*Hanlin Yüan*) which safeguarded Confucian orthodoxy and perhaps corresponded to a congregation of the papal *Curia*. Accordingly, legal administration remained largely "Cadi" and possibly "Cabinet justice."[33]

This was also the case of the judicial relation between English sheriffs and the lower classes. But in England in order to transact the fortunes important for capitalism there was the law of precedent with its corresponding bailing justice. It had been created under the steady influence of the interested parties whose influence was guaranteed through the recruitment of judges from among lawyers. While not rational this law was calculable, and it made extensive contractual autonomy possible.

However, in patriarchal Chinese justice, the advocate, in the occidental sense, was singularly out of place. Sib members, possibly educated in literature, functioned as lawyers for their kin. Otherwise a "low brow" consultant made out written documents. This phenomenon was characteristic of all specifically patrimonial states, particularly theocratic and ethico-ritualistic states of oriental stamp. That is, in addition to non-capitalistic sources of accumulated wealth, such as the pure political office and tax prebend, a political capitalism of purveyors to the state and tax farmers flourished. Under certain conditions this capitalism had true orgies. Furthermore, the purely commercial capitalism of middlemen developed.

However, the rational industrial capitalism which is specific for modern development originated nowhere under this régime. Capital investment in industry is far too sensitive to such irrational rule and too dependent upon the possibility of calculating the steady and rational operation of the state machinery to emerge under an administration of this type. But why did this administration and judiciary remain so irrational from a capitalist point of view? That is the decisive question. We have become acquainted with some of the interests which played a part, but they deserve closer attention.

Just as capitalism lacked a judiciary independent of substantive individualization and arbitrariness, so it lacked political prerequisites. To be sure, the feud was not lacking. On the contrary, the whole of Chinese history is replete with great and small feuds, including the numerous struggles of individual villages, associations, and sibs. Since the pacification of the world empire, however, there has been no rational warfare, and what is more important, no armed peace during which several competing autonomous states constantly prepare for war. Capitalist phenomena thus conditioned through war loans and commissions for war purposes did not appear.

The particularized state authorities of the Occident had to compete for freely mobile capital in Antiquity (before the World Empire) as well as during the Middle Ages and modern times. As in the Roman Empire, political competition for capital disappeared following the unification of the Chinese Empire.[34] The

Chinese Empire also lacked overseas and colonial relations and this handicapped the development of those types of capitalism common to occidental Antiquity, the Middle Ages, and modern times. These were the varieties of booty capitalism, represented by colonial capitalism and by Mediterranean overseas capitalism connected with piracy. While the barriers to overseas expansion partly depended on the geographical conditions of a great inland empire, in part, as we have seen, they resulted from the general political and economic character of Chinese society.

Rational entrepreneurial capitalism, which in the Occident found its specific locus in industry, has been handicapped not only by the lack of a formally guaranteed law, a rational administration and judiciary, and by the ramifications of a system of prebends, but also, basically, by the lack of a particular mentality. Above all it has been handicapped by the attitude rooted in the Chinese "ethos" and peculiar to a stratum of officials and aspirants to office. This brings us to our central theme.

CHAPTER V

THE LITERATI°

F OR twelve centuries social rank in China has been determined more by qualification for office than by wealth. This
qualification, in turn, has been determined by education, and
especially by examinations. China has made literary education
the yardstick of social prestige in the most exclusive fashion, far
more exclusively than did Europe during the period of the
humanists, or as Germany has done. Even during the period of
the Warring States, the stratum of aspirants for office who were
educated in literature—and originally this only meant that they
had a scriptural knowledge—extended through all the individual
states. Literati have been the bearers of progress toward a rational
administration and of all "intelligence."

As with Brahmanism in India, in China the literati have been
the decisive exponents of the unity of culture. Territories (as
well as enclaves) not administered by officials educated in
literature, according to the model of the orthodox state idea,
were considered heterodox and barbarian, in the same way as
were the tribal territories that were within the territory of Hinduism but not regulated by the Brahmans, as well as landscapes
not organized as *polis* by the Greeks. The increasingly bureau-

* "The Chinese Literati" reprinted by permission of Hans H. Gerth and
C. Wright Mills and Oxford University Press from *From Max Weber: Essays
in Sociology.* Copyright 1946 by Oxford University Press, Inc.

cratic structure of Chinese polities and of their carriers has given to the whole literary tradition of China its characteristic stamp. For more than two thousand years the literati have definitely been the ruling stratum in China and they still are. Their dominance has been interrupted; often it has been hotly contested; but always it has been renewed and expanded. According to the Annals, the Emperor addressed the literati, and them alone, as "My lords"[1] for the first time in 1496.

It has been of immeasurable importance for the way in which Chinese culture has developed that this leading stratum of intellectuals has never had the character of the clerics of Christianity or of Islam, or of Jewish Rabbis, or Indian Brahmans, or Ancient Egyptian priests, or Egyptian or Indian scribes. It is significant that the stratum of literati in China, although developed from ritual training, grew out of an education for genteel *laymen.* The "literati" of the feudal period, then officially called *po-shih,* that is, "living libraries," were first of all proficient in ritualism. They did not, however, stem from the sibs of a priestly nobility, as did the *Rishi* sibs of the *Rig-Veda,* or from a guild of sorcerers, as did in all likelihood the Brahmans of the *Atharva-Veda.*

In China, the literati go back, at least in the main, to the descendants, probably the younger sons, of feudal families who had acquired a literary education, especially the knowledge of writing, and whose social position rested upon this knowledge of writing and of literature. A plebeian could also acquire a knowledge of writing, although, considering the Chinese system of writing, it was difficult. But if the plebeian succeeded, he shared the prestige of any other scholar. Even in the feudal period, the stratum of literati was not hereditary or exclusive—another contrast with the Brahmans.

Until late historical times, Vedic education rested upon oral transmissions; it abhorred the fixing of tradition in writing, an abhorrence which all guilds of organized professional magicians are apt to share. In contrast to this, in China the writing of the ritual books, of the calendar, and of the *Annals* go back to prehistoric times.[2] Even in the oldest tradition the ancient scriptures were considered magical objects,[3] and the men conversant with them were considered holders of a magical charisma. As we shall see, these have been persistent facts in China. The prestige of the literati has not consisted in a charisma of magical powers of sorcery, but rather in a knowledge of writing and of literature as such; perhaps their prestige originally rested in addition upon a knowledge of astrology. But it has not been their task to aid private persons through sorcery, to heal the sick, for instance, as the magician does. For such purposes there were special professions, which we shall discuss later. Certainly the significance of magic in China, as everywhere, was a self-understood presupposition. Yet, so far as the interests of the community were concerned, it was up to its representatives to influence the spirits.

The emperor as the supreme pontifex, as well as the princes, functioned for the political community. And for the family, the head of the sib and the housefather influenced the spirits. The fate of the community, above all of the harvest, has been influenced since olden times by rational means, that is, by water regulation; and therefore the correct "order" of administration has always been the basic means of influencing the world of the spirits.

Apart from knowledge of scriptures as a means of discerning tradition, a knowledge of the calendar and of the stars was required for discerning the heavenly will and, above all, for knowing the *dies fasti* and *nefasti,* and it seems that the position of the literati has also evolved from the dignified role of the court astrologer.[4] The scribes, and they alone, could recognize this important order ritually (and originally probably also by means of horoscopes) and accordingly advise the appropriate political authorities. An anecdote of the Annals[5] shows the results in a striking manner.

In the feudal state of the Wei, a proved general—Wu Ch'i, the alleged author of the textbook in ritually correct strategy which was authoritative until our time—and a literary man competed for the position of first minister. A violent dispute arose between the two after the literary man had been appointed to the post. He readily admitted that he could neither conduct wars nor master similar political tasks in the manner of the general. But when the general thereupon declared himself to be the better man, the literary man remarked that a revolution threatened the dynasty, whereupon the general admitted without any hesitation that the literary man was the better man to prevent it.

Only the adept of scriptures and of tradition has been considered competent for correctly ordering the internal administration and the charismatically correct life conduct of the prince, ritually and politically. In sharpest contrast to the Jewish prophets, who were essentially interested in foreign policy, the Chinese literati-politicians, trained in ritual, were primarily oriented toward problems of internal administration, even if these problems involved absolute power politics, and even though while in charge of the prince's correspondence and of the chancellery they might personally be deeply involved in the guidance of diplomacy.

This constant orientation toward problems of the "correct" administration of the state determined a far-reaching, practical, and political rationalism among the intellectual stratum of the feudal period. In contrast to the strict traditionalism of the later period, the Annals occasionally reveal the literati to be audacious political innovators.[6] Their pride in education knew no limit,[7] and the princes—at least according to the lay-out of the Annals —paid them great deference.[8] Their intimate relations to the service of patrimonial princes existed from ancient times and has been decisive for the peculiar character of the literati.

The origin of the literati is veiled from us in darkness. Apparently they were the Chinese *augurs*. The pontifical cesaro-papist character of the imperial power has been decisive for their position, and the character of Chinese literature has also been determined by it. There were official Annals, magically proved hymns of war and sacrifice, calendars, as well as books of ritual and ceremony. With their knowledge the literati supported the character of the state, which was in the nature of an ecclesiastic and compulsory institution; they took the state for granted as an axiomatic presupposition.

In their literature, the literati created the concept of "office," above all, the ethos of "official duty" and of the "public weal."[9] If one may trust the Annals, the literati, being adherents of the bureaucratic organization of the state as a compulsory institution, were opponents of feudalism from the very beginning. This is quite understandable because, from the standpoint of their interests, the administrators should be only men who were personally qualified by a literary education.[10] On the other hand, they claimed *for themselves* to have shown the princes the way toward autonomous administration, toward government manufacture of arms and construction of fortifications, ways and means by which the princes became "masters of their lands."[11]

This close relation of the literati to princely service came about during the struggle of the prince with the feudal powers. It distinguishes the Chinese literati from the educated laymen of Hellas, as well as from those of Ancient India *(Kshatriya)*. It makes them similar to the Brahmans, from whom, however, they differ greatly in their ritualist subordination under a cesaro-papist pontifex. In addition, no caste order has existed in China, a fact intimately connected with the literary education and the subordination under a pontifex.

The relation of the literati to the *office* has changed its nature [in the course of time]. During the period of the feudal states, the various courts competed for the services of the literati, who were seeking opportunities for power and, we must not forget, for the best chances for income.[12] A whole stratum of vagrant "sophists" *(che-she)* emerged, comparable to the wayfaring knights and scholars of the occidental Middle Ages. As we shall later see, there were also Chinese literati who, in principle, remained unattached to any office. This free and mobile stratum of literati were carriers of philosophical schools and antagonisms, a situation comparable to those of India, of Hellenic Antiquity, and of the Middle Ages with its monks and scholars. Yet, the literati as such felt themselves to be a unitary status group. They claimed common status honors[13] and were united in the feeling of being the sole bearers of the homogeneous culture of China.

The relation of the Chinese literati to princely service as the normal source of income differentiated them as a status group from the philosophers of Antiquity and from at least the educated laymen of India, who, in the main, were socially anchored in fields remote from any office. As a rule, the Chinese literati strove for princely service both as a source of income and as a normal field of activity. Confucius, like Lao-tzu, was an official before he lived as a teacher and writer without attachment to office. We shall see that this relation to state-office (or office in a "church state") was of fundamental importance for the nature of the mentality of this stratum. For this orientation became increasingly important and exclusive. The opportunities of the princes to compete for the literati ceased to exist in the unified empire. The literati and their disciples then came to compete for the existing offices, and this development could not fail to result in a unified orthodox doctrine adjusted to the situation. This doctrine was to be *Confucianism*.

As Chinese prebendalism grew, the originally free mental mobility of the literati came to a halt. This development was fully underway even at the time when the Annals and most of the systematic writings of the literati originated and when the sacred books, which Shih Huang Ti had destroyed, were "rediscovered."[14] They were "rediscovered" in order that they might be revised, retouched, and interpreted by the literati and therewith gain canonical value.

It is evident from the Annals that this whole development came about with the pacification of the empire, or rather that it was pushed to its conclusions during this period. Everywhere war has been the business of youth, and the sentence *sexagenarios de ponte* has been a slogan of warriors directed against the "senate." The Chinese literati, however, were the "old men," or they represented the old men. The Annals, as a paradigmatic public confession of the prince Mu Kung (of Ch'in), transmitted the idea that the prince had sinned by having listened to "youth" (the warriors) and not to the "elders," who, although having no strength, did have experience.[15] In fact, *this* was the decisive point in the turn toward pacifism and therewith toward traditionalism. Tradition displaced charisma.

1. Confucius

EVEN the oldest sections of the classic writings connected with the name of K'ung-tzu, that is, with Confucius as editor, permit us to recognize the conditions of charismatic warrior kings. (Confucius died in the year 478 B.C.) The heroic songs of the hymn-book *(Shih Ching)* tell of kings fighting from war chariots, as do the Hellenic and Indian epics. But considering their character as a whole, even these songs are no longer heralds of individual, and in general, purely human heroism, as are the Homeric and Germanic epics. Even when the *Shih Ching* was edited, the king's army had nothing of the romance of the warrior followings or the Homeric adventures. The army already had the character of a disciplined bureaucracy, and above all it had "officers." The kings, even in the *Shih Ching*, no longer win simply because they are the greater heroes. And that is decisive for the spirit of the army. They win because before the Spirit of Heaven they are morally right and because their charismatic virtues are superior, whereas their enemies are godless criminals who, by oppression and trespass upon the ancient customs, have wronged their subjects' weal and thus have foregone their charisma. Victory is the occasion for moralizing reflections rather than heroic joy. In contrast to the sacred scriptures of almost all other ethics, one is struck at once by the lack of any "shocking" expression, of any even conceivably "indecent" image. Obviously, a very systematic expurgation has taken place here, and this may well have been the specific contribution of Confucius.

The pragmatic transformation of the ancient tradition in the Annals, produced by official historiography and by the literati, obviously went beyond the priestly paradigms performed in the Old

Testament, for example, in the Book of Judges. The chronicle expressly ascribed to Confucius' authorship contains the driest and most sober enumeration of military campaigns and punitive expeditions against rebels; in this respect it is comparable to the hieroglyphic protocols of Assyria. If Confucius really expressed the opinion that his character could be recognized with special clarity from this work—as tradition maintains—then one would have to endorse the view of those (Chinese and European) scholars who interpret this to mean that his characteristic achievement was this systematic and pragmatic correction of facts from the point of view of "propriety." His work must have appeared in this light to his contemporaries, but for us its pragmatic meaning, in the main, has become opaque.[16]

The princes and ministers of the classics act and speak like paradigms of rulers whose ethical conduct is rewarded by Heaven. Officialdom and the promotion of officials according to merit are topics for glorification. The princely realms are still ruled hereditarily; some of the local offices are hereditary fiefs; but the classics view this system skeptically, at least the hereditary offices. Ultimately they consider this system to be merely provisional. In theory, this pertains even to the hereditary nature of the dignity of the emperor. The ideal and legendary Emperors (Yao and Shun) designate their successors (Shun and Yü) without regard to birth, from the circle of their ministers and over the heads of their own sons, solely according to their personal charisma as certified by the highest court officials. The emperors designate their ministers in the same way, and only the third Emperor, Yü, does not name his first minister (Yi) but his son (Ch'i) to become his successor.

In contrast with the old and genuine documents and monuments, one looks in vain for genuinely heroic minds in most of the classic writings. The traditional view held by Confucius is that caution is the better part of valor and that it ill behooves the wise man to risk his own life inappropriately. The profound pacification of the country, especially after the rule of the Mongols, greatly enhanced this mood. The empire became an empire of peace.

According to Mencius, there were no "just" wars within the frontiers of the empire, as it was considered as one unit. Compared to the size of the empire, the army had finally become very tiny. After having separated the training of the literati from that of the knights, the emperors retained sport and literary contests and gave military certificates[17] in addition to the state examinations of the literati. Yet for a long time the attainment of such military certificates had hardly any connection with an actual career in the army.[18] And the fact remained that the military were just as despised in China as they were in England for two hundred years, and that a cultivated literary man would not engage in social intercourse on an equal footing with army officers.[19]

2. The Development of the Examination System

DURING the period of the central monarchy, the mandarins became a status group of certified claimants to office prebends. All categories of Chinese civil servants were recruited from their midst, and their qualification for office and rank depended upon the number of examinations they had successfully passed.

These examinations consisted of three major degrees,[20] which were considerably augmented by intermediary, repetitive, and preliminary examinations as well as by numerous special conditions. For the first degree alone there were ten types of examinations. The question usually put to a stranger of unknown rank was how many examinations he had passed. Thus, in spite of the ancestor cult, how many ancestors one had was not decisive for social rank. The very reverse held: it depended upon one's official rank whether one was allowed to have an ancestral temple (or a mere table of ancestors, which was the case with illiterates). How many ancestors one was permitted to mention was determined by official rank.[21] Even the rank of a city god in the Pantheon depended upon the rank of the city's mandarin.

In the Confucian period (sixth to fifth century B.C.), the possibility of ascent into official positions as well as the system of examinations was still unknown. It appears that as a rule, at least in the feudal states, the "great families" were in the possession of power. It was not until the Han dynasty—which was established by a parvenu—that the bestowal of offices according to merit was raised to the level of a principle. And not until the T'ang dynasty, in 690 A.D., were regulations set up for the highest degree. As we have already mentioned, it is highly probable that literary education, perhaps with a few exceptions, was at first actually, and perhaps also legally, monopolized by the "great families," just as the Vedic education in India was monopolized. Vestiges of this continued to the end. Members of the imperial sib, although not freed from all examinations, were freed from the examination for the first degree. And the trustees, whom every candidate for examinations, until recently, had to name, had to testify to the candidate's "good family background." During modern times this testimony has only meant the exclusion of descendants of barbers, bailiffs, musicians, janitors, carriers, and others. Yet alongside this exclusion there was the institution of "candidates for the mandarinate," that is, the descendants of mandarins enjoyed a special and preferred position in fixing the maximum quota of examination candidates from each province. The promotion lists used the official formula "from a mandarin family and from the people." The sons of well-deserved officials held the lowest degree as a title of honor. All of which represent residues of ancient conditions.

The examination system has been fully carried through since the end of the seventh century. This system was one of the means the patrimonial ruler used in preventing the formation of a closed estate, which, in the manner of feudal vassals and office nobles, would have monopolized the rights to the office prebends. The first traces of the examination system *seem* to emerge about the time of Confucius (and Huang K'an) in the sub-state of Ch'in, a locality which later became autocratic. The selection of candidates was determined essentially by military merit. Yet, even the *Li Chi* and the *Chou Li*[22] demand, in a quite rationalist way, that the district chiefs examine their lower officials periodically with regard to their morals, and then propose to the emperor which of them should be promoted. In the unified state of the Han Emperors, pacifism began to direct the selection of officials. The power of the literati was tremendously consolidated after they had succeeded in elevating the correct Kuang Wu to the throne in 21 A.D. and in maintaining him against the popular "usurper" Wang Mang. During the struggle for prebends, which raged during the following period and which we shall deal with later, the literati developed into a unified *status group*.

Even today the T'ang dynasty irradiates the glory of having been the actual creator of China's greatness and culture. The T'ang dynasty, for the first time, regulated the literati's position and established colleges for their education (in the seventh century). It also created the *Hanlin Yüan*, the so-called "academy," which first edited the Annals in order to gain precedents, and then controlled the emperor's correct deportment. Finally, after the Mongol storms, the national Ming dynasty in the fourteenth century decreed statutes which, in essence, were definitive.[23] Schools were to be set up in every village, one for every twenty-five families. As the schools were not subsidized, the decree remained a dead letter—or rather we have already seen which powers gained control over the schools. Officials selected the best pupils and enrolled a certain number in the colleges. In the main, these colleges have decayed, although in part they have been newly founded. In 1382, prebends in the form of rice rents were set aside for the "students." In 1393, the number of students was fixed. After 1370, only examined men had claims to offices.

At once a fight set in between the various regions, especially between the North and the South. The South even then supplied candidates for examinations who were more cultured, having experienced a more comprehensive environment. But the North was the military foundation stone of the empire. Hence, the emperor intervened and *punished* (!) the examiners who had given the "first place" to a Southerner. Separate lists for the North and the South were set up, and moreover, a struggle for the patronage of offices began immediately. Even in 1387 special examinations were given to officers' sons. The officers and officials, however, went further, and demanded the right to designate their successors.

which meant a demand for re-feudalization. In 1393 this was conceded, but in the end only in a modified form. The candidates presented were preferentially enrolled in the colleges, and prebends were to be reserved for them: in 1465 for three sons, in 1482 for one son. In 1453 we meet with the purchase of college places, and in 1454 with the purchase of offices. During the fifteenth century, as is always the case, these developments arose from the need for military funds. In 1492 these measures were abolished, but in 1529 they were reintroduced.

The *departments* also fought against one another. The Board of Rites was in charge of the examinations after 736, but the Board of Civil Office appointed the officials. The examined candidates were not infrequently boycotted by the latter department, the former answering by going on strike during the examinations. Formally, the minister of rites, actually, the minister of offices (the major-domo) were in the end the most powerful men in China. Then merchants, who were expected to be less "stingy," came into office.[24] Of course, this hope was quite unjustified. The Manchus favored the old traditions and thus the literati and, as far as possible, "purity" in the distribution of offices. But now, as before, three routes to office existed side by side: (1) imperial favors for the sons of the "princely" families (examination privileges); (2) easy examinations (officially every three to six years) for the lower officials by the higher officials who controlled patronage; this inevitably led each time to advancement also to higher positions; (3) the only legal way: to qualify effectively and purely by examination.

In the main, the system of examinations has actually fulfilled the functions as conceived by the emperor. Occasionally (in 1372), it was suggested to the emperor—one can imagine by whom —that he draw the conclusion from the orthodox charisma of virtues by abolishing the examinations, since virtue *alone* legitimizes and qualifies. This conclusion was soon dropped, which is quite understandable. For after all, both parties, emperor and graduates, had a stake in the examination system, or at least they thought they had. From the emperor's standpoint, the examination system corresponded entirely to the role which the *mjestnit-shestvo*, a technically heterogeneous means, of Russian despotism played for the Russian nobility. The system facilitated a competitive struggle for prebends and offices among the candidates, which stopped them from joining together into a feudal office nobility. Admittance to the ranks of aspirants was open to everybody who was proved to be educationally qualified. The examination system thus fulfilled its purpose.

3. The Typological Position of Confucian Education

WE SHALL now discuss the position of this educational system among the great types of education. To be sure, we cannot here, in passing, give a sociological typology of pedagogical ends and means, but perhaps some comments may be in place.

Historically, the two polar opposites in the field of educational ends are: to awaken charisma, that is, heroic qualities or magical gifts; and, to impart specialized expert training. The first type corresponds to the charismatic structure of domination; the latter type corresponds to the *rational* and bureaucratic (modern) structure of domination. The two types do not stand opposed, with no connections or transitions between them. The warrior hero or the magician also needs special training, and the expert official is generally not trained exclusively for knowledge. However, they are polar opposites of types of education and they form the most radical contrasts. Between them are found all those types which aim at cultivating the pupil for a *conduct of life,* whether it is of a mundane or of a religious character. In either case, the life conduct is the conduct of a status group.

The charismatic procedure of ancient magical asceticism and the hero trials, which sorcerers and warrior heroes have applied to boys, tried to aid the novice to acquire a "new soul," in the animist sense, and hence, to be reborn. Expressed in our language, this means that they merely wished to *awaken* and to test a capacity which was considered a purely personal gift of grace.

For one can neither teach nor train for charisma. Either it exists *in nuce,* or it is infiltrated through a miracle of magical rebirth— otherwise it cannot be attained.

Specialized and expert schooling attempts to *train* the pupil for practical usefulness for administrative purposes—in the organization of public authorities, business offices, workshops, scientific or industrial laboratories, disciplined armies. In principle, this can be accomplished with anybody, though to varying extent.

The pedagogy of cultivation, finally, attempts to *educate* a cultivated type of man, whose nature depends on the decisive stratum's respective ideal of cultivation. And this means to educate a man for a certain internal and external deportment in life. In principle this can be done with everybody, only the goal differs. If a separate stratum of warriors form the decisive status group—as in Japan—education will aim at making the pupil a stylized knight and courtier, who despises the pen-pushers as the Japanese Samurai have despised them. In particular cases, the stratum may display great variations of type. If a priestly stratum is decisive, it will aim at making the disciple a scribe, or at least an intellectual, likewise of greatly varying character. In reality, none of these types ever occurs in pure form. The numerous combinations and intermediary links cannot be discussed in this context. What is important here is to define the position of Chinese education in terms of these forms.

The holdovers of the primeval charismatic training for regeneration, the milk name, the previously discussed initiation rites of youth, the bridegroom's change of name, and so on, have for a long time in China been a formula (in the manner of the Protestant confirmation) standing beside the testing of educational qualifications. Such tests have been monopolized by the political authorities. The educational qualification, however, in view of the educational means employed, has been a "cultural" qualification, in the sense of a general education. It was of a similar, yet of a more specific nature than, for instance, the *humanist* educational qualification of the Occident.

In Germany, such an education, until recently and almost exclusively, was a prerequisite for the official career leading to positions of command in civil and military administration. At the same time this *humanist* education has stamped the pupils who were to be prepared for such careers as belonging socially to the *cultured* status group. In Germany, however—and this is a very important difference between China and the Occident—rational and specialized *expert* training has been added to, and in part has displaced, this educational status qualification.

The Chinese examinations did not test any special skills, as do our modern national and bureaucratic examination regulations for jurists, medical doctors, or technicians. Nor did the Chinese examinations test the possession of charisma, as do the typical "trials" of magicians and bachelor leagues. To be sure, we shall presently see the qualifications which this statement requires. Yet it holds at least for the technique of the examinations.

The examinations of China tested whether or not the candidate's mind was thoroughly steeped in literature and whether or not he possessed the *ways of thought* suitable to a cultured man and resulting from cultivation in literature. These qualifications held far more specifically with China than with the German humanist gymnasium. Today one is used to justifying the gymnasium by pointing to the practical value of formal education through the study of Antiquity. As far as one may judge from the assignments[25] given to the pupils of the lower grades in China, they were rather similar to the essay topics assigned to the top grades of a German gymnasium, or perhaps better still, to the select class of a German girls' college. All the grades were intended as tests in penmanship, style, mastery of classic writings,[26] and finally—similar to our lessons in religion, history, and German —in conformity with the prescribed mental outlook.[27] In our context it is decisive that this education was on the one hand purely secular in nature, but, on the other, was bound to the fixed norm of the orthodox interpretation of the classic authors. It was a highly exclusive and bookish literary education.

The literary character of education in India, Judaism, Christianity, and Islam resulted from the fact that it was completely in the hands of Brahmans and Rabbis trained in literature, or of clerics and monks of book religions who were professionally trained in literature. As long as education was Hellenic and not "Hellenist," the Hellenic man of culture was and remained primarily ephebe and hoplite. The effect of this was nowhere thrown into relief more clearly than in the conversation of the Symposium, where it is said of Plato's Socrates that he had never "flinched" in the field, to use a student term. For Plato to state this is obviously at least of equal importance with everything else he makes Alcibiades say.

During the Middle Ages, the military education of the knight, and later the genteel education of the Renaissance salon, provided a corresponding though socially different supplement to the education transmitted by books, priests, and monks. In Judaism and in China, such a counterbalance was, in part altogether, and in part as good as altogether, absent. In India, as in China, the literary means of education consisted substantially of hymns, epic tales, and casuistry in ritual and ceremony. In India, however, this was underpinned by cosmogonic as well as religious and philosophical speculations. Such speculations were not entirely absent from the classics and from the transmitted commentaries in China, but obviously they have always played only a very minor role there. The Chinese authors developed rational systems of social ethics. The educated stratum of China simply has never been an autonomous status group of scholars, as were the Brahmans, but rather a stratum of officials and aspirants to office.

Higher education in China has not always had the character it has today. The public educational institutions *(Pan kung)* of the feudal princes taught the arts of the dance and of arms in addition to the knowledge of rites and literature. Only the pacification of the empire into a patrimonial and unified state, and finally, the pure system of examinations for office, transformed this older education, which was far closer to early Hellenic education, into what has existed into the twentieth century. Medieval education, as represented in the authoritative and orthodox *Hsiao Hsüeh,* that is "schoolbook," still placed considerable weight upon dance and music. To be sure, the old war dance seems to have existed only in rudimentary form, but for the rest, the children, according to age groups, learned certain dances. The purpose of this was stated to be the taming of evil passions. If a child did not do well during his instruction, one should let him dance and sing. Music improves man, and rites and music form the basis of self-control.[28] The magical significance of music was a primary aspect of all this. "Correct music"—that is, music used according to the old rules and strictly following the old measures—"keeps the spirits in their fetters."[29] As late as the Middle Ages, archery and charioteering were still considered general educational subjects for genteel children.[30] But this was essentially mere theory. Going through the schoolbook one finds that from the seventh year of life, domestic education was strictly separated according to sex; it consisted essentially of instilling a ceremonial, which went far beyond all occidental ideas, a ceremonial especially of piety and awe toward parents and all superiors and older persons in general. For the rest, the schoolbook consisted almost exclusively of rules for self-control.

This domestic education was supplemented by school instruction. There was supposed to be a grade school in every *hsien*.. Higher education presupposed the passing of the first entrance examination. Thus two things were peculiar to Chinese higher education. First, it was entirely non-military and purely literary, as all education established by priesthoods has been. Second, its literary character, that is, its *written* character, was pushed to extremes. In part, this appears to have been a result of the peculiarity of the Chinese script and of the literary art which grew out of it.[31]

As the script retained its pictorial character and was not rationalized into an alphabetical form, such as the trading peoples of the Mediterranean created, the literary product was addressed at once to both the eyes and the ears, and essentially more to the former. Any "reading aloud" of the classic books was in itself a translation from the pictorial script into the (unwritten) word. The visual character, especially of the old script, was by its very nature remote from the spoken word. The monosyllabic language requires sound perception as well as the perception of pitched tone. With its sober brevity and its compulsion of syntactical logic, it stands in extreme contrast to the purely visual character of script. But in spite of this, or rather—as Grube has shown in an ingenious way—in part because of the very rational qualities of its structure, the Chinese tongue has been unable to offer its services to poetry or to systematic thinking. Nor could it serve the development of the oratorical arts as have the structures of the Hellenic, Latin, French, German, and Russian languages, each in its own way. The stock of written symbols remained far richer than the stock of monosyllabic words, which was inevitably quite delimited. Hence, all phantasy and ardor fled from the poor and formalistic intellectualism of the spoken word and into the quiet beauty of the written symbols. The usual poetic speech was held fundamentally subordinate to the script. Not speaking but writing and reading were valued artistically and considered as worthy of a gentleman, for they were receptive of the artful products of script. Speech remained truly an affair of the plebs. This contrasts sharply with Hellenism, to which conversation meant everything and a translation into the style of the dialogue was the adequate form of all experience and contemplation. In China the very finest blossoms of literary culture lingered, so to speak, deaf and mute in their silken splendor. They were valued far higher than was the art of drama, which, characteristically, flowered during the period of the Mongols.

Among the renowned social philosophers, Meng Tzu (Mencius) made systematic use of the dialogue form. That is precisely why he readily appears to us as the one representative of Confucianism who matured to full "lucidity." The very strong impact upon us of the "Confucian Analects" (as Legge called them) also rests upon the fact that in China (as occasionally elsewhere) the doctrine is clothed in the form of (in part, probably authentic) sententious responses of the master to questions from the disciples. Hence, to us, it is transposed into the form of speech. For the rest, the epic literature contains the addresses of the early warrior kings to the army; in their lapidar forcefulness, they are highly impressive. Part of the didactic *Analects* consists of speeches, the character of which rather corresponds to pontifical "allocutions." Otherwise speech plays no part in the official literature. Its lack of development, as we shall see presently, has been determined by both social and political reasons.

In spite of the logical qualities of the language, Chinese thought has remained rather stuck in the pictorial and the descriptive. The power of *logos,* of defining and reasoning, has not been accessible to the Chinese. Yet, on the other hand, this purely scriptural education detached thought from gesture and expressive movement still more than is usual with the literary nature of any education. For two years before he was introduced to their meaning, the pupil learned merely to paint about 2,000 characters. Furthermore, the examiners focused attention upon style, the art of versification, a firm grounding in the classics, and finally, upon the expressed mentality of the candidate.

The lack of all training in calculation, even in grade schools, is a very striking feature of Chinese education. The *idea* of positional numbers, however, was developed[32] during the sixth century before Christ, that is, during the period of Warring States. A calculative attitude in commercial intercourse had permeated all strata of the population, and the final calculations of the administrative offices were as detailed as they were difficult to survey, for reasons mentioned above. The medieval schoolbook (*Hsiao Hsüeh* 1, 29) enumerates calculation among the six "arts." And at the time of the Warring States, there existed a mathematics which allegedly included trigonometrics as well as the rule of three and commercial calculation. Presumably this literature, apart from fragments, was lost during Shih Huang Ti's burning of the books.[33] In any case, calculation is not even mentioned in later pedagogy. And in the course of history, calculation receded more and more into the background of the education of the genteel mandarins, finally to disappear altogether. The educated merchants learned calculation in their business offices. Since the empire had been unified and the tendency toward a rational administration of the state had weakened, the mandarin became a genteel literary man, who was not one to occupy himself with the "σχολή" of calculation.

The mundane character of this education contrasts with other educational systems, which are nevertheless related to it by their literary stamp. The literary examinations in China were purely political affairs. Instruction was given partly by individual and private tutors and partly by the teaching staffs of college foundations. But no priest took part in them.

The Christian universities of the Middle Ages originated from the practical and ideal need for a rational, mundane, and ecclesiastic legal doctrine and a rational (dialectical) theology. The universities of Islam, following the model of the late Roman law schools and of Christian theology, practiced sacred case law and the doctrine of faith; the Rabbis practiced interpretation of the law; the philosophers' schools of the Brahmans engaged in speculative philosophy, in ritual, as well as in sacred law. Always ecclesiastic dignitaries or theologians have formed either the sole teaching staff or at least its basic corps. To this corps were attached mundane teachers, in whose hands the other branches of study rested. In Christianity, Islam, and Hinduism, prebends were the goals, and for the sake of them educational certificates were striven after. In addition, of course, the aspirant wished to qualify for ritual activity and the curing of souls. With the ancient Jewish teachers (precursors of the Rabbis), who worked "gratis," the goal was solely to qualify for instructing the laymen in the law, for this instruction was religiously indispensable. But in all this, education was always bound by sacred or cultic scriptures. Only the Hellenic philosophers' schools engaged in an education solely of laymen and freed from all ties to scriptures, freed from all direct interests in prebends, and solely devoted to the education of Hellenic "gentlemen" (Caloicagathoi).

Chinese education served the interest in prebends and was tied to a script, but at the same time it was purely lay education, partly of a ritualist and ceremonial character and partly of a traditionalist and ethical character. The schools were concerned with neither mathematics nor natural sciences, with neither geography nor grammar. Chinese philosophy itself did not have a speculative, systematic character, as Hellenic philosophy had and as, in part and in a different sense, Indian and occidental theological schooling had. Chinese philosophy did not have a rational-formalist character, as occidental jurisprudence has. And it was not of an empirical casuist character, as Rabbinic, Islamite, and, partly, Indian philosophy. Chinese philosophy did not give birth to scholasticism because it was not professionally engaged in logic, as were the philosophies of the Occident and the Middle East, both of them being based on Hellenist thought. The very concept of logic remained absolutely alien to Chinese philosophy, which was bound to script, was not dialectical, and remained oriented to purely practical problems as well as to the status interests of the patrimonial bureaucracy.

This means that the problems that have been basic to all occidental philosophy have remained unknown to Chinese philosophy, a fact which comes to the fore in the Chinese philosophers' manner of categorical thought, and above all in Confucius. With the greatest practical matter-of-factness, the intellectual tools remained in the form of parables, reminding us of the means of expression of Indian chieftains rather than of rational argumentation. This holds precisely for some of the truly ingenious statements ascribed to Confucius. The absence of speech is palpable, that is, speech as a rational means for attaining political and forensic effects, speech as it was first cultivated in the Hellenic *polis*. Such speech could not be developed in a bureaucratic patrimonial state which had no formalized justice. Chinese justice remained, in part, a summary Star Chamber procedure (of the high officials), and, in part, it relied solely on documents. No oral pleading of cases existed, only the written petitions and oral hearings of the parties concerned. The Chinese bureaucracy was interested in conventional propriety, and these bonds prevailed and worked in the same direction of obstructing forensic speech. The bureaucracy rejected the argument of "ultimate" speculative problems as practically sterile. The bureaucracy considered such arguments improper and rejected them as too delicate for one's own position because of the danger of innovations.

If the technique and the substance of the examinations were purely mundane in nature and represented a sort of "cultural examination for the literati," the popular view of them was very different: it gave them a magical-charismatic meaning. In the eyes of the Chinese masses, a successfully examined candidate and official was by no means a mere applicant for office qualified by knowledge. He was a proved holder of magical qualities, which, as we shall see, were attached to the certified mandarin just as much as to an examined and ordained priest of an ecclesiastic institution of grace, or to a magician tried and proved by his guild.[34]

The position of the successfully examined candidate and official corresponded in important points, for example, to that of a Catholic chaplain. For the pupil to complete his period of instruction and his examinations did not mean the end of his immaturity. Having passed the "baccalaureate," the candidate came under the discipline of the school director and the examiners. In case of bad conduct his name was dropped from the lists. Under certain conditions his hands were caned. In the localities' secluded cells for examinations, candidates not infrequently fell seriously ill and suicides occurred. According to the charismatic interpretation of the examination as a magical "trial," such happenings were considered proof of the wicked conduct of the person in question. After the applicant for office had luckily passed the examinations for the higher degrees with their strict seclusion, and after, at long last, he had moved into an office corresponding to the number and rank of examinations passed and depending on his patronage, he still remained throughout his life under the control of the school. And in addition to being under the authority of his superiors, he was under the constant surveillance and criticism of the censors. Their criticism extended even to the ritualist correctness of the very Son of Heaven. The impeachment of the officials[35] was prescribed from olden times and was valued as meritorious in the way of the Catholic confession of sins. Periodically, as a rule every three years, his record of conduct, that is, a list of his merits and faults as determined by official investigations of the censors and his superiors, was to be published in the *Imperial Gazette*.[36] According to his published grades, he was allowed to retain his post, was promoted, or was demoted.[37] As a rule, not only objective factors determined the outcome of these records of conduct. What mattered was the "spirit," and this spirit was that of a life-long pennalism by office authority.

4. *The Status-Honor of the Literati*

AS A STATUS group, the literati were privileged, even those who had only been examined but were not employed. Soon after their position had been strengthened, the literati enjoyed *status privileges*. The most important of these were: first, freedom from the *sordida munera*, the *corvée;* second, freedom from corporal punishment; third, prebends (stipends). For a long time this third privilege has been rather severely reduced in its bearing, through the financial position of the state. The *Sheng* (baccalaureate) still got stipends of $10.00 yearly, with the condition that they had to submit every three to six years to the *Chü jen* or Master's examination. But this, of course, did not mean anything decisive. The burden of the education *and* of the periods of nominal pay actually fell upon the sib, as we have seen. The sib hoped to recover their expenses by seeing their member finally enter the harbor of an office. The first two privileges were of importance to the very end; for the *corvée* still existed, although to a decreasing extent. The rod, however, remained the national means of punishment. Caning stemmed from the terrible pedagogy of corporal punishment in the elementary schools of China. Its unique character is said to have consisted in the following traits, which remind one of our Middle Ages but were obviously developed to even greater extremes.[38] The fathers of the sibs or of the villages compiled the "red cards," that is, the list of pupils *(Kuan-tan)*. Then for a certain period they engaged a schoolmaster from among the oversupply of literati without office, which always existed. The ancestral temple (or other unused rooms) was the preferred schoolroom. From early until late the howling in unison of the written "lines" was to be heard. All day long the pupil was in a condition of mental daze, which is denoted by a Chinese character, the component parts of which signify a pig in the weeds (*meng*). The student and graduate received slaps on the palm of his hand, no longer on what, in the terminology of German mothers of the old hue, was called "the God-ordained spot."

The graduates of high rank were entirely free from such punishment so long as they were not demoted. And in the Middle Ages freedom from the *corvée* was firmly established. Nevertheless, in spite and also because of these privileges, the development of feudal ideas of honor was impossible on their basis. Moreover, as has been observed, these privileges were precarious because they were immediately voided in the case of demotion, which frequently occurred. Feudal honor could not be developed on the bases of examination certificates as a qualification for status, possible degradation, corporal punishment during youth, and the not quite infrequent case of degradation even in old age. But *once*, in the past, such feudal notions of honor had dominated Chinese life with great intensity.

The old Annals praise "frankness" and "loyalty" as cardinal virtues.[39] "To die with honor" was the old watchword. "To be unfortunate and not to know how to die is cowardly." This applied particularly to an officer who did not fight "unto the death."[40] Suicide was a death which a general, having lost a battle, valued as a *privilege*. To permit him to commit suicide meant to forego the right to punish him and therefore was considered with hesitation.[41] The meaning of feudal concepts was changed by the patriarchal idea of *hsiao*. *Hsiao* meant that one should suffer calumny and even meet death as its consequence if it served the honor of the master. One could, and in general should, compensate for *all* the mistakes of the lord by loyal service. The *kotow* before the father, the older brother, the creditor, the official, and the emperor was certainly not a symptom of *feudal* honor. For the correct Chinese to kneel before his love, on the other hand, would have been entirely taboo. All this was the reverse of what held for the knights and the *cortegiani* of the Occident.

To a great extent, the official's honor retained an element of student honor regulated by examination achievements and public censures by superiors. This was the case even if he had passed the highest examinations. In a certain sense, it is true of every bureaucracy (at least on its lower levels; and in Württemberg, with its famous "Grade A, Fischer," even in the highest positions of office); but it held to quite a different extent in China.

5. The Gentleman Ideal

THE peculiar spirit of the scholars, bred by the system of examinations, was intimately connected with the basic presuppositions from which the orthodox and also, by the way, nearly all heterodox, Chinese theories proceeded. The dualism of the *shen* and *kuei*, of good and evil spirits, of heavenly *Yang* substance as over against earthly *Yin* substance, also within the soul of the individual, necessarily made the sole task of education, including self-education, to appear to be the unfolding of the *Yang* substance in the soul of man.[42] For the man in whom the *Yang* substance has completely gained the upper hand over the demonic *kuei* powers resting within him also has power over the spirits; that is, according to the ancient notion, he has magical power. The good spirits, however, are those who protect order and beauty and harmony in the world. To perfect oneself and thus to mirror this harmony is the supreme and the only means by which one may attain such power. During the time of the literati, the *chün tzu*, the "princely man," and once the "hero," was the man who had attained all-around self-perfection, who had become a "work of art" in the sense of a classical, eternally valid, canon of psychical beauty, which literary tradition implemented in the souls of disciples. On the other hand, since the Han period at the latest,[43] it was a firmly established belief among the literati that the spirits reward "beneficence," in the sense of social and ethical excellence. Benevolence tempered by classical (canonical) beauty was therefore the goal of self-perfection.

Canonically perfect and beautiful achievements were the highest aspiration of every scholar as well as the ultimate yardstick of the highest qualification certified by examination. Li Hung-chang's youthful ambition was to become a perfect literary man,[44] that is, a "crowned poet," by attainment of the highest degrees. He was, and he remained, proud of being a calligrapher of great craftsmanship and of being able to recite the classics by heart, especially Confucius' "Spring and Autumn." This ability occasioned his uncle, after having tested it, to pardon the imperfections of his youth and to procure him an office. To Li Hung-chang all other branches of knowledge (algebra, astronomy) were only the indispensable means of "becoming a great poet." The classical perfection of the poem he conceived in the name of the Empress-Dowager, as a prayer in the temple of the tutelary goddess of silk-culture, brought him the Empress' favor.

Puns, euphemisms, allusions to classical quotations, and a refined and purely literary intellectuality were considered the conversational ideal of the genteel man. All politics of the day were excluded from such conversation.[45] It may appear strange to us that this sublimated "salon" cultivation, tied to the classics, should enable man to administer large territories. And in fact, one did not manage the administration with mere poetry even in China. But the Chinese prebendary official proved his status quality, that is, his charisma, through the canonical correctness of his literary forms. Therefore, considerable weight was placed on these forms in official communications. Numerous important declarations of the emperors, the high priests of literary art, were in the form of didactic poems. On the other hand, the official had to prove his charisma by the "harmonious" course of his administration; that is, there must be no disturbances caused by the restless spirits of nature or of men. The actual administrative "work" could rest on the shoulders of subordinate officials. We have noticed that above the official stood the imperial pontifex, his academy of literati, and his collegiate body of censors. They publicly rewarded, punished, scolded, exhorted, encouraged, or lauded the officials.

Because of the publication of the "personal files" and all the reports, petitions, and memorials, the whole administration and the fateful careers of the officials, with their (alleged) causes, took place before the broadest public, far more so than is the case with any of our administrations under parliamentary control, an administration which puts the greatest weight upon the keeping of "official secrets." At least according to the official fiction, the official *Gazette* in China was a sort of running account of the emperor before Heaven and before his subjects. This *Gazette* was the classic expression for the kind of responsibility which followed from the emperor's charismatic qualification. However dubious in reality the official argumentation and the completeness of publication may have been—that, after all, also holds for the communications of our bureaucracy to our parliaments—the Chinese procedure at least tended to open a rather strong and often a quite effective safety-valve for the pressure of public opinion with regard to the official's administrative activities.

6. The Prestige of Officialdom

THE hatred and the distrust of the subjects, which is common to all patrimonialism, in China as everywhere turned above all against the lower levels of the hierarchy, who came into the closest practical contact with the population. The subjects' apolitical avoidance of all contact with "the state" which was not absolutely necessary was typical for China as for all other patrimonial systems. But this apolitical attitude did not detract from the significance of the official education for the character formation of the Chinese people.

The strong demands of the training period were due partly to the peculiarity of Chinese script and partly to the peculiarity of the subject matter. These demands, as well as the waiting periods which were often quite long, forced those who were unable to live on a fortune of their own, on loans, or on family savings of the sort discussed above, to take up practical occupations of all sorts, from merchant to miracle doctor, before completing their educational careers. Then they did not reach the classics themselves, but only the study of the last (the sixth) textbook, the "schoolbook" *(Hsiao Hsüeh),*[46] which was hallowed by age and contained mainly excerpts from the classic authors. Only this difference in the *level* of education and not differences in the *kind* of education set these circles off from the bureaucracy. For only classic education existed.

The percentage of candidates who failed the examinations was extraordinarily high. In consequence of the fixed quotas,[47] the fraction of graduates of the higher examinations was proportionately small, yet they always outnumbered many times the available office prebends. They competed for the prebends by personal patronage,[48] by purchase money of their own, or by loans. The sale of prebends functioned here as in Europe; it was a means of raising capital for the purposes of state, and very frequently it replaced merit ratings.[49] The protests of the reformers against the sale of offices persisted until the last days of the old system, as is shown by the numerous petitions of this sort in the *Peking Gazette.*

The officials' short terms of office (three years), corresponding to similar Islamic institutions, allowed for intensive and rational influencing of the economy through the administration as such only in an intermittent and jerky way. This was the case in spite of the administration's theoretical omnipotence. It is astonishing how few permanent officials the administration believed to be sufficient. The figures alone make it perfectly obvious that as a rule things must have been permitted to take their own course, as long as the interests of the state power and of the treasury remained untouched and as long as the forces of tradition, the sibs, villages, guilds, and other occupational associations remained the normal carriers of order.

Yet in spite of the apolitical attitude of the masses, which we have just mentioned, the views of the stratum of applicants for office exerted a very considerable influence upon the w̟e̟j of the middle classes. This resulted, first and above all, from the popular magical-charismatic conception of the qualification for office as tested by examination. By passing the examination, the graduate proved that he was to an eminent degree a holder of *shen*. High mandarins were considered magically qualified. They could always become objects of a cult, after their death as well as during their lifetime, provided that their charisma was "proved." The primeval magical significance of written work and of documents lent apotropaic and therapeutic significance to their seals and to their handwriting, and this could extend to the examination paraphernalia of the candidate. A province considered it an honor and an advantage to have one of its own sons selected by the emperor as the best graduate of the highest degree,[50] and all whose names were publicly posted after having passed their examinations had "a name in the village." All guilds and other clubs of any significance had to have a literary man as a secretary, and these and similar positions were open to those graduates for whom office prebends were not available. The officeholders and the examined candidates for office, by virtue of their magical charisma and of their patronage relations—especially when they stemmed from petty bourgeois circles—were the natural "father confessors" and advisers in all important affairs of their sibs. In this they corresponded to the Brahmans *(Gurus)* who performed the same function in India.

Alongside the purveyor to the state and the great trader, the officeholder, as we have seen, was the personage with the most opportunities for accumulating possessions. Economically and personally, therefore, the influence on the population of this stratum, outside as well as inside their own sibs, was approximately as great as was the combined influence of the scribes and priests in Egypt. Within the sib, however, the authority of old age was a strong counterweight, as we have already emphasized. Quite independent of the "worthiness" of the individual officials, who were often ridiculed in popular dramas, the prestige of this literary education as such was firmly grounded in the population until it came to be undermined by modern Western-trained members of the mandarin strata.

7. *Views on Economic Policy*

THE social character of the educated stratum determined its stand toward economic policy. According to its own legend, for millennia, the polity had the character of a religious and utilitarian welfare-state, a character which is in line with so many other typical traits of patrimonial bureaucratic structures bearing theocratic stamps.

Since olden times, to be sure, actual state policy, for reasons discussed above, had again and again let economic life alone, at least so far as production and the profit economy were concerned. This happened in China just as in the ancient Orient—unless new settlements, melioration through irrigation, and fiscal or military interests entered the picture. But military interests and interests in military finance had always called forth liturgical interventions in economic life. These interventions were monopolistically or financially determined, and often they were quite incisive. They were partly mercantilist regulations and partly in the nature of regulations of status stratification. Toward the end of national militarism, such planned "economic policy" eventually fell into abeyance. The government, conscious of the weakness of its administrative apparatus, confined itself to the care of the tide and the maintenance of the water routes, which were indispensable for provisioning the leading provinces with rice; for the rest, to the typically patrimonial policy of dearth and consumption. It had no "commercial policy" in the modern sense.[51] The tolls the mandarins had established along the waterways were, so far as is known, merely fiscal in nature and never served any economic policy. The government on the whole pursued only fiscal and mercantilist interests, if one disregards emergency situations which, considering the charismatic nature of authority, were always politically dangerous. So far as is known, the most grandiose attempts to establish a unified economic organization were planned by Wang An-shih, who during the eleventh century tried to establish a state trading monopoly for the entire harvest. In addition to fiscal gains, the plan was intended to serve the equalization of prices and was connected with a reform in land taxes. The attempt failed.

As the economy was left to itself to a large extent, the aversion against "state intervention" in economic matters became a lasting and basic sentiment. It was directed particularly against monopolistic privileges,[52] which, as fiscal measures, are habitual to patrimonialism everywhere. This sentiment, however, was only one among the quite different attitudes which resulted from the conviction that the welfare of the subjects was dependent upon the charisma of the ruler. These ideas often stood in unmediated fashion beside the basic aversion to state intervention, and continually, or at least occasionally, made for bureaucratic meddling in everything, which again is typical of patrimonialism. Moreover, the administration of course reserved the right to regulate consumption in times of dearth—a policy which is also part of the theory of Confucianism [as reflected] in numerous special norms concerning all sorts of expenditures. Above all, there was the typical aversion against too sharp a social differentiation as determined in a purely economic manner by free exchange in markets. This aversion, of course, goes without saying in every bureaucracy. The increasing stability of the economic situation under conditions of the economically self-sufficient and the socially homogeneously composed world-empire did not allow for the emergence of such economic problems as were discussed in the English literature of the seventeenth century. There was no self-conscious bourgeois stratum which could not be politically ignored by the government and to whose interests the "pamphleteers" of the time in England primarily addressed themselves. As always under patrimonial bureaucratic conditions, the administration had to take serious notice of the attitude of the merchants' guilds only in a "static" way and when the maintenance of tradition and of the guilds' special privileges were at stake. Dynamically, however, the merchant guilds did not enter

into the balance, because there were no expansive capitalist interests *(no longer!)* of sufficient strength, as in England, to be
capable of forcing the state administration into their service.

8. Sultanism and the Eunuchs as
Political Opponents of the Literati

THE total *political* situation of the literati can be understood only
when one realizes the forces against which they had to fight. We
may disregard the heterodoxies here, for they will be dealt with
below.

In early times the main adversaries of the literati were the
"great families" of the feudal period who did not want to be
pushed out of their office monopolies. Having to accommodate
themselves to the needs of patrimonialism and to the superiority
of the knowledge of script, they found ways and means of paving
the way for their sons by imperial favor.

Then there were the capitalist purchasers of office: a natural
result of the leveling of status groups and of the fiscal money
economy. Here the struggle could not lead to constant and absolute success, but only to relative success, because every demand
of war pushed the impecunious central administration toward
the jobbery of *office-prebends* as the *sole* means of war finance.
This held until recent times.

The literati also had to fight the administration's rationalist
interests in an expert officialdom. Specialist, expert officials came
to the fore as early as 601 under Wen Ti. During the distress of
the defensive wars in 1068 under Wang An-shih, they enjoyed a
short-lived and full triumph. But again tradition won out and this
time for good.

There remained only one major and permanent enemy of the
literati: sultanism and the eunuch-system which supported it.[53]
The influence of the harem was therefore viewed with profound
suspicion by the Confucians. Without insight into this struggle,
Chinese history is most difficult to understand.

The constant struggle of the literati and sultanism, which lasted

THE LITERATI » 139 «

for two millennia, began under Shih Huang Ti. It continued under all the dynasties, for of course energetic rulers continually sought to shake off their bonds to the cultured status group of the literati with the aid of eunuchs and plebeian parvenus. Numerous literati who took a stand against this form of absolutism had to give their lives in order to maintain their status group in power. But in the long run and again and again the literati won out.[54] Every drought, inundation, eclipse of the sun, defeat in arms, and every generally threatening event at once placed power in the hands of the literati. For such events were considered the result of a breach of tradition and a desertion of the classic way of life, which the literati guarded and which was represented by the censors and the "Hanlin Academy." In all such cases "free discussion" was granted, the advice of the throne was asked, and the result was always the cessation of the unclassical form of government, execution or banishment of the eunuchs, a retraction of conduct to the classical schemata, in short, adjustments to the demands of the literati.

The harem system was of considerable danger because of the way in which successorship to the throne was ordered. The emperors who were not of age were under the tutelage of women; at times, this petticoat-government had come to be the very rule. The last Empress-Dowager, Tz'u Hsi, tried to rule with the aid of eunuchs.[55] We will not discuss at this point the roles which Taoists and Buddhists have played in these struggles, which run through all of Chinese history—why and how far they have been natural coalitionists, specifically of the eunuchs, and how far they have been coalitionists by constellation.

Let us mention in passing that, at least by modern Confucianism, astrology has been considered an unclassical superstition.[56] It has been thought to compete with the exclusive significance of the emperor's *Tao* charisma for the course of government. Originally this had not been the case. The departmental competition of the Hanlin Academy against the board of astrologers may have played a decisive part;[57] perhaps also the Jesuit origin of the astronomic measures had a hand in it.

ın the conviction of the Confucians, the trust in magic which the eunuchs cultivated brought about all misfortune. Tao Mo in his Memorial of the year 1901 reproached the Empress that in the year 1875 the true heir to the throne had been eliminated through her fault and in spite of the censors' protest, for the censor Wu Ko-tu had acknowledged this by his suicide. Tao Mo's posthumous memorial to the Empress and his letter to his son were distinguished by their manly beauty.[58] There cannot be the slightest doubt of his sincere and profound conviction. Also the belief of the Empress and of numerous princes in the magical charisma of the Boxers, a belief which alone explains her whole policy, was certainly to be ascribed to the influence of eunuchs.[59] On her death bed this impressive woman left as her counsel: (1) never again to let a woman rule in China, and (2) to abolish the eunuch system forever.[60] This counsel was fulfilled in a different way than she had undoubtedly intended—if the report is accurate. But one may not doubt that for the genuine Confucian everything that has happened since, above all the "revolution" and the downfall of the dynasty, only confirms the correctness of the belief in the significance of the charisma of the dynasty's classic virtue. In the improbable but possible event of a Confucian restoration, the belief would be exploited in this sense. The Confucianists, who are ultimately pacifist literati oriented to inner political welfare, naturally faced military powers with aversion or with lack of understanding. We have already spoken of their relationship to the officers, and we have seen that the whole Annals are paradigmatically filled with it. There are protests to be found in the Annals against making "praetorians" into censors (and officials).[61] As the eunuchs were especially popular as favorites and generals in the way of Narses, the enmity against the purely sultanist patrimonial army suggested itself. The literati took pride in having overthrown the popular military usurper Wang Mang. The danger of ruling with plebeians has simply always been great with dictators, yet only this one attempt is known in China. The literati, however, have submitted to de facto established power even when it was created purely by usurpation, as was the power of the Han, or by conquest, as was the power of the Mongol Manchus. They submitted even though they had to make sacrifices—the Manchus took over 50 per cent of the offices without having the educational qualifications. The literati have submitted to the ruler *if* the ruler in turn submitted to their ritualist and ceremonial demands; only *then,* in modern language, have they accommodated themselves and taken a "realistic" stand.

"Constitutionally"—and this was the theory of the Confucians— the emperor could rule *only* by using certified literati as officials; "classically" he could rule only by using orthodox Confucian officials. Every deviation from this rule was thought capable of bringing disaster and, in case of obstinacy, the downfall of the emperor and the ruin of the dynasty.

CHAPTER VI

THE CONFUCIAN LIFE
ORIENTATION

1. Bureaucracy and Hierocracy

JUST as it was spared the power of an increasingly expro-
priated feudalism or a bourgeois stratum which never developed,
so also patrimonial bureaucracy was spared the competition of
an autonomous hierocracy. Nothing whatever is known of socially powerful prophecy, be it of Middle Eastern, Iranian or
Indian character.[1] There were no prophets raising ethical "demands" in the name of a supra-mundane God; the nature of
religiosity remained unbroken and precluded the very existence
of such demands. The pontifical, cesaro-papist authority had only
feudal lords, not prophets, to fight seriously. The mere thought of
prophets led it to eliminate violently and systematically every
heterodox movement as heresy.

The Chinese "soul" has never been revolutionized by a
prophet.[2] There were no "prayers" of private individuals. The
ritualist and literary officeholder and, above all, the emperor
took care of everything, and they alone were able to do so.

Allowing for reservations with regard to Taoism, no powerful
priesthood has ever existed so far as is known historically. Above
all, there were no independent religious forces to develop a doctrine of salvation or an autonomous ethic and education. Hence,
the intellectualistic rationalism of a stratum of officials could
freely unfold itself; here as elsewhere this intellectualism inwardly

despised religions unless they were needed for the taming of the masses. Intellectualism allowed the professional religionists only that measure of official prestige which was indispensable for its taming purposes, a prestige which was ineradicable in the face of the powerful associations of local sibs bound by tradition. All further external and internal development, however, was radically cut off. The cult of the great deities of heaven and earth, with which some deified heroes and special spirits[3] were connected, was an affair of the state. These cults were not managed by priests but by the holders of political power. The one "lay religion" prescribed by the state was the belief in the power of ancestral spirits and its cult. Popular religion otherwise remained, in principle, a completely unsystematic pluralism of magical and heroistic cults. Patrimonial bureaucracy, in its rationalism, was far from seeking to transform systematically these chaotic conditions which it inwardly despised. The bureaucracy rather accepted the situation.

On the one hand, when viewed in the perspective of Confucian reasons of state, religion had to be "upheld for the people." The order of the world, according to a word of the Master, could not be maintained without belief. Therefore, the retention of religious belief was politically even more important than was the concern for food. On the other hand the imperial power was the supreme and religiously consecrated structure; in a sense it stood above the crowd of popular deities. The emperor's personal position, as we have seen, was based exclusively on his charisma as the plenipotentiary ("Son") of Heaven where his ancestors resided. But the veneration and significance of the individual deities were still subject to the charismatic principle of success, just like a Neapolitan driver's or a boatman's Saint. This charismatic character of the religion suited officialdom's interest in self-preservation. For any evil which befell the country did not disavow officialdom *per se,* but at most the individual official and the individual emperor whose divine legitimation appeared to be forfeited; otherwise it disavowed the special deity. By the special and irrational anchorage of the mundane orders, an optimal fusion was effected

he legitimate power of officialdom and the supra-
powers minimally represented on earth; for independ-
he latter might conceivably compete with officialdom.

Any rationalization of popular belief as an independent religion of supra-mundane orientation would inevitably have constituted an independent power opposed to officialdom. This
exigency repeatedly made itself felt in the resolute resistance of
the officials toward any attempt to loosen a stone in this historic
edifice.

Chinese language has no special word for "religion." There was
first: "doctrine"—of a school of literati; second: "rites"—without
distinguishing whether they were religious or conventional in
nature. The official Chinese name for Confucianism was "doctrine
of the Literati" *(ju chiao)*.

Whether magical or cultic in nature, religion remained of a
this-wordly turn of mind. This attitude was far stronger and
more principled than is usually the rule. The hope for long life
played a major role in the very cults which, besides the state cult
of the great spirits, were the most favored ones. It is possible that
the original meaning of every concept of "deity" in China has
rested in the belief that the men of greatest perfection have succeeded in eluding death and in living forever after in a realm of
bliss.[4] In any case, in general, it may be said that the orthodox
Confucian Chinese, but not the Buddhist, performs his rites for
the sake of his fate in this world—for long life, children, wealth,
and to a very slight degree for the good of the ancestors, but not
at all for the sake of his fate in the "hereafter." This is in sharp
contrast with the Egyptian care of the dead which was wholly
oriented toward man's destiny in the hereafter. For a long time
it was the unofficial but prevailing view of the enlightened Confucians that after death the soul evaporated, flew away in the
mist, or otherwise perished.

This doctrine was supported by Wang Ch'ung's authority and,
as has been said, his concept of God was inconsistent. God, according to him, must not be conceived in anthropomorphic terms.
Yet God is "body," a shapeless fluid into which the essentially

similar human spirit merges at death, and death is an extinction of the individual personality.

The definitive disappearance of ideas of a personal God and of immortality was attained by the materialist and atheist Chu-Fu-tzu during the twelfth century. This did not prevent the emergence of later orthodox philosophers who believed in a personal God. Still official Confucianism, which was articulated in the sacred edict of Emperor K'ang Hsi in the seventeenth century, has retained the materialist and atheist standpoint mentioned before.

In Confucianism there prevailed, anyway, an absolutely agnostic and essentially negative mood opposed to all hopes for a beyond. Even where this stand had not permeated or where it was outweighed by Taoist or Buddhist influences (to be discussed below) the interest in man's fate in the beyond remained quite subordinate to the possible influence of the spirits on life here and now.

The "Messianic" hope for a this-worldly Savior-Emperor is found in China, as in almost all patrimonial associations.[5] But this hope is not hope for an absolute utopia, as was the case in Israel.

In the absence of any other eschatology or doctrine of salvation, or any striving for transcendental values and destinies, the religious policy of the state remained simple in form. In part, the policy was to transfer the management of the cult to the state; in part, it was a policy of tolerating the private practitioners of magic inherited from the past and indispensable to the private citizen.

The state cult was deliberately sober and plain; it consisted of sacrifice, ritualist prayer, music, and rhythmic dance. Obviously all orgiastic elements were strictly and intentionally eliminated. This held also for official pentatonic music. In the official cult almost all ecstasy and asceticism, as well as contemplation,[6] were absent and were considered elements of disorder and irrational excitement. This, bureaucratic rationalism could not stand and deemed it as dangerous as the Roman nobility of office considered the cult of Dionysos. Official Confucianism, of course, lacked individual prayer in the occidental sense of the word and knew only ritual formula. The master, when sick, is said to have declined prayers on his behalf and it is reported that he had not prayed for long years.[7] However, the prayers which princes and high officials said for the good of the political association have always been cherished as effective up to the very present.

Confucianism, for these reasons, necessarily lacked the notion that men are differently qualified in a religious way, and beyond these reasons Confucianism was indifferent to religion. Hence, any religious idea differentiating a "state of grace" was absent. The very concept had to remain unknown to Confucianism.

The patrimonial bureaucracy was politically antagonistic to feudalism and to any status structure based on descent. This antagonism was correspondingly found in classical Confucian ethical theory in which the principled equality of man was presupposed. This assumption was not primitive in origin, as we have seen above.

The feudal period rested upon the idea of the charismatic difference between the "noble" sibs and the people. The rule of the literati created the sharp cleavage between the educated and the uneducated or "stupid people" *(yü min)*, as the founder of the Ming dynasty called them during the fourteenth century. Official theory, however, maintained that not birth but education, in principle accessible to all, should be decisive. "Equality" did not, of course, mean unconditional equality in all natural endowments. One man might well have "greater" natural disposition for doing what another could do only by exertion. But everybody could at least attain what was demanded by Confucian bureaucratic reasons-of-state and social ethics—an ethic which never reached for the stars.

Given a good state administration, then, every man had to search for the reasons of external or internal success or failure within himself. Man was good; evil was internalized from without through the senses; and differences in quality were differences in the harmonic development of the individual, a view which characteristically followed upon the absence of a supra-mundane deity. These ideas, moreover, reflected the status conditions in the patrimonial state. The cultured man, to be sure, wished to have his name honored after death but only for reasons of personal merit.

2. Absence of Natural Law and Formal Logic of Legal Thought

IN PRINCIPLE, living conditions alone differentiated people. Identical economic position and education made for essentially identical character. To anticipate: in sharp contrast to the unanimous view of all Christian confessions, material wealth was not ethically considered a primary source of temptation though, of course, temptations were recognized. Rather, wealth was held to be the most important means for promoting morals. We shall learn the reasons below.

On the other hand, in terms of natural law, no sphere of personal liberty was sanctioned. The very word "liberty" was foreign to the language. This can readily be explained from the nature of the patrimonial state and from historical vestiges.

Actually private property in goods was the one institution which was fairly well fenced in. But this institution emerged after long periods of liturgically negating the private sphere, and it was not guaranteed in the occidental sense. For the rest, there were no legally guaranteed liberties. Actually "private property" in goods was only relatively secure, and it did not enjoy that nimbus of sanctity found, for instance, in the statements of Cromwell against the Levellers.[8]

Patrimonialist theory, to be sure, held that the emperor could be no one's guest and that the superior official could not be the guest of the subordinate since all possessions of the inferior belonged rightfully to the superior. This, however, had essentially no more than ceremonial significance. On occasion the authorities interfered severely with the tillage and distribution of land, mostly for plain fiscal reasons. However, among other things, for centuries these interferences had animated the nimbus of the semi-legendary *ching-t'ien* system with its patrimonially regulated "right to the land."

Interest in maintaining social tranquillity led to the predilection for the most equal distribution of property possible which in turn was expressed in such ideals as a subsistence economy. In the interest of preventing a dearth of food, the subsistence economy was dovetailed with a storage policy in the Egyptian manner. The ideal of patrimonialism in this field, as in others, was substantive justice not formal law. Hence, property and income remained, on the one hand, problems of practical expediency and, on the other hand, problems of social-ethical concern for feeding the masses. This must not be understood in the occidental sense of an individualist social ethic of natural law which originated in modern times precisely out of the tension between formal law and substantive justice. For in their view, understandably, the educated and the ruling strata should also be the wealthiest strata. Still the ultimate goal was to have property as widely distributed as possible in the interest of universal contentment.

A divine, unchangeable law of nature existed only in the form of sacred ceremonies, the magical efficacy of which had been tested since time immemorial, and in the form of sacred duties toward the ancestral spirits. A development of natural law of modern occidental stamp, among other things, would have presupposed a rationalization of the existing law which the Occident had in the form of Roman law.

Roman law, however, was first a product of autonomous urban business life which required fixed schemata of complaint; second, of the rationalization through the juridical technology of the Roman notables; and third, the rationalization of the bureaucracy of the Eastern Roman Empire.

In China, no estate of jurists existed because there was no advocateship in the occidental sense. It was absent because the patrimonialism of the Chinese welfare state, with its weak office authority, did not appreciate the formal development of secular law. We should add to what was said earlier that local custom held even *contra legem* by virtue of the principle "arbitrariness breaks common law" *(Willkür bricht Landrecht)*. Furthermore, the Chinese judge, a typical patrimonial judge, discharged business in thoroughly patriarchal fashion. That is, insofar as he was given leeway by sacred tradition he precisely did not adjudicate according to formal rules and "without regard to persons." Just the reverse largely obtained; he judged persons according to their concrete qualities and in terms of the concrete situation, or according to equity and the appropriateness of the concrete result. This "Solomonic" Cadi-justice also lacked a sacred book of laws such as Islamism had. The systematic imperial collection of laws was considered inviolate only insofar as it was supported by compelling magical tradition.

Under such conditions the tension between sacred and secular law was competely absent, a tension which exists in the Occident, in Islamism, and to a certain extent even in India. A doctrine of natural law in the sense of Antiquity, especially Stoicism, and of the Middle Ages would have presupposed what evidently could not emerge in Confucianism. This was the tension between philosophical or religious postulates and the "world" which resulted in the doctrine of an "original state." The central and prerequisite ethical concepts for such a doctrine were alien to Confucianism. About this later.

Our modern occidental rationalization of law has been the result of two forces operating side by side. On the one hand, capitalism was interested in strictly formal law and legal procedure. It was interested in having law function in a predictable way, possibly like a piece of machinery. On the other hand, the rationalism of officialdom in absolutist states led to the interest in codified systems and in homogeneous law to be handled by a rationally trained bureaucracy striving for equal, interlocal opportunities of promotion. No modern system of law has emerged when one of these two forces was lacking. Modern capitalism, as is shown by Anglo-Saxon common law, could indeed prosper on the soil of an unsystematic law guaranteeing the autonomy of the economically powerful stratum. It was a law that lacked a strict logico-legal articulation but was formal law created by a class of lawyers whose mode of legal thought was conditioned by Roman and Canonical law. Formally, on the other hand, rationalist bureaucracy had a heartfelt interest in the compendious collection of statutes, in the ubiquitous employability of the official, in homogeneous law, above all, in the paramountcy of authoritative enactment over inviolate tradition and over the arbitrary autonomy of locally and socially differentiated law. Bureaucracy, wherever it held sway alone, was not only interested in the juridical perfection of legal forms but rather in their substantive "justice" which alone could correspond to the immanent ethos of bureaucracy.

Bureaucracy has substantively rationalized and systematized law unless checked by economically powerful capitalist interests or a socially powerful estate of jurists. Otherwise bureaucracy has destroyed formal juristic technology which is indifferent to substantive "justice." Chinese patrimonialism, after the unification of the empire, had neither to reckon with powerful and indomitable capitalist interests nor with an autonomous estate of jurists. But it had to take account of the sanctity of tradition which alone guaranteed the legitimacy of patrimonialism; and it had to realize the limited intensity of its administrative organization. Therefore, not only did formal jurisprudence fail to develop, but a systematic, substantive, and thorough rationalization of law was never attempted. In general, the administration of law retained the nature which usually characterizes theocratic welfare justice. Thus a juristic, theological, and philosophical "logic" failed to develop.

3. Absence of Natural Sciences

SYSTEMATIC and naturalist thought also failed to mature. Occidental natural science, with its mathematical foundation, is a combination of rational forms of thought grown on the soil of ancient philosophy and the technical "experiment" which originated on the soil of the Renaissance. The specifically modern element of all naturalist disciplines did not first develop in the field of science but in art. The "experimenting," great art of the Renaissance was the child of a unique blend of two elements: the empirical skill of occidental artists based on craftsmanship, and their historically and socially determined rationalist ambition. They sought eternal significance for their art and social prestige for themselves by raising art to the level of "science." The latter point was specific to the Occident. Here also was the strongest incentive for a "return" to Antiquity, as this was understood. Besides the type represented by Leonardo, music, especially sixteenth century music with its experimental keyboards (Zarlino), was central to this tremendous endeavor which operated with the characteristically Renaissance artistic concept of "nature." Special conditions for the highly competitive elaboration of artistic practice came into play as in Antiquity.

Economic and technological interests of the Northern European economy, above all, the needs of the mining industry assisted intellectual forces in transferring the experiment to the natural sciences. Details are out of place here.

In its masterly refinement Chinese art lacked all these understood incentives to rationalist ambition. Under the conditions of patrimonial bureaucracy, the contest of the ruling stratum was discharged entirely into competition among prebendary and degree-hunting literati and all other pursuits were stifled.

Moreover, the relatively slight development of industrial capitalism did not allow the emergence of those economic premiums which were necessary for the transition from empirical to rational technology.[9] Thus all remained sublimated empiricism.

Consequently, practical rationalism, the intrinsic attitude of bureaucracy to life, free of all competition, could work itself out fully. There was no rational science, no rational practice of art, no rational theology, jurisprudence, medicine, natural science or technology; there was neither divine nor human authority which could contest the bureaucracy. Only an ethic congruent with bureaucracy could be created and this was limited solely by consideration of the forces of tradition in the sibs and by the belief in spirits. Unlike Western civilization, there were no other specifically modern elements of rationalism standing either in competition or in support of bureaucracy. Western culture in China was grafted upon a base which, in the West, had been essentially overcome with the development of the ancient polis. Hence, the culture of this bureaucracy can be considered an experiment which approximately tests the practical rationalism of government by office prebendaries and its effects. Orthodox Confucianism resulted from this situation.

The rule of orthodoxy followed from the unity of the theocratic world empire and its authoritative regulation of doctrine. During the Period of the Warring States with its violent struggles we find mobile intellectual currents contesting for dominance just as in the polis-culture of occidental Antiquity. Chinese philosophy, in all its contrast, was developed roughly during the same span of time as the philosophy of Antiquity. Since the unification, at about the beginning of the Christian era, no entirely independent thinker has appeared. Only Confucians, Taoists, and Buddhists continued the struggles. Within the recognized or licensed Confucian doctrine there remained the struggles of philosophical and their related administrative-political schools. The rule of the Manchu definitively canonized Confucian orthodoxy.

4. The Nature of Confucianism

CONFUCIANISM, like Buddhism, consisted only of ethics and in this Tao[10] corresponds to the Indian *dharma*. However, in sharp contrast to Buddhism, Confucianism exclusively represented an innerworldly morality of laymen. Confucianism meant adjustment to the world, to its orders and conventions. Ultimately it represented just a tremendous code of political maxims and rules of social propriety for cultured men of the world. This was in still greater contrast to Buddhism.

The cosmic orders of the world were considered fixed and inviolate and the orders of society were but a special case of this. The great spirits of the cosmic orders obviously desired only the happiness of the world and especially the happiness of man. The same applied to the orders of society. The "happy" tranquillity of the empire and the equilibrium of the soul should and could be attained only if man fitted himself into the internally harmonious cosmos. If man in the individual case did not succeed, human unreasonableness and, above all, disorderly leadership of state and society were to be blamed. Thus, in a nineteenth century edict the prevalence of bad winds in a province was traced to negligence in certain police duties, namely, in surrendering suspects and unduly drawing out trials. This had caused the spirits to become restless.

The charismatic conception of imperial prerogative and the identity of order in the cosmos and in society determined these basic presuppositions. Everything depended upon the behavior of the officials and these men were responsible for the leadership of a society which was conceived as one large, patrimonially ruled community. The monarch should deal with the uneducated mass of the people as children. His primary duties were to care for officialdom materially and spiritually and to maintain good and respectful relations with them.

The individual best served Heaven by developing his true nature for in this way the good within every man would unfailingly appear. Thus, everything was an educational problem and the educational aim was the development of the self from one's natural endowment. There was no radical evil.

One has to go back to the third century B.C. to find philosophers who taught the heterodox doctrine of the original wickedness of man.[11] There were only faults and these were the result of deficient education. Certainly the world, the social world in particular, was, as it were, just as imperfect as man. Evil demons existed alongside the good spirits but, given respectively the educational level of man and the charismatic quality of the ruler, the world was as good as could be. The order of the world resulted from the natural development of cultural needs and the unavoidable division of labor, which in turn led to collision of interests. According to the Master's realistic conceptions, the basic impulses of human conduct were economic and sexual. Hence, creatural wickedness and a "state of sin" were not necessary reasons either for coercive power or social subordination. The latter were considered simply as the economic state of affairs where means of subsistence were scarce in relation to ever-growing needs. Without coercive power a war of all against all would result. Therefore, the coercive order *per se*, the differentiation of property, and the struggles of economic interests were not, in principle, problems at all.

Although the school developed a cosmogony, Confucianism was in large measure bereft of metaphysical interest. The scientific claims of the school were no less modest. The development of mathematics had progressed to trigonometry[12]—but this soon decayed because it was not used.[13] Confucius evidently had no knowledge of the precession of the equinoxes[14] which had been known in the Middle East for a long time. The office of the court astronomer, that is the calendar maker, must be distinguished from the court astrologer who was both an annalist and an influential adviser. The former was a carrier of secret knowledge and his office was hereditarily transmitted. But relevant knowledge can hardly have developed, witness the great success of the Jesuits' European instruments. Natural science as a whole remained purely empirical. Only quotations seem to have been preserved from the old botanical, that is pharmacological work, allegedly the work of an emperor.

The historical disciplines benefited from the importance given to early times. The archeological contributions seem to have flourished during the tenth and twelfth centuries as did the art of annalism soon after. In vain Wang An-shih attempted to create an estate of professional jurists to occupy the offices. For orthodox Confucianism took no interest in any but purely antiquarian or purely practical subjects. (This statement will be qualified in Chapter VII.)

5. *Freedom from Metaphysics and Innerworldly Nature of Confucianism*

THE CONFUCIANS, in principle, doubted the reality of magic as little as did the Jews, Christians, and Puritans. Witches were also burned in New England, but magic had no significance for salvation and that was important. The Rabbis maintained that "For Israel the stars are not decisive," and thus astrological determination was powerless before Yahwe's will for the pious. Confucianism correspondingly maintained that magic was powerless in the face of virtue. He who lived the classical way of life need not fear the spirits; only lack of virtue in high places gave power to the spirits.

Moreover, Confucianism was completely distanced from the Buddhist Saint's contemplation and its Taoist imitators. Tradition makes the Master reject "living in hiding and performing miracles in order to win fame among later generations," which is not without polemical point against Lao-tzu's mystical Taoism. The attitude toward some of the great Confucian sages of the past, who according to tradition withdrew into solitude, to be sure, became somewhat twisted. It was held that one might withdraw only from a poorly governed state. For the rest, the Master occasionally promised the gift of knowing the future as a reward of virtuous perfection, the only turn of phrase which indicates mystical foundations. Upon closer observation one notices that only the ability to interpret *omina* correctly was meant. This was said in order not to lag behind the professional divinatory priests. The one Messianist hope was for a future model emperor. This hope, as mentioned above, was diffused all over the world and was of popular origin. It was neither rejected nor touched by Confucianism. After this fairy tale of a model emperor had been accepted, it was elaborated that he was to be preceded by a phoenix.[15] Confucianism was only interested in affairs of this world such as it happened to be.

he Central Concept
of Propriety

...ionally educated man will participate in the old
...ies with due and edifying respect. He controls all his
...tivities, physical gestures, and movements as well with politeness and with grace in accordance with the status mores and the
commands of "propriety," a basic concept (!) of Confucianism.
The sources like to dwell on describing the Master as one who
moved about with perfect elegance, a man of the world who
knew how to greet all participants according to rank and according to the most intricate forms of etiquette. "Cultivated man,"
"princely," or "noble" man is a central concept which recurs in
many transmitted statements of the Master. He is a man who is
both inwardly and in relation to society harmonically attuned and
poised in all social situations, be they high or low; he behaves
accordingly and without compromising his dignity. Controlled
ease and correct composure, grace and dignity in the sense of a
ceremonially ordered court-salon characterize this man.

In contrast to the passion and ostentation of the feudal warrior
in ancient Islam we find watchful self-control, self-observation,
and reserve. Above all, we find repression of all forms of passion,
including that of joy, for passion disturbs the equilibrium and the
harmony of the soul. The latter is the root of all good. However,
detachment does not, as in Buddhism, extend to all desire but to
all irrational desire, and it is not practiced as in Buddhism for
the sake of salvation from the world but for the sake of integra-
tion into the world. Confucian ethic, of course, had no idea of salvation. The Confucian had no desire to be "saved" either from
the migration of souls or from punishment in the beyond. Both
ideas were unknown to Confucianism. The Confucian wished
neither for salvation from life, which was affirmed, nor salvation
from the social world, which was accepted as given. He thought
of prudently mastering the opportunities of this world through
self-control. He desired neither to be saved from evil nor from a
fall of man, which he knew not. He desired to be saved from

nothing except perhaps the undignified barbarism of social rudeness. Only the infraction of piety, the one basic social duty, could
constitute "sin" for the Confucian.

7. Piety

FEUDALISM rested on honor as the cardinal virtue, patrimonialism on piety. The reliability of the vassal's allegiance was
based upon the former; the subordination of the lord's servant
and official was based upon the latter. The difference is not a contrast but a shift of accent. The vassal of the Occident "commended" himself and too, like the Japanese vassal, he had duties
of piety. The free official also has a status honor which must be
counted as a motive of conduct. This was identical in China and
in the Occident, but in contrast to the Middle East and Egypt
where officials rose from a state of slavery. Everywhere the relationship of the officer and official to the monarch retains certain
feudal traits. Even today the oath which is rendered personally to
the monarch is characteristic of this relationship. Monarchs
usually emphasize these elements of the official relation for
dynastic reasons; the officials do so out of status interests. Residues
of feudalism still inhere rather strongly in Chinese status ethics.
Piety *(hsiao)* toward the feudal lord was enumerated along with
piety toward parents, superiors in the hierarchy of office, and
officeholders generally, for the identical principle of *hsiao* applied
to all of them.

   In substance, feudal allegiance was transferred to the patronage
relationships of officials. And the basic character of allegiance was
patriarchical, not feudal. The absolutely primary virtue, constantly inculcated in children, was filial piety toward parents.[16]
In case of conflict, piety preceded all other virtues.[17]

   In a statement of the Master, praise is given to a high official
who continued to tolerate indisputable abuses out of piety and in
order not to disavow his father. He tolerated them because his
father had done so when occupying the same position. However,
this is in contrast to a paragraph of the *Shu Ching* which tells

ιperor continues a son in his father's office that he
ᵖensate for his father's trespasses.[18] No man's conduct
st of the Master until his way of mourning his parents
ved. In a patrimonial state where filial piety was transferred to all relations of subordination, it can be readily understood that an official—and Confucius for a time was a minister—
would consider filial piety as the virtue from which all others
issue. Filial piety was held to provide the test and guarantee of
adherence to unconditional discipline, the most important status
obligation of bureaucracy.

The sociologically basic change of the army from the combat
of heroes to disciplined formations was consummated in China
in pre-historic times. The universal belief in the omnipotence of
discipline is found in very old anecdotes and was firmly established even among the contemporaries of Confucius. "Insubordination is worse than low thinking." Thus "extravagance," that is
to say lavish expenditure, is worse than thrift. The reverse, however, also holds; thrift leads to "low" or plebeian thinking which
is unbecoming to a cultured man's station. Therefore, thrift must
not be positively valued. We see that the attitude toward things
economic, here as in every status ethic, is a problem of consumption and not of work. It is not worth while for a "superior" man to
learn economic management; actually it is not proper for him
to do so. This does not result from a principled rejection of
wealth *per se:* on the contrary, a well-administered state is the
state in which people are ashamed of their poverty. In a poorly
administered state people are ashamed of their wealth which in
some cases might have been dishonestly acquired in office. There
were only reservations concerning the acquisition of wealth.
Economic literature was a literature of mandarins.

The ethic of Confucianism, like every bureaucratic ethic, rejected the direct or indirect participation of officials in profita᷉
enterprise. This was regarded as morally dubious and unbeco.
ing to one's station. The more the official actually had to depen᷉
upon exploiting his office position the more was this insisted upon.
His income was not high and was, as in Antiquity, income in kind.

However, this neither feudal nor ascetic but utilitarian ethic has developed no principled anti-chrematistic theories. On the contrary, Confucianism has produced theories of supply and demand, of speculation and profit, which sound very modern. In contrast to the Occident the profitability of money went without saying, and theory apparently knew no barriers to interest. Interest, in Chinese as in Greek, is called the "infant" of capital. Certain imperial statutes, to be sure, rejected certain kinds of "usury." But the capitalist, as a privately interested man, was not to become an official and the educated literati were to stay away from chrematistics. Where social doubts about the profit motive *per se* emerged they were essentially political in nature.

8. The Confucian Attitude toward the Economy and Confucianism's Rejection of the Professional Expert

THE Master considered acquisitiveness a source of social unrest. Obviously, he meant the rise of the typical, pre-capitalist class conflict between the interests of the buyers or the monopolists and the consumers' interests. Naturally, Confucianism was predominantly oriented toward a consumers' policy. Still hostility toward economic profit was quite remote, as it was also in the popular mind. Extortionist and unfair officials, especially tax and other petty officials, were bitterly chastized on the stage, but not much seems to have been made of the accusations or mockery of merchants and usurers. The hostile wrath of Confucianism toward Buddhist monasteries led to Emperor Wu Tsung's campaign of annihilation in the year 844. But Confucianism primarily justified itself by the argument that the monasteries distracted people from useful work. Actually, as we have seen, "currency policy" played a role in this.

Economic activity is highly appreciated throughout orthodox literature. Confucius, too, might strive for wealth, "even as a servant, with whip in hand," if only the success of the endeavor were fairly guaranteed. But the guarantee does not hold and this fact leads to the one really essential reservation concerning economic acquisitiveness: namely, the poise and harmony of the soul are shaken by the risks of acquisitiveness. Thus, the position of the office prebendary appears in ethically hallowed form. It is the one position becoming to a superior man because the office alone allows for the perfection of personality. Mencius reasons that without permanent income the educated man can be of constant mind only with difficulty, and the people not at all. Economic, medical, priestly income represent the "little path." This leads to professional specialization, a very important point and closely connected with what has been said above. The cultured man, however, strives for that universality which in the Confucian sense education alone provides and which the office precisely requires. This view characterizes the absence of rational specialization in the official functions of the patrimonial state.

Yet, as in politics Wang An-shih's attempted reform indicated specialization so in literature it was recommended that specialized competencies of officials in the modern bureaucratic manner replace the traditional universality of official business which no single man could possibly master.

The old educational ideal of the Chinese, however, stood in sharp contrast to these functional demands and, concomitantly, to the execution of a functional administrative rationalization in the manner of our European mechanisms.

The Confucian aspirant to office, stemming from the old tradition, could hardly help viewing a specialized, professional training of European stamp as anything but a conditioning in the dirtiest Philistinism.[19] This was undoubtedly the locus of much of the important resistance to "reform" in the occidental sense. The fundamental assertion, "a cultured man is not a tool" meant that he was an end in himself and not just a means for a specified useful purpose. The all-round educated Confucian "gentleman," as Dvořak has translated the term *chün-tzu*, or the "princely man," supported a status ideal of cultivation that was directly opposed to the socially oriented Platonic ideal.

The Platonic ideal was established on the soil of the polis and proceeded from the conviction that man can attain fulfillment by being good at only one task. There was even stronger tension between the Confucian ideal and the vocational concept of ascetic Protestantism.

Confucian virtue, based upon universality or self-perfection, was greater than the riches to be gained by one-sided thoroughness. Not even in the most influential position could one achieve anything in the world without the virtue derived from education. And vice versa, one could achieve nothing, no matter what one's virtue, without influential position. Hence, the "superior" man coveted such a position, not profit.

Such, in brief, are the basic propositions concerning the attitude to vocational life and property, generally ascribed to the Master.

9. The Gentleman Ideal

THE Confucian attitude toward vocational life and possessions is opposed to that feudal enjoyment of lavish expenditure prominent in statements of the prophet in early Islam, and it is opposed to the Buddhist rejection of attachment to worldly goods. It is opposed to the strictly traditionalist, vocational ethic of Hinduism and to the Puritan hallowing of inner-worldly ascetic and profitable work in a rationally specialized vocation. If, for once, we may disregard this fundamental contrast, there are all sorts of particularized affinities to be found between Confucianism and the sober rationalism of Puritanism.

The princely man avoids the temptations of beauty. As the Master correctly said, "No man loves virtue as one loves a beautiful woman."[20] According to tradition, the jealous neighboring prince had pressured the Master out of his position with the prince of Lu by donating to the overlord of Lu a collection of beautiful girls which gave the morally ill-advised prince greater pleasure than did the doctrines of his political father-confessor. In any case, Confucius viewed woman as a thoroughly irrational creature often as difficult to deal with as servants.[21] Condescension makes both women and servants forget their distance, strictness in turn makes them ill-humored. The Buddhist horror of women, which was determined by flight from the world, thus found its counterpart in Confucianism's lack of esteem for women, determined by rational sobriety. Confucianism has, of course, never considered outlawing concubines who were necessarily accepted along with the legitimate wife for the sake of producing descendants. The repeatedly mentioned cartel of the feudal princes was directed solely against giving the sons of concubines equal rights as heirs, and the struggle against the illegitimate influences of the harem cloaked itself as a struggle against the threatening predominance of the *Yin* (feminine) substance over the *Yang* (masculine) substance.

Constancy in friendship is highly praised. Man needs friends, but one should select friends from one's peers. To status inferiors benevolent kindness should be extended. For the rest, all ethics in this sphere go back to the principled mutuality of the neighborhood association of peasants, "I shall do unto you as you do unto me." That is the "reciprocity" which the Master, when questioned, presented as the very foundation of social ethics.

However, the love of one's enemy among the radical mystics (Lao-tzu, Mo Ti) was decidedly rejected as running counter to fundamental state interests. Justice toward enemies, love for friends—what in addition could one offer friends were one to offer love to one's enemies? All in all, the cultured gentleman of Confucianism was a man who combined "benevolence" with "energy," and "knowledge" with "frankness." All this, however, was delimited by "judicious caution" which the common man lacked, wherefore he was denied the path to the "correct middle." Moreover, what gave this ethic its special stamp was that everything was to proceed within the confines of social propriety. For only the sense of propriety molds the "princely" man into a "personality" in the Confucian sense. Therefore, the barrier to the cardinal virtue of frankness was the command of propriety. Not only duties of piety had an unconditional precedence (a fib was permissible for reasons of piety) but social proprieties had precedence, too, according to the Master's practice and as trans-mitted by tradition. "Where we are three I find my master," Con-fucius has allegedly said, which meant, I bow to the majority. He selected the classical writings according to this "propriety." Ssu-ma Ch'ien presumably knew of 3,000 (?) *Shi Ching* odes from which Confucius is said to have selected 306 odes.

Perfection could be reached only by unceasing study, and that meant literary studies. The "princely" man reflects and "studies" everything incessantly and anew. Allegedly ninety year old candi-dates were by no means rare at official state examinations. Still this incessant study consisted of the mere assimilation of existing ideas. According to a communication ascribed to him, the Master even in old age tried vainly to create from his own mind only to fall back again upon reading. In his view, unless one read, the mind operated in neutral gear as it were. The phrase "concepts without percepts are empty" was replaced by "thought without reading is sterile." For without study, as was said, the quest for knowledge squanders intelligence, benevolence makes for stu-pidity, candor for injudiciousness, energy for rudeness. Audacity leads to insubordination, and firmness of character leads to er-raticism. The "correct middle," which for this ethic of social ad-justment was the supreme good, was then missed.

Piety, the mother of discipline, was the one truly absolute duty and a literary education was the one universal means of perfec-tion. The prince's wisdom of state, however, was thought to be the selection of the "correct" minister in the classical sense, so Confucius is reported to have said to the Duke of Nagi.

10. The Significance of the Classics

THIS education was transmitted only through the study of the old classics whose absolutely canonical prestige and purified form of orthodoxy went without question.

To be sure, one occasionally finds a statement to the effect that a man consulting Antiquity about problems of the present may easily do harm. Yet this should be interpreted as a rejection of the old feudal conditions rather than anti-traditionalism, as Legge assumes. The whole of Confucianism became a relentless canonization of tradition.

Li Ssǔ's famous ministerial Memorial which was truly anti-traditionalist, was directed against Confucianism and led to the great catastrophe of the burning of the books after the creation of the bureaucratic and unified state in 213 B.C. The guild of the literati, we read, praises Antiquity at the expense of the present, hence teaches contempt for the emperor's laws and criticizes the laws in terms of the allegedly authoritative books of literati. The only useful books are those on economics, medicine, and divination—a characteristic reversal of Confucian values. This was the completely utilitarian rationalism of the destroyer of feudalism who for the sake of his power position, divested himself of all those fetters of tradition which were always a barrier to Confucian rationalism. But in so doing he upset the prudent compromise between the interest of the ruling stratum in power and its interest in legitimacy. On this compromise the *raison d'état* of the system was based.

Undoubtedly, reasons of security made the Han dynasty duly fall back upon Confucianism soon afterward. A patrimonial officialdom, finding itself in a position of absolute power and monopolizing both the official and priestly functions, could indeed have none but a traditionalist mentality regarding literature. The sanctity of literature alone guaranteed the legitimacy of the order which supported the position of officialdom.

At this point bureaucracy had to restrict its rationalism; likewise, in confronting the religious belief of the people it had to do so. Popular belief guaranteed the docility of the masses and, as noted, set limits to the criticism of the system of government. The individual ruler could be a poor ruler, hence devoid of charisma. In that case the ruler did not rule by divine right and was to be deposed just like any incompetent official. The system, however, had to rest on piety, which was endangered with every shattering of tradition. For these well-known reasons Confucianism has not made the slightest attempt ethically to rationalize the existing religious beliefs. It presupposed as an element of the given secular order the official cult which was managed by the emperor and the officials, and the ancestor cult of the house-father. The monarch of the *Shu Ching* reached decisions not only after consulting the lords of the realm and the "people" (then, undoubtedly, the army) but also after using two traditional means of divination. The course of conduct was merely casuistically debated if these sources contradicted one another. Especially because of the attitude of the educated stratum, the private need for advisory cure of soul and religious orientation remained on the level of magical animism and the worship of functional deities. These are always to be found unless prophecies intervene and in China prophecies did not arise.

Chinese thought has brought magical animism into a system which de Groot has named "Universism." But Confucianism has not alone contributed to its creation and we must consider the participating forces which, from the Confucian viewpoint, were heterodox.

11. Historical Development of Orthodoxy

FIRST, we have to realize that Confucianism was the only doctrine among the theories of the literati which was ultimately also absorbed by the other schools. But Confucianism has not always been the only accepted doctrine, nor the exclusively state-approved philosophy of China. *Hung-fan,* that is "the great plan," is the technical term for this. The further back one goes in history the less identified with Confucian orthodoxy are the literati. The Period of the Warring Kingdoms knew of competing philosophical schools and their competition did not vanish even in the unified Empire. It was especially keen whenever imperial power reached a low point. The victory of Confucianism was decided only about the eighth century of the Christian era. This is not the place to recapitulate the history of Chinese philosophy; nevertheless, the development of orthodoxy may be illustrated by the following data.

For the time being we may by-pass the position of Lao-tzu and his school since it stood very much apart. After Confucius there are still such philosophers to be found as Yang Chu, an Epicurean fatalist who, in opposition to the Confucians, eliminated the significance of education because the uniqueness of a person was held to be his irremediable "fate." There was Mo Ti, who emancipated himself from tradition to a considerable degree. Before and during Mencius' time in the fourth century B.C., imperial power was at a low and Sung K'eng, an active official of one of the Warring Kingdoms, stood on an anti-Confucian platform maintaining the wickedness of human nature. The dialecticians, the asceticists, and the pure physiocrats such as Hsü Hsing opposed one another with programs widely differing in economic policy. As late as the second century A.D. the *Chung Lun* of Chu Hsi took a strictly anti-pacifist position, arguing that degeneration of mores during long periods of peace leads to debauchery and lasciviousness.[22]

All these were non-classical heresies and Mencius fought those of his time. But his contemporary, Hsün-tzu, took the Confucian view that human goodness was an artificial product not of God but of man. Thus, politically, he maintained: "God is the expression of the heart of the people."

Also the absolute pessimist, Yang Chu, stood aloof from Mencius and considered the end of all wisdom to be the bearing of life and casting off the fear of death. A reason often presented for the sufferance of the pious was that God's will is "unsteady."

A system of the antagonist literati schools of his time is to be found in Ssu-ma Ch'ien, whose father seems to have been a Taoist.[23] Six schools are distinguished: First, metaphysicians, with their *Yin* and *Yang* speculations based upon astronomy; second, Mo Ti (Mocius and his school), influenced by mysticism believing in plain burials and absolute simplicity of conduct even for the emperor; third, the school of the philologists, with their interpretation of words and conceptual realism, who were relatively apolitical and had survived from the time of the sophists; fourth, the Legists, men who represented, as Tsui Shui later did, the theory of determent; fifth, the Taoists, to be discussed later; sixth, the school of the literati, the Confucians, whom Ssu-ma Ch'ien follows. Yet Ssu-ma Ch'ien represents the Confucian standpoint in a way which later appeared, in several respects, to be non-classical.

12. The "Pathos" of Early Confucianism

SSU-MA CH'IEN esteemed the well-known Emperor Huang Ti who became an anchoret in a way suggestive of Taoism.[24] His cosmogony, a doctrine of five elements, is evidently of astrological origin. The orthodox Confucians would surely go along with his appreciation of wealth; they would also endorse the notion that only the rich are motivated to adhere correctly to the rites. Though the recommendation of trade as a means of income was shocking to the Confucians,[25] some of them would not have objected to Ssu-ma Ch'ien's doubts about the absolute determinism of "providence" for it was known that virtuous people do die of starvation. The monuments of the Han period bear similar statements. For example an inscription from a tombstone of the Han period (about 25 B.C.) bemoaning the premature death of a man reads: "There have been men since Antiquity who have led an impeccable life without having been rewarded for it." "His memory lives on" (cf. Ssu-ma Ch'ien). "He will ennoble his descendants." (This is the old conception of hereditary charisma; the newer conception differs from this, as mentioned above.) "He has departed for a cold shadowy realm."

An inscription from a tomb of 405 A.D. reads: "All life must die." Perfect man has no individual characteristics. (He is united with Tao. Cf. Chapter VII. Is this Chuang-tzu's influence?) Praise is given to indifference toward promotion or loss of office. Promotion is determined by frankness, filial piety, and piety toward the dead.

But generally it was felt that, "Heaven knows no mercy, he fell sick and died." A "god" is never mentioned. The mentality and mood on the whole is related to that of Ssu-ma Ch'ien and the forced optimism of the later period is absent.[26]

Yet, Ssu-ma Ch'ien's position was not acceptable without reservation. That heroism might be "useless" corresponded to the later doctrine and was ascribed to the Master. But it was hardly classical that the celebrated name was everything, that virtue was presented as an "end in itself," or that the prince was to be pedagogically directed. Yet this was what the castrate Ssu-ma Ch'ien taught. The absolute equanimity of tone in the Annals was practiced by Ssu-ma Ch'ien in a masterful manner and accorded excellently with Confucius' practice. The letter which Ssu-ma Ch'ien wrote to his friend Jen Yen,[27] who was in custody and who in vain sought his help, strikes us as being in the most orthodox Confucian style. Ssu-ma Ch'ien, at one time suspect politically, had been castrated.[28] He was later employed but wrote that he actually could not or would not help him for fear of incurring risks. For the soul of one "who has taken to the long path"[29] might harbor wrath against him, i.e., Ssu-ma Ch'ien, and hence might harm him. He wished to state his reasons for not helping Jen Yen, for the "virtuous man puts himself out for one who knows how to esteem him," a truly Confucian expression. Instead of discussing the fate of the unfortunate in detail, he merely presents his own misfortune, that is his castration. How did the writer manage to get over his sufferance? He lists four main points:

First, by not dishonoring one's ancestors; second, by not losing one's own honor; third, by not violating reason and dignity; four, by not trespassing the "rules binding upon all." As for Ssu-ma Ch'ien, he would wash off the stain by writing his book.

The whole letter reminds us of Abaelard's letters to Héloïse which hurt us by their cold didactic manner (for presumably similar reasons!). Yet this cool temperature of inter-human relations is truly Confucian. There are things which may run counter to our feelings but we should not forget that the magnificent and proud documents, cited at the end of the preceding chapter, are done in the Confucian spirit. Shih Huang Ti's inscription, reproduced by Ssu-ma Ch'ien,[30] defines acting against "reason" as objectionable. This would be interpreted by Ssu-ma Ch'ien and the Confucians to mean that guidance for reasonable conduct can be attained only through study[31] and knowledge. For Confucianism the last word was "knowledge," and that meant knowledge of tradition and of the classical norm as acquired through literary studies. In this emphasis, as we shall see, Confucianism was separated from other systems of Chinese attitudes toward the world.

13. The Pacifist Character of Confucianism

THE "reason" of Confucianism was a rationalism of order. Chen Ki Tong says, "Rather be dog and live in peace than be man and live in anarchy."[32] As this statement indicates, Confucian reason was essentially pacifist in nature.[33] Historically, this peculiarity was accentuated to the point where Emperor Ch'ien Lung could write in the history of the Ming dynasty, "Only he who seeks to shed no human blood can hold the realm together."[34] For, "The ways of Heaven are changeable and reason alone is our aid." This was the final product of the unified Empire. In contrast, Confucius had demanded vengeance for the killing of parents, older brothers, and friends and regarded this as a manly duty. But the ethic remained pacifist, inner-worldly, and solely oriented to the fear of the spirits.

The spirits were not without moral qualifications. On the contrary, we have seen that in China, as in Egypt, the irrationality of the judiciary was founded in the belief that the cry of the oppressed inevitably induced the vengeance of the spirits. It was especially true when the victim had died of suicide, grief, and despair. Emerging at the latest under the Han dynasty, this firm belief grew out of the idealized projection of the bureaucracy and the right of appeal to Heaven. We have also seen the great power of howling masses accompanying a real or supposed victim of oppression in the train of officials. An identical belief in the vengeance of spirits compelled every official to give way before mass hysteria with its danger of suicide.

A crowd forced a capital verdict to be passed against a mandarin who had beaten his kitchen boy to death (in 1882).[35] The belief in spirits and their way of functioning was the one and very effective official Magna Charta of the masses in China. But the spirits also kept watch over contracts of all sorts. They denied protection to coerced or immoral contracts.[36] Legality as a virtue was thus animistically guaranteed *in concreto* and not merely as a total habituation of the whole personality. Yet, the central force of a salvation religion conducive to a methodical way of life was non-existent.

CHAPTER VII

ORTHODOXY AND HETERODOXY

1. Doctrine and Ritual in China

THE official Chinese state cult everywhere served only the interests of the community; the ancestor cult served those of the sibs. With both of them individual interests *per se* remained out of the picture. The great spirits of nature were increasingly depersonalized. Their cult was reduced to official ritual, the ritual was gradually emptied of all emotional elements and finally became equated with mere social convention. This was the work of the cultured stratum of intellectuals who left entirely aside the typical religious needs of the masses. The proud renunciation of the beyond and of religious guarantees of salvation for the individual in the here and now could be sustained only among cultured intellectuals.[2]

This gap (between the masses and the intellectuals) could not be filled by imposing the Confucian attitude upon non-mandarins, that is to say inculcating them with classical doctrine, the only available instruction.

Shortly after Confucius, a variety of functional deities and apotheosized heroes suddenly appeared in literature. It is hardly conceivable that the process of developing such divine figures was only then initiated, for elsewhere these formations belong to earlier stages. Certain typical functional deities ("masters") of thunder, winds, etc., are characteristic of the earlier religion of peasants; apotheosized heroes bespeak of feudal hero combat and belong to a period long since passed in China. But the specialization and fixation of the functional deities down to the goddess of the privy, like the similar specialization of *numina* in ancient Rome, may have resulted from increasing cultic conventionalism under the rule of bureaucracy.

The canonization of Confucius is the first certain example of a historical figure becoming a subject of worship.[3] Pictorial representations, even more than numerous features of the ambiguous official terminology, allow us to discern in the God of Heaven a being originally conceived as a person. As we have seen, not until the twelfth century of the Christian era was his depersonalization brought to a materialistically determined end. The masses were blocked from direct access to the impersonalized highest being in the prayer and sacrifice of the state cult. For them the primeval "Lord of Heaven," legends of whose birth, government, hermitage, and ascent to Heaven were later elaborated, seems to have lived ever after and has been worshiped in the household. The representatives of the official cult of Heaven naturally ignored this.

Other popular deities known in modern times may well be similarly derived from ancient functional deities. These the official cult ignored and Confucianism merely counted them among the crowd of "spirits." Only an expert could approach the difficult problem of relating the original character of these deities to their later form, i.e., to assign a place to "animism." Only an expert could conceive the miraculous nature and the efficacy ascribed to natural and artificial objects and thereby assign a place to "fetishism." We are not concerned with these problems here. We are interested in the cleavage between the official institution of grace and non-classical popular religion. And we wish to inquire whether the latter could have or has been the source of a methodical way of life differing from the official cult in orientation. Such might appear to be the case. The cults of most popular deities, unless they were Buddhist in origin, were considered part of a religious current which Confucianism and the

institution of grace under its control have always treated as heterodox. This current, like the institution of grace oriented to Confucianism, on the one hand consisted of cultic and magical practice and on the other hand, doctrine. This we shall soon discuss.

First, however, it seems useful to clarify further the principled
relationship of the old popular deities to the ethical doctrine of
Confucianism.

We may use the example closest at hand: let us consider the
relation of the Hellenic philosophical schools of social ethics to
the old Hellenic popular deities. Again we can observe the awkward situation which, in principle, has been shared by the cultured intellectual strata of all times when confronting historically
given, robust folk belief. The Hellenic state gave ample •leeway
to metaphysical and social-ethical speculations. The state merely
demanded the observance of the cultic duties which were bequeathed, for neglect of them could bring misfortune to the polis.
The Greek philosophical schools corresponded to Confucianism
in their social-ethical orientation and the main representatives of
the classical period, like the Chinese intellectuals of the Confucian
school, essentially left the gods aside. On the whole they simply
went along with the transmitted rites, as the circles of genteel
intellectuals in China did and as such circles generally do with
us. At one point, though there was a significant difference.

For pedagogical purposes, the Confucian edition of classical
literature had succeeded in eliminating not only these folk deities
but also all matters offensive to their ethical conventionalism. This
was perhaps the most important contribution made by Confucius, as already indicated.

One need only read Plato's famous discussion of Homer in
the *Republic* to recognize how much classical Hellenic philosophy
would have liked to do in social pedagogy as Confucianism had
done. Though there was no place for Homer in the ethically
rational state, he was a tremendous force in knightly education
and was considered classical. In the military polis the role of
Homer and his hero-gods could not possibly have been ignored
by public authorities and educators. Nor was it possible to estab-

lish a rule of literati based on an ethically purified literature (and music) such as Patrimonialism has executed in its interest in China. Moreover, even after the polis had been subdued and political inhibitions thus removed within the pacified empire, none of the co-existing philosophical schools succeeded in attaining the exclusive canonical prestige which Confucianism had attained in China. For the analogy would have been the acceptance of a special philosophy as the only correct state philosophy, i.e., as if the Caesars had tolerated only Stoic philosophy and had appointed only Stoic philosophers to office. This was impossible in the Occident because no philosophical school claimed or could claim the legitimacy of absolute traditionalism. But Confucius, finding himself in such a position, deliberately did this. For this reason occidental philosophy could not be of political service to a world ruler and his officials in the way Confucian doctrine could be.

The Greek philosophers in their inner nature were oriented to problems of the free polis. Duties of citizens, not duties of subjects, was their basic theme. An internal connection with ancient and sacred religious commandments of piety was lacking; such commandments might have been of service to a patrimonial ruler interested in legitimacy. In their zeal, the politically most influential philosophers were quite remote from that absolute adjustment to the world and from the rejection of all dubious metaphysical speculations whose absence recommended Confucianism so urgently to the Chinese overlord. Stoicism down to the Antonines remained the doctrine of the opposition hostile toward opportunism. Only the disappearance of the opposition after Tacitus facilitated the acceptance of Stoic theories by the Caesars. This followed from the uniqueness of the ancient polis and was perhaps its most important result for the history of ideas.

Thus the tension between philosophical theory and social ethics, as opposed to the popular cult of the pre-Christian Occident, continued to exist in the following sense. The cult of the heroic and folk deities of "Homeric" times was correspondingly developed as the official institution; but the teachings of the philosophers were the optional concern of private citizens. It was exactly opposite to what was found in China. There a canonical doctrine and religiously sanctioned state rites co-existed with deities whose cult was in part only officially practiced, in some degree merely tolerated, and in part suspiciously viewed as a private affair. Of course, officially unauthorized, partially suspect cults also existed in occidental Antiquity alongside the official cult of the gods. Certain of these private cults were distinguished by a soteriology of their own and a corresponding ethic. Beginning with Pythagoreanism, this continued through the cults of saviors during the time of the Caesars. The same held for some unofficial cults in China.

In contrast, development in the Occident led to the world historical alliance between public authorities and one of these soteriological communities—i.e., Christendom—an alliance still influential today. Chinese development followed a different course. For a time in China it seemed as if Buddhism might play a similar role since it had been formally accepted by the emperors. Buddhism, however, was confined to the position of a tolerated, though influential, cult practiced alongside others. This was due to the interests which we have indicated, such as the resistance of the Confucian bureaucracy, mercantilist and currency policies, and finally to a tremendous catastrophe. Above all, as we shall see later, the influence of Buddhism in China had relatively little bearing on the matter which is of special interest here, namely, economic mentality. In China, most of the old folk deities, as well as a whole swarm of new creations, had come under the patronage of a priesthood which was tolerated because it claimed to have originated with a philosophical personage, Lao-tzu, and his doctrine. Originally the meaning of this doctrine did not differ in the main from that of Confucianism. Later it became antagonistic to Confucianism and was finally considered thoroughly heterodox. We cannot dispense with a review of this heterodoxy.

The individual's mystic or ascetic quest for salvation was an interest entirely alien to (classical) Confucianism. In India, this search for salvation flowed from strata of educated laymen, especially nobles who were learned or semi-learned in the Vedic scriptures, and whose education was not bound to a priesthood. The quest for individual salvation had, of course, just as little place in Chinese bureaucratic rationalism as it had in the way of life of any bureaucracy.

2. Anchoretism and Lao-tzu

ANCHORETS[4] have always existed in China, and not only according to Chuang-tzu.[5] For their existence has also been preserved in pictorial representations[6] and the Confucians themselves acknowledge them. There are even notes leading us to assume that originally the early heroes and literati retired in old age to a solitary life in the woods. In a pure society of warriors, the "aged," considered worthless, were often left to exposure and it is quite possible that the anchorets were first recruited from among these age groups. These assumptions are, however, uncertain.

In historical times, unlike India, a Vanaprastha existence of the aged was never considered normal. Nevertheless, only withdrawal from the "world" gave time and strength for "thinking" as well as for mystic feeling. Confucius, like his counterpart, Lao-tzu, lived alone and without office. The only difference was that the mystics, Lao-tzu and Chuang-tzu, declined office-holding because of their quest for salvation, whereas Confucius felt himself deprived of office. For politically unsuccessful literati, the anchoret existence was considered the normal form of retirement from politics rather than committing suicide or petitioning for punishment.[7] The brother of the prince of one of the Warring Kingdoms, Chang Yang in Yü, withdrew into anchoretism.[8] Chuang-tzu also reported that the successful emperor, Huang Ti, abdicated and became an anchoret. One may only conceive of the early anchorets' goal of salvation as oriented first, macrobiotically and second, magically. Long life and magic powers were the goals of the masters and of a small number of disciples who resided with them in their service.

3. Tao and Mysticism

TO THIS point of view a mystical attitude toward the world could be enjoined. A philosophy could be based upon it, and this actually happened. Emperor Huang Ti, upon questioning, received the answer that the sage could teach only men who had retired from the world, especially from the secular station and office. They were the "scholars, who sit at home," i.e., did not accept office. The later contrast with the Confucian aspirants to office is already indicated here, for the "philosophy" of the anchorets went far beyond this. As with all true mysticism, absolute indifference to the world was self-implied; and, it is not to be forgotten that the macrobiotic goal was, as said before, one of the anchorets' strivings. According to the primitive "metaphysics" a thrifty and rational management (one might say economy) of the obvious bearer of life, i.e., one's breath, seemed important.

The physiologically ascertainable fact that the regulation of breathing may facilitate mental conditions of a specific sort led further afield. The "saint" must be "neither dead nor alive" and should behave as if not alive. "I am a stupid man," hence I have eluded worldly wisdom, said Lao-tzu in affirming his sanctity. Chuang-tzu did not wish to be "harnessed" to an office but rather to exist "like a pig in a muddy ditch."

The aim was "to make one's self equal to ether," to "throw off the body." Experts hold different opinions when asked whether Indian influences have been present in this rather old phenomenon of regulation of breathing.[9] Indian vestiges do not seem to be absent in the case of the most famous of these anchorets who fled from office, namely Lao-tzu, alleged by tradition to be older but contemporary with Confucius.[10]

4. The Practical Consequences
of Mysticism

HERE we are not concerned with Lao-tzu as a philosopher[11] but with his sociological position and his influence. The opposition to Confucianism is evident even in terminology. The harmonic state appropriate to the charismatic emperor was designated in the *Chung Yung* by Confucius' grandson, Tzu Ssu, as a state of equilibrium. In the writings influenced by Lao-tzu or claiming to follow him, the state is called emptiness *(hu)*, or non-existence *(wu)*, which is attainable by *wu-wei* (doing nothing) and *pu-yen* (saying nothing). Obviously, these are typically mystic and by no means exclusively Chinese categories. According to Confucian doctrine the *Li*, the rules of ceremony and ritual, are the means for producing *chung*;[12] but the mystics viewed these means as being quite worthless. The inner attitude by which one can achieve the power of a *Tao shih*, a doctor of *Tao* so to say, is to behave as if one did not have a soul, thereby liberating the soul from the senses. Like the Confucians the *Tao Teh Ching*,[13] ascribed to Lao-tzu, teaches that life is equal to the possession of a *"shen"*; hence macrobiotics is equated with cultivation of the *shen*. The macrobiotic point of view was the same, but the means differed.

We have met repeatedly with the basic category, *Tao*, in terms of which heterodox Taoists were later separated from Confucians. Both schools, and generally all Chinese thought, held the concept of *Tao* in common. All the old deities were likewise common to them. But Taoism has enriched the pantheon with numerous deities who are essentially apotheosized men —a facet of macrobiotics, whereas orthodoxy considered these deities as non-classical. Both had in common the classical literature; but the heterodox school added Lao-tzu's *Tao Teh Ching* and Chuang-tzu's writings which the Confucians rejected as non-classical. Confucius himself did not reject the basic categories of his opponents, as de Groot greatly emphasizes. Also Confucius has not rejected *wu-wei (laissez-faire)* and obviously he has been quite close on occasion to the doctrine of the magical charisma of men, which in *Tao* means abstention from all action. Let us pursue the contrast somewhat further.

5. The Contrast Between the Orthodox and Heterodox Schools

CONFUCIANISM had eliminated all ecstatic and orgiastic vestiges of the cult and, like the Roman nobility of office, rejected these as undignified. Still magical practice here as everywhere knew ecstasy and orgy. The *wu* (men or women) and *shih* (men), the old medicine men and rainmakers, still exist today and are mentioned in the literature of all times. At temple festivities they are still ecstatically active. Originally they absorbed the magical "power," then the "spirit," then the "god" and worked through him. The *wu* and *shih* represented themselves later as "Taoists" and until the present were considered so. But in the initial phase, Lao-tzu and his disciples did not seek the orgiastic ecstasy which they would certainly have rejected as undignified; rather, like all mystic intellectuals, they sought apathetic ecstasy. As we shall see below, only later did all the magicians agree to consider themselves as "Taoist" successors of Lao-tzu and to regard him as their *archegetes* because he happened to be or was considered to be one of the literati. The mystics were in their worldliness, i.e., their macrobiotics, still more radical than the Confucians. What was the substance of their central theories and in what way did they differ? In relation to Confucianism one tends to designate all heterodoxy as "Taoism."

"*Tao*" *per se* is an orthodox Confucian concept. It means the eternal order of the cosmos and at the same time its course, an identification frequently found in a metaphysics which lacks a thorough dialectical structure.[14] With Lao-tzu, *Tao* was brought into relationship with the typical god-seeking of the mystic. *Tao* is the one unchangeable element and therefore it is the absolute value; it means the order as well as the god-head of matter and the all-inclusive idea of the eternal arch-symbols of all being. In short, it is the divine All-One of which one can partake—as in all contemplative mysticism—by rendering one's self absolutely void of worldly interests and passionate desires until release from all activity is attained *(wu wei)*. Not only Confucius, but also his school could and did accept this. *Tao* was the same and was equally valid for both Confucius and Lao-tzu.

The Confucians, however, were not mystics. Interest in union with the divine substance and in the state attainable by contemplation should have led Lao-tzu, like most of the mystics, to the complete devaluation of inner-worldly culture as a source of religious salvation. To some extent this held for Lao-tzu, too. To him the supreme good was a psychic state, a *unio mystica*, and not a state of grace to be proved in active conduct like occidental asceticism.

As with all mysticism this state was determined psychologically and did not operate externally in a rational way. Universal acosmistic charity typically results from the objectless euphoria of these mystics and their characteristic apathetic ecstasy; perhaps it had been created by Lao-tzu. This purely psychic state was also rationally interpreted here. Heaven and earth were legitimated as the greatest deities because of the absolute unselfishness of their services to man and because of the unconditional goodness peculiar to divinity. The macrobiotic element of the doctrine constitutes the basis for the permanence of forces of nature which at least approximate that of the solely eternal *Tao*. The mystic's conduct followed this model.

The physiologically determined internal condition was likewise rationally interpreted. Everywhere the substance of mysticism is to maintain one's goodness and humility by leading an incognito existence in the world. This constitutes the mystic's specifically broken relationship with the world. If action is not absolutely suspended it is minimized, for therein lies the only possible proof of the mystic's state of grace. And only in this manner is it possible to demonstrate that the world cannot touch him. In accord with Lao-tzu's theories it is at the same time the best guarantee for the permanence of one's life on earth, perhaps

even permanence beyond life on earth. Lao-tzu or his interpreter did not develop a true doctrine of immortality; this seems
to be a product of later times. Though the thought of being removed to eternal paradise once the individual had attained
perfect *Tao* is a rather early idea, it was not a dominant one.

With Lao-tzu the minimization of action resulted, at least
primarily and directly, from the nature of the mystic possession
of the holy. Lao-tzu has only indicated, not consummated, certain
implications of mystic religiosity. The "saint" whom Lao-tzu
places above the Confucian "gentleman" ideal, not only has no
need for worldly virtue, but basically this is dangerous since it
may deflect him from the pursuit of the holy. In the paradoxical
formulation favored by the Chinese, Lao-tzu regards worldly
virtue and its esteem as a sign that the world has become unholy
and godless. For him a world which is held together by the
cardinal virtue of Confucian *Li,* that is "propriety," stands at
the lowest level. This world happens to exist, however, and
what matters is to accommodate one's self to its ways.

Such accommodation is possible only through relativities of
some sort. Lao-tzu did not take as his conclusion the resolute
rejection of the world. Nor, above all, did he reject in principle
the ideal of the educated gentleman *(chün tzu)* which was vital
for the mandarins as a status group. Had he done so, traces
of his thoughts might never have come down to us.

To be sure, he demanded the "great" virtue as opposed to
the "little" virtue of Confucianism, i.e., accommodation to the
world. This means he demanded the ethic of absolute perfection
as against the socially relativist ethic. This demand, however,
could ultimately lead him neither to asceticist conclusions nor to
positive demands in the field of social ethics. In part this was
so because contemplative mysticism cannot give birth to such
demands; in part also because the ultimate conclusions were not
drawn.

According to a tradition, the real content of which is questionable but which some eminent experts still maintain, the
personal antagonism of Confucius toward Lao-tzu was deter-

mined only by certain relativist consequences which Lao-tzu's mysticism had for political ideals. On the one hand the rationalist literati tended toward the centralism of the rationally and bureaucratically governed welfare-state. On the other hand the mystic advocated the greatest possible autonomy and self-sufficiency for the individual parts of the state, those small communities which might form a locus of plain peasant or civic virtue. The mystics upheld the slogan: as little bureaucracy as possible, for their self-perfection could not possibly be promoted by the busy state policy of civilization. At the famous meeting of Lao-tzu and Confucius, tradition ascribes to the former the warning to Confucius, "may the Master banish his [own] proud spirit, his many wants, his flattering bearing, his grandiose plans." To this is added the argument which is as implicit for the mystic as it is inadequate for the rationalist man of social ethics. "All this is useless for you personally," i.e., useless for attaining the *unio mystica* with the divine principle of *Tao*. Mystical illumination *(ming)* meant that all things come by themselves to man. But if one may draw conclusions from his transmitted statements, this was a personally unattainable goal for the founder of Confucianism and one that lay beyond his endowments. Confucius in astonishment is said to have referred to Lao-tzu as the "dragon," thus indicating his limitatior

The concept of sanctity *(hsing)*, basic for Lao-tzu, plays no part in the Confucian system. It is by no means unknown, but Confucius considered this state as never having been attained, not even by himself. Hence, this concept remains unconnected with the Confucian ideal of *chün tzu,* the "cultured" man. Sanctity, as is the case with Mencius, is basically viewed as a gentlemanly virtue enhanced to perfection.

The scriptural symbol for Lao-tzu's sanctity expresses humility. As a category of strictly individualist self-salvation Lao-tzu's concept of sanctity points in its consequences to a direction opposite the Confucian ideal. The latter is guided by the yardstick of cultivation and accommodation to world and society as they happen to be. Lao-tzu rejected the scriptural scholars, who in China represent theology, for the same reason that occidental mystics rejected theology: because it leads away from God. Men of social ethics out to master and order real life typically and naturally reproached Lao-tzu's mystic salvation, as they would reproach all consistent mystic salvation, for its "egotism." Consistently carried through, the mystic could indeed search only for his own salvation; he could seek to influence others only by example, not by propaganda, or by social action. When fully consistent, mysticism would have to reject inner-worldly action completely because it is irrelevant for the salvation of the soul. Some beginnings of principled abstention from politics are to be found in rather distinct form. It is, however, the characteristic trait and the source of all paradoxes and difficulties in Lao-tzu's system that in this it is not consistent.

Lao-tzu (or his interpreter) belonged to the same stratum as Confucius and therefore, like all Chinese, took certain things for granted. The first of these was the positive value of government which inevitably contradicted the assumption that salvation lay beyond this world. This value followed from what was generally presupposed as the charismatic vocation of the ruler. For Lao-tzu, too, the good of man ultimately depended upon the qualities of the ruler. From this the mystic concluded that the ruler ought to have the charisma of one mystically united with the *Tao,* and further, that mystic redemption was to be imparted to all subjects as "gift of grace" through the charismatic efficacy of the ruler's qualities. However, for the social, ethical man it was sufficient that the ruler *per se* be approved by Heaven and that his virtues be adequate as social ethical qualities from the standpoint of the spirits.

Confucius and Lao-tzu, or at least their successors, nevertheless shared the belief in spirits and the whole official Pantheon, whereas the *Tao Teh Ching* was apparently largely free of magic. An educated Chinese, oriented to practical politics could not reject all this. The ideas of the supra-mundane, personal god, who was creator and ruler of this world, who held sway over all creatures as he saw fit and before whom all creatures were unsanctified, could be consummated neither by Chinese education, nor in the main, by Indian education. Therefore, the approach to an asceticist ethic which contrasts God and creature was precluded. It goes without saying that the given, essentially animist religion ultimately meant little to the mystic in search of salvation. We noticed and we shall note repeatedly that the same held for the social ethical man educated in Confucianism.

Both held the conviction that good order in worldly government would best serve to keep the demons at rest. This charismatic turn of the belief in demons was one of the reasons which also made it impossible for Lao-tzu's disciples to draw radically apolitical conclusions. On the other hand it is understandable that an intellectual stratum of officials and aspirants to office in a patrimonial state could neither accept the individualist quest for salvation nor the broken humility of the mystic. Above all they could not accept the demand for a charismatic, mystic qualification for the overlord and the administrators, which would be like requiring a personal pneuma and charisma for the Roman bishop's church. Moreover, it was perfectly understood that the bureaucratic power state of the rationalists would hold the field in practical politics. This was so much the case that while it might be repeatedly felt that only a Chinese could correctly interpret Confucianism in detail, a similar thing could not be said of Taoism. European scientists usually agree that nowadays no correct Chinese could understand with complete empathy Lao-tzu's (or his interpreter's) views in their original, inwardly experienced context.

Among his successors or those who pretended to be successors, the ethical consequences of Lao-tzu's mysticism contributed to securing the predominance of Confucianism. The internal inconsistency of the mystic's attitude assisted this.

All religiously motivated, active antagonism to the world is lacking in Lao-tzu as is mostly the case with contemplative mysticism. The contemplatively determined demand for rational self-sufficiency is motivated by the argument that it prolongs life. But all tension between the divine and the creatural is lacking, a tension which would have been guaranteed only by the retention of an absolutely super-creatural, supra-mundane, personal creator and ruler of the world. For Lao-tzu, too, the goodness of human nature was the self-evident point of departure. The conclusion drawn was not true indifference to the world or even rejection of the world but only minimization of worldly action. Only Confucian economic utilitarianism elevated to hedonism could have practical results for social ethics in the world as it happened to be.

The mystic "enjoys" *Tao*. The rest who cannot or will not do so, may enjoy what is accessible to them. In this, a principled antagonism toward Confucianism evidently found expression with regard to the ethical and religious qualification of men. For the Confucian, the common man in contrast to the superior man was also the man who thinks only of bodily needs. He wished to see this undignified condition alleviated through the creation of prosperous living conditions and through education from above. For virtue *per se* was accessible to every man. As we have noticed, no fundamental qualitative differences existed among men. For the mystic Taoist, however, the difference between the illuminated mystic and the man of the world had to be a difference in charismatic endowment. The immanent aristocracy and the particularism of grace in all mysticism express the experience that men are differently qualified in a religious way. He who lacked illumination stood—in occidental terms—outside the state of grace. He had to remain the way he was.

There was one consummate mystic hostile to the literati and usually considered as belonging to Lao-tzu's school who reached the peculiar conclusion that "The rulers may fill their subjects' bellies not their minds; they may strengthen their limbs but not their character."

Even one of Lao-tzu's views was that the state would do well to confine itself to caring for the mere sustenance of men. This view is rooted in his disinclination for literary knowledge since it hindered true illumination. If the mystically illumined ruler could not exert a charismatic and exemplary influence by his mere existence it was better for him to abstain from all action.

One should let things and men go as they can. Too much knowledge on the part of the ruler's subjects and too much government by the state are truly dangerous evils. Only absolute compliance with the unchangeable cosmic and social order leads to "acquiescence," to subduing of the passions. In Lao-tzu's doctrine of salvation this was also promoted by music, edifying practice of the ceremonials, taciturnity, and training in ataraxy. The *Tao Teh Ching*, ascribed to Lao-tzu with the reservations made above, demanded in consequence the greatest non-intervention possible. This demand was opposed to the prevailing inclination toward patriarchical tutelage of the subjects in classical Confucian doctrine. The *Tao Teh Ching* argued that the happiness of the people would be promoted most safely through the natural laws of the harmonic cosmos.

We noticed that theories of non-intervention were also to be found in orthodox doctrine. They could be deduced with extraordinary ease from the idea of providential harmony (the *Tao*) in the world. Very early they led to theories of the harmony of class interests almost in the manner of Bastiat. These theories corresponded to the genuinely low intensity and steadiness of the administration in relation to economic life. The position of heterodox Taoism was even more consistent. The active motive of a "vocational ethic" was of course entirely lacking in this Chinese and especially Taoist "Manchesterism." This was due to the contemplative mystic base of Taoism. Only an asceticist ethic of laymen, originating from a tension between God's will and the orders of the world, could have offered such an activating note. Therefore the strongly emphasized Taoist virtue of thriftiness did not have an asceticist but an essentially contemplative character; the major concrete issue in the dispute with orthodoxy was the question of reducing costs of funerals.

Having repeatedly spoken of "successors" and "disciples" of Lao-tzu we should realize that this designation does not quite agree with the facts. Lao-tzu, whatever his personal teaching may actually have been, has hardly left a "school." However, there were philosophers quite some time before Ssu-ma Ch'ien who referred to Lao-tzu as an authority. In far later historical times in China, mysticism found some eminent representatives who at least partially considered themselves as "disciples" of Lao-tzu. This development is only of limited interest here.

Semi-legendary tradition describes the personal antagonism between Confucius and Lao-tzu. But as yet one could hardly have spoken of a "contrast of schools," especially of one clearly, separating these two antagonists. Rather there existed a sharp difference of temperaments, ways of life, and attitudes, especially attitudes toward the practical state-problem—the office. The contrast of schools obviously (cf. de Groot) was articulated only by Confucius' grandson, Tzu Ssu, on the one hand, and in Chuang's sharply pointed polemic on the other. It is certain and experts like de Groot emphasize that the typical mystic's rejection of rational knowledge as a means of working for one's own or the general good was the thesis theoretically most important yet unacceptable to the Confucians and even to their Master. Everything else might have been tolerable. De Groot emphasizes that "quietism" *(wu-wei)* was not altogether alien to the Confucian. The common descent from the early, solitary ways of the "thinkers" was responsible for this. The early attitude of the sages had changed considerably under the political pressures of the "sophists" during the Period of the Warring Kingdoms. How should one adjust to the *Tao* without certain knowledge of the true rites, which the "old men" possessed and which was acquired only by study? Underlying this change in attitude was of course the profound contrast between mystic indifference and the accommodation or the will to reform the world.

Chuang-tzu formulated the opposition to the Confucians by sharpening Lao-tzu's formulations as follows: first, search for "intelligence" means attachment to externals; second, search for "reason" means attachment to sound (words); third, search for the "love of man" means confusion in one's practice of virtue; fourth, seeking to do one's duty means to rebel against laws of nature (the omnipotence of *Tao*); fifth, adherence to *"Li"* (rules) means attachment to externals; sixth, love of music means to be given to immorality; seventh, adherence to sanctity means adherence to affectation; eighth, quest for knowledge means hairsplitting.[15]

Points one, two, five, and eight, may well have been the ones which the Confucians abhorred most strongly, for the four cardinal virtues of Confucian man were: *shen*, that is, love of man; *li*, that is, rules of living; *I*, that is, liberality (duties); *chi*, that is, knowledge. Among these *li* and *chi* were most important. Anything which deviated from this was heretic and non-classical (*pu ching*), incorrect (*pu tuan*), morally dubious and wrong *Tao (tso Tao)*.

The split between the followers of Confucius and Lao-tzu has existed since Tzu Ssu's attacks. But the bitterness of the dispute was created only by the development of the schools and by the competition for prebends and power. The later literati who felt themselves to be Lao-tzu's successors at least occasionally attempted to establish an organization similar to that of the Confucian literati, and this despite the principle of *wu-wei* and the abhorrence of holding office.

The *Tao Teh Ching* is not absolutely and *in toto* condemned as heretic by the Confucians, but like the works of Chuang-tzu and Kuan Chung, it is always rejected as non-classical. That is, the *Tao Teh Ching* is not counted among the "sacred" scriptures. Once and at least for a short time, the emperors placed the *Tao Teh Ching* among the classics which the candidates had to study for the examination.

The Confucians in turn maintained that "knowledge" was important and also virtuous for the emperor. The emperor might behave "quietly" if he were a scholar and only in that case would he do so. The Confucians put this thesis into practice by establishing the gigantic official encyclopedia (*Ku chin t'u shu chi ch'en*, published in 1715). Neither of the two parties has doubted the decisive importance of imperial charisma, which the *Shu Ching* already contained explicitly, but the interpretation differed.

6. Taoist Macrobiotics

A GENERAL tendency in the Chinese value scheme facilitated the development of a special school on the basis of Lao-tzu's teachings. This was the appreciation of physical life *per se,* hence of long life and the belief that death is an absolute evil. For when rightly considered death should be avoidable for a truly perfect man. The truly perfect man *(chen, ching, hsin)* must be endowed with invulnerability and magical powers;[16] for in what other way could his perfection be proved?[17] This yardstick was very old. There was high esteem for the common milfoil, combinations of which play such a conspicuous part in the well known oracular lines of the *I Li.* This was likewise true of the turtle as an oracular animal. Both attained their role through their longevity. According to Confucian belief practice of virtue and, in particular, studies had macrobiotic effect; so, too, had silence and the avoidance of bodily exertion without absolute abstention from activities. The gymnastics of breathing, mentioned above, were especially developed as a macrobiotic means. Macrobiotic plants became specific medicaments and the search for the elixir of life was systematically practiced. We have seen that Shih Huang Ti for this very reason extended his favor to this school. According to all experience the restriction of excitement and quiet living were macrobiotically effective. The thesis seemed to be unassailable that abstention from passionate desires was the primary macrobiotic means and the cardinal virtue—hence the *wu wei* of the anchorets and mystics.

With this as a point of departure, the development led further afield through the doctrine of demons shared by both parties. Systematization of macrobiotics once undertaken, the way was clear for conceiving the rationalization of all apotropaic and therapeutic magic. That has indeed happened and the theoretical results have essentially become the common property of both schools. The practical exploitation, however, was left to the non-classical school. This was because for the Confucian every departure from the Dogma of (classically oriented) omnipotent *virtue* simply endangered the unity of ethics. Besides, we cannot forget that the emperor was constantly pressed in the direction of magic through the harem.

The purely magical aspect of Lao-tzu's doctrine facilitated and elicited an influx of all the old magicians into the community of the Taoists. They were most numerous in the South, the richest agricultural area, and it was there that this development was preeminent.

The union of teacher and pupils in solitude outside the cities, was the nuclear cell of the "Taoist" monasteries in China as in India (and in contrast to the Occident). To be sure, the extent of Indian influence on Lao-tzu (however independent-minded he was) is disputed; this problem can hardly be solved in regard to Taoist formation of monasteries. Taoism with its hermitages probably paved the way for Buddhism, and Buddhist competition brought about the Taoist monastic movement, a movement for the organized association of the anchorets which probably had a quick pace. The autonomy of Taoism seems most distinctly guaranteed by the fact that not all of the functionaries, but only the most characteristic of them—the magicians—lived outside monastic communities.[18] Taoism had emerged when the escapist doctrine of intellectuals was fused with the primeval, this-worldly trade of the magicians. The *"Tao-shih,"* the practitioners, lived a worldly life, married and managed their art as a vocation. They had altars founded *en masse* for all sorts of saints but these were often deserted after a short time because the saints failed to prove themselves. They created the great official collection of prescriptions and liturgies during the sixteenth century[19] and, given the opportunity, they engaged in politics.

7. The Taoist Hierocracy

TAOISM was hardly generally diffused when it accepted a fixed hierocratic organization. In the province of Kiangsi a hereditary charismatic sib had monopolized the manufacture or life elixirs[20] and had appropriated the name of *t'ien shih* (heavenly master). A descendant of Chang Ling, who had been councilor of the Han and had written about the art of breathing, created an organization during the days of unrest and weakness of the Han dynasty. This organization had an administrative staff, collected taxes, enforced strict discipline, and successfully competed with the political authorities. In the end it created in Szechwan a truly autonomous "church state." At first, to be sure, it existed in the form of a camorra-like secret organization, namely the *t'ai-p'ing tao,* the "Kingdom of Peace." It was the predecessor of a modern organization which we will have to discuss below.

The church state was denounced in the year 184 by an apostate and was outlawed and persecuted by the Han. This church state, a typical organization of the South against the North, maintained itself against the government by the so-called "rebellion of the yellow kerchiefs," a ferocious religious war (the first of its kind). This lasted until the hereditary hierarch in 215 A.D. thought it prudent to submit as a princely tributary to General Wei.[21] In that role he was confirmed and acknowledged with high honors. His secular power waned considerably by the doings of the government; officially he became only, in Grube's happy phrase, the "keeper of the files of the gods" who took care of cases of canonization. He, by the way, was not the only man in such a position. In addition to the ancestral cult, the apotheosis of men was the source of "non-classical," "Taoist," gods. The number of these had greatly swollen but they were ignored by the official cult. The highest god P'an Ku, the God of Heaven, was enthroned with his wives on the Jaspis mountain of the West. His image is taken from the ancient conception of a personal god as the lord of Heaven.

The political career of the *tao shih* now began and it was based upon their claim to have power over the demons. For in the struggle between the literati and the powers hostile to them, we always find the Taoists with the party opposing the literati. First the Taoists were "aristocratic." The uneducated feudal pressure groups used them as their tools. Their opposition to the

Confucian rites and ceremonies[22] and craze for order and educa-tion enabled them to take the position that "the people shall re-main uneducated." This was their position during Ssu-ma Ch'ien's epoch and the literati succeeded only as late as 124 in gaining mastery over the Taoists. They saw to it that all prebends were reserved for themselves and that the *pépinière* of the seventy court literati was recruited from all parts of the empire.[23]

However, once feudalism had come to an end the main ad-versary of the literati was Sultanism, supported by the eunuchs, generals, and "a-literate" favorites. The Taoists regularly took the side of the latter. Every upsurge of the power of the eunuchs led to political influence by the magicians. This struggle repeatedly ended in the victory of the literati, a victory most decisive under the pacifist Manchu, but it continued down to the rule of the Empress Dowager.

One should not entertain mistaken notions based upon our concept of religious denominations. The Confucian mandarin also claimed the Taoist for certain services,[24] just as classical Hellenic man had enrolled the otherwise despised "prophet" and (later) horoscopist. The very ineradicability of Taoism rested upon the fact that the victorious Confucians themselves never seriously aimed at uprooting magic in general and Taoist magic in particu-lar. They only sought to monopolize office prebends.

They did not even entirely succeed in this. We shall demon-strate below the geomantic reasons which frequently blocked the complete removal of once existent buildings. However, having once allowed monasteries to exist, one had willy nilly to allow for their inmates. This, as we shall see, also held for the Buddhists. All strata of literati given to demonology and magic repeatedly shied away from provoking the "spirits," including the non-classical spirits. Hence, the Taoists were tolerated and in a certain sense recognized by the state. The official position of the Tao Lu Ssu, subordinate to the Chang T'ien Shih—the Taoist heredi-tary hierarch—was obviously modeled after the position of Bud-dhist superiors. In certain state temples, Taoist priestly positions existed. There were, as a rule, first, a director; second, a hierophant; third, a thaumaturgist (for drought and inundation); fourth, ordinary priests.[25] There are certainly Taoist traits in the inscriptions of some of the neighboring[26] princes who had become independent. The absolute rejection of Taoism by K'ang Hsi's sacred edict and by all Manchu rulers changed nothing in this respect.

Before resuming the discussion of the specifically Chinese "image of the world," created jointly by the orthodox and the heterodox, we wish merely in anticipation to record that the position of Buddhism, viewed politically, was very similar.[27]

8. The General Position of Buddhism in China

BUDDHISM was imported from India as a means of gaining convenient, literate, administrative forces and as a means of taming the masses.

The "a-literate" character of reformed Buddhism (Mahayana Buddhism),[28] appealing especially to the feminine emotive aspect, made it a favorite faith of the harem. Again and again we find eunuchs as its patrons, just as with Taoism. This was especially true during the eleventh century under the Ming.[29]

There were various motives for the terrible persecution of Buddhism. Among these were the currency and mercantilist interests of Confucianism; and, naturally, the widespread competition for prebends. There was also the antagonism of Confucians toward Sultanism which was supported by the Buddhists. Nonetheless, Buddhism was as little eradicated in practice as Taoism was, despite the sharply worded edicts of the emperors and despite the many secret societies which were linked to Buddhism ("white Lotos"). In addition to geomantic reasons which will be discussed further below, there were ceremonials which the Chinese certainly did not wish to forego and which were alone offered by Buddhism—the masses for the dead. Belief in the migration of souls remained one of the popular conceptions of a beyond once Buddhism had gained a foothold. Therefore, recognized Buddhist prebends were to be found just like the Taoist prebends.[30] Their position does not concern us as yet and we shall resume the discussion of Taoism.

The "a-literate" and anti-literate character of later Taoism accounts for the interesting fact that it took strong (though not exclusive) root among the circles of traders. This is a very distinct example of a fact which we shall learn repeatedly: the nature of a stratum's religiosity has nowhere been solely determined by economic conditions.[31] But *vice versa* the peculiar nature of Taoism could not be irrelevant for the way of life of the merchants. For Taoism had become absolutely irrational and, frankly speaking, had turned to very inferior magical macrobiotics, therapy, and apotropaia. Taoism promised to prevent premature death which was considered a punishment for sins;[32] it promised to move in the supplicant's favor the (Taoist, non-classical) god of wealth and the numerous apotheosized bureaucratic and functional deities. Anything resembling a "civic ethic" was of course most unlikely to be found in Taoism. Here we are not at all interested in this aspect of Taoism, but rather in its indirect, negative effects.

9. The Systematic Rationalization of Magic

THE toleration of magical and animist conceptions by both orthodoxy and heterodoxy and their positive cultivation by Taoism have been decisive for their continued existence and their tremendous power in Chinese life. Let us briefly consider their effects.

In general, one may say that every sort of rationalization of the archaic empirical knowledge and craft in China has moved toward a magic image of the world. Astronomy became astrology insofar as it was not a calendric science. The latter was archaic and first served to allocate agricultural functions to the proper seasons. Technology was primitive and in no way approximated Babylonian accomplishments. With the revision of the calendar under Shih Huang Ti, who was hostile to the literati, chronomantics began its ascent. That is, purely in terms of analogies and macrocosmic notions tasks were allocated to the months, to *dies fasti et nefasti*, not generally but for concrete matters in each case. The *Ta Shih* ("superior writer"), a board of calendar makers who were originally identical with the annalists, was transformed into the official department of astronomy and astrology. However, the management of chronomantics by means of numerous copies of the government-produced *Shih Hsien Shu* (calendar, chronomantic land register) became a source of profit for the "day-masters" who were to be consulted when choosing a day for a task.

Astrology, on the other hand, was connected with archaic meteorology, conjecture, visibility of Venus, the nature of stellar light, and the determination of the winds. Originally, as de Groot assumes,[33] the latter was important because of the trade-winds. Furthermore earthquakes, mountain slides, aeroliths, monstrous births, interpretations of fortuitous utterances of children (as especially direct media) and magical "meteorology" of all sorts produced an immense literature. It served exclusively to examine whether or not the spirits were in order; if they were not the state leadership had to be concerned with the consequences. The *wu* and *shih*, the primeval meteorological magicians and rainmakers who engaged in this, were considered "Taoists." Not infrequently hysterical (clairvoyant) women engaged in this trade with special success.

Medicine, and connected with it pharmacology, once manifested estimable empirical accomplishments. They were completely rationalized in an animistic direction. We have mentioned before that macrobiotic plants provided the *shen-jo* medicaments and like the tree of life of the Hebrews, they grew in enormous quantities in the "Paradise of the West," the grove of Queen Hsi Wang Mu. The extent to which Chinese expansion was codetermined by hope for the discovery of this paradise, such as Shih Huang Ti's sea expedition for the life elixir, is hardly debatable. Characteristic of early conditions was the firmly believed legend of the prince who heard (!) the spirits of disease in his entrails debating how best to settle down. These may be interpreted as animistically rationalized fever dreams and were still relatively primitive as against other rationalizations.

Elements, seasons, kinds of taste and weather were brought into relation with the five (!) human organs—thus, in turn, macrocosm and microcosm—and magical therapy was oriented to such notions. The old breathing technique which the *Tao Teh Ching* advised was directed toward "storing up" breath, the carrier of life, and continued to exist along with gymnastics as a therapy. Already Tang Chuan-shu during the second century B.C. rejected passionate desire as dangerous to efficient breathing. The *Su Wen,* of post-Christian origin according to de Groot, was considered a classical text on the scientific method of breathing. To this method were added *fu, i.e.,* brushstrokes of the charismatic mandarins on amulets and the like. We wish, however, to put aside these matters which are taken from de Groot. To us the tremendous geomantic development of the *jang shu* or *fêng-shui* ("wind and water") is of incomparably greater significance.

We noticed with de Groot that the chronomancers *(shih)* determined the time for all sorts of building. But it was of greatest import that they came to determine the forms and location of construction. After a struggle between several geomantic schools during the ninth century the school of "forms" triumphed over the more substantively animist opponent.[34] The far greater opportunities for these geomancers to receive fees may have been important in this.

Ever since then the forms of mountains, heights, rocks, plains, trees, grass, and waters have been considered geomantically significant. A single piece of rock by its form could protect whole areas against the attacks of evil demons. Nothing at all could be irrelevant. Moreover the geomantically very sensitive tombs were considered seats of pestilential influence. And geomantic control became indispensable for all construction, even for such internal construction as water mains in homes. Hence every death at a neighbor's might be traced back to one's building, or might signify revenge; any new funeral place might disturb all the spirits of the tombs and cause terrible misfortunes.

With regard to innovations, the manner of mining was always thought especially apt to incense the spirits. Finally, railroad and factory installations with smoke were thought to have magically infested whole areas (anthracite coal in China was used in pre-Christian times). The magic stereotyping of technology and economics, anchored in this belief and in the geomancers' interests in fees, completely precluded the advent of indigenous modern enterprises in communication and industry. To overcome this stupendous barrier occidental high capitalism had to sit in the saddle aided by the mandarins who invested tremendous fortunes in railroad capital. The *wu* and the *shih*, as well as the chronomancers and geomancers, were relegated more and more to the category of "swindlers." But this could never have come about through China's own resources.

Often detours of many miles were made because, from the geomantic viewpoint, the construction of a canal, road, or bridge was deemed dangerous. Not infrequently Buddhist, that is heretic monasteries, were licensed for the sake of *fêng shui*. They were geomantic "improvements" of nature and the monks were obliged to engage in geomantically important ceremonials which were highly compensated. Moreover, the profits of the geomancers are said to have reached fabulous sums indeed and every party paid for its geomancer when a building dispute or such like was at issue.

Thus a superstructure of magically "rational" science, survivals of which we find everywhere, cloaked the simple empirical skills of early times as well as considerable technical endowments, as is evident from the "inventions." This super-structure consisted of chronometry, chronomancy, geomancy, meteoromancy, annalistics, ethics, medicine, and classical mantically-determined statecraft. In these the magician's position among the people was foremost and his profit interests were often practically predominant (hence heterodoxy). The caste of the literati in their turn, though, took a decisive part in this rationalization.

Cosmogonic speculation with the sacred number five operated in terms of five planets, five elements, five organs, etc., macrocosm

and microcosm being correspondent (apparently in an entirely
Babylonian manner, but every comparison demonstrates it as
absolutely indigenous).[35] This Chinese "universist" philosophy
and cosmogony transformed the world into a magic garden. Every
Chinese fairy tale reveals the popularity of irrational magic. Wild
and unmotivated *dei ex machina* swarm through the world and
can do anything; only countercharms help. In the face of this
the ethical rationality of the miracle is out of the question.

All this—to state it clearly—was not only tolerated and permitted but was enhanced by acknowledging the magic image of
the world. It was anchored in the profit opportunities available *en
masse* to the *wu* and *shih* of all sorts. Taoism, because of its
a-literate and irrational character was even more traditionalist
than Confucianism. Taoism knew no "ethos" of its own; magic,
not conduct, was decisive for man's fate. In the final stage of its
development this separated Taoism from Confucianism which, as
we have seen, maintained the reverse and considered magic as
impotent in the face of virtue. Confucianism was helpless when
confronted with the magic image of the world, however much it
disdained Taoism. This helplessness prevented the Confucians
from being internally capable of eradicating the fundamental,
purely magical conceptions of the Taoists. To tackle magic always
appeared dangerous for the Confucian's own power. To the sug-
gestion that such nonsense be stopped, one of the literati once
decisively answered: "Who will hinder the emperor from doing as
he pleases when he no longer believes in the *omina* and *portenta?*"
In China the belief in magic was part of the constitutional foundation of sovereign power.

Taoist doctrine may also be differentiated from these magical
crudities and from "universist" theory. Even so it did not operate
more rationally, nor did it form a counterbalance. The doctrine
of "actions and compensations," a product of the Middle Ages,
was considered Taoist. As we noticed, the same name was applied to the management of magic which was not practiced by
the Buddhist bonzes. This was vested according to all known

history in the hands of a special class of priests, or rather magicians who were recruited among plebeians.

As is to be expected from what has been said, Taoism shared part of its non-ritualistic literature with Confucianism. Thus a "book of secret bliss" was allegedly both Confucian and Taoist. The same held for the general magical presuppositions.

However, as described previously, these were highly developed. Besides, in contrast to Confucianism, they were linked with certain positive promises for the here and now and the beyond. Disdained by the cultured intellectual stratum, the folk deities were valued by the masses for these very promises.

Therefore, what Confucianism failed to do the plebeian priesthood of Taoism did. They satisfied the need for a certain systematization of the pantheon on the one hand and the canonization of proved human benefactors or spirits on the other. Hence Taoism grouped together the triad of the "three pure ones." This consisted of the old personal God of Heaven, de-personified by the official doctrine as Yü-huang-shang-ti, Lao-tzu, and a third figure of unknown derivation. It schematized the ubiquitously worshiped and popular eight main genies (partly historical persons) as well as the other hosts of heaven. The god of the city, who was frequently a canonized mandarin, was guaranteed his function as official keeper of files concerning the fate of the inhabitants in the beyond; thus his function as lord over paradise and hell was guaranteed. It took in hand the organization of his cult (if a permanently organized cult emerged at all) and that of the other canonized spirits of nature and of heroes. The means were mostly raised through subscription by the local interest groups and they took turns; masses were read by the priests only at the great festivals.

Thus an unofficial, though tolerated and genuine cult was established. Since the time of the earliest writers whc professed to be Lao-tzu's "disciples" an esoteric Taoism existed alongside it, treating those endowed with the gift of *Tao* as carriers of superhuman forces of all sorts and passing on to them the task of providing magical goods to the needy.

This development was by no means astonishing if, after what has been said, there was a real historical connection between this esoteric Taoism and Lao-tzu or other mystics. Here no path could be found from the aristocratic charisma of man endowed with grace to rational asceticism. Here as elsewhere the development of non-classical contemplation *per se* and of early anchoretism necessarily led directly from the mystic pantheist union with the divine to sacramental magic. That is, it led to magical influence over the world of the spirits and practical adjustment to the magical lawfulness of their operation. As we have already discussed in the introduction,* the aristocratic salvation of men partaking of illumination could scarcely have taken any other road to folk-religiosity.

For political reasons, anthropolatry was as little tolerated by the Chinese government in the nineteenth century as it had been earlier. Such anthropolatric development usually appears when a turn toward ritualism is made and when aristocratic redemption by illumination is adjusted to the needs of the masses. Then the charismatic magician, as a carrier of the "Yang"-substance becomes an object of worship and a living "redeemer." Adoration and prayer for good harvests along with cultist worship of a living bearer of charisma is reported from the fourth century B.C.[36] The later practice of orthodoxy, however, allowed this only were the persons deceased and preferably were they charismatically proven officials. There were careful attempts to forestall naming any living man a prophet or savior. This was in case he proceeded beyond the ineradicable magical techniques of the specialists or in case his practices suggested a tendency toward hierocratic formation.

Nevertheless, Taoism repeatedly succeeded in gaining the acknowledgment of the emperors. In the eleventh century a Taoist system of examinations with five grades was established alongside

* [Cf. *From Max Weber, Essays in Sociology,* tr. edited and with an Introduction by Hans H. Gerth and C. Wright Mills, Oxford University Press, New York, 1946, Ch. XI, pp. 267-301.]

the orthodox examinations and modeled after them. In such cases the question was one of making offices and prebends accessible to students educated in Taoism. However, the Confucian school unanimously protested every case and succeeded in driving the Taoists from their enjoyment of prebends. For in its economic and social aspects, the dispute revolved about the tax yields of the empire and who was to enjoy them. Yet in these conflicts, also, the profound internal antagonism of Confucianism toward all emotional religiosity and toward magic had its effects. As we have seen, it was almost always through the eunuchs and the harem, the traditional enemies of the literati, that the Taoist sorcerers found their way to the palace.

In 741, a eunuch succeeded in becoming the president of the Academy. Always the proud, masculine, rational, and sober spirit of Confucianism, similar to the mentality of the Romans, struggled against interference in the guidance of the state when such interference was based upon the hysterical excitation of women given to superstition and miracles. The contrast continued to exist in this form up to the last days of the dynasty. We have quoted in a different connection a Hanlin professor's report of 1878 concerning the general unrest due to a great drought. He expressly recommended to the two ruling Empresses that to maintain and restore the cosmic order not excitement, but only a "composed and unshaken spirit" and beyond that the correct discharge of the ethical and ritualistic duties of state were necessary. In true Confucian manner the petitioner added that he claimed neither the gift of revealing the secrets of the demons and spirits nor of divining signs; and he continued with the distinctly polemical point that the eunuchs and servants of the still youthful emperor should beware of the superstitious prattle which is an inherent danger of heterodoxy. He concluded, with the above-quoted admonition, that the Empresses should do justice to the situation in no way other than practicing virtue. This document of the Confucian spirit is impressive in its proud frankness and at the same time it reveals unmistakable echoes of the old antagonism.[37]

10. The Ethic of Taoism

AS WE HAVE seen, it was decisive for the adherence of mer-
cantile circles to Taoism that their special god of wealth, the
vocational god of the merchants, was cultivated by the Taoists.
Taoism brought quite a number of such special deities to a position of honor. Thus the hero of the imperial troops was canonized
as a god of war; student deities, gods of erudition and especially
gods of longevity were honored. As with the Eleusian mysteries
the center of gravity for Taoism was its promise of health, wealth,
and happy life in this world and in the beyond. In theory, the
spirits held out rewards and punishments for all deeds, be it in
this world or in the beyond; be it for the actor or, in contrast to
the doctrine of migration of souls, his descendants. The promises
of a beyond were especially attractive to a large public. For both
the Taoist and the Confucian, it was implicitly understood that
just as "correct living" is decisive for the individual's behavior, so
the "correct living" of the prince is decisive for the fate of the
realm and the cosmic order. Therefore Taoism, too, had to raise
ethical demands, but its unsystematic beginnings toward connect-
ing the fate in the beyond with an ethic remained inconsequential.

Naked magic, never seriously fought by the stratum educated in
Confucianism, was rampant again and again. For this reason and
in the way described, Taoist doctrine was increasingly developed
as sacramental therapy, alchemy, macrobiotics, and a technique
for gaining immortality. The enemy of the literati who instigated
the burning of the books was united with the literati through the
immortality-brews of the Taoists. His expedition in search of the
isles of the immortals in the Eastern Sea is reported in the Annals.
Other rulers turned to the Taoists because of their attempts at
producing gold. Among the officials educated in literature—the
stratum which dominated the way of life of the educated—the
original meaning of Lao-tzu's teaching was not understood
and its consequences were sharply rejected. The magic of the
priests bearing his name, however, was treated with tolerant disdain and regarded as a diet suitable for the masses.

In general, sinologists do not doubt that Taoism in its hierarchical organization, its formation of a pantheon (especially the triad of supreme gods), and its cultic forms has copied much if not everything from Buddhism, but the degree of dependency is disputable.

11. The Traditionalist Character of Chinese Orthodox and Heterodox Ethics

TAOISM, in its effects, was essentially even more traditionalist than orthodox Confucianism. Nothing else could be expected from its magically oriented technique of salvation nor from its sorcerers. For their entire economic existence made them directly interested in conserving tradition and especially the transmitted demonology. Hence, it is not surprising to find ascribed to Taoism the explicit and principled formulation: "Do not introduce innovations." In any case not only was there no path leading from Taoism to a rational method of life, be it inner or other-worldly, but Taoist magic necessarily became one of the most serious obstacles to such a development. For laymen the genuine ethical imperatives in later Taoism were substantially the same as those in Confucianism; while the Taoist expected personal advantages the Confucian expected rather the good conscience of the gentleman from their fulfillment. While the Confucian operated with the polar opposites "right" and "wrong" the Taoist, like all magicians, operated rather with "clean-unclean." Despite the interest in immortality and in rewards and punishments in the beyond the Taoist retained a worldly orientation like the Confucian. The founder of the Taoist hierarchy is said to have expressly appropriated the words of the philosopher Chuang-tzu, which surpass Achilles' statement* in the netherworld: "The turtle prefers living and dragging its tail through dirt to being dead and worshipped in a temple."

Indeed we have to remind ourselves that magic also retained

* Cf. Homer, *The Odyssey*, Book XI, 489, Tr.

its acknowledged place in orthodox Confucianism, and that it had its traditionalist effects. We have mentioned that as recently as 1883 a censor protested utilizing modern techniques in building dykes at the Huang Ho because this would deviate from the way planned by the classics. Undoubtedly the fear of causing unrest among the spirits was decisive in this. Confucianism strictly rejected the emotional ecstasy to be found only among the popular magicians, the apathetic ecstasy among the Taoists, and every form of monachal asceticism. In general, all magic was rejected as "irrational" in this psychological sense.

Neither in its official state cult nor in its Taoist aspect could Chinese religiosity produce sufficiently strong motives for a religiously oriented life for the individual such as the Puritan method represents. Both forms of religion lacked even the traces of a satanic force of evil against which the pious Chinese, whether orthodox or heterodox, might have struggled for his salvation. The truly Confucian wisdom of life was "civic" in the sense that officialdom possessed an optimist rationalism. It had its superstitious elements as is the case with all enlightenment. As a "status" religion it was a morale of literary intellectualism whose specific note was pride in education.

In view of the actual distribution of fortunes and the unpredictability of man's destiny the fact was necessarily faced that the greatest utilitarian optimism and conventionalism imaginable did not satisfy even modest demands for justice in this best of all possible social orders. Misfortunes and injustice in this order were supposed to be the result only of individual educational deficiencies or governmental charismatic deficiencies or, according to Taoist doctrine, the result of magical trespasses. The eternal problem of theodicy also necessarily emerged here. For the Confucian, at least, neither a beyond nor a migration of souls was conceivable. But indications of a somewhat esoteric belief in predestination are traceable in the classic scriptures. The conception was rather dualist in meaning since the Chinese bureaucracy was characteristically a stratum of literati who were essentially distanced from the heroism of warriors and at the same time a status group which was segregated from purely bourgeois life.

Folk belief apparently lacked any conception of providence. However, it developed a distinct, if incipient, astrological belief that the stars ruled over the individual's fate. The belief in providence does not seem entirely foreign to Confucian esoterics, insofar as one may speak of such esoterics. In general, however, providence did not refer to the concrete fate of the individual man, as is evident especially in Mencius. It referred only to the harmony and the eventual destiny of the social collectivity *per se,* as is the case with all primitive community cults. But Confucianism did not really work out the specific concept of predestination, for example, in the sense of the Hellenic *moira,* an irrational, impersonal, and fateful power determining the great *peripeteia* of individual life. This conception is specific to all purely human heroism which has always proudly refused to believe in a benevo-' lent providence. Both elements existed side by side.

Confucius obviously regarded his mission and its underlying influences as positively and providentially ordered. To be sure, beside this is found the belief in irrational *moira,* with a characteristic twist. Only the "superior man," it is said, knows of fate; and without belief in fate, one cannot be a cultured man. Here as elsewhere, the faith in providence served to underpin the kind of Stoic heroism which alone is accessible to the intellectual literati, namely, a "preparedness" approximating Montaigne's attitude. That meant accepting the unalterable with equanimity and in so doing the attitude of the cultivated and educated cavalier was proved. Common man, without fate or fearsome of fate, pursues happiness and goods; or he faces the change of fortune with resignation as *fatum*—not as *kismet,* even though in practice the latter seemed to be the case according to missionary reports. Confucian "superior" man, however, learned to live in the knowledge of fate and to face up to it inwardly with proud equanimity. For he was devoted to his personality and its perfection.[38]

In addition to other irrational elements of Confucian rationalism known to us it is evident that this faith in irrational predestination also served to support gentility. This faith rejected a completely rational this-worldly theodicy, at least for the individual. Therefore, some philosophers rejected as ethically dangerous a faith which produced tension within the otherwise rationalist system of Confucianism. The Confucian belief in predestination, however, differs in meaning from the Puritan belief in predestination which is oriented to a personal god and his omnipotence. Also the Puritan firmly and clearly rejects the benevolence of providence but in so doing, he looks out for himself in the beyond. In Confucianism, however, neither the cultured nor the common man bothered about the beyond. The cultured Confucian's one interest beyond death was that his name be honored; to protect this honor he had to be prepared to endure death. Confucian rulers and generals indeed knew how to die proudly when Heaven was against them in the high gamble of war and human destiny. They knew better how to die than their Christian colleagues, as we in Germany know.* The strongest motive for highminded deportment known to Confucianism[39] may well have been this specific sense of honor, which characterized a cultured man and was linked essentially to a man's accomplishments not to his birth. In this regard the Confucian way of life was oriented to status and not to "bourgeois" values in the sense of the Occident.

This implies that such an ethic of intellectuals was necessarily limited in its significance for the broad masses. First, the local and next the social differences in education were enormous. The traditionalist and hitherto strong subsistence economy was maintained among the poorer strata of the people by a masterful art of thrift (in the sense of consumption). This almost unbelievably intensive thrift was unequaled anywhere else in the world. It was possible only with a standard of living which precluded any internal relationship to the gentleman ideals of Confucianism. Here as elsewhere only the gestures and external forms of behavior of the ruling stratum could be generally assimilated.

* Weber refers to the rulers of imperial Germany and their exit in 1918. Tr.

In all probability the educated stratum decisively influenced the way of life of the masses through negative effects. On the one hand, the emergence of a prophetic religiosity was completely inhibited and, on the other, the orgiastic elements of animist religiosity were almost completely expurgated. Possibly this determined at least part of those traits which are sometimes considered racial qualities of the Chinese. Above all the cool temperature of Confucian social ethics might be so considered as well as its rejection of other than purely *personal* ties among family members, students or companions.

The retention of personalism is especially evident in its effect on social ethics. Hitherto in China no sense of obligation has existed toward impersonal communities, be they of political, ideological, or any other nature.[40] All social ethics in China merely transferred the organic relations of piety to other relations considered similar to them. Within the five natural social relations the duties to master, father, husband, older brother (including the teacher), and friend comprised the sum total of the ethically binding. There was no element of devotion in the Confucian principle of reciprocity, which was basic to all natural functional obligations outside these relationships. There are duties which have always been firmly rooted in the genuine social ethics of the neighborhood association. Especially is there the obligatory liberal hospitality and charity of the propertied, everywhere praised by sacred singers as a sign of noble living. This has been assimilated by all religious ethics.

Under the impact of Confucian rationalism and conventionalism in life-conduct these duties assumed a strongly formalist character. This was especially true of the "practicing of virtue," the characteristic and usual expression for the form of hospitality for the poor held on the eighth day of the twelfth month. Almsgiving, the primitive and central imperative of all religious ethics, had become a traditional tribute which it was dangerous to withhold. The Christian significance of alms led to regarding the "poor" as a god-ordained "estate" within the Christian community, since their existence was necessary for saving the souls of the rich. In China the poor had gathered into well-organized guilds which no one lightly risked having as his principled enemy.

In general, it may well represent the normal case for it is not only in China that charity is expected to begin solely where there is a concrete personal or functional cause. Experts knowing the country can alone judge whether this alleged charity is actually stronger in China than elsewhere. As all magical religion originally did, Chinese folk religion considered permanent bodily ailments a result of some ritual sin. Since no motive of religious sympathy came into the balance it may well be the case that this sentiment was not particularly developed, despite the great praise which ethics (Mencius) bestowed upon the social value of sympathy. In any case sympathy was not greatly developed on the soil of Confucianism. Even the (heterodox) representatives of love for one's enemies (Mo Ti, for instance) justified sympathy on essentially utilitarian grounds.

Since the sacred personal duties of social ethics could conflict with one another, they had to be relativized. This is evident in the compulsory division of familial and fiscal interests, in suicides and the refusals of fathers to arrest their sons (for high treason). Bamboo canings were decreed for officials who mourned too little and in turn for those who mourned too much. The latter were troublesome to the administration because they refused office.

A conflict in the Christian manner between the interest in the salvation of one's soul and the demands of the natural social order was inconceivable. Any contrast between "god" or "nature" and "statutory law" or "convention" or any other binding force was absent. Therefore, any religious or religiously substructured natural law which might have produced tension or led to compromise with a sinful or nonsensical world was absent. The only exceptions were the slight beginnings of natural law mentioned above, as is at once obvious from the instances in the classics which occasionally refer to the "natural." In these instances, what is meant is always the cosmos of the internally harmonic order of nature and society. Certainly, hardly anyone was really expected to attain the level of absolute perfection. Every man, however, is quite adequate for acquiring a sufficient degree of personal perfection within the social orders. He is not in the least hindered from this in practicing the official social virtues: namely, human kindness, righteousness, frankness, ritual piety and knowledge, whether with a more active (Confucian) or more contemplative (Taoist) coloration. As we have repeatedly noticed, the ruler insufficiently endowed with charisma is personally guilty if the social order fails in regard to the welfare and contentment of all, regardless of whether or not he has fulfilled the above-mentioned duties.

Confucianism, therefore, knew no blissful original state at least according to classical doctrine. It merely knew uncultured bar-barism at the pre-civilized stage, for which there was the ready example of the savage mountain tribes who always threatened invasion.

When questioned how man was to be improved in the short-est time, the Master stonily replied that one should first enrich, then educate man. As a matter of fact, the English formalistic "How do you do?" characteristically corresponded to the greeting formula of the Chinese, "Have you eaten rice?" Since poverty and stupidity were the sole original sins, so to say, and since education and economic life were all-powerful in stamping man, Confucian-ism necessarily viewed the possibility of a golden age not as an innocent and primitive state of nature but rather as an optimal state of culture.

Now, a striking passage of the classical scriptures describes a condition in which imperial dignity is not determined by hered-ity but by election. Parents do not love their children simply because they are theirs or *vice versa;* and children, widows, the aged, the childless, and the diseased are maintained from com-mon funds. Men have their work and women their homes. Goods, to be sure, are saved but not accumulated for private ends; work does not serve individual advantage and thieves and rebels do not exist. All doors are open and the state is not a power state. This is the "great path" and it results in the "great homogeneity." In contrast, the empirical coercive order with the individual right of inheritance, the individual family, the military power state, and the exclusive rule of individual interest is called, in characteristic terminology, the "little tranquility." The description of this anarchist social ideal falls so far outside the framework of empirical Confucian social thought and, especially, is so irreconcilable with the filial piety basic to all Confucian ethics that orthodoxy has partly inferred textual corruption and partly sensed "Taoist" heterodoxy (as Legge did, by the way).

Nowadays, for understandable reasons, K'ang Yu-wei's modern school would quote this statement in proof of the Confucian legitimacy of the ideal socialist future. Actually this statement, like many other of the *Li Chi,* may well be expressive of the view which de Groot presents especially clear. That is: many doctrines, often considered heterodox or at least non-classical or even considered a special religion, were originally related to orthodoxy in about the way Christian mysticism was related to Catholicism and Sufist mysticism to Islamism.

Only artificially could the grace of an ecclesiastic institution be brought to compromise with the mystic's individual search for salvation. But the ecclesiastic institution must not in principle reject mysticism *per se.*

Confucian optimism ultimately concluded and hoped to attain perfection on earth solely through the individual's ethical strength and through the power of orderly administration. Eventually this created tension since it is an equally basic Confucian view that the material and ethical welfare of the individual and the whole people is ultimately determined by the charismatic qualities of the ruler who is legitimated by Heaven and by the welfare policy of his officials. This very doctrine, however, led Taoism to its own conclusions. The doctrine that the source of all good was abstention from action was held to be heterodox. But it was only the final conclusion of orthodox Confucian optimism turned into mysticism. Its acosmistic trust in its own qualification and the resultant devaluation of institutional grace led immediately to the danger of heresy. To surpass the this-worldly morality of laymen by searching for special paths to salvation was dubious for institutional grace just as in the case of ecclesiastic non-asceticist Protestantism.

We have seen that Tao as the "path" to virtue was perfectly understood and was also a central orthodox Confucian concept. Mysticism could refer to the significance of the god-willed, the natural, cosmic, and social harmony from which the principle of non-interference could be deduced. Mysticism could do this as well as the aforementioned, more or less consistent *laissez-faire* theories of some Confucians. The latter reserved state intervention for cases of all too dubious excess in the differentiation of wealth. For Confucianism to ascertain whether these doctrines were still orthodox was just as difficult and doubtful as it was for the medieval church to determine whether or not a mystic was still orthodox. Thus, it is understandable why de Groot rejects altogether the usual treatment of Taoism as a special religion alongside Confucianism. The religious edicts of the emperors repeatedly and expressly mention Taoism alongside Buddhism as a merely tolerated, non-classical faith. In contrast to this, the sociologist has to consider in fact the special hierocratic organization.

Ultimately, the substantive differences between orthodox and heterodox doctrines and practices, as well as any decisive peculiarities of Confucianism, had two sources. On the one hand, Confucianism was a status ethic of the bureaucracy educated in literature; on the other hand, piety and especially ancestor-worship were retained as politically indispensable foundations for patrimonialism. Only when these interests appeared to be threatened did the instinct of self-preservation in the ruling stratum react by attaching the stigma of heterodoxy.[41]

12. *Sects and the Persecution of Heresies in China*

THE most important and absolute limit to practical tolerance for the Confucian state consisted in the fundamental importance of the ancestor cult and this-worldly piety for the docility of the patrimonial subject.[42] The tolerance of the state evinced both affinities with and differences from the comparable attitude in occidental antiquity. The state cult knew only the official great spirits. However, on given occasions the emperor saluted the Taoist and Buddhist shrines, too, with the qualification that a polite bow was deemed sufficient instead of a Kotow which was even made to St. Confucius. The state paid for geomantic services[43] and the *fêng shui* were officially recognized.[44]

Occasional suppressions of exorcists from Tibet were to be found; the ancients called them *wu*—so it was said in the decrees concerning them.[45] These suppressions, to be sure, occurred simply for police reasons. The city mandarin officially participated in the cult of the Taoist city god and the canonizations by the Taoist patriarch required the imperial *placet*. No claims to "freedom of conscience" were guaranteed, nor were purely religious views persecuted as a rule, unless either magical reasons (similar to the religious trials of the Hellenes) or political considerations called for such persecutions. These considerations, however, were rather exacting.

The religious edicts of emperors made the persecution of heresy a duty. Even a writer like Mencius agreed with this. The means, intensity, concept, and scope of "heresy" changed. The Chinese state fought heresies, which in its view were hostile to the state, partly through indoctrination (as late as the nineteenth century by an officially distributed educational poem of a monarch). Partly it did so by fire and sword, like the Catholic Church fighting the denial of sacramental grace and the Roman Empire fighting the rejection of the cult of the emperor.

Despite the legend of unlimited toleration in the Chinese state almost every decade of the nineteenth century has seen all-out persecutions of heresies, including the torture of witnesses. On the other hand almost every rebellion was intimately connected with a heresy. In comparison with the ancient Roman state, for instance, the Chinese state was in a special position. For it had an exclusively and officially recognized doctrine after Confucianism was definitively placed beside the official state cult and the obligatory ancestor cult of the individual. To that extent the Chinese state approached a "denominational" state and stood in contrast to the pre-Christian ancient *imperium*. The "sacred edict" of 1672 (in the seventh of its sixteen sections) expressly ordered the rejection of false doctrines. The orthodox doctrine, however, was not a dogmatic religion but a philosophy and wisdom of life. The relation would indeed have been similar if, for example, the Roman emperors of the second century had officially adopted the Stoic ethic as orthodox and had made the acceptance of Stoic ethic prerequisite for delegation to state offices.

In contrast to this the popular form of sectarian religiosity consisted in the ministrations of sacramental grace as in India. And everywhere this happened on the soil of religiosity leading to mystic redemption. Whether turning prophet, propagandist, patriarch, or father confessor, the mystic in Asia inevitably became also a mystagogue. Imperial charisma of office, however, tolerated powers with an independent authority of grace at its side as little as the institutional grace of the Catholic Church could have done. Accordingly, in their arguments, the imperial edicts almost always reproached the heretics with identical facts. First, of course, the fact was mentioned that novel and non-licensed deities were worshiped. However, this point was not decisive, for basically the whole popular pantheon deviated from the state cult and was considered non-classical and barbaric. The truly decisive points were rather the following three:[46]

(1) The heretics banded together, allegedly in order to practice a virtuous life. However, they formed non-licensed associations and managed collections.

(2) They had leaders, partly incarnate gods, partly patriarchs, who preached compensation and promised salvation of soul in the beyond.

(3) They removed the ancestral tablets from their houses and separated themselves from their parental families for the sake of monachal or otherwise non-classical way of life.

The first point was an offense against the political police who prohibited non-licensed associations. The Confucian subject was expected to practice virtue privately in the five classical social relations. He did not require a sect for this and the very existence of a sect violated the patriarchical principle on which the state rested.

The second point for the Confucian meant defrauding the people openly, for there was no compensation in the beyond and no special salvation of the soul. But it also meant contempt for the this-worldly charisma of the Confucian state office. The care for the (this-worldly) salvation of soul within the Chinese state was the concern of the ancestors. For the rest it was the concern of the officials and their emperor who alone was legitimated by Heaven. Hence, any belief in redemption and any striving for sacramental grace threatened not only piety toward the ancestors but the prestige of the administration.

For a similar reason the third reproach was the most decisive of all. To reject the ancestor cult meant to threaten the cardinal virtue of politics, i.e., piety and on this depended discipline in the hierarchy of offices and obedience of subjects. A religiosity which emancipated [the subjects] from believing in the all-decisive power of imperial charisma and the eternal order of pious relations was unbearable in principle.

The motives of the decrees, according to circumstances, might also be mercantilist or ethical.[47] Contemplative life, the individual contemplative search for salvation, and especially the monachal existence were viewed by the Confucians as parasitical laziness. It drew income from the productive citizens, for the Buddhist men did not plough (because of the *"ahimsa,"* i.e., the prohibition against endangering living beings, worms, and insects) and Buddhist women did not weave. Moreover, monkdom was quite often a mere pretext for escaping the public *corvée*. Occasionally even rulers who owed their thrones to the Taoists or Buddhists at a time when the latter were powerful turned against them in due course. Begging was the true kernel of Buddhist monachal asceticism and was repeatedly forbidden to the clergy; so, too, was redemptory preaching outside the monasteries. After having been placed under obligatory licenses, the monasteries were numerically sharply curtailed, as we shall point out. In contrast, the decisive favors temporarily bestowed upon Buddhism were based on the hope that this doctrine of meekness might be used for taming the subjects. It was similar to the introduction of Lamaism under the Mongol Khans.

Afterward the tremendous diffusion of monasteries and the rampant interest in redemption very soon led to sharp repression. Then in the ninth century the Buddhist Church received the blow from which it has never completely recovered. Part of the Buddhist and Taoist monasteries were retained and were even placed on the state budget, with the strict rule that every monk be publicly certified. That is, a sort of "cultural examination" was demanded in the manner of the Prussian *Kulturkampf.* According to de Groot's very plausible assumption, the *fêng shui* were decisive in this, for it was impossible to remove places once licensed for worship without incurring a perhaps dangerous excitement of the spirits. This essentially determined the relative toleration which was granted to heterodox cults for reasons of state. This tolerance by no means meant positive esteem but rather the disdainful "toleration" which is the natural attitude of every secular bureaucracy toward religion. It is an attitude moderated only by the need for taming the masses.

The "superior" man confronted these as he did all other beings who were not officially worshiped for reasons of state. He followed the very modern principle ascribed to the Master, who advised appeasing the spirits by the proven ceremonials but "keeping them at their proper distance." In these tolerated heterodox religions participation of the masses had nothing in common with our concept of "religious affiliation." Depending on circumstances, occidental man of Antiquity worshiped Apollo or Dionysos and the Southern Italian worshiped competing saints and religious orders. So, too, according to need and proven efficacy, the Chinese paid respect to or withdrew it from Taoist mantics and Buddhist masses alike. The latter were always popular even among the highest circles. In Peking folk customs, Buddhist and Taoist sacraments were used side by side and the classical ancestor cult furnished the ground coloration. In any case it was nonsense to enumerate the Chinese as "Buddhist" by religious affiliation though this often used to be done. By our yardstick only the registered monks and priests may be called "Buddhists."

The monachal form of heterodoxy did not by itself determine the opposition of public authorities. But when Buddhism, and Taoism under its influence, developed communities of laymen with married secular priests, that is, when religious affiliations of a sort began to emerge, the government naturally intervened quite sharply. It placed before the priests the choice of being interned in the licensed monasteries or of returning to profane vocations. Some customs copied by the sects from Indian models were singled out for suppression by the government. Such was the case when distinguishing signs in painting and dress were adopted for initiation ceremonies by way of ordering the novices according to religious worth and the rank of the mysteries to which they were admitted. At this point, the specific aspect of sectarianism began to develop. The value and worth of the "personality" were guaranteed and legitimated not by blood ties, status group, or publicly authorized degree, but by being a member of and by proving oneself in a circle of specifically qualified associates. This basic function of all sect religiosity is far more odious to any compulsory institution of grace, to the Catholic Church as well as to the cesaro-papist state, than is the easily controlled monastery.

Here we disregard the temporary, politically determined promotion of Lamaism, which meant little historically. We likewise disregard the destiny of Chinese Islamism,[48] which was quite important, and the lot of Jewry, which was reduced in a peculiar way and, unlike anywhere else in the world, strongly divested of its character. The Islamite lords in the far West of the empire are mentioned in some edicts with a characteristic request that criminals be sold to them as slaves.

The persecution of the "European worship of the Lord from Heaven" which was the official name of Christianity, will not be discussed here, an omission which requires no further explanation. This persecution would have occurred despite greater tactfulness among the missionaries. Only military force led to contractually stipulated toleration once the meaning of Christian propaganda had been recognized. The old religious edicts to the people argued for the toleration of the Jesuits by explicitly mentioning their astronomical services.

The number of sects (de Groot enumerates fifty-six) was not small and their following was large, especially in Honan, and in some other provinces. Sectarian adherents were often found among the servants of mandarins and among the personnel of the rice fleet. The fact that orthodox *(ching)* Confucianism treated every heterodoxy *(i tuan)* as attempted rebellion—such is the way of the church-state—has impelled most of them to use force. Quite a few sects go back half a millennium and some are even older, despite the persecution.

13. The T'ai P'ing Rebellion

IT WAS not an insurmountable "natural disposition" that hindered the Chinese from producing religious structures comparable to those of the Occident. In recent times this has been proved by the impressive success of Hung Hsiu-ch'uan's iconoclastic and anti-magical prophecy of the *T'ien Wang* ("Heavenly King") of the *T'ai P'ing*[49] *T'ien Kuo* (Heavenly Kingdom of Peace; from 1850-1864). To our knowledge it was by far the most powerful and thoroughly hierocratic, politico-ethical rebellion against the Confucian administration and ethic which China has ever experienced.[50] The founder allegedly[51] belonged to a rusticated sib of nobles and was a severely epileptic[52] and ecstatic man. Like the Byzantine iconoclasts of Islamism, and perhaps stimulated in part through the influence of Protestant missions and the Bible, he radically and puritanically rebuked every belief in spirits, magic, and idolatry. His ethic was half mystic-ecstatic and half ascetic. He was educated in Confucianism, had failed to pass his state examination, and was influenced by Taoism. The Genesis and the New Testament belonged to the canonical books of the sect which he had founded with the support of his sib. Among the customs and symbols of the sect were: a water bath copied from baptism, instead of the Lord's Supper, a sort of tea-eucharist due to abstention from alcohol, the modified Lord's Prayer, and a likewise characteristically modified Decalogue. Besides, he quoted the *Shih Ching* and other classical works by selecting a medley of passages to suit his purposes. In so doing, he fell back, of course, like all reformers, on announcements and orders of the emperors of the legendary archaic period.

The result was a peculiar mixture of Christian and Confucian forms, reminiscent of Mohammed's eclecticism. We find the God Father of Christianity[53] and Jesus[54] at his side—though "holy," not in substance his equal. Finally, we find the prophet as Christ's "younger brother" and upon him the holy spirit rested.[55] There was profound horror of the veneration of saints and images and especially of the cult of the Virgin Mother. Prayers were at fixed hours, sabbatical rest was on Saturdays with two services which included Bible reading, litany, sermon, reading of the Decalogue, and hymns. We find the Christmas festival, the ministerial ceremony of (insoluble) wedlock, the admissibility of polygamy, prohibition of prostitution under pain of capital punishment, and rigid segregation of unmarried women and men. We find also strict abstinence from alcohol, opium, and tobacco; the abolition of the braid and of the crippling of women's feet; and propitiary sacrifices at the tomb of the dead.[56]

Like the orthodox emperor, the T'ien Wang was *supreme pontifex*. The officials of the five highest boards next to him had the titles of "King" of the West, East, South, North, and a fifth King served as an assistant. The three examination degrees were also to be found in the T'ai P'ing empire. Traffic in offices was abolished and all officials were nominated by the Emperor. The magazine storage policy and the *corvée* were taken from the old orthodox practice, but important differences existed in some points such as the strict separation of "external" and "internal" administration. For the latter, women were drawn into economic life as leaders. The policy of communication, road building and commerce was relatively "liberal." The contrast in principle was

about the same as that between Cromwell's regiment of Saints—
with some traits reminiscent of early Islamism and the anabaptist
régime of Münster—and Laud's cesaro-papist state.

In theory the state was the commonwealth of an ascetic order
of warriors. A typical military booty communism was intermixed
with acosmistic charity in the early Christian manner; nationalist
instinct was pushed into the background in favor of international
religious fraternization. Officials were to be selected according to
religious charisma and proven moral worth. The administrative districts were districts for military recruitment and provisioning on the one hand; on the other, they were church parishes with
prayer halls, state schools, libraries, and clerics appointed by
the T'ien Wang. Military discipline was as puritanically strict as
the order of life. Jewelry and all precious metals were confiscated
in order to defray collective expenditures.[57] Suitable women were
also enrolled in the army. Payments from a common fund were
made to families drafted for administrative functions.[58]

In ethics the Confucian belief in fate was brought into connection with vocational virtue[59]—a transposition made in the spirit
of the New Testament. Moral "rectitude," in lieu of the ceremonial
correctitude of the Confucian, "differentiates man from animal";[60]
and with the prince too, everything depended on rectitude.[61] For
the rest Confucian "reciprocity" held, except for the commandment which prohibited one from saying that he did not wish to
love his enemy. With this ethic "happiness is easily obtainable."
In contrast to Confucianism, however, human nature by itself was
considered incapable of really fulfilling all the commandments.[62]
Repentance and prayer were means of redemption from sin. Military bravery was held to be the most important and god-pleasing
virtue.[63] Taoist magic and Buddhist idolatry were as sharply rejected as the orthodox cult of spirits. This was in contrast to the
friendly attitude toward Jewry and Protestant Christianity. Protestant missionaries of the Dissenting and of the Low Church
repeatedly held services in T'ai P'ing prayer halls. But from the
beginning the Anglican High Church and the Jesuits were hostile
because of the iconoclasm and the sharp rejection of the cult of

the Virgin Mother. Due to the religious discipline behind their crusade, the T'ai P'ing armies were as superior to the armies of the orthodox government as Cromwell's army was to that of the King.

For political and commercial[64] reasons, Lord Palmerston's government saw fit to prevent this church-state from gaining the upper hand and especially to prevent the treaty harbor of Shanghai from falling into its hands.[65] With the aid of Gordon and the Navy the T'ai P'ing power was broken. Given to visionary ecstasies and a seraglio existence,[66] the T'ien Wang had secluded himself for years in the palace. After the fourteen years his realm had lasted he finished his life and that of his harem by self-cremation in his Nanking residence. As much as a decade later "rebel" leaders were still taken prisoners.[67] The human loss, the financial weakness, and the devastation of the particular provinces were not fully retrieved for a much longer time.

The T'ai P'ing ethic, after what was said above, was a peculiar mixture of chiliastic-ecstatic and ascetic elements. The latter was outstanding and was unsurpassed anywhere else in China. Moreover, the magical and idolatrous fetters were broken and this was unknown elsewhere in China. The personally benign and universal god of the world, freed of national barriers, was adopted. And this god would otherwise have remained entirely alien to Chinese religion. To be sure, one can hardly say what developmental course this religion might have taken in case of victory. Sacrifices at the ancestral tombs had to be retained just as the Jesuit missions had to allow them until the curia intervened upon the denunciation of competing orders. The beginning emphasis on correctness in good works might have led again into ritualist tracks. The increasing ceremonial regulation of all public order[68] might well have restored the principle of institutional grace. Nevertheless, the movement signified a break with orthodoxy in important points and it allowed an indigenous religion to arise which inwardly was relatively close to Christianity. This opportunity was incomparably greater than that offered by the hopeless missionary experiments of the occidental denominations. And it may well have been the last opportunity for such a religion in China.

Politically, the concept of "private association" was strongly suspect even before this; afterward it came to be largely identified with "high treason." Despite the tough struggle the bureaucracy opposed a merciless persecution of this "silent China." It was a persecution at least externally successful in the cities and for understandable reasons less conspicuous in the open country. The quiet and correct-living man anxiously stayed away from such affairs. This attitude reinforced the trait of "personalism" which we have treated above.

The Confucian literati-bureaucracy largely succeeded in confining sect formation to an occasional flare-up. This it did by using force and by appealing to the belief in spirits. Moreover, all sects about which detailed information is available were absolutely heterogeneous as compared with the sectarian movement with which occidental Catholicism or Anglicanism had to deal. It was always a matter of incarnation prophecy or of prophets of the mystagogue type who were often in possession of this hereditary dignity for generations. They lived secretively and promised advantages to their followers in this world as well as in the beyond. Their redemptory prerequisites, however, were of an exclusively magical, sacramental, ritualist, or at the most, contemplative-ecstatic character. The regularly recurrent soteriological means were ritual purity, devout repetition of the same formula, or certain contemplative exercises. As far as is known, rational asceticism is never found.[69]

As we have seen, genuine heterodox Taoist humility and rejection of all feudal ostentation were essentially motivated by contemplation. The same held undoubtedly for the abstention from certain kinds of luxury consumption (perfumes, precious ornaments) which the Lung-hua sect, e.g., imposed upon its believers, in addition to the regular rules of Buddhist sects. Asceticism was also absent where sects considered using force in fighting their oppressors and therefore systematically practiced boxing, like the famous sect in modern times.[70] The "League of righteous energy," the real name of the "Boxers" in English, sought invulnerability through magical training.[71]

All these sects were derivatives and eclecticist fusions of heterodox Taoist and Buddhist soteriology. They did not contribute any important new elements to the latter.

The sects apparently did not follow class lines. Naturally, the mandarins were the most strictly orthodox Confucians. But heterodox Taoists and especially the followers of the Lung-hua sect—essentially practicing a house cult with prayer-formula— appeared to be rather numerous among the propertied classes from which the mandarins were also recruited.

Women obviously formed a strong contingent here as in all soteriological religions. This is easy to understand because their religious evaluation by the (heterodox, hence unpolitical) sects in China as in the Occident rated, in most instances, significantly above their level of esteem in Confucianism.

14. The Result of the Development

THE elements borrowed from or influenced by Taoism or Buddhism obviously played a considerable role in the workaday life of the masses. In the Introduction* it was stated generally that religions of salvation and saviors always found their permanent and pre-eminent locus among the "civic" classes and usually displaced magic among them. At first they offered the only retreat available to the suffering and needy individual *per se*. The purely religious communities of mystagogues usually grew out of the individual search for salvation with the magician.

In China, where the state cult also took no note of individual distress, magic has never been displaced by a great prophecy of salvation or by an indigenous savior-religion. Only a substratum of redemptory religiosity emerged which corresponded partly to the Hellenic mysteries and partly to Hellenic orphics. This religiosity in China was stronger than in Hellas but it remained purely magical in character. Taoism was merely an organization

* Cf. *From Max Weber: Essays in Sociology*, pp. 284 ff.

of magicians. Buddhism in its imported form was no longer the redemptory religion of early Indian Buddhism, but had become the magical and mystagogical practice of a monastic organization. Hence, in both cases the formation of religious communities, at least for laymen, was lacking; and that is sociologically decisive. The popular, redemptory religions which were stuck in magic were usually quite unsocial. The individual qua individual turned to the Taoist magician or Buddhist bonze. Only the Buddhist festivities formed occasional communities; only the heterodox sects, often pursuing political ends and hence politically persecuted, formed enduring communities. Anything corresponding to our cure of souls was absent. Moreover, there was not a trace of "church discipline," which meant in turn that the means for a religious control of life were lacking. Instead, as in the Mythras mysteries, there were stages and degrees of sanctification and of hierocratic rank.

From the sociological viewpoint these beginnings of redemptory religiosity were rather pitiful. Nevertheless from the viewpoint of moral history they had considerable ramifications. Despite the persecutions to which it was exposed, Buddhism imported about all that Chinese folk life knew of the religious sermon and individual search for salvation, belief in compensation and a beyond, religious ethic and inward devotion. The same holds for Japan. In order to be called a "folk religion" at all this monachal soteriology of Indian intellectuals had to undergo the most profound internal transition imaginable. Hence, we shall first have to consider Buddhism on its native ground. Only then can it be fully understood why no bridges could connect its monachal contemplation with rational routine conduct. And only then can we comprehend why the role conceded to Buddhism in China deviated so widely from the role which Christianity could assume in late Antiquity, despite the seeming analogy.

CHAPTER VIII

CONCLUSIONS:
CONFUCIANISM AND PURITANISM

I<small>N THIS</small> context we may best gain perspective on the foregoing by clarifying the relationship between Confucian rationalism—for the name is appropriate—and what is geographically and historically closest to us, namely, Protestant rationalism.

To judge the level of rationalization a religion represents we may use two primary yardsticks which are in many ways interrelated. One is the degree to which the religion has divested itself of magic; the other is the degree to which it has systematically unified the relation between God and the world and therewith its own ethical relationship to the world. In the former respect the varying expressions of ascetic Protestantism represent a last phase. The most characteristic forms of Protestantism have liquidated magic most completely. In principle, magic was eradicated even in the sublimated form of sacraments and symbols, so much so that the strict Puritan had the corpses of his loved ones dug under without any formality in order to assure the complete elimination of superstition. That meant, in this context, cutting off all trust in magical manipulations. Nowhere has the complete disenchantment of the world been carried through with greater consistency, but that did not mean freedom from what we nowadays customarily regard as "superstition." Witch trials also flourished in New England. Still while Confucianism left untouched the significance of magic for redemption, Puritanism came to consider all magic as devilish. Only ethical rationalism was defined as religiously valuable, i.e., conduct according to God's commandment and at that, proceeding from a God-fearing attitude. Finally, from our presentation it should be perfectly clear that in the magic garden of heterodox doctrine (Taoism) a rational economy and technology of modern occidental character was simply out of the question. For all natural scientific knowledge was lacking, partly as a cause and partly as an effect of these elemental forces: the power of chronomancers, geomancers, hydromancers, meteoromancers; and a crude, abstruse, universist conception of the unity of the world. Furthermore, Taoism was interested in the income opportunities of prebendal office, the bulwark of magical tradition.

The preservation of this magic garden, however, was·one of the tendencies intimate to Confucian ethics. To this, internal reasons were added which prevented any shattering of Confucian power.

In strong contrast to the naïve stand of Confucianism toward things of this world, Puritan ethics construed them as a tremendous and grandiose tension toward the "world." As we shall see further in detail, every religion which opposes the world with rational, ethical imperatives finds itself at some point in a state of tension with the irrationalities of the world. These tensions with individual religions set in at very different points, and the nature and intensity of the tension varies accordingly. With the individual religions this depends largely on the path of salvation as defined by metaphysical promises. We must note that the degree of religious devaluation of the world is not identical with the degree of its rejection in actual practice.

Confucianism, we have seen was (in intent) a rational ethic which reduced tension with the world to an absolute minimum. This was true of its religious depreciation as well as its practical rejection. The world was the best of all possible worlds; human nature was disposed to the ethically good. Men, in this as in all things, differed in degree but being of the same nature

f unlimited perfection, they were in principle
ulfilling the moral law. Philosophical-literary edu-
upon the old classics was the universal means of
ction, and insufficient education along with its main
cause, insufficient economic provision, were the only sources of
shortcoming. Such faults, however, and especially the faults of
government, were the esssential reason for all misfortunes since
they caused the unrest of the purely magically-conceived spirits.
The right path to salvation consisted in adjustment to the eternal
and supra-divine orders of the world, Tao, and hence to the requirements of social life, which followed from cosmic harmony.
Pious conformism with the fixed order of secular powers reigned
supreme. The corresponding individual ideal was the elaboration
of the self as a universal and harmoniously balanced personality,
in this sense a microcosm. For the Confucian ideal man, the
gentleman, "grace and dignity" were expressed in fulfilling traditional obligations. Hence, the cardinal virtue and goal in self-
perfection meant ceremonial and ritualist propriety in all circumstances of life. The appropriate means to this goal were
watchful and rational self-control and the repression of whatever
irrational passions might cause poise to be shaken.

The Confucian desired "salvation" only from the barbaric lack
of education. As the reward of virtue he expected only long life,
health, and wealth in this world and beyond death the retention
of his good name. Like for truly Hellenic man all transcendental
anchorage of ethics, all tension between the imperatives of a
supra-mundane God and a creatural world, all orientation toward
a goal in the beyond, and all conception of radical evil were
absent. He who complied with the commandments, fashioned
for the man of average ability, was free of sin. In vain Christian
missionaries tried to awaken a feeling of sin where such presuppositions were taken for granted. Then, too, an educated Chinese
would simply refuse to be continually burdened with "sin."
Incidentally, the concept of "sin" is usually felt as rather shocking and lacking in dignity by genteel intellectuals everywhere.
Usually it is replaced by conventional, or feudal, or aestheti-

cally formulated variants such as "indecent" or "not in good taste." There were sins, certainly, but in the field of ethics these consisted of offenses against traditional authorities, parents, ancestors, and superiors in the hierarchy of office. For the rest they were magically precarious infringements of inherited customs, of the traditional ceremonial, and, finally, of the stable social conventions. All these were of equal standing. "I have sinned" corresponded to our "I beg your pardon" in violating a convention. Asceticism and contemplation, mortification and escape from the world were not only unknown in Confucianism but were despised as parasitism. All forms of congregational and redemptory religiosity were either directly persecuted and eradicated, or were considered a private affair and little esteemed, as were the orphic priests by the noble Hellenic men of classic time. This ethic of unconditional affirmation of and adjustment to the world presupposed the unbroken and continued existence of purely magical religion. It applied to the position of the emperor who, by personal qualification, was responsible for the good conduct of the spirits and the occurrence of rain and good harvest weather; it applied to ancestor worship which was equally fundamental for official and popular religiosity; and it applied to unofficial (Taoist) magical therapy and the other survival forms of animist compulsion of spirits (i.e., anthropo- and herolatric belief in functional deities).

Like the educated Hellene, the educated Confucian adhered to magical conceptions with a mixture of skepticism while occasionally submitting to demonology. But the mass of the Chinese, whose way of life was influenced by Confucianism, lived in these conceptions with unbroken faith. With regard to the beyond the Confucian might say with old Faust, "Fool who turns his eyes blinking in that direction"; but like Faust he would have to make the reservation, "If only I could remove magic from my path . . ." Also the high Chinese officials, educated in the old Chinese way, did not hesitate to be edified by the stupidest miracle. Tension toward the "world" had never arisen because, as far as known, there had never been an ethical prophecy of a supramundane God who raised ethical demands. Nor was there a substitute for this in the "spirits" who raised demands and insisted upon faithful fulfillment of contract. For it was always a matter of specific duty placed under the spirits' guardianship, oath, or whatever it happened to be; never did it involve inner formation of the personality *per se* nor the person's conduct of life. The leading intellectual stratum, officials and candidates for office, had consistently supported the retention of ancestor worship as absolutely necessary for the undisturbed preservation of bureaucratic authority. They suppressed all upheavals arising from religions of redemption. Besides Taoist divination and sacramental grace, the only religion of salvation permitted was that of the Buddhist monks for, being pacifist, it was not dangerous. In China, its practical effect was to enrich the scope of psychic experience by certain nuances of moody inwardness as we shall see. For the rest, it was a further source of magical-sacramental grace and tradition-strengthening ceremony.

This means that such an ethic of intellectuals was necessarily limited in its significance for the broad masses. First, local and, above all, social differences in education were enormous. The traditionalist and, until modern times, strongly subsistence-oriented pattern of consumption among the poorer strata of the people was maintained by an almost incredible virtuosity in thrift (in consumption matters), which has nowhere been surpassed and which precluded any intimate relation to the gentleman ideals of Confucianism.

As usual, only the gestures and forms of external conduct among the master stratum became the object of general diffusion. In all probability the educated stratum has decisively influenced the way of life of the masses. This influence seems to have been consummated especially through negative effects: on the one hand, completely blocking the emergence of any prophetic religiosity, and on the other hand, eradicating almost all orgiastic elements in the animist religion. It is possible that at least part of the traits which some authors are occasionally wont to refer to as the racial qualities of the Chinese are co-determined by these factors. Nowadays, here as elsewhere, even experienced and knowing men can say nothing definite about the extent to which biological heredity is influential. For us, however, there is an important observation which can easily be made and is confirmed by eminent sinologists. In the traits relevant for us, the further back one goes in history the more similar the Chinese and Chinese culture appear to what is found in the Occident. The old popular beliefs, the old anchorets, the oldest songs of the *Shih Ching*, the old warrior kings, the antagonisms of the philosophical schools, feudalism, the beginnings of capitalist developments in the Period of the Warring States—all of which are considered characteristic—are more closely related to occidental phenomena than are the traits of Confucian China. Hence, one has to reckon with the possibility that many of the Chinese traits which are considered innate may be the products of purely historical and cultural influences.

Regarding such traits, the sociologist essentially depends upon the literature of missionaries. This certainly varies in value but in the last analysis remains relatively the most authentic. Always emphasized are such observations as these: the striking lack of "nerves" in the specifically modern European meaning of the word; the unlimited patience and controlled politeness; the strong attachment to the habitual; the absolute insensitivity to monotony; the capacity for uninterrupted work and the slowness in reacting to unusual stimuli, especially in the intellectual sphere. All this seems to constitute a coherent and plausible unit but other seemingly sharp contrasts appear. There is an extraordinary and unusual horror of all unknown and not immediately apparent things which finds expression in ineradicable distrust. There is the rejection or lack of intellectual curiosity about things not close at hand and immediately useful. These traits stand in contrast to an unlimited and good-natured credulity in any magical swindle, no matter how fantastic it may be. In the same way the strong lack of genuine sympathy and warmth, often even among people who are personally close, stands in apparent contrast to the great and close-knit cohesion of social organizations. The absolute docility and ceremonial piety of the adult toward his parents hardly seems compatible with the alleged lack of love and respect for authority in small children. Likewise what is repeatedly maintained as the incomparable dishonesty of the Chinese, even toward their own defense attorneys, could scarcely be reconciled with the obviously remarkable reliability of merchants in big business—compared to countries with a feudal past such as Japan, for example. Retail trade, to be sure, seems to know little of such honesty; the "fixed" prices appear to be fictitious even among native Chinese. The typical distrust of the Chinese for one another is confirmed by all observers. It stands in sharp contrast to the trust and honesty of the faithful brethren in the Puritan sects, a trust shared by outsiders as well. Finally, the unity and unshakability of the general psychophysical bearing constrasts sharply with the often reported instability of all those features of the Chinese way of life which are not regulated from without by fixed norms. Most traits, however, are so fixed. More sharply formulated, the bondage of the Chinese, which is produced by their innumerable conventions, contrasts basically with the absence of an inward core, of a unified way of life flowing from some central and autonomous value position. How can all this be explained?

The absence of hysteria-producing, asceticist religious practices and the rather thorough elimination of toxic cults could not fail to influence the nervous and psychic constitution of a human group. As regards the use of toxics the Chinese belong to the relatively "sober" peoples. This has been since the pacification as compared to the former carousing in the old long house and at princely courts. Frenzy and orgiastic "obsession" were divested of the charismatic value attaching to sacredness and were only considered symptomatic of demonic rule. Confucianism rejected the use of alcohol except for rudimentary use at sacrifices. That the alcoholic orgy was not rare among the lower strata of the people in China, as elsewhere, does not change the *relative* significance of the difference. Opium, the toxic considered specifically Chinese, has been imported only in modern times. As is well known, it was imposed by war from without, despite the sharpest resistance of the ruling strata. Its effects, moreover, lie in the direction of apathetic ecstasy, a straight continuation of the line of *"wu wei,"* and not in the direction of heroic frenzy or the unchaining of active passions. The Hellenic *sophrosyne* did not prevent Plato in *"Phaidros"* from considering beautiful ecstasy as the source of everything great. In this the rationalist Roman nobility of office—who translated *"ekstasis"* as *"superstitio"* — and the educated stratum of China were of different mind. The "naïveté," as well as what is felt to be indolence, is perhaps partly connected with this complete lack of Dionysion element in Chinese religion, a lack which resulted from the deliberate sobering of the cult by the bureaucracy. In the bureaucracy nothing existed and nothing was allowed that might bring the psyche out of its equilibrium. Every inordinate passion, especially wrath, *ch'i*, produced evil charms; thus, on feeling any pain, the first question to ask was to what *ch'i* it might be ascribed. Animistic magic, as the only remaining form of popular religion, determined the traditionalist fear of any innovation which might bring evil charms or stir up the spirits. To be sure, this magic was despised by the educated Chinese; but it was the form of religion supported because of the character of the official cults. The preservation of this animistic magic explains the great credulity of the Chinese. Thus, magical also is the belief that disease and misfortune are symptoms of divine wrath which the individual has brought upon himself. In turn this belief facilitated a certain inhibition of those sympathetic emotions which, in the face of suffering, usually originate from the we-feeling of salvation religions. These emotions have always strongly governed popular ethics in India.

From the retention of magic in China there also resulted the specifically cool temper of Chinese humanity and formal kindliness toward one's fellow man. Even in intra-familial relationships there was a ceremonious punctilio and a selfish fear of the spirits.

Immeasurable ceremonial fetters surround the life of the Chi-

nese, from the stage of the embryo to the cult of the dead. In
their unexampled elaborateness and inviolability of detail they
constitute a treasure house for folklorist research. W. Grube's
works have especially exploited this material. Part of this ceremonial is evidently magical, especially apotropaic in origin. Part
is to be attributed to Taoism and popular Buddhism, to be discussed elsewhere. Both Taoism and popular Buddhism have left
profound traces in the workaday life of the masses. But there remains a very considerable residue of the purely conventional and
ceremonial. Ceremonial prescription regulated questions and an-
swers, indispensable offers as well as the exact manner of grateful
decline, also visits, presents, expressions of respect, condolence,
and joyful sympathy. This surpassed anything preserved from
ancient peasant tradition, such as is found in Spain where that
tradition was influenced by feudalism and probably also by
Islamism. In the field of gesture and of "face" one may assume
Confucian origins to be predominant even where the origin cannot be traced.

While the Confucian ideal of propriety did not always exert
its influence in the form of prevailing customs it revealed itself
in the "spirit" in which they were practiced. The aesthetically
cool temper caused all duties bequeathed from feudal times,
especially duties of charity, to be frozen into a symbolic ceremonial. On the other hand, the belief in spirits bound the
sib members more closely together. Undoubtedly, as in Egypt,
the much bewailed dishonesty was partly a direct product of
that patrimonial fiscalism which everywhere proved a training
ground for dishonesty. For both in Egypt and China the process
of tax collection involved raids, flogging, assistance of sib members, howlings of the oppressed, fear of the oppressors, and
compromise. To this must certainly be added the exclusive cult
of ceremonial and conventional propriety in Confucianism. Still
there were lacking the feudal instincts which branded all trade
with the adage "*Qui trompe t'on?*" Among the monopolistically
secure and cultured status group of wealthy oversea traders of
the *Ko Hang* guild, a much vaunted business integrity could

develop out of the exigencies of their interest-situation. This honesty, if it existed, seems to have been a factor of acculturation rather than an internal development like the Puritan ethic. This, however, applies to all ethical traits of the Chinese.

A true prophecy creates and systematically orients conduct toward one internal measure of value. In the face of this the "world" is viewed as material to be fashioned ethically according to the norm. Confucianism in contrast meant adjustment to the outside, to the conditions of the "world." A well-adjusted man, rationalizing his conduct only to the degree requisite for adjustment, does not constitute a systematic unity but rather a complex of useful and particular traits. In Chinese popular religion the animistic ideas which perpetuate the belief in plural souls of the individual could almost stand as a symbol of this fact. Not reaching beyond this world, the individual necessarily lacked an autonomous counterweight in confronting this world. Confucianism facilitated the taming of the masses as well as the dignified bearing of the gentleman, but the style of life thus achieved must necessarily be characterized by essentially negative traits. Such a way of life could not allow man an inward aspiration toward a "unified personality," a striving which we associate with the idea of personality. Life remained a series of occurrences. It did not become a whole placed methodically under a transcendental goal.

The contrast between this socio-ethical position and the whole religious ethic of the Occident was unbridgeable. Outwardly some patriarchical aspects of the Thomist and the Lutheran ethic might appear to resemble Confucianism, but this is merely an external impression. The Confucian system of radical world-optimism succeeded in removing the basic pessimistic tension between the world and the supra-mundane destination of the individual. But no Christian ethic, however entangled in mundane compromises, could attain this.

Completely absent in Confucian ethic was any tension between nature and deity, between ethical demand and human shortcoming, consciousness of sin and need for salvation, conduct on earth and compensation in the beyond, religious duty and socio-political reality. Hence, there was no leverage for influencing conduct through inner forces freed of tradition and convention. Family piety, resting on the belief in spirits, was by far the strongest influence on man's conduct. Ultimately family piety facilitated and controlled, as we have seen, the strong cohesion of the sib associations. This was likewise true of the above-mentioned cooperative associations which may be considered as enlarged family enterprises with specialization of labor. This firm cohesion was in its way religiously motivated and the strength of the truly Chinese economic organization was roughly co-extensive with these personal associations controlled by piety. Chinese ethic developed its strongest motives in the circle of naturally grown, personalist associations or associations affiliated with or modeled after them. This contrasts sharply with the Puritan ethic which amounts to an objectification of man's duties as a creature of God. The religious duty toward the hidden and supra-mundane God caused the Puritan to appraise all human relations—including those naturally nearest in life—as mere means and expression of a mentality reaching beyond the organic rela-tions of life. The religious duty of the pious Chinese, in contrast, enjoined him to develop himself within the organically given, personal relations. Mencius rejected the universal "love of man" with the comment that it would extinguish piety and justice and that it is the way of animals to have neither father nor brother. In substance, the duties of a Chinese Confucian always consisted of piety toward concrete people whether living or dead, and toward those who were close to him through their position in life. The Confucian owed nothing to a supra-mundane God; therefore, he was never bound to a sacred "cause" or an "idea." For Tao was neither; it was simply the embodiment of the bind-ing, traditional ritual, and its command was not "action" but "emptiness." For the economic mentality, the personalist principle was undoubtedly as great a barrier to impersonal rationaliza-tion as it was generally to impersonal matter of factness. It tended to tie the individual ever anew to his sib members and to bind him to the manner of the sib, in any case to "persons" instead of functional tasks ("enterprises"). This barrier was intimately connected with the nature of Chinese religion, as our whole presentation has shown. For it was an obstacle to rationalizing the religious ethic, an obstacle which the ruling and educated stratum maintained in the interest of their position. It is of considerable economic consequence whether or not confidence, which is basic to business, rests upon purely personal, familial, or semi-familial relationships as was largely the case in China.

The great achievement of ethical religions, above all of the ethical and asceticist sects of Protestantism, was to shatter the fetters of the sib. These religions established the superior community of faith and a common ethical way of life in opposition to the community of blood, even to a large extent in opposition to the family. From the economic viewpoint it meant basing business confidence upon the ethical qualities of the individual proven in his impersonal, vocational work. The economic ramifications of universal and mutual distrust must probably be rated high, though we have no yardstick for this. Thus, universal distrust resulted from the official and exclusive sway of conventional dishonesty and from the Confucian emphasis on keeping face.

Confucianism and Confucian mentality, deifying "wealth," could facilitate political-economic measures of a sort comparable to the worldliness of the Renaissance in the Occident. At this point, however, one can observe the limited significance of economic policy as compared to economic mentality. In no other civilized country has material welfare ever been so exalted as the supreme good.[1] The politico-economic views of Confucianism were comparable to those of our Cameralists. The oldest document of Chinese political economy[2] is a tract by the Confucian Ssu-ma Ch'ien on the "balance of trade" in which the usefulness of wealth, including commercial profit, is emphasized. Economic policy alternated between fiscal and *laissez-faire* measures; in any case it was not deliberately anti-chrematistic. The merchants of the occidental Middle Ages were and are "despised" by German literati just as in China. Still economic policy did not create the economic mentality of capitalism. The money profits of the traders in the Period of the Warring States were political profits of commissioners to the state. The great mining *corvées* were used to search gold. Still no intermediate link led from Confucianism and its ethic—as firmly rooted as Christianity—to a civic and methodical way of life. This was all-important. Puritanism did create it, and unintentionally at that. This strange reversion of the "natural," which is strange only on first, superficial glance, instructs us in the paradox of unintended consequences: i.e., the relation of man and fate, of what he intended by his acts and what actually came of them.

Puritanism represents the polar opposite type of rational dealing with the world, a somewhat ambiguous concept as we have shown elsewhere. The *"ecclesia pura,"* in practice and in true meaning, represented the Christian communion at the Lord's Supper in honor of God and purged of all morally rejected participants. This honor might have a Calvinist or Baptist foundation, its church constitution might be more synodical or more congregationalist. Broadly understood, Puritanism may refer to the morally rigoristic and Christian asceticist lay communities in general. This includes the Baptist, Mennonite, Quaker, ascetic Pietist, and Methodist communities which had spiritual mystical beginnings.

As against the Confucian type, it was peculiar to these types that they should oppose the flight from the world in order to rationalize it, despite or indeed because of their asceticist rejection of the world. Men are equally wicked and fail ethically; the world is a vessel of sin; and there can be no differences in creatural wickedness in the face of the Lord. Adjustment to vanity fair would be a sign of rejection; self-perfection in the sense of Confucianism would be idolatrous blasphemy. Wealth and surrender to its enjoyment would be the specific temptation, reliance on philosophy and literary education would be sinful and creatural pride; all trust in magical coercion of spirits and deities would be not only despicable superstition but impudent blasphemy. All things reminiscent of magic, all vestigial ritualism and priestly powers were eradicated. The Quakers, in theory, did not even

the result of differing disposition for spiritual endowment. Finally,
inequality of religious opportunity was due to the varying intensity and success of the endeavor to attain "conversion" (decisive with the old Pietists), "penitance," "winning through," or
whatever the nature of rebirth might be. However, besides the
unreasoning, unmerited, "free" grace of a supra-mundane God,
Providence was always instrumental in these differences. Thus
the belief in predestination was but one, though by far the most
consistent, dogmatic form of this religion of virtuosi.

Only a few of the *massa perditionis* were called to attain the
holy whether they alone were destined for it by virtue of a predestination of yore, or whether all—according to the Quakers
this included non-Christians—had received the offer but only
a small company, capable of seizing it, could reach the goal.
According to some Pietist doctrines, salvation was offered only
once in a lifetime; according to others, the so-called Terminists,
it was offered once and for all. Men always had to prove himself capable of grasping the holy. Hence, everything was directed
toward God's free grace and the destiny in the beyond; life in
the here and now was either a vale of tears or a mere transition.
Therefore, a tremendous emphasis was placed upon this tiny
span of time and upon what happened during it. This was perhaps encompassed by Carlyle's words: "Millennia had to pass
ere thou camest to life and millennia wait in silence for what
thou shalt do with this thy life." It was not that it was possible
to attain eternal grace by one's own achievement. The latter
was impossible. The individual could receive and above all recognize his call to salvation only through consciousness of a central

and unitary relation of this short life toward the supra-mundane God and His will in "sanctification." Sanctification in turn could prove itself only through God-ordained activities, and as in all active asceticism, through an ethical conduct blessed by God. Thus, the individual could gain certainty of salvation only in being God's tool. The strongest premium imaginable was thereby placed upon a rational and moral way of life. Only life conduct abided by firm principles and controlled at a unitary center could be considered a God-pleasing way of life. Though naïve surrender to the world unconditionally led away from salvation, nevertheless the creatural world and creatural man were God's creation and to them He addressed certain demands. According to Calvinist conception God had created the world "in His honor." Therefore, however creaturally wicked men might be, He wished to see His honor realized by subduing sin, possibly also sufferance and wished to subject them to ethical discipline through rational order. To "work the works of him that sent me, while it is day" here became a duty and the works posited were not ritual but rational-ethical in nature.

The contrast to Confucianism is clear: both ethics had their irrational anchorages, the one in magic, the other in the ultimately inscrutable resolves of a supra-mundane God. But from magic there followed the inviolability of tradition as the proven magical means and ultimately all bequeathed forms of life-conduct were unchangeable if the wrath of the spirits were to be avoided. From the relation between the supra-mundane God and the creaturally wicked, ethically irrational world there resulted, however, the absolute unholiness of tradition and the truly endless task of ethically and rationally subduing and mastering the given world, i.e., rational, objective "progress." Here, the task of the rational transformation of the world stood opposed to the Confucian adjustment to the world. Confucianism demanded constant and vigilant self-control in order to maintain the dignity of the universally accomplished man of the world; Puritan ethics demanded this self-control in order methodically to concentrate man's attitudes on God's will. The Confucian ethic intentionally left people

in their personal relations as naturally grown or given by relations of social super- and subordination. Confucianism hallowed
alone those human obligations of piety created by inter-human
relations, such as prince and servant, higher and lower official,
father and son, brother and brother, teacher and pupil, friend
and friend. Puritan ethic, however, rather suspected these purely
personal relationships as pertaining to the creatural; but Puritanism, of course, did allow for their existence and ethically controlled them so far as they were not against God. The relation to
God had precedence in all circumstances. Overly intensive idolatrous relations of men *per se* were by all means to be avoided.
Trust in men, and precisely in those closest to one by nature,
would endanger the soul. Thus, the Calvinist Duchess Renate
d'Este might curse her next of kin if she knew them rejected by
God through arbitrary predestination. From this, very important
practical differences of the two ethical conceptions resulted even
though we shall designate both of them as rationalist in their
practical turn of mind and although both of them reached
"utilitarian" conclusions. These differences did not alone result
from the autonomy of the laws of political structures. In part
the cohesion of the sibs was an essential result of forms of
political and economic organization which were themselves tied
to personal relations. To a striking degree they lacked rational
matter-of-factness, impersonal rationalism, and the nature of an
abstract, impersonal, purposive association. True "communities"
were absent, especially in the cities, because there were no
economic and managerial forms of association or enterprise
which were purely purposive. Almost none of these originated[3]
from purely Chinese roots. All communal action there remained
engulfed and conditioned by purely personal, above all, by
kinship relations. This applied also to occupational associations.
Whereas Puritanism objectified everything and transformed it
into rational enterprise, dissolved everything into the pure business relation, and substituted rational law and agreement for
tradition, in China, the pervasive factors were tradition, local
custom, and the concrete personal favor of the official. Another

factor seems still more important. In conjunction with the tremendous density of population in China, a calculating mentality
and self-sufficient frugality of unexampled intensity developed
under the influence of worldly-minded utilitarianism and belief
in the value of wealth as a universal means of moral perfection.
The Chinese shopkeeper haggled for and reckoned with every
penny, and he daily counted over his cash receipts. Reliable
travelers reported that the conversation of the native Chinese
was about money and money affairs, apparently to an extent
seldom found elsewhere. But it is very striking that out of this
unceasing and intensive economic ado and the much bewailed
crass "materialism" of the Chinese, there failed to originate on
the economic plane those great and methodical business conceptions which are rational in nature and are presupposed by
modern capitalism. Such conceptions have remained alien to
China, except, for instance, in Canton where past or present
foreign influence and the incessant advance of occidental capitalism have taught them to the Chinese.

In the past, especially in times of political division, political
capitalism arose independently in the form of usury connected
with office, emergency loans, wholesale trade and industrial
ergasteria. This Chinese political capitalism was comparable to
the capitalism of late Antiquity, Egypt, and Islam. Recently
there has also been the usual dependency upon the merchant and
buyer. In general, however, the Chinese lacked the strict organization of the *sistema domestico,* such as existed even during the
late Middle Ages in the Occident. But in spite of the rather
intensive internal and, for a time at least, considerable foreign
trade, there existed no bourgeois capitalism of the modern or
even late Medieval type. There were no rational forms of late
Medieval and scientific European capitalist enterprise in industry,
and no formation of capital in the European manner. Chinese
capital, which took part in exploiting modern opportunities, was
predominantly the capital of mandarins; hence, it was capital
accumulated through extortionist practices in office. There was
no rational method of organized enterprise in the European

fashion, no truly rational organization of commercial news services, no rational money system—the development of the money economy did not even equal that of Ptolemean Egypt. There were only beginnings of legal institutions and these compare with our law of firms, of commercial companies, of checks, bonds, shares. (These beginnings were characterized essentially by their technical imperfection.) The numerous technical inventions were little used for economic purposes.[4] Finally, there was no genuine, technically valuable system of commercial correspondence, accounting, or bookkeeping.

Thus, we meet with conditions very similar to those of Mediterranean Antiquity, though in consequence of the pacification of the empire slavery was insignificant. In some respects, however, these conditions were even more remote from the "spirit" of modern capitalism and its institutions than those of Antiquity. In spite of all the heresy trials, there was extensive religious tolerance, at least compared to the intolerance of Calvinist Puritanism. Peace existed and there was a far reaching freedom of commodity trade, freedom of mobility, freedom of occupational choice and methods of production. There was no tabooing whatsoever of the shopkeeper spirit. All of this has not favored the rise of modern capitalism in China. In this typical land of profiteering, one may well see that by themselves neither "acquisitiveness," nor high and even exclusive esteem for wealth, nor utilitarian "rationalism" have any connection as yet with modern capitalism. The Chinese petty and middle class business man, as well as the big business man who adhered to the old tradition, ascribed success and failure, like the Puritan, to divine powers. The Chinese, however, ascribed them to the Taoistic god of wealth. For him success and failure in business were not symptomatic of a state of grace but of magically and ceremonially significant merit or offense, and compensation was sought in terms of ritually "good" works. The Chinese lacked the central, religiously determined, and rational method of life which came from within and which was characteristic of the classical Puritan. For the latter, economic success was not an ultimate goal or end in itself

but a means of proving one's self. The Chinese did not deliberately cut himself off from the impressions and influences of
the "world"—a world which the Puritan sought to control, just
as he did himself, by means of a definite and one-sided rational
effort of will. The Puritan was taught to suppress the petty acquisitiveness which destroys all rational, methodical enterprise
—an acquisitiveness which distinguishes the conduct of the
Chinese shopkeeper. Alien to the Confucian was the peculiar
confinement and repression of natural impulse[5] which was
brought about by strictly volitional and ethical rationalization
and ingrained in the Puritan.

For the Confucian the pruning of freely expressed and original
impulse was of a different nature. The watchful self-control of
the Confucian was to maintain the dignity of external gesture
and manner, to keep "face." This self-control was of an aesthetic
and essentially negative nature. Dignified deportment, in itself
devoid of definite content, was esteemed and desired. The equally
vigilant self-control of the Puritan had as its positive aim a
definitely qualified conduct and, beyond this, it had as an inward
aim the systematic control of one's own nature which was regarded as wicked and sinful. The consistent Pietist would take
inventory, a sort of bookkeeping practiced daily even by such
an *Epigonus* as Benjamin Franklin, for the supra-mundane, omniscient God saw the central internal attitude. However, the world
to which the Confucian adjusted merely observed the graceful
gesture. The Confucian gentleman, striving simply for dignified
bearing, distrusted others as generally as he believed others distrusted him. This distrust handicapped all credit and business
operations and contrasted with the Puritan's trust, especially
his economic trust in the absolutely unshakable and religiously
determined righteousness of his brother in faith. Faced with the
creatural wickedness of the world and of man, especially of
those in high places, this confidence just sufficed to prevent his
profoundly realistic and thoroughly unrespecting pessimism from
becoming a blockage to the credit indispensable for capitalist
commerce. It merely caused him to assess soberly the objective

external and internal ability of the partner, to take stock of the constancy of motives indispensable for business according to the adage "honesty is the best policy."

The Confucian's word was a beautiful and polite gesture as an end in itself; the Puritan's word was an impersonal and businesslike communication, short and absolutely reliable: "Yea, yea; Nay, nay: for whatsoever is more than these cometh of evil."

The thriftiness of the Confucian was narrowly circumscribed by the status proprieties of the gentleman. The excessive thrift found in the mystically determined humility of Lao-tzu and some other Taoists was fought by the Confucian school. Thrift, for the Chinese petty bourgeois classes, meant hoarding. This was fundamentally comparable to the peasant's way of hoarding wealth in his stocking. It served to safeguard burial rites and good name, honor and enjoyment of possession *per se*, as is usual where asceticism has not yet broken the enjoyment of wealth.

For the Puritan, however, possessions were as great a temptation as they were for the monk. Like the income of monasteries, his income was a secondary result and symptom of successful asceticism. John Wesley said: "We have no choice but to recommend that men be pious, and that means," as an unavoidable effect, "getting rich." But obviously the dangerous nature of riches for the pious individual was the same as it had been for the monasteries. Wesley expressly focused upon the observed and apparent paradox between the rejection of the world and acquisitive virtuosity.

For the Confucian, as a statement handed down by the Master expressly teaches, wealth was the most important means for a virtuous, i.e., dignified life and for the ability to dedicate oneself to self-perfection. Hence inquiry as to means of improving men was answered by, "enrich them," for only a rich man could live according to rank and station. However, for the Puritan, income was an unintended result, an important symptom of virtue. The expenditure of wealth for purposes of personal consumption easily constituted idolatrous surrender to the world. Confucius might not disdain the acquisition of riches but wealth seemed insecure and could upset the equilibrium of the genteel soul. Thus, all truly economic and vocational work was the Philistine activity of expert professionals. For the Confucian, the specialistic expert could not be raised to truly positive dignity, no matter what his social usefulness. The decisive factor was that the "cultured man" (gentleman) was "not a tool"; that is, in his adjustment to the world and in his self-perfection he was an end unto himself, not a means for any functional end. This core of Confucian ethics rejected professional specialization, modern expert bureaucracy, and special training; above all, it rejected training in economics for the pursuit of profit.

To this "idolatrous" maxim Puritanism contrasts the task of proving oneself in vocational life and in the special functions of the world. The Confucian was the man of literary education, more precisely the man of bookish education, a man of scripture in the highest form. Confucianism was as foreign to the Hellenic valuation and development of speech and conversation as it was to the energy of rational action in military or economic affairs. Though they did so with differential intensity most Puritan denominations opposed philosophic literary education since it conflicted with an indispensable grounding in the Bible. The Bible was cherished as a sort of book of statutes and a managerial doctrine. Thus, philosophical literary education, the highest ornament of the Confucian, was, for the Puritan, an idle waste of time and a danger to religion. Scholasticism and dialectics, Aristotle and his derivatives, were a horror and a menace to the Puritan; thus Spener, for instance, preferred mathematically-founded Cartesian rational philosophy. Useful and naturalist knowledge, especially empirical knowledge of natural sciences, geographical orientation as well as the sober clarity of a realist mind and specialized expert knowledge were first cultivated as planned educational ends by Puritans—in Germany particularly by Pietist circles.

S··· ˡ ⁻ wledge was the only avenue to knowledge of God's e providence embodied in His creation. On the other nowledge served as a means of rationally mastering the world in one's vocation and it enabled one to do one's duty in honor of God. Hellenism and, essentially also, the Renaissance at its height were equally distant from both Confucianism and Puritanism. The indispensable ethical qualities of the modern capitalist entrepreneur were: radical concentration on God-ordained purposes; the relentless and practical rationalism of the asceticist ethic; a methodical conception of matter-of-factness in business management; a horror of illegal, political, colonial, booty, and monopoly types of capitalism which depended on the favor of princes and men as against the sober, strict legality and the harnessed rational energy of routine enterprise; the rational calculation of the technically best way, of practical solidity and expediency instead of the traditionalist enjoyment of transmitted skill or the beauty of product characteristic of the old artisan craftsman. This must be added to the pious worker's special will for work. The relentlessly and religiously systematized utilitarianism peculiar to rational asceticism, to live "in" the world and yet not be "of" it, has helped to produce superior rational aptitudes and therewith the spirit of the vocational man which, in the last analysis, was denied to Confucianism. That is to say, the Confucian way of life was rational but was determined, unlike Puritanism, from without rather than from within. The contrast can teach us that mere sobriety and thriftiness combined with acquisitiveness and regard for wealth were far from representing and far from releasing the "capitalist spirit," in the sense that this is found in the vocational man of the modern economy.

The typical Confucian used his own and his family's savings in order to acquire a literary education and to have himself trained for the examinations. Thus he gained the basis for a cultured status position. The typical Puritan earned plenty, spent little, and reinvested his income as capital in rational capitalist enterprise out of an asceticist compulsion to save. "Rationalism" —and this is our second lesson—was embodied in the spirit of both ethics. But only the Puritan rational ethic with its supramundane orientation brought economic rationalism to its consistent conclusion. This happened merely because nothing was further from the conscious Puritan intention. It happened because inner-worldly work was simply expressive of the striving for a transcendental goal. The world, as promised, fell to Puritanism because the Puritans alone "had striven for God and his justice." In this is vested the basic difference between the two kinds of rationalism. Confucian rationalism meant rational adjustment to the world; Puritan rationalism meant rational mastery of the world. Both the Puritan and the Confucian were "sober men." But the rational sobriety of the Puritan was founded in a mighty enthusiasm which the Confucian lacked completely; it was the same enthusiasm which inspired the monk of the Occident. The rejection of the world by occidental asceticism was insolubly linked to its opposite, namely, its eagerness to dominate the world. In the name of a supra-mundane God the imperatives of asceticism were issued to the monk and, in variant and softened form, to the world. Nothing conflicted more with the Confucian ideal of gentility than the idea of a "vocation." The "princely" man was an aesthetic value; he was not a tool of a god. But the true Christian, the other-worldly and inner-worldly asceticist, wished to be nothing more than a tool of his God; in this he sought his dignity. Since this is what he wished to be he was a useful instrument for rationally transforming and mastering the world.

The Chinese in all probability would be quite capable, probably more capable than the Japanese, of assimilating capitalism which has technically and economically been fully developed in the modern culture area. It is obviously not a question of deeming the Chinese "naturally ungifted" for the demands of capitalism. But compared to the Occident, the varied conditions which externally favored the origin of capitalism in China did not suffice to create it. Likewise capitalism did not originate in occidental or oriental Antiquity, or in India, or where Islamism held sway. Yet in each of these areas different and favorable circumstances seemed to facilitate its rise. Many of the circumstances which could or had to hinder capitalism in China

similarly existed in the Occident and assumed definite shape in
the period of modern capitalism. Thus, there were the patrimonial
traits of occidental rulers, their bureaucracy, and the fact that
the money economy was unsettled and undeveloped. The money
economy of Ptolemaic Egypt was carried through much more
thoroughly than it was in fifteenth or sixteenth century Europe.
Circumstances which are usually considered to have been obstacles to capitalist development in the Occident had not existed
for thousands of years in China. Such circumstances as the fetters
of feudalism, landlordism and, in part also, the guild system were
lacking there. Besides, a considerable part of the various trade-
restricting monopolies which were characteristic of the Occident
did not apparently exist in China. Also, in the past, China knew
time and again the political conditions arising out of preparation
for war and warfare between competing states. In ancient Babylon and in Antiquity, there were conditions conducive to the rise
of political capitalism which the modern period also shares with
the past. It might be thought that modern capitalism, interested
in free trading opportunity, could have gained ground once the
accumulation of wealth and profit from political sources became
impossible. This is perhaps comparable to the way in which,
in recent times, North America has offered the freest space for
the development of high capitalism in the almost complete absence of organization for war.

Political capitalism was common to occidental Antiquity until
the time of the Roman emperors, to the Middle Ages, and to the
Orient. The pacification of the Empire explains, at least indirectly,
the non-existence of political capitalism but it does not explain
the non-existence of modern capitalism in China. To be sure
the basic characteristics of the "mentality," in this case the practical attitudes toward the world, were deeply co-determined by
political and economic destinies. Yet, in view of their autonomous
laws, one can hardly fail to ascribe to these attitudes effects
strongly counteractive to capitalist development.

NOTES

I. City, Prince and God

1. The great central works of classical Chinese literature will not be cited separately when reference is made to a passage. They have been translated and edited with textual criticism by J. Legge in the series *Chinese Classics*. Some of them have been incorporated in Max Mueller's *Sacred Books of the East*.

The most convenient introduction to the personal or (what here amounts to the same thing) presumably personal views of Confucius and his authoritative disciples may well be the three writings which Legge has edited with an introduction, the small volume entitled *The Life and Teachings of Confucius* (London, 1867). They comprise the *Lun Yü* (translated as *Confucian Analects*), the *Ta Hsüeh (The Great Learning)*, and the *Chung Yung (Doctrine of the Mean)*. In addition there are the famous annals of Lu *(Ch'un Ch'iu: "Spring and Autumn Annals")*. For translations of Mencius' writings see *Sacred Books of the East* and Faber, *The Mind of Mencius*. The *Tao Teh Ching* has appeared in many translations. The German translation by v. Strauss (1870) is masterly and an English translation by Carus appeared in 1913. Meanwhile, von Wilhelm has edited a good selection of Chinese mystics and philosophers (Diederichs, Jena). Of late, a preoccupation with Taoism has become almost fashionable. The older popularizing work of Williams, *The Midden Empire,* is still a useful introductory treatise on political and social conditions. Then there is von Richthofen's grandiose and predominantly geographical work which on the side takes these conditions into consideration. Otto Franke gives an excellent sketch in *Die Kultur der Gegenwart* (II, II, 1) along with bibliography. [Franke's unfinished *magnum opus Geschichte des Chinesischen Reiches, Eine Darstellung seiner Entstehung, seines Wesens und seiner Entwicklung bis zur Neuesten Zeit* 3 vols. appeared at Berlin-Leipzig in 1930, 1936, 1937. The first two volumes include the rise of the Han empire and the establishment of the Confucian state; the third volume (pp. 576) contains annotations, supplements and corrections to vols. I and II, as well as indices of subject matter and names. Ed.]

For literature on the Chinese city see H. Plath, "Ueber die Verfassung und Verwaltung Chinas unter den drei ersten Dynastien," *Abhandlungen der Koeniglichen Bayrischen Akademie der Wissen-*

schaften, 1865, I. Cl. X, Abt. 2, p. 453 ff. The best work thus far on the economic life of a (modern) Chinese city is that of a disciple of Karl Buecher, Dr. Nyok Ching Tsur, "Die gewerblichen Betriebsformen der Stadt Ningpo," *Zeitschrift fuer die Gesamte Staatswissenschaft,* Supplement 30 (Tuebingen, 1909).

For ancient Chinese religion (so-called "Sinism") see E. Chavannes, *Revue de l'Histoire des Religions,* vol. 34, p. 125 ff. For the religion and ethic of Confucianism and Taoism, commendable are Dvořak's two treatises in *Darstellungen aus dem Gebiet der nichtchristlichen Religionsgeschichte.* For the rest, see Wilhelm Grube, "Die Religion der alten Chinesen" *Religionsgeschichtliches Lesebuch,* A. Bertholet ed., (Tübingen, 1908) pp. 1-69 and Buckeley on China in *Lehrbuch der Religionsgeschichte,* Chantepie de La Saussaye ed., 3rd ed. (Tuebingen, 1904). At present [in 1920 Ed.] de Groot's great work on the official religion is outstanding.

Cf. his main work, *The Religious System of China* (dealing thus far mainly with ritual, especially with the rites of death). De Groot gives a comprehensive survey of the religious systems of China in *Kultur der Gegenwart.* For the tolerance of Confucianism, see his spirited polemical treatise "Sectarianism and Religious Persecution in China," *Verh. der Kon. Ak. van Wetensch. te Amsterdam,* Afd. letterk. N. Reeks, IV, I, 2. For the history of religious affairs see his essay in vol. VII of the *Archiv fuer Religionswissenschaft* (1904). See also the review of Pelliot in the *Bulletin de l'École française de l'Extrême Orient,* vol. III (1903), p. 105. Concerning Taoism see Pelliot, *loc. cit.* p. 317. Concerning the sacred edict of the founder of the Ming dynasty (the precedent for the "sacred edict" of 1671) see Chavannes, *Bulletin de l'École francaise de l'Extrême Orient* vol. III (1903), p. 549 ff.

For a presentation of the Confucian doctrine from the viewpoint of the modern reform party of K'ang Yu-wei see Chen Huan-chang, *The Economic Principles of Confucius and His School* (Doctoral thesis, Columbia University, New York, 1911).

The impact of the various religious systems on style of life is elucidated in Wilhelm Grube's beautiful essay "Zur Pekinger Volkskunde," *Veroeffentlichungen aus dem Koeniglichen Museum fuer Voelkerkunde* (Berlin, vol. VII, 1901). Cf. also Grube's "Religion und Kultur der Chinesen, Ueber chinesische Philosophie," *Kultur und Gegenwart,* I, 5. Grube, *Geschichte der chinesischen Literatur* (Leipzig, 1902).

From the missionary literature see Jos. Edkins, *Religion in China* (3rd ed. 1884). It is rather valuable because it reproduces numerous conversations. Douglas' *Society in China* contains some valuable material. For further literature one has to peruse the great and well-known English, French and German periodicals, as well as the *Zeitschrift fuer vergleichende Rechtswissenschaft* and the *Archiv fuer Religionswissenschaft*.

For a descriptive introduction of modern Chinese conditions see Freiherr von Richthofen's *Tagebuecher aus China* and the books by Lauterer, Lyall, Navarra and others. Concerning Taoism cf. the notes to Chapter VII below.

For a modern history of ancient China see A. Conrady in *Weltgeschichte* ed. by Pflugk-Harttung (Berlin, 1911), vol. III, pp. 459-567. The new work of de Groot, *Universismus, Die Grundlage der Religion und Ethik, des Staatswesens und der Wissenschaft Chinas* (Berlin, 1918), came to my attention only when this book was in press. Among short introductory sketches we wish especially to refer to a small brochure by one of the best experts, Freiherr von Rosthorn, *Das soziale Leben der Chinesen* (1919). Of the older similar literature we should name J. Singer's *Ueber soziale Verhaeltnisse in Ostasien* (1888).

More instructive than many a book is the study of the collection of imperial decrees. Originally intended for internal administrative use, these have interested Englishmen for decades and have been translated under the title of *Peking Gazette*. Further literature and translated sources are cited below.

Only a small portion of the documentary sources and inscriptions have been translated and that is a great handicap for the non-sinologist. Unfortunately, I did not have an expert sinologist to cooperate on the text or check it. For that reason the volume is published with misgivings and with the greatest reservation.

2. This is also the conclusion of H. B. Morse in *The Trade and Administration of the Chinese Empire* (New York, 1908), p. 74. Basic facts which justify the judgment are: the absence of excise taxes and all taxes on mobile wealth, very low custom tariffs until modern times, and a grain policy which was handled exclusively from the point of consumption. Furthermore, given the nature of officialdom, the wealthy trader could actually have his own way—for money.

3. The transition to this system, which corresponded to our bank currency as exemplified by the Hamburg Bank, was only brought about through the emperors' debasement of coinage and paper issues. Hence the transition is secondary. The report and imperial decree published by the *Peking Gazette* of 2 June, 1896, demonstrate the essential confusion which could be produced even in recent times by a sudden contraction of copper money at a given place. It led to the increased issue of local bank notes and resulted in agio differences and speculation in bullion silver. Moreover, government intervention was completely inept. For the best presentation of currency conditions see H. B. Morse, *The Trade and Administration of the Chinese Empire*, (New

York, 1908), Chapter V, p. 119 ff. Cf. also J. Edkins, *Banking and Prices in China* (1905). From ancient Chinese literature we may refer to Ssu-ma Ch'ien (Se Ma Tsien), Chavannes ed., vol. III, Chapter XXX.

4. The term for money is *huo,* means of exchange. *Pu huo* means valuable means of exchange.

5. Besides the chapter in H. B. Morse, *op. cit.,* and Jos. Edkins, *Chinese Currency* (London 1913) see the publication of Biot, *Journal Asiatique* (3rd Série, vol. 3, 1837) which is still useful. Biot relies essentially on the authority of Ma Tuan-lin. The New York doctoral thesis of W. P. Wei, "The Currency Problem in China," *Studies in History, Economics,* etc. No. 59 (1914), the first chapter of which contains some material, came to my attention only during proofreading.

6. With every earthquake geomantic superstition (discussed below) led to the suppression of mining operations. But it is a ridiculous exaggeration for Biot, *loc. cit.,* to compare these mines to those of Potosi. Richthofen definitely settled this issue. The mines in Yunnan reportedly yielded only about 13 million taels from 1811 to 1890, despite the relatively low royalty of 15%. Even in the 16th century (1556) a silver mine was opened at the cost of 30,000 taels which subsequently yielded 28,500 taels. The recurrent prohibitions of lead mining precluded the yield of silver as a by-product. Only during Chinese rule of farther India (Cambodia, Annam) and Burma, which were rich in silver, did the permanent influx of silver increase. Also Western trade via Bokhara, especially during the 13th century, brought an influx of silver for silk exports. Then, again, since the 16th century, trade with Europeans has brought silver. From the Annals, it may be concluded that an important reason for the usually low profitability of the silver mines was the great uncertainty, besides an imperfect technology.

7. Emperor Ch'ien Lung's history of the Ming dynasty reports tremendous corvées for the exploitation of gold mines [*Yu tsiuan tung ki n kang mu,* tr. by Delamarre (Paris, 1865) p. 362]. In the year 1474, 550,000 (?) people were allegedly regimented for such corvées.

8. According to Weil, *loc. cit.* p. 17, minting profits are said to have been unknown in early Chinese minting policy. But this is unbelievable since the notoriously tremendous counterfeit minting would not have then been profitable. Besides the Annals expressly report the contrary (see below).

9. Concerning the impact of the *fêng-shui* see *Variétés Sinologiques* No. 2 (H. Havret, "La Province de Ngan Hei," 1893), p. 39.

10. According to a comment of the *Wen hian tong kao,* reproduced by Biot (*Journal Asiatique,* 3rd Série, vol. 6, 1838, p. 278), the coinage of the entire country under Yuan Ti (48-30 B.C.) is supposed to

have been estimated at 730,000 *yüan* at 10,000 *ch'ien* (copper coins) of which 330,000 were held by the state (!). Ma Tuan-lin considers this amount to be low.

11. The Annals (Ma Tuan-lin) state that copper, at that time by weight, was 1,840 times more valuable than grain (other sources state 507 times as much), whereas under the Han copper was allegedly 1 to 8 times more valuable than rice. In Rome, too, during the last century of the Republic, the exchange rate of wheat was surprising.

12. The *"p'ien-ch'ien"* paper money of the 10th century was redeemed by the treasury.

13. The heavy iron money in Szechwan, even in the first century, caused the Guild of the Sixteen to issue certificates *(ch'ao-tzu),* i.e. bank money which later became irredeemable through insolvency.

14. An older Chinese statement of state income from the Annals (Ma Tuan-lin) appeared as follows:

	997 B.C. (in thousands)	1021 A.D. (in thousands)
grain	21,707 *shih*	22,782 *shih*
copper coins	4,656 *kuan* (1,000 *ch'ien* each)	7,364 *kuan*
heavy silk goods	1,625 *p'i* (pieces)	1,615 *p'i*
light silk goods	273 *p'i*	181 *p'i*
silk thread	1,410 ounces	902 ounces
gauze (very fine silk)	5,170 ounces	3,995 ounces
tea	490 pounds	1,668 pounds
hay, fresh and dried .	30,000 *shih*	28,995 *shih*
fire wood	280 *shou*	?
coal	530 *sheng*	26 *sheng*
iron	300 pounds	. . .

In addition in 997 B.C.: items for arrow wood, goose feathers (for arrows) and vegetables.

However, in 1021 A.D.: items for leather (816,000 *sheng*), hemp (370,000 pounds), salt (577,000 *shih*), paper (123,000 *sheng*).

In 1077 A.D.: the year of the monetary and monopolistic trade reform of Wang An-shih (see below).

silver	60,137	ounces
copper	5,585,819	*kuan*
grain	18,202,287	*shih*
heavy silk material	2,672,323	*p'i*
silk thread and light materials . . .	5,847,358	ounces
hay	16,754,844	*shou*

To this is added a mixture of items such as tea, salt, cheese, bran, wax, oil, paper, iron, coal, safflower, leather, hemp, etc., which the annalist, for no clear reason, states in terms of total weight (3,200,253 lbs.). As regards grains, one figured 1½ *shih* to be the monthly per capita allowance (the *shih*, however, varied considerably in size). The silver income on the last balance, which is absent in the two first ones is to be explained either as the result of the trade monopoly, or as a result of the tax collectors having continued to figure copper money in silver, or because the latter account states net receipts, the former supposed receipts (?).

In contrast, the first account of the Ming dynasty in 1360 shows only three items:

grain .... 29,433,350 *shih*
money (in copper and paper) ... 450,000 ounces (of silver)
silk materials .... 288,546 pieces

This means a considerable increase in the silver horde and an elimination of the numerous, specified taxes in kind, which at that time obviously figured only in the budgets of the provinces where the receipts were spent. Not much can be done with these figures because the initial deductions cannot be ascertained.

From 1795 to 1810 the central government received 4.21 million *shih* of grain (of 120 Chinese pounds each). This was accompanied by a considerable increase, both relative and absolute, in the silver receipts, facilitated by the strongly active balance of Chinese trade with the West after the godsend of American silver. (Recent developments are of no interest here.)

According to the Annals, in olden times it was customary to demand tax deliveries of increasingly valuable goods with increasing distance from the capital; less valuable goods were required from the environs of the capital. [For the above figures see Biot, *op. cit.* pp. 315, 316, 319, 330. A few obvious mistakes in the German edition have been corrected. Ed.]

15. This happened, for instance, in 689 A.D., according to Ma Tuan-lin.

16. Cf. the export of grain in 683 A.D. to Japan which then had a copper standard.

17. According to the Annals this happened, for instance, in 702 A.D.

18. For the first time in 780 A.D.

19. During the eighth century the minting masters argued that 1,000 units of copper transformed into works of art (vases) were equivalent to 3,600 units and, thus, that the industrial use of copper was more profitable than its monetary use.

20. In 817, and often since that time, no more than 5,000 *kuan* (of 1,000 *ch'ien* each) were allowed. Time limits on the sale of surplus copper holdings were stipulated according to their size.

21. Apparently this was first used for the official seals. After Shi Huang Ti it became the external mark of the transition from feudalism to the patrimonial state.

22. Thus in 1155 the Tatarian rulers of Northern China demanded 1½ percent.

23. This happened even in 1107. The notes were devalued to one hundredth of their face value by inflation.

24. Thus, in 1111, when paper money was issued for the frontier war.

25. This was the regular form which, initially, had also been recommended by interested traders. These notes were in the nature of treasury bills.

26. Old or worn paper issues occasionally were exchanged at only 1/10 to 1/3 of their face value.

27. Even in 1107, because of the war against the Tartars, one half of every payment of sums over 10,000 *ch'ien* had to be paid in paper. This often happened.

28. Marco Polo's description cannot be accepted. A 3% deduction on the worn notes turned in and exchanged for new (paper!) notes and the issue of gold and silver for notes upon anybody's request is impossible. This remains so even were one to understand Marco Polo to mean—which the text would permit—that the industrial purpose had to be stated. Marco Polo also reports the compulsory sale of precious metal for notes.

29. By the middle of the 19th century the ratio allegedly dropped from 500:1 to 1100:1.

30. J. Edkins, *Chinese Currency* (1890), p. 4.

31. The prebends of the officials of the Ch'in and Han were graded in sixteen classes of partly fixed sums of money and partly fixed payments in rice, as stated by Chavannes in vol. II, Appendix I of his edition of Ssu-ma Ch'ien. To be refused the privilege of offering sacrificial meat as payment in kind was considered a sign of imperial disfavor. This happened, for instance, to Confucius, according to Ssu-ma Ch'ien's biography. To be sure, documents containing pure pecuniary accounts were to be met with in what was then Chinese Turkestan.

32. Stone construction replaced wood construction during the fourth century B.C. Earlier the stockaded capitals were removed frequently and easily.

33. L. Gaillard's S. J.'s work on Nanking does not yield much knowl-

edge of Chinese urbanism. Cf. *Variétés Sinologiques,* vol. 23 (Shanghai, 1903).

34. We shall discuss below the great significance of the Chinese guilds. Their differences, which form a contrast to the West, as well as the reasons for these differences, will be clarified. The significance of the guilds is even more striking because their economic control and their social power over the individual were far more extensive than in the Occident.

35. Naturally, also in China, it was far from the case that every urban resident maintained connection with the ancestral shrine of his native place.

36. The god of wealth was considered the universal city god in the official pantheon.

37. On the Chinese city cf. Eugene Simon, *La Cité Chinoise* (Paris, 1885, lacking conciseness).

38. The honorary official (Giles calls him "headborough"), who was responsible to the government for the peace of a place, otherwise merely forwarded petitions and acted as a notary. He had a (wooden) seal but was not considered an official and he ranked below the lowliest mandarin in the locality. Cf. H. A. Giles, *China and the Chinese* (New York, 1912), p. 77.

Besides, there was not a special municipal tax but rather governmentally prescribed contributions for schools, charities, and water service.

39. Peking consisted of five administrative districts.

40. To be sure, the compass was mainly used for inland traffic.

41. Cf. Plath, *China vor 4,000 Jahren* (Muenchen, 1869), p. 125.

42. According to the tradition, Shih Huang Ti for instance ordered a compulsory *synœcism* of the 120,000 (?) wealthiest families of the entire country to his residence. Emperor Ch'ien Lung's chronicle of the Ming dynasty reports synœcisms of wealthy people to Peking in 1403. Cf. *Yu tsiuan tung kian kang mu, op. cit.,* p. 150.

43. See H. B. Morse, *The Gilds of China* (London, 1909). From the older literature see MacGowan "Chinese Guilds," *Journal of the North China Branch of the Royal Asiatic Society,* 1888/9, and Hunter, *Canton Before Treaty Days 1821-44* (London, 1882).

44. The guild of the goldbeaters from Ningpo in Wenchow denied guild membership and teaching of the craft to those who were native born. This emphasizes the derivation from the inter-ethnic specialization of tribal crafts.

45. Cf. the above mentioned instance of Ningpo which has numerous parallels.

46. Cf. footnote 41 above.

47. Under the Chou dynasty the personal God of Heaven, with his six dignitaries beside him, was allegedly replaced in the cult by the impersonal expressions of "Heaven and Earth," as Legge also assumes. (Cf. *Shu Ching, Prolegomena,* p. 193 ff.) The spirit of the emperor and the spirits of those among his vassals who were of good conduct proceeded to heaven. There the spirit could appear in order to give warnings. (Legge, p. 238.) There was no hell.

48. The instability of this development toward impersonalism is shown, for instance, in a curse inscribed in the year 312 by the King of Ch'in' against the hostile King of Ch'u, who had allegedly violated moral codes and broken a contract. As witnesses and avengers the King of Ch'in called upon 1. Heaven, 2. the ruler on high (hence, a personal God of Heaven), 3. the spirit of a river (where presumably the contract had been concluded). Cf. the inscription in Appendix III, vol. II of Chavannes' edition of Ssu-ma Ch'ien and Chavannes in the *Journal Asiatique,* May-June, 1893, p. 473 f.

49. Cf. the excellent Leipzig doctoral thesis (1913) of M. Quistorp (a disciple of Conrady) "Maennergesellschaft und Altersklassen im alten China," *Mitteilungen des Seminars für Orientalische Sprachen,* vol. XVIII (1915), p. 1 ff. Only an expert could judge whether totemism has ever prevailed in China, as Conrady assumes. [Otto Franke, after having examined the sources and the literary controversy, concludes that there is evidence enough of totemist survivals up to the twelfth century. "Today they have vanished." *Op. cit.* vol. III, p. 377. See also vol. I, p. 74; vol. II, 403; vol. III, pp. 51, 311, 375 ff. See also Chapter IV, footnote 3, below. Ed.]

50. Quistorp, *op. cit.* finds traces in certain rudimentary mythologies of Lao-tzu.

51. [Otto Franke has documented and greatly enlarged on this comparison. He cites Boniface's bull *Unam sanctam* of 1302 "as demonstrating quite clearly the identity of traits which characterize the Catholic world-church and Chinese universal state." *Op. cit.,* vol. III, p. 104. Cf. also vol. I, 120 ff., 161; vol. III, p. 83 f., 167. Ed.]

52. Hou T'u, one of the six ministers of Emperor Huang Ti, was deified under the name "Genius of the Earth" (Cf. *Schih Luh Kiang Yuh Tschi, Histoire Géographique des XVI Royaumes,* translated and edited with annotations by Michels (Paris, 1891, p. LII, fn. 215). According to this, a chthonian cult could hardly have yet existed or such a title would have been blasphemy.

53. The source of "universalism" in the idea of Tao obviously rested in this very fusion. The idea has been elaborated into a cosmic system of analogies with far greater sophistication than were the Babylonian

concepts derived from the inspection of the liver, not to mention the "metaphysical" ideas of ancient Egypt. For a philosophical interpretation see Chapter VII below and the detailed discussion in de Groot's beautiful book on *Universismus, op. cit.*, a systematic treatise which does not explore the question of origin. But the chronomantic interpretation of calendar making and of the calendar *per se* is obviously secondary. Likewise secondary is the absolute stereotyping of the ritual. Connected with both is the rational philosophy of Tao which departed from mysticism and will be discussed below. The oldest calendar (*Hsiah siao cheng*, "small regulator") seems least burdened with such *theologumena*, and was obviously developed after the calendar reform of Shih Huang Ti. Later the government produced a basic text on chronomancy, *Shih hsien shu*, and severely persecuted all private and unauthorized calendar making. The *Shih hsien shu* has often been reprinted as a popular book and provides material to the "day masters," the professional chronomancers. The ancient calendar board of the *la shih* (superior writers) was the historical source for the offices of astronomers (calendar makers) as well as the astrologers (interpreters of portent). It also was a source for the purely exemplary and paradigmatically conceived court annals. Originally the latter was joined with calendar making (see below), the annalists being calendar makers.

54. For the following cf. de Groot, *Religion of the Chinese*, especially p. 33 f., 55 f.

55. This argument was occasionally used to close the ranks to the all too powerful concubines of emperors. Petticoat government was said to mean preponderance of the *Yin* over the *Yang*.

56. According to de Groot's clear and painstakingly accurate presentation of the official cult in his *Universismus*, the following were worshipped:

1. "Heaven," which, however, according to de Groot, appeared at the great sacrificial act as *primus inter pares* among the ancestral spirits of the emperor. 2. Earth ("Empress Earth"). 3. The imperial ancestors, also their cults. 4. *She Chi*, the tutelatory spirit of the soil and the fruits of the field. 5. The sun and the moon. 6. *Shen Nung*, the archegetes of agriculture. 7. The *archegethis* of silk-culture (the sacrifice was given by the empress). 8. The great emperors. However, since 1722, this included all emperors of former dynasties except those who had suffered violent deaths or were overthrown by successful rebellion, for these were indications of the lack of charisma. 9. Confucius and some coryphées of his school. In principle, all of these were worshipped by the emperor in person.

To these were added, 10. The Gods of Rain and of the Winds (*T'ien Shen*) and the Gods of the Mountains, Seas, and Rivers (*Ti Ke*). 11.

Jupiter as the God of the Calendar (the spirit of the great—Jupiter-year). 12. The *archegetes* of the art of healing together with the God of Springtime (which may suggest former chthonian orgies as the source of magical therapy). 13. The God of War (the canonized general Kuan-ti, 2nd-3rd century A.D.). 14. The God of the classical studies (the tutelary god against heresy). 15. The Spirit of the North Pole (canonized in 1651). 16. The God of Fire, *Huo Shen.* 17. The gods of the guns. 18. The gods of the fortresses. 19. "The Holy Mountain of the East." 20. The dragon and water deities, or the deities of building, tile-works and grain storage. 21. The canonized provincial officials. All these were (normally) ministered to by the authorized officials. Eventually, it is clear, almost the entire external machinery of state was canonized. But the supreme sacrifices were obviously offered to impersonal spirits.

57. The *Peking Gazette* contains reams of official requests for such canonizations. There is further correspondence to Catholic procedures in that advancement follows step by step and in accordance with proof of further miracles. Thus, in 1873, a governor reported on the attitude of a "presiding Spirit of the Yellow River" when inundations threatened. Admission of the spirit to the cult was granted, but the motion to bestow an honorific title upon the spirit was left *in suspense* until such time as further merit might be reported. In 1874 (*Peking Gazette*, 17 Dec.), after it had been reported that the procurement of his effigy had brought the threatening flood to a standstill, the spirit received the title. The *Peking Gazette* of 13 July, 1874, carried a motion which would grant recognition to the miraculous power of a temple of the Dragon God in Honan. On 23 May, 1878, a new title of the "Dragon Spirit" was granted (*Peking Gazette* of that date). Likewise, according to the *Peking Gazette* of 4 April, 1883, the authorized officials requested the promotion of a canonized deceased mandarin of the river area, since his spirit had been seen hovering over the water and, in supreme danger, was actively seeking to quiet the water. Similar requests by officials who are very well known in Europe are frequently to be found, among others that of Li Hung-chang in the *Peking Gazette* of 2 December, 1878. On 31 November, 1883, a censor, as *advocatus diaboli,* protested the canonization of a mandarin whose administration had been by no means excellent (cf. *Peking Gazette* of the date).

58. It is impossible to distinguish strictly between "charm" and non-charm in the world of pre-animist and animist ideas. Even ploughing, or any other ordinary act which was a means to an end, was "magic" in the sense of taking into service specific "forces" (later on

"spirits"). Here only sociological distinctions can be made. The possession of extraordinary qualities differentiated the state of ecstasy from that of workaday life, the professional magician from ordinary people. "Extraordinariness," then, was rationalistically transformed into the "supernatural." The artistic craftsman who produced the paraments of the Temple of Yahwe was possessed of the *"ruach"* of Yahwe, just as the medicine man was possessed of the force which qualified him for his accomplishments.

59. This does not suffice as the sole explanation, because otherwise the same development would have occurred in Mesopotamia. It has to be accepted that—as G. Jellinek has already stated on occasion—the centrally important development of the relations between *imperium* and *sacerdotium* has often rested simply on "accidental" historical fates and these we can no longer assess.

60. Therefore, the absence of rain (or of snow) leads to the most spirited discussions and proposals in the circle of court and ritualist officials. The *Peking Gazette,* in such cases, is full of all sorts of magical and remedial proposals. Cf. for instance, the *Peking Gazette* of 11 and 24 June, 1878, during the threatening drought of that year. The *Yamen* (committee) of state astronomers turned to the classical astrological authorities who referred to the coloration of sun and moon, whereupon a member of the Hanlin Academy pointed out that this must have aroused excitement. He demanded that the memorial be publicized but that the still youthful Emperor be protected from the prattle of eunuchs about evil premonitions and even asked that the palace be guarded. For the rest, the Empress Dowagers were to attend to their moral duties, and rain would follow. This report was published with reassuring explanations concerning the way of life of the high ladies and it referred to the rain which, in the meanwhile, had fallen.

Earlier in the same year a "girl angel" (anchoret, deceased in 1469) had been proposed for canonization because she had frequently given aid during famine (*Peking Gazette,* 14 January, 1878). Several similar promotions had occurred previously.

61. This fundamental assertion of Confucian orthodoxy is emphasized repeatedly in numerous imperial edicts, memorials, or proposals of the Hanlin Academy. Thus, the memorial of the Hanlin "professor," which was cited in footnote 60 and will be cited repeatedly below, contains the sentence "It is the practice of virtue alone that can influence the power of Heaven . . ." (See also the following notes.)

62. Tschepe, *op. cit.,* p. 53.

63. The *Peking Gazette* of 6 October, 1899, carried a decree of the Emperor (who had been placed under guardianship by the coup d'état

of the Empress Dowager) in which he bewails his sins as the probable reason for drought. He added that the princes and ministers had burdened themselves with a share of guilt through their incorrect conduct. In the same situation in 1877, the two Empress Dowagers promised to heed the admonition of a censor that they preserve their "reverential attitude," which had already contributed to ending the drought.

64. Cf. the end of footnote 63. In 1894, when a censor had criticized intervention into state affairs as unbecoming to the Empress Dowager (cf. the report of the *Peking Gazette,* 28 December, 1894), he was dismissed from office and condemned to hard labor on the mail roads of Mongolia. This was not because his criticism was *per se* inadmissible, but because it was allegedly based "on mere hearsay," rather than proof. In 1882, a member of the Hanlin Academy knew better how to handle the aims of this energetic woman when he expressed the wish that the Empress Dowager (*Peking Gazette,* 19 August, 1882) devote herself rather to the affairs of government, since the Emperor was still young and tender and since work for the members of the dynasty was best. Otherwise, too, those surrounding the Empress might begin to criticize her guidance.

65. This theory concerning the responsibility of the monarch was, by the way, in opposition to other theories which declared that "vengeance" toward the emperor was not admissible (sixth century B.C.), and that grave (magical) evils would befall anyone who laid hands on a crowned head. (E. H. Parker, *Ancient China Simplified,* London, 1908, p. 308.) The theory, like the whole predominantly pontifical position of the emperor, had simply not always been established. Apparently, there is only one emperor whom the army alone proclaimed a legitimate monarch. But, besides designation, originally acclamation by the "hundred families," that is the great feudal vassals, was undoubtedly the legal prerequisite for successorship to the throne.

66. Wherever Chinese civilization gained a foothold this whole charismatic conception of the prince has permeated. After the Prince of Nan Chao had thrown off the Chinese rule an inscription published by Chavannes (*Journal Asiatique,* 9th Série, vol. 16 [1900], p. 435) states that the king had "a force which contains balance and harmony" (borrowed from the *Chung Yung*), that he had the ability "to cover and to feed" (like Heaven). As signs of his virtue are mentioned "meritorious works" (alliance with Tibet). Like the Chinese model emperor, he sought out and surrounded himself with the "old families" (p. 443). This should be compared with the *Shu Ching*.

67. Cf. footnote 65. Below, mention will have to be made of the fact that the mandarins were considered carriers of magical forces.

II. The Feudal and Prebendal State

1. E. H. Parker, *Ancient China Simplified* (London, 1908), p. 57.

2. See for the data, Fr. Hirth, *The Ancient History of China* (New York, 1908). Translations from the "Bamboo-Annals" are to be found by Biot in the *Journal Asiatique*, 3rd Série, vol. XII, p. 537 ff., XIII, p. 381 ff. The inscriptions on bronze vases and the odes of the *Shu Ching*, as sources for the period from the 18th to the 12th century B.C., are discussed in Frank H. Chalfant, "Early Chinese Writing," *Memoirs of the Carnegie Museum*, vol. IV, No. 1 (Pittsburgh, September, 1906). [Since 1928-29 archaeological work of the *Academia Sinica* (in Peiping) has unearthed a great many objects—turtle shells covered with many characters, urns, tripods, vases, bones, etc. For a discussion of the especially important bronze objects, their material, form, and decoration see H. G. Creel, *"On the Origins of the Manufacture and Decoration of Bronze in the Shang Period,"* Monumenta Serica, vol. I, p. 39 ff. For a discussion of the literature see Otto Franke, *op. cit.*, vol. III, p. 52 ff. Ed.]

3. Cf. Chavannes, *Journal Asiatique*, 14th Série, vol. X (1909), p. 33, note 2.

4. Cf. Kun-Yu *(Discours des Royaumes)*, de Harlez, ed. (Louvain, 1895), pp. II, V, 110.

5. Cf. Ssu-ma Ch'ien's (Se Ma Tsien) biography of Shih Huang Ti (Schi-Hoang-Ti), Chavannes, ed. (1897), p. 139.

6. *Yu tsiuan tung kian kong mu, op. cit.*

7. Chavannes' edition of Ssu-ma Ch'ien II, Appendix I, note 1, p. 526.

8. Ssu-ma Ch'ien's biography of Shih Huang Ti, Chavannes, ed., p. 149, note.

9. *Le Tscheou-li, ou rites des Tscheou*, Tr. by Biot, 2 vols (Paris, 1851). Allegedly, it derives from the government of Ch'eng Wang, 1115-1079 B.C. Only the nucleus of it is believed to be authentic.

10. Designations of the Major Domo, Minister of Agriculture, Master of Ceremonies, Minister of Justice, of War, of Labor as Minister of Heaven, Earth, Spring, Summer, Autumn, Winter are doubtlessly the product of literati. The notion that the budget was determined by the mandarin of Heaven is certainly unhistorical.

11. Ssu-ma Ch'ien has recorded the actual administrative organization of the Ch'in and Han. (Cf. Part II of Chavannes' edition of Ssu-ma Ch'ien, Appendix II.) The *t'ai wei*, as military chief of the generals, was placed beside two viziers (until Emperor Wu). The *tsung sheng*

was chancellor and head of the *missi dominici* and provincial officials. The *fung cheng* was in charge of sacrificial rites. At the same time he was Grand Astrologer, Grand Augur, Grand Physician and—characteristically—responsible for dykes and canals. Then follow the *po she* (literati); the *lang chung ling*, i.e., the superintendent of the palace; the *wei wei*, the commandant of the palace guards; the *t'ai p'u*, chief of the armory, the *t'ing wei*, the minister of justice; the *tien k'o*, chief of the vassals and barbarian princes; the *tsung sheng*, overseer of the imperial family; the *chi su nei shih*, overseer of magazines and hence minister of agriculture and commerce; the *shao fu*, the chief of the imperial household [a "vice-chief," Ed.]. Under the *shao fu* stood: the *shang shu*, a eunuch [the financial administrator of the court, Ed.]; the *shung wei*, the police chief of the capital; the *chiang cho shao fu*, the superintendent of buildings; the *chung she*, overseer of the household of the empress and the successor to the throne; the *nei she*, the prefect of the capital; the *chu chüeh chung wei*, supervisor of the vassals, an office which was later combined with that of the *tien k'o* (see above). In contrast to the rational and hence historically unreliable constructions of the *Chou Li*, this list portrays all the irrationalism of a patrimonial officialdom emerging from the management of the household and the conduct of ritual. Then by accretion came the management of the army, the administration of justice, the control of the irrigation economy, and finally, purely political interests.

12. "Patriarchal" is not to be equated with sultanism, but refers to the patriarchalism of hereditary sib charisma as manifested in a ritualist pontifex. Perhaps the latter originally transmitted his charisma by designating a successor, as the classical books postulate, and only later did his charisma become hereditary.

13. The Annals of Ssu-ma Ch'ien (first century B.C.) have in part been translated and edited by Edouard Chavannes. P. Tschepe (*loc. cit.* p. 7) has described the political development of the feudal states of Chin, Han, Wei, Chou, and Wu on the basis of the Annals. (Tschepe's work is useful despite the unavoidable "Christian" reflections, which often strike us as somewhat naïve.) When Tschepe is quoted alone the reference is to the Chin Annals. In addition, we shall refer to the *"Discours des Royaumes"* which we have repeatedly quoted.

14. For these conditions, see E. H. Parker, *op. cit.*, p. 144 f.

15. Cf. P. A. Tschepe (S. J.), *Histoires du Royaume de Tsin*, 777-207.

16. That is, they were figured per 1,000 consumers of salt in the state of Chin which was the first to be rationalized. This is based on Hirth's interpretation of a paragraph of *Kuan-tzu*. See Hirth's *Ancient History of China* (New York, 1908).

17. By now, statements of E. H. Parker (*op. cit.*, p. 83) seem unacceptable.

18. Of this, more will follow in our discussion of the land tax.

19. Cf. Ssu-ma Ch'ien's tract *"Rites,"* vol. III, Chavannes, ed.

20. Tschepe, *op. cit.*, p. 54.

21. *Ibid.*, p. 66.

22. We cannot discuss here the technical nature of these old "books." Paper is a product which was imported at a much later time. Reading and writing were practiced long before, and doubtlessly long before the time of Confucius. Von Rosthorn's assumption (to be mentioned), that the ritual literature was orally transmitted and hence that the "burning of the books" was a legend apparently is not acknowledged by de Groot, who accepts the latter as fact even in his latest work.

23. The Annals (Tschepe, *op. cit.*, p. 133) contain from a plan for alliance calculations of the military strength of the various states. According to these figures, an area of 1,000 square *li* (1 *li* = 537 meters) could presumably muster 600 chariots, 5,000 horses, and 50,000 men of whom 40,000 were fighters, the rest service troops. An (alleged) tax reform plan from the 12th century B.C. called for 10,000 war chariots from an area of the same size. Analogies from the Middle East lead us to assume that this was several centuries after the introduction of the war chariot.

24. Cf. Tschepe, *op. cit.*, p. 67.

25. During the Period of the Warring States a strong patriotism aroused by the barbarians prevailed in the border states, especially the state of Ch'in. When the king of Ch'in was taken prisoner "2,500" families subscribed the funds for continuing the war. In 112 A.D., a Han emperor, in financial straits, sought such a "cavalier loan"—in Leopoldian Austria a similar attempt was made even in the seventeenth century—but apparently had faint success.

26. Tschepe, *loc. cit.*, p. 142.

27. Both are mentioned in a lecture of one of the literati reproduced by Tschepe, *loc. cit.*, p. 77.

28. *Ibid.*, p. 61.

29. *Ibid.*, p. 59.

30. *Ibid.*, p. 14.

31. *Ibid.*, p. 38.

32. "The nobles and the people preserve their rank and station," says the emperor in an inscription recorded in the Annals (Tschepe, *op cit.*, p. 261). Another inscription distinguishes between "nobles, officials, and people."

33. See the paragraph in Tschepe (to be discussed presently) in

his "Histoire du Royaume de Han," *Variétés Sinologiques,* vol. 31, p. 43 (for the principality of Wei in 407 B.C.).

34. *Ibid.*

35. Tradition has the scholar Li Ssu, the powerful minister of old, state in a memorial the importance of the literati (and generally also, of the foreign-born, including the merchants) for princely power, *ibid.*, p. 231.

36. For instance, the inscription preserved by Ssu-ma Ch'ien in his biography (Chavannes, ed. vol. V, p. 166) states that all conduct contrary to reason is objectionable. Numerous other inscriptions *(ibid.)* praise the rational order, which the Emperor established in the realm. This "rationalism" did not prevent him from sponsoring the search for the elixir of life.

37. This statement of Shih Huang Ti is transmitted in his biography by Ssu-ma Ch'ien (Chavannes, ed. vol. II, p. 162). By the way, the literati ministers of the Warring States, and even Wang An-shih (eleventh century A.D.), were not always disinclined in principle to a similar view.

38. Apparently court eunuchs first appeared during the eighth century B.C.

39. Forced laborers working on the Great Wall reportedly numbered 300,000 (?). Even higher figures are stated for servitude as a whole. To be sure, the Great Wall was erected over long periods of time. The requisite labor might well be estimated since the wall comprises at least 160 million cubic meters of massive structure, according to Elisée Reclus' calculation.

40. The main concern was to furnish the necessary provisions for the soldiers and convicts doing corvée. The annalists (Tschepe *loc. cit.*, p. 275) calculated the costs of transportation to the place of consumption at 18,200% of shipment. Because of consumption on the way only one of 182 loads is said to have reached its destination, which of course may occasionally have been the case.

41. Tschepe, *loc. cit.*, p. 363 f. The eunuch stemmed from a noble family which had previously been convicted.

42. The Annals and especially Ssu-ma Ch'ien in his biography of Shih Huang Ti (Chavannes, ed. vol. II, p. 178), present some data on this attempt. The originator of the plan apparently was "Master Lu," a Taoist, whom Shih Huang Ti had commissioned to search for the herb of life. "True man," it was said, "is hiding himself and does not show himself," which is a special application of certain principles of Lao-tzu, to be discussed below. But Shih Huang Ti actually ruled personally and the complaint of "sages" of all persuasions was that he failed duly to seek their advice (*loc. cit.*, p. 179). The successor Erh Shih

Huang Ti, lived as *"ch'en,"* i.e., as a "hidden man" under the guardian-ship of his favorite and consequently did not receive officials (*ibid.,* p. 266). This was the typical complaint of the Confucians when the Taoists and the eunuchs were in power. Their alliance will be discussed below. Even under the founder of the Han dynasty, the "following," that is the feudal lords, returned to power after the Emperor's down-fall. This happened even though the entire bureaucracy of Shih Huang Ti was retained and even when the literati were restored to influential positions.

43. Tschepe, *op. cit.,* p. 259 f. (allegedly an inscription).

44. *Ibid.,* p. 267 f.

45. *Ibid.,* p. 67. See also the discussion of Yang with the vassals at the court of Prince Hsiao Kung, *ibid.,* p. 118.

46. Characteristic are the figures for the gross income of the treasury as stated by Ma Tuan-lin. Chinese authors ascribe to this their tre-mendous and entirely unmotivated differences (especially during the sixteenth century). (Cf. Biot, *Journal Asiatique,* 3rd Série, vol. 5, 1838, and *ibid.,* vol. 6, 1838, p. 329.) After all, it is obvious what it means if even in 1370, 8.4 million *ch'ing* (equal to 48 million *ha*) of taxable land had been registered, in 1502, however, 4.2 million, in 1542, 4.3 million, but in 1582, again 7 million *ch'ing* (equal to 39.5 million *ha*) were counted. (In 1745, 30 years after the introduction of tax quotas, al-legedly 161.9 million *ha* were counted.)

47. At the end of the *Peking Gazette* for 1879, we find an estimate of the number of living candidates for office who had been promoted to the second civilian degree and hence were fully qualified for office. There are estimates, too, on the average age of the candidates, on whom a maximum quota was fixed for each of the two degrees, and their probable longevity. There are too many, unless the number of promoted candidates of advanced age is quite small; there are too few because the number of transfers from military careers, especially the Manchus, has to be added. Moreover, there were candidates who had purchased their qualification for office. Even assuming 30,000 instead of roughly 21,200 living candidates and assuming a population of 350 millions, there would be but one candidate per 11-12,000 population. In the 18 provinces, including Manchuria, there were only 1,470 ad-ministrative districts of the lowest rank under an independent state official (the *chih hsien*). *Ceteris paribus,* there was roughly one official per 248,000 population. If we include the higher independent offices, which are provided for in the budget, there would be one higher official per 200,000 population. Even were one to add part of the dependent and temporary officials, a ratio would result which would allow Ger-many, e.g., to function with only 1,000 administrative and judicial offi-

cials with second law degrees. Quite different figures result if one extrapolates the family and population figures of the Chinese police. The figures from these materials for the year 1895/6 were placed at the disposal of Sacharov (*Arbeiten der Kaiserlich Russischen Gesandtschaft*, a Christian mission, translated by Abel and Meckenberg, Berlin 1858). According to these figures, in the district of Peking and in two other districts there were resident (hence not employed) in 1845 about 26,500 military and civilian officials; in 1846, 15,866 active officials were provided for in the budget and 23,700 officials were classified as candidates, two hardly reconcilable figures. Obviously not only the holders of second degrees but also the aspirants, and all Manchu officers, are included.

48. For some high officials a breach of this principle was frequently necessary: Li Hung-chang, for instance, remained chief administrator of Chihli for several decades. A single prolongation of three years has been permitted but otherwise the principle has been adhered to rather strictly until now.

49. Often there were as many as six ministers, but the only officials of any importance other than the Viceroy were the provincial governors, judges, and chancellors of the exchequer. The chancellor of the exchequer originally was the sole and highest administrative official, for the governor was a *missus dominicus* (formerly often a eunuch) who ultimately became a resident agent. All departments other than those of finance and justice were unofficial. Even the lowest official (*chien*), whose formal title means "herdsman," had two secretaries—for justice and for finance. His superior, the prefect of the *fu*, retained visible or at least demonstrable functions (the management of waterways, agriculture, studs, grain, shipments, provision of quarters for troops, and general police administration), though his office was considered essentially a supervisory board and a channel of communications to higher offices. The functions of the lowest official, however, were simply encyclopedic in nature, for he was virtually in charge of and responsible for everything. With the large provincial boards special *taotai* were employed for the gabelle, road construction, etc., as in all patrimonial states where special officials may be commissioned and authorized *ad hoc*. Concerning the concept of a "jurist" (knower of precedents) and the legal profession in China, cf. Alabaster, *Notes and Commentaries on Chinese Criminal Law*, which is not available to me now.

50. Its official name was "Canal of the Tribute Transports." Cf. P. Dom. Gandar S.J., "Le Canal Imperial," *Variétés Sinologiques*, No. 4 (Shanghai, 1894).

51. The memoranda and receipts concerning these enterprises are

in part preserved in the documents which Aurel Stein has gathered in Turkestan. In some places the reclamation of dry land advanced three steps daily, cf. Chavannes, *Les Documents Chinois découverts par Aurel Stein dans le sable du Turkestan Oriental* (Oxford, 1913).

52. Cf. Chavannes, *loc. cit.*, p. XI ff.

53. Despite the common assumption, it is quite uncertain whether climatic changes played any part in this. In any event the disintegration of the corvée system would be sufficient explanation, for in these areas land could be kept under cultivation only if the question of "costs" was never raised. With special crops a worker could subsist on this soil but could never extract a full livelihood. Obviously the land was kept under the plough, despite certainly tremendous subsidies, only in order to provision the garrisons and missions with easily perishable goods.

54. P. D. Gandar, S.J., *op. cit.*, p. 35.

55. *Yu tsiuan kian kang mu, op. cit.*, p. 351.

56. See above, p. 330-32, footnote 14, for budgetary accounts of the central government from the 10th, 11th, and 14th century. According to the Annals, the taxes in kind on the whole appeared to be scaled by distance from the capital. Thus, for example, the first zone sent grain with straw, the second only grain, and every following zone sent goods of higher specific value, i.e., embodying more labor. This is quite believable and accords with other reports.

57. Cf. Aurel Stein's findings covering the period 98-137 A.D. (Chavannes, ed., *op. cit.*). The officers receive their military pay in money but it is questionable whether this is also true of the troops (No. 62) though their clothing was at least partly purchased with money (No. 42). Moreover, the book of expenditures of a Buddha temple (of a later time, though) shows a full money economy with the hiring of artisans as wage workers and the recording of all payments in terms of money (*ibid.*, No. 969). Later these practices relapsed.

58. In the year 1883, the imperial factories delivered 405,000 taels worth of silk and porcelain at cost-price to the court (*Peking Gazette,* 23, 24, 27, 30 January; 13, 14 June, 1883). Added to this were the deliveries in kind from the provinces, which at least partly were destined for the court (silk, precious paper, etc.) and partly for political purposes (iron, sulphur, etc.). In 1883, the province of Shansi vainly petitioned for supplementary funds, since the goods to be delivered (except iron) had to be purchased first.

59. On the land tax see Biot's work, which is still useful in many ways. *Journal Asiatique*, 3rd Série, vol. 6 (1838).

60. To be sure, these figures are very unreliable. One has to consider that, before the tax compromise of 1713, the officials were interested in minimizing or fixing the number of taxable subjects (there was

a head tax then). With the fixing of tax quotas this interest subsided (see below). After that, the reverse obtained and it was in the official's interest to boast of big population figures. Since then, only the gods— to whom they were communicated—were interested in these figures. High figures thus proved the charisma of the particular official. Even figures from the 19th century are quite dubious, for instance, the abnormal increase of the population in the province of Szechwan. Still Dudgeon, *On the Population of China* (1895), computes the population figure of the 14 provinces for the 1880's at 325 million.

61. During the last 30 years all schemes for direct taxation have failed, for they would have mainly proposed taxes on the prebends of mandarins. The patrimonial conception of the income of the official comes to preeminence in all the ramifications of mourning his death. According to the ancient meaning, which was preserved in Chinese officialdom with special distinctiveness, mourning was to ward off the wrath and envy of the spirit of the departed toward those who, as heirs, had appropriated his possessions. Disregarding the fact that originally a considerable part of his belongings were to accompany him to Hades (including the widow and other human sacrifices), the heirs had to avoid the dead-house and the touching of his possessions for a long time. Poorly clad, they lived in another hut and abstained from enjoyment of their possessions.

Now, the office being as much valued as a mere prebend and the prebend as much as the mere private possession of the prebendary, a case of death with obligatory mourning unconditionally resulted in retirement from office. The constant and numerous vacancies, the temporary unemployability of numerous officials, and the piling up of candidates who had lost their offices through mourning, constituted a great political calamity. This was especially so during epidemics, hence, for reasons of state the emperors alternately prohibited too greatly extended mournings, or, fearsome of the spirits, they enjoined mournings —both entailing corporal punishment.

Li Hung-chang was sharply though vainly ordered by the Empress Dowager to take a vacation from office, instead of retiring upon the death of his mother (*Peking Gazette*, 1 May, 1882).

62. This is suggestive of the way the American party boss taxes officials whom the elected head of the victorious party has appointed. He does so for his own as well as his party's benefit, the difference being that these taxes are usually fixed.

63. Jamieson, Parker. Cf. the latter's computations and estimates in his *Trade and Administration of the Chinese Empire*, p. 85 ff.

64. This conception is clearly revealed in the rescript reproduced in the *Peking Gazette*, 11 January, 1895. The complaint is that certain

(lower) officials retain the prebends for more than three years and thus deny others "their turn" *("nicht drankommen")*.

65. On the rentier spirit, see for instance, E. H. Parker, *China, Her History, Diplomacy and Commerce* (London, 1901). "He is a 2,000-hundredweight-(rice-) man," i.e., he receives an annual rent of this amount, the usual classification of a rich man.

III. Administration and Rural Structure

1. It is not possible to discuss prehistoric China here, particularly the original nomadism which has been supposed by sinologists. Naturally, the nomadic peoples of inner Asia repeatedly invaded and conquered the river plains even in prehistoric times. Only the Mongols seriously prepared to maintain themselves as nomads before the superior culture of the agriculturists, and they did so for a time by forbidding the cultivation of land surrounding the capital. Consumption of milk, however, remained alien to the Chinese and this speaks more clearly than any tradition for the continuity of the primeval hoe and garden culture. Besides, the ceremony of handling the plough was among the ritual acts of the imperial *pontifex maximus*. In view of this, the nomadic derivation of part or even all of the old ruling stratum may well be insignificant. The existence of the "bachelor house" (see above), of course, has nothing to do with "nomadism," but indicates that in these communities the men engaged in hunting and warfare while the women cultivated the land. Milk consumption has obviously been absent in China a long time and this fact contradicts the nomadic hypothesis. Large cattle were used for work or were sacrificed; only small cattle were normally consumed.

For the history of the rural structure in connection with the fiscal system see N. J. Kochanovskuj, "Semljevladjenie i semljedjelje w Kitaje (*Isvjestija Vostotschnavo Instituta d.g. isd.*, 1907/8, vol. XXIII, 2 (Vladivostok, 1909) and A. J. Iwanoff, *Wang-An-Schi i jevo reformy* (St. Petersburg, 1906). Unfortunately other Russian literature was not available to me. I did not have access to A. M. Fielde, "Land Tenure in China," *Journal of the China Branch of the Royal Asiatic Society*, vol. 23, p. 110 (1888), and scarcely to any other publications of this journal. For further references see below.

2. Reproduced by Biot, *loc. cit.*

3. Cf. R. Leonhard's statements which are correct in this point if not in others, especially not anything concerning Antiquity. See his review of the valuable but somewhat one-sided book of Lacombe, "L'évolution de la propriété foncière," *Schmollers Jahrbuch*.

4. This would be certain if totemist associations could be shown to have existed in China, as Conrady maintains. With the development of the sib, the emergent ruling stratum has universally withdrawn from the essentially plebeian totem association. [See Chapter I, note 49, Ed.]

5. For instance, in the state of Lu, the model Confucian state, the following levies were at one time prescribed for the existing registration unit of 64 *ch'ing:* 1 chariot, 4 horses, 10 head of cattle, 3 armored and 64 non-armored foot soldiers. Obviously this register presupposed that the sibs, associated in a registration unit, would in their turn meet the military requirement by providing the soldiers' pay. Presumably, recourse to direct compulsory draft remained subsidiary. Elsewhere we shall show, how in India, similar conditions led to prebendal landlordism. In other places in China the army draft extended directly to the individual family. In the state of Lu even this arrangement shows a preliminary phase of army recruitment by the patrimonial prince instead of a summons of vassals, and hence indicates the elimination of feudalism as a military system. European analogies are to be found in Delbrück's excellent presentation of these conditions for the feudal army.

6. *Suan fa tong tsang,* cf. Biot, *Journal Asiatique,* 3rd Série, vol. 5, 1838 (the presentation is based on the *Wen hsien t'ung k'ao*).

7. It must always be kept in mind that the first fairly well ascertained date in Chinese history (Chavannes) is the year 841 B.C.

8. Today it is figured that a family of five could live on 15 *mou* (about 85 *ar*) of cultivated land that is not exclusively used for gardening. To us this is still an almost unbelievably low figure.

9. Cf. Chapter I, above.

10. *Peking Gazette* of 14 June, 1883.

11. Examples of Japanese household registers including a calculation of their allotments, are furnished by O. Nachod in his history of Japan, *Weltgeschichte,* ed. by Pflugk-Hartung (Berlin, 1910), vol. III, p. 592 ff.

12. These groups of ten are to be understood as associations of ten sibs each. The attempts to revert to the family or to the individual, instead of the sib, have only lately been successful.

13. While Russian authors may wish to rediscover the *nadjel* of the Russian *optshina* in the normal land claim, it should not be overlooked that a village communism resulted from these purely tax-determined measures only under Russian conditions, particularly the tax liability of the village community. But the latter has apparently been absent in China.

14. Presumably the "well" system was named from the Chinese character which represents a square partitioned into nine fields. However, it was so named, too, because irrigation ditches, pipes, and a long-lasting

inundation of the dammed-up area were indispensable to rice cultivation. Throughout Asia (including Java), this involved thoroughgoing innovations in property relations and everywhere it particularly meant fiscal intervention, the basis of which lay in the indispensable channelization of water. But it is quite possible that the system, which is usually considered quite old, rationally evolved from the original cultivation of the chieftain's land by sib members.

15. Proprietors living close to the Imperial Canal and burdened with Canal liturgies played a considerable role in the T'ai P'ing Rebellion.

16. See Wang An-shih's memorial reproduced by Iwanoff, *op. cit.*, p. 51 f.

17. Cf. the two reports of Su Shih against Wang An-shih, *ibid.*, p. 167 ff., 190 f. and the objections of other opponents, among them, Ssu-ma Kuang, *ibid.*, p. 196.

18. These matters are connected with the structure of internal administration and will be discussed below.

19. Even in the 8th century magazines for silk and linen are said to have existed.

20. Cf. the excerpts from the Annals in P. A. Tschepe (S.J.) "Histoire du Royaume de Tsin, 777-207," *Variétés Sinologiques*, vol. 27, especially p. 118 f.

21. This prohibition would seem to have actually arrested the development of the *colonate*. For even nowadays small tenancy does not seem to be widespread.

22. Here, banner fiefs of the Manchu garrisons, the hereditary land prebends of the border troops drafted for liturgies, and the proprietors living close to canals, streets, etc., may be bypassed.

23. And this was enforced by the courts! The judge, to be sure, had to reject the complaint, usually "admonishing" the buyer not to be "hard-boiled" but to pay. Only influential people could escape. See Hoang, *loc. cit.*, and the text below.

24. Thus P. Pierre Hoang translates the term. Cf. his "Notion technique sur la propriété en China" (Shanghai, 1897), *Variétés Sinologiques*, vol. 11 § 20.

25. The ancestral land is frequently referred to in the *Peking Gazette*.

26. Hoang, *loc. cit.*, for instance, Appendix XXIII, p. 119. We have mentioned above that tenancy is not, relatively speaking, very extensive. Besides the general prohibition of the *colonate* in 1205, the difficulty of collecting farm rents seems to have been primarily decisive.

27. Hoang, *op. cit.*, p. 12, No. 31, p. 152, 157 f.

28. An example is: "family of the eternal peace."

29. In this connection, the system of registration and the land regis-

ter were first elucidated in a note of Bumbaillif, "Land Tenure in China," *China Review* (1890/91). The unit of registration was a sib property designated at the time of the registration by the ancestral head of a sib. In case division had already occurred, the part holdings were listed. Even in the event of land division or change of ownership, the original registration number with its designation was retained, and only the amount of the tax and the family which was to pay part or all of it were recorded. Ten heads of sibs (or about this number) formed a group and, according to ancient law, were responsible for the tax. They were guardians of the peace and they also owned in common land which was either farmed or leased by the head of the sibs. The head of each sib collected the taxes of his sib, and whosoever might fail to present his tax receipt by November 16 could be deprived of his land by the group of ten. If the households of a sib could not raise the tax, the sib's ancestral land was seized. The composition of the groups of ten was subject to change. The above-mentioned note reports the request of the head of a sib (or part sib) to form jointly with nine others a new group of ten. The size of the sib holdings varied considerably. A varying number of groups of ten was organized into a higher unit, again for meeting what were originally military and liturgical charges. More on the sibs follows.

30. It is maintained that unified property holdings of 300 *ha* were to be found but that essentially larger property units of individual landlords were rare. The (Frankfurt) doctoral dissertation of Wen Hsian Liu, *Die Vorteile des laendlichen Grund und Bodens und seine Bewirtschaftung in China* (Berlin, 1920), which came to my attention at the last moment, does not present figures.

[J. L. Buck has computed the average farm of owners to be 4.22 acres, of part owners 4.25, and of tenants 3.56 acres. He estimates that 17% of the farmers are tenants, less than one third part-owners, and over one half owners. See his *Land Utilization in China* (Chicago, 1937), p. 192. According to Ch'en Han-seng, as much as 40% of all farm land in certain areas of Kwangtung is owned by landed sibs. Cf. his *Landlord and Peasant in China* (New York, 1936), pp. 37-41. H. T. Fei contains some material on sib landlordism in Yunnan. See his *Earthbound China* (Chicago, 1945). Chronic conditions of warfare, inflation, and usury capitalism, of course, have greatly increased the burden of the peasantry, many of whom have been forced into debt, bankruptcy and the loss of their lands. Even in 1936, Leonard T. K. Wu stated that "the choice for them is either continued collapse of their economy or a complete alteration of the usury-merchant-landlord system." Cf. his "Merchant Capital and Usury Capital in Rural China." *Far Eastern Survey*, March 25, 1936, p. 68, Ed.]

31. There were some 15 official holidays but no Sunday rest.

32. At the beginning of the twentieth century in the gardening areas of the plains, credits amounted to $750-1,000 *per ha*. This does not take account of the much larger purchasing power of the Western money in the Orient. Interest was calculated at 7-9% on loans, or better, the yield of labor, for according to available figures, as the quality of the soil increased the percentage of this "rent" decreased.

33. It amounted to 8-9% in agriculture and 12-30% in retail trade and industry.

IV. Self-government, Law and Capitalism

1. We may refer to the nucleus of the T'ai P'ing "rebels" (1850-64). According to the *Peking Gazette*, the Hung Yi Tang, the sib of the founder of the T'ai P'ing rebellion, was persecuted as a secret society as late as 1895.

2. According to Conrady, *loc. cit.*, *Chang chia tsung* means the "village of the Chang family."

3. Possibly both forms of the bachelor house, the "cooperative" and the "authoritarian" one, existed side by side in different regions. On the whole, evidence compiled by Quistorp, *loc. cit.*, speaks rather for the former type. But note that the legendary Emperor Yao handed the government over to his successor Shun in the ancestor-hall. One emperor threatened his vassals by pointing to the wrath of their ancestral spirits. Such examples, compiled by Hirth in his *Ancient History of China*, support the assumption of the authoritarian type of bachelor house as do Emperor P'an Keng's in the *Shu Ching* (cf. Legge, *op. cit.*, p. 238), and the apparition of an emperor's ancestral spirits demanding an explanation from the emperor for his abuse of power. Totemist survivals are listed by Conrady, *loc. cit.* Although important, they are not entirely convincing. [See Chapter I, note 49, Ed.]

4. The above-mentioned sparing of the last descendant of an overthrown dynasty is rooted in the concern that the ancestral spirits should not be disturbed. The spirits, after all, were those of former emperors and hence powerful.

The *Peking Gazette* of 13 April and 31 July, 1883, reports the complaint of the Chang Tuan, the representative of the Ming dynasty, concerning cultivation of the ancestral sites of the Ming. We may refer to adoptions and recall the above-mentioned state sacrifices for the spirits of those who died without leaving descendants.

5. Cf. the speech of the Prince of Chou in the *Shu Ching* (Legge,

p. 175). The prayer on behalf of the sick Emperor was made not to Heaven but to the ancestors. *Ibid.*, p. 391 ff.

6. De Groot's references in his *Universismus* show clearly that the Spirit of Heaven is treated as *primus inter pares*. According to the rescript published in the *Peking Gazette* of 29 September, 1898, the "spirits of the ancestors" had condemned the abortive attempts at reform of the Emperor and of K'ang Yu-wei. Besides a person's own merits, Heaven considers those of the ancestors (de Groot, *The Religion of the Chinese*, New York, 1910, p. 27 f.). Hence Confucian doctrine maintained that for a time Heaven may watch the sins of a dynasty and interfere only at the point of complete degeneration, which, of course, is quite a convenient "theodicy."

7. There are cases in which adoption has been revoked because the death sacrifices for the natural father were endangered (*Peking Gazette*, 26 April, 1878).

8. Patricide was considered such a terrible event (punishable by "slow death") that the governor of the province was removed from office just as in cases of natural catastrophe (*Peking Gazette*, 7 August, 1894). In 1895, when a drunkard killed his grandfather the father was also punished for having failed to educate the son to "endure even the most severe punishments from his elder."

9. Occasionally sub-sibs had their "sub-ancestor halls."

10. According to classical ritual, adoption could be consummated only within the sib. Even in the same village, however, family statutes made widely varying dispositions. Parts of the old ritual had been almost universally abrogated. Thus, the daughter-in-law no longer mourned only her parents-in-law, as prescribed, but also her own parents. There was "deep" mourning not only of the father's death, as was officially prescribed, but also of the mother's.

11. Therefore A. Merx's version is highly probable. He reads μηδένα ἀπελπίζοντες instead of μηδὲν ἀπελπίζοντες. Here, too, we confront the fear of "crying" to God, and in case of suicide, fear of the "spirit" of the desperate man.

12. Feuds against outsiders were occasioned by tax repartition, death feuds, and especially conflicts which the *fêng shui*, i.e. geomancers, provoked among neighbors. Every building, and especially every new grave, could harm the ancestral spirits of the existing graves or could upset the spirits of the rocks, rivulets, hills, etc. To settle such feuds was often well-nigh impossible because of the geomantic interests at stake on both sides.

13. The *Peking Gazette* of 14 December, 1883 reports, for instance, the purchase of 2,000 *mou* (1 mou = 5.62 *ar*) for 17,000 taels. Besides

sacrifices, explicit mention is made of supporting widows and orphans and financing the school from rents.

14. We may refer to Eugene Simon, *La Cité Chinoise* (Paris, 1885), and to Leong and Tao, *Village and Town Life in China* (London, 1915).

15. As late as 1899, the police were enjoined not to treat as "unknown strangers" people who had a claim to their ancestral land but who had gone abroad. (*Peking Gazette,* 12 October, 1899.)

16. As a result of hereditary partitions individual property often consisted of scattered holdings of five to fifteen lots.

17. As noted above, in the city they were the guilds that had often usurped extensive self-governing functions.

18. This should be compared to the book by the two Chinese bachelors which has already been cited. The part dealing with the village is far better than that dealing with the city. One simply cannot say much about the "city" as a social structure. Analogies can be found in Germanic law.

19. The village temples were not considered "Taoist" shrines. (Cf. Chapter VII.)

20. Especially, the temple priest held landed property. If the temple had been founded by donors honorific titles such as *shan chu,* i.e., Master of Youth, were given in compensation. The priest lived from fees and grain stipends, hence the more numerous the temples, the poorer the village. However, only one of the temples was *the* village temple.

21. To raise loans through the temple was considered meritorious. For this see Doolittle, *Social Life of the Chinese* (London, 1866).

22. Data on the existence of the sib elders can apparently be found for all periods. Under the Han variously composed sub-groups functioned at their side. As a rule they were elected officials in their fifties who were entrusted with security police, joint liability, the duty of reprimanding, supervision of sacrifices, allocation of the corvée, tax collection and hence also tax liability. Under certain conditions they might be justices of the peace or they might administer adult education; occasionally they might also be responsible for recruiting and training the militia. According to the new arrangements under the Han, nine by eight families officially constituted a *li;* ten *li* comprised one *t'ing* under an elected elder; ten *t'ing* made one *san* headed by an elected *san-lao* whose main task was popular education. To this must be added the *shih fu,* i.e., the tax supervisor and justice of the peace, and the *ju tse,* the police commissioner. The main purpose was military. Cf. the discussion of A. J. Iwanoff, *Wang-An-Shi i jevo reformy,* (St. Petersburg, 1906).

23. For this point see A. H. Smith, *Village Life in China* (Edinburgh, 1899).

24. Usually the *kuang kun* was athletically trained. Like the member of the *Camorra* or *Maffia* he sought unofficial relations with the *yamen* of the *hsien-official* who had no power over him. A village employee, the village head, a justice of the peace, or at the opposite end, a beggar could function as a *kuang kun*. The situation for the rest of the villagers could become hopeless if he had a literary education and was possibly related to an official.

25. The decrees of the *Peking Gazette* refer to them as "gentry and notables" whose advice ought to be sought.

26. Cf. the report of the *Peking Gazette* of 14 April, 1895. Two sib associations freed a man who had been arrested by the tax collector.

27. S. Hoang, "Mélanges sur l'administration," *Variétés Sinologiques,* 21 (Shanghai, 1902), p. 120 f.

28. I did not have access to the several recent and good doctoral dissertations on these associations.

29. The forms of the associations were suggestive of the ἔρανοι. A credit association *(she)* might accumulate a money fund and auction it off for use or distribute it by lot (Smith, *loc. cit.*). Credit might be provided by friends in which case the debtor was made president of a club and by honor of the club repaid his debts in installments to the members (his creditors). Doolittle *(op. cit.,* p. 147) gives examples of such clubs. Those who received refunds were often determined by lot, an artificial substitute for the old neighborhood credit association and for bankruptcy proceedings.

30. According to Doolittle, *loc. cit.*

31. The government was interested in this question with reference to applications for examinations since a quota of prebends was allocated to the provinces. Even during the Han period the candidate's home town and district were always added to the name or official registers such as that of the army. At that time the district was undoubtedly the home of the sib.

32. For this see E. H. Parker, *Ancient China Simplified* (London, 1908), p. 112 f.

33. Even in recent decades the imperial rescripts took issue with judicial decisions made on the basis of private letters from influential persons *(Peking Gazette,* 10 March, 1894). The interminability of trials was such that imperial rescripts ascribed to their length unfavorable weather and droughts or the ineffectiveness of prayers *(Peking Gazette,* 9 March, 1899). Legal guarantees were completely lacking. Between the lines of imperial rescripts can be read the party intrigues

which created antagonisms within officialdom upon the founding of a factory (*Peking Gazette*, 4 March, 1895).

34. Meanwhile, to my knowledge, only J. Plenge has occasionally and independently argued in such a way that it is certain he has largely recognized the significant reason for the collapse of politically oriented capitalism. Unfortunately, I cannot locate the passage at the moment.

V. The Chinese Literati

1. Yu tsiuan tung kian kang mu [*Ming History of Emperor Ch'ien Lung*], trans. by Delamarre (Paris, 1865), p. 417.

2. As eminent an authority as von Rosthorn disputes this point in his "The Burning of the Books," *Journal of the Peking Oriental Society*, vol. IV, Peking, 1898, pp. 1 ff. He believes that the sacred texts were orally transmitted until the Han period, and hence that they are in the same tradition that prevailed exclusively in early India. The outsider is not entitled to pass judgment, but perhaps the following may be said. The annalistic scriptures at least cannot rest on oral tradition and, as the calculation of the eclipses of the sun shows, they go back into the second millennium. Very much of what elsewhere is (according to the usual assumption, reliably) reported of the archives of the princes and the importance of script and the written communication of the literati could just as little be reconciled with the above, *if* one were to extend the view of the eminent expert *beyond* the ritual literature (that is, literature which has been brought into poetic form). Here, of course, only expert sinologists have the last word, and a "criticism" on the part of a non-expert would be presumptuous. The principle of strictly *oral* tradition has almost everywhere applied only to charismatic revelations and to charismatic commentaries of these, and not to poetry and didactics. The great age of script as such comes out in its pictorial form and also in its arrangement of the pictorial characters: at a late period the vertical columns divided by lines still referred back to the origin from scored disks of bamboo sticks which were placed side by side. The oldest "contracts" were bamboo scores or knotted cords. The fact that *all* contracts and documents were made out in duplicate form is probably rightly considered a survival of this technique (Conrady).

3. This explains also the stereotyping of script in such an extraordinarily early stage of development, and hence it produces an after-effect even today.

4. E. de Chavannes, *Journal of the Peking Oriental Society*, vol. III, 1, 1890, p. IV, translates *Tai che ling* by "grand astrologer," instead of "court annalist," as it is usually rendered. Yet, the later, and especially

the modern period knows the representatives of literary education to be sharp opponents of the astrologers. Cf. below.

5. P. A. Tschepe (S.J.), "Histoire du Royaume de Han," *Variétés Sinologiques*, 31 (Shanghai, 1910), p. 48.

6. During the fourth century the representatives of the feudal order, foremost among them the interested princely sibs, argued against the intended bureaucratization of the state Ch'in by pointing out "that the forebears had improved the people by education, not by administrative changes" (this harmonizes fully with the later theories of Confucian orthodoxy). Thereupon the new minister Yang, belonging to the literati, comments in highly un-Confucian manner: "the ordinary person *lives* according to tradition; the higher minds, however, *create* tradition, and for extraordinary things the rites give no precepts. The weal of the people is the highest law," and the prince accedes to his opinion. (Cf. the passages in Tschepe's "Histoire du Royaume de Tsin," *Variétés Sinologiques*, 27, p. 118.) It is quite probable that when Confucian orthodoxy articulated and purified the Annals it very strongly erased and retouched these features in favor of the traditionalism which was later considered correct. On the other hand, one must beware of simply taking at face value all the reports referred to below which testify to the astonishing deference paid to the early literati!

7. Although the princely heir of Wei alights from the chariot he receives no response to his repeated salutations from the king's courtier and literary man, who is a parvenu. To the question "whether the rich or the poor may be proud" the *literatus* replies "the poor," and he motivates this by saying that he might find employment any day at another court. (Tschepe, "Histoire du Royaume de Han," *op. cit.*, p. 43.) One of the literati is seized by a great rage about a brother of the prince being preferred over him for the post of a minister. (Cf. *ibid.*)

8. The prince of Wei listens only in standing to the report of the court *literatus*, a disciple of Confucius (*loc. cit.;* cf. preceding note).

9. Cf. the statements of Tschepe, "Histoire du Royaume de Tsin," p. 77.

10. The hereditary transmission of the ministerial position is considered ritually objectionable by the literati (Tschepe, *loc. cit.*). When the prince of Chao orders his minister to scrutinize and find some land suitable as fiefs for several worthy literati the minister thrice declares after having thrice been warned, that he has as yet not found any land worthy of them. Thereupon the prince finally understands and makes them officials. (Tschepe, "Histoire du Royaume de Han," pp. 54-5.)

11. Cf. the passage concerning the respective question by the King of Wu in Tschepe, "Histoire du Royaume de U," *Variétés Sinologiques* 10 (Shanghai, 1891).

12. That also income was an end sought goes without saying, as the Annals show.

13. Once when a prince's concubine laughed at one of the literati, all the prince's literati went on strike until she was executed (Tschepe, "Histoire du Royaume de Han," *loc. cit.*, p. 128).

14. The event reminds one of the "finding" of the sacred law under Josiah with the Jews. The contemporary great annalist, Ssu-ma Ch'ien, does not mention the find.

15. Tschepe, "Histoire du Royaume de Tsin," *loc. cit.*, p. 53.

16. Individual concealments are confirmed (for instance, the attack of the state Wu upon its own state Lu). For the rest, in view of the scantiness of the material, one may seriously raise the question as to whether one should not rather consider the great, strongly moralizing *commentary* to the Annals as his work.

17. In 1900 the Empress Dowager still took very unfavorable notice of a censor's request to abolish them. Cf. the rescripts in the *Peking Gazette* concerning the "orthodox army" (10 January, 1899), concerning the "review" during the Japanese war (21 December, 1894), concerning the importance of military ranks (1 and 10 November, 1898), and from an earlier period, e.g. (23 May, 1878).

18. Concerning this practice cf. Etienne Zi (S.J.), "Pratique des Examens Militaires en Chine," *Variétés Sinologiques*, No. 9. Subjects for examination were archery and certain gymnastic feats of strength; and, formerly, the writing of a dissertation; since 1807, however, the writing of a section of one hundred characters from the *Wu Ching* (theory of war), allegedly dating from the time of the Chou dynasty, was required. A great many officers did not acquire degrees and the Manchus were freed from taking them altogether.

19. A *taotai* (prefect) for his military merits had been taken over from the officers' ranks into the civil administration. In response to a complaint an imperial rescript (*Peking Gazette*, 17 September, 1894) comments as follows: although the officer's conduct in the matter in question has substantively been found free from fault, he nevertheless has shown his "rough soldierly manners" by his conduct, "and we have to ask ourselves whether he possesses the *cultivated manners* which for a person of his rank and position must appear indispensable." Therefore it is recommended that he resume a military position.

The abolition of age-old archery and of other very old sports as elements of "military" training was made almost impossible by the rites, which in their beginnings probably were still connected with the "bachelor house." Thus the Empress, when rejecting the reform proposals, makes reference to these rites.

20. The French authors for the most part designate *shêng yüan, hsiu*

ts'ai by "baccalaureate" [bachelor's degree], *chü jên* by "licentiate" [master's degree], *chin shih* by "doctorate." The lowest degree gave a claim to a stipend only to the top graduates. The bachelors who had received a stipend were called *lin sheng* (magazine prebendaries), bachelors selected by the director and sent to Peking were called *pao kung*, those among them who were admitted to the college *yü kung*, and those who had acquired the bachelor degree by purchase were called *chüan sheng*.

21. The charismatic qualities of the descendant simply were proof for those of his sib, hence of the forebears. At the time, Shi Huang Ti had abolished this custom, as the son was not to judge the father. But since then almost every founder of a new dynasty has bestowed ranks to his ancestors.

22. By the way, this is a rather certain symptom of its *recent origin!*

23. Cf. for this: Biot, *Essai sur l'histoire de l'instruction publique en Chine et de la corporation des Lettrés* (Paris, 1847). (It is still useful.)

24. Complaints at Ma Tuan-Lin, translated in Biot, p. 481.

25. Themes for them are given by Williams, cf. Zi, *loc. cit.*

26. This held especially for the examinations for the master's degree, where the theme of the dissertation often called for an erudite, philological, literary, and historical analysis of the respective classical text. Cf. the example given by Zi, *loc. cit.*, p. 144.

27. This held especially for the highest degree ("doctorate") for which the emperor, often in person, gave the themes and for which he classified the graduates. Questions of administrative expediency, preferably connected with one of the "six questions" of Emperor T'ang, were customary topics. (Cf. Biot, p. 209, note 1, and Zi, *loc. cit.*, p. 209, note 1.)

28. *Siao Hioh*, ed. de Harlez, vol. V, p. 11, vol. I, pp. 29, 40. Cf. the quotation from Chu Hsi, *ibid.*, p. 46. Concerning the question of generations, cf. 1, 13.

29. *Loc. cit.*, I, 25, furthermore 2. Introduction No. 5 f.

30. There were literary prescriptions also for this.

31. It need hardly be mentioned that what is here said about language and script reproduces *exclusively* what such eminent sinologists, as especially the late W. Grube, teach the layman. It does *not* result from the author's own studies.

32. J. Edkins, "Local Values in Chinese Arithmetical Notation," *Journal of the Peking Oriental Society*, I, No. 4, pp. 161 f. The Chinese abacus used the (decimal) positional value. The older positional system which has fallen into oblivion seems to be of Babylonian origin.

33. De Harlez, *Siao Hioh*, p. 42, note 3.

34. Also, Timkovski, *Reise durch China* (1820-21), *German by Schmid* (Leipzig, 1825), emphasizes this.

35. For such a self-impeachment of a frontier officer who had been inattentive, see No. 567 of Aurel Stein's documents, edited by E. de Chavannes. It dates from the Han period, hence long before the introduction of examinations.

36. The beginnings of the present *Peking Gazette* go back to the time of the second ruler of the Tang dynasty (618-907).

37. Actually one finds in the *Peking Gazette*, with reference to the reports partly of censors, partly of superiors, laudations and promotions (or the promise of such) for deserving officials, demotions of insufficiently qualified officials for other offices ("that he may gather experiences," *loc. cit.*, 31 December, 1897 and many other issues), suspension from office with half pay, expulsion of totally unqualified officials, or the statement that the good services of an official are balanced by faults which he would have to remedy before further promotion. Almost always detailed reasons are given. Such announcements were especially frequent at the end of the year but there was also a great volume at other times. There are also to be found posthumous sentences to be whipped for (obviously) posthumously demoted officials (*Peking Gazette*, 26 May, 1895).

38. Cf. A. H. Smith, *Village Life in China* (Edinburgh, 1899), p. 78.

39. For the following see Kun Yu, *Discours des Royaumes, Annales Nationales des Etats Chinoises de X au V siècles,* ed. de Harlez [London, 1895], pp. 54, 75, 89, 159, 189, and elsewhere.

40. Tschepe, *Variétés Sinologiques,* 27, p. 38. He *begs* to be punished. Similarly in A. Stein's documents, *loc. cit.*, No. 567.

41. See, however, the rescript in the *Peking Gazette* of 10 April, 1895, by which promotions were posthumously given to officers who chose death after the surrender of Weihaiwei (obviously because they took the guilt *upon themselves* and thus prevented the compromise of the Emperor's charisma by the disgrace).

42. There was, however, at least in one district, also a temple of *Tai Chi,* the primary matter (chaos), from which the two substances are said to have developed by division ("Schih Luh Kuoh Kiang Yuh Tschi," translated by Michels, p. 39.)

43. According to de Groot.

44. Cf. the excerpts translated from his memoirs by Gräfin Hagen (Berlin, 1915), pp. 27, 29, 33.

45. Cf. the elegant and ingenious, though quite shallow, notes of Cheng Ki Tong, which were intended for Europeans. (*China und die*

Chinesen, German by A. Schultze [Dresden und Leipzig, 1896], p. 158). Concerning Chinese conversation, there are some observations which well agree with what has been said above in Hermann A. Keyserling, *The Travel Diary of a Philosopher,* trans. by J. Holroyd Reece (New York, 1925).

46. "Siao Hsüeh" (trans. by de Harlez, *Annales du Musée, Guimet* XV, 1889) is the work of Chu Hsi (twelfth century A.D.). His most essential achievement was the definitive canonization of Confucianism in the systematic form he gave to it. For Chu Hsi cf. Gall, "Le Philosophe Tchou Hi, sa doctrine, etc.," *Variétés Sinologiques,* 6 (Shanghai, 1894). It is essentially a popular commentary to the *Li Chi,* making use of historical examples. In China every grade school pupil was familiar with it.

47. The number of "masters" was allocated to the provinces. If an emergency loan was issued—even after the T'ai P'ing rebellion—higher quotas were promised occasionally to the provinces for the raising of certain minimum sums. At every examination only ten "doctors" were allowed to graduate, the first three of whom enjoyed an especially high prestige.

48. The paramount position of personal patronage is illustrated by the comparison between the extraction of the three highest graduates and that of the highest mandarins as given by Zi, *loc. cit.,* Appendix II, p. 221, note 1. Disregarding the fact that of the 748 high official positions, occupied from 1646 to 1914, 398 were occupied by Manchus although but three of them were among the highest graduates (the three *tien she* put in the first place by the Emperor), the province of Honan procured 58, that is, one sixth of all high *officials,* solely by virtue of the powerful position of the Tseng family, whereas almost two thirds of the highest *graduates* stemmed from other provinces which altogether had a share of only 30 per cent in these offices.

49. This means was first systematically used by the Ming Emperors in 1453. (But, as a financial measure, it is to be found even under Shih Huang Ti.) The lowest decree originally cost 108 piasters, equal to the capitalized value of the study prebends, then it cost 60 taels. After an inundation of the Huang Ho, the price had been reduced to about 20 to 30 taels in order to expand the market and thereby procure ample funds. Since 1693 the purchasers of the bachelor's degree were also admitted to the higher examinations. A *taotai* position with all secondary expenses cost about 40,000 taels.

50. That is why the emperors under certain conditions when placing the candidates took into consideration whether or not the candidate belonged to a province which as yet had no graduate who had been put in first place.

51. Ssu-ma Ch'ien's treatise on the balance of trade (*ping sheng*) (No. 8, Chap. 30, in vol. III of Chavannes' edition) represents a rather good example of Chinese cameralism. It is also the oldest document of Chinese economics that has been preserved. Topics which in our view do not belong to the "balance of trade" are: big trading profits during the period of the Warring States, degradation of the merchants in the unified empire, exclusion from office, fixation of salaries and, *in accordance with them*, fixation of land taxes, taxes of commerce, forest, water (appropriated by the "great families"), the question of private monetization, the danger of too large an enrichment of private persons (but: where there is wealth there is *virtue*, which is quite Confucian in thought), costs of transport, purchases of titles, monopolies of salt and iron, *registering* of merchants, internal tariffs, policies of price stabilization, struggles against commissions being given to wholesale purveyors to the state instead of direct commissions being given the artisans. The objective of this cameralist financial policy was *internal* order through stability, and not a favorable balance of foreign trade.

52. The Co-hong merchants' monopoly of the trade of Canton harbor, the only one opened to foreigners, existed until 1892 and had been set up in order to choke any intercourse of the Barbarians with the Chinese. The enormous profits which this monopoly yielded caused the concerned office prebendaries to be disinclined to any voluntary change in this condition.

53. Not only the official Ming history (cf. the following note) is full of this but so is the "Chi li kuo chiang yü chih" (*Histoire géographique des XVI Royaumes*, ed. Michels [Paris, 1891]). Thus, in 1368 the harem is excluded from affairs of state at the request of the Hanlin Academy (p. 7); in 1498 representation of the Hanlin Academy at the occasion of the palace fire and the demand (typical for accidents) to "speak freely" against the favorite eunuch (cf. following note).

54. Numerous cases illustrating this struggle are to be found, for instance in the "Yüchuan t'ung chien kang mu," *op. cit.* Consider the fifteenth century: in 1404 a eunuch is at the head of the army (p. 155). Since then this occurs repeatedly; thus, in 1428 (p. 223). Hence, the intrusion of palace officials into the administration in 1409 (p. 168). In 1443 a Hanlin doctor demands the abolition of cabinet rule, a reduction of the *corvée*, and above all, council meetings of the emperor, with the literati. A eunuch kills him (p. 254). In 1449 the favorite eunuch is killed at the request of the literati (p. 273), in 1457, however, *temples* are established in his honor.

In 1471 the counselors have to communicate with the emperor through the eunuch (p. 374). The very same is reported by Hsiao Kang (361-28 B.C.). In 1472 we meet eunuchs as secret policemen (p. 273), which in 1481 is abolished at the request of the censors (p. 289). in 1488 the old ritual is restored (the same occurs in numerous instances).

The removal of a eunuch in 1418 took an awkward course for the literati when the list was found on the eunuch of the literati who had bribed him. The literati were successful in having the list secreted and in seeing to it that a different pretext was found for the removal of the literati who had done the bribing (*ibid.* p. 422).

55. Cf. E. Backhouse and J. O. P. Bland, *China under the Empress Dowager* (Heinemann, 1910) and, against this, the famous memorial of Tao Mo from the year 1901.

56. When in 1441 a sun eclipse predicted by the astrologers failed to occur, the Board of Rites congratulated him—but the Emperor rejected this.

57. See the (previously cited) memorial, 1878, of the Hanlin Academy to the Empress.

58. *Loc. cit.*, Chap. 9, pp. 130 f.

59. See the decree of the Empress of February, 1901.

60. *Loc. cit.* p. 457.

61. For instance, "Yu tsiuan tung kien kang mu" (*loc. cit.* pp. 167, 223), 1409 and 1428. An edict forbidding in a similar manner interference in the administration was given the military even in 1388 (*ibid.*).

VI. The Confucian Life Orientation

1. Concerning the anchorets of the early period, cf. Chapter VII.

2. Concerning Buddhism cf. below and Max Weber, *Hinduismus und Buddhismus* (*Gesammelte Aufsaetze zur Religionssoziologie* vol. II) (Tübingen, 1921).

3. Cf. Chapter I.

4. Cf. Chavannes in the preface to his edition of Ssu-ma Ch'ien's tracts concerning the Fang and Chang sacrifices, *Journal of the Peking Oriental Society*, vol. III, No. 1 (1890).

5. Cf. also the poem "Chiu Yung" of the third century. Cf. Conrady in *Hochschulvortraege fuer Jedermann*, vol. XIX, XX (Leipzig, 1903).

6. For a discussion of the beginnings, cf. Chapter VII.

7. Weber's interpretative statement seems to be controversial, a point to which Professor L. Chen of the National Chekiang University, Hangchow, was good enough to draw my attention. Professor Chen (with others, e.g., William Edward Soothhill) translates the passage of the dirge (*Analects, Book VII,* 34) "I have prayed for

long." Arthur Waley's translation "The Master said, 'My expiation began *long ago!*'" and his annotation would seem to confirm Weber's point. Waley's note reads: "What justifies me in the eyes of Heaven is the life I have led. *There is no need for any rite now.*" In a fragment of one of the lost books of Chuangtzu there is a parallel story in which Tzu-lu wants to take the omens about Confucius' chance of recovery, and Confucius says "My omen-taking *was done long ago!*" See T'ai P'ing Yu Lan 849, fol. I. verso. *The Analects of Confucius,* translated and annotated by Arthur Waley (London, 1938), p. 131. (Our Italics, Ed.)

8. This is to be found in the stenographic reports of the Clarke papers from the military camp where equal franchise was discussed in terms of natural law for the first time in world history.

9. The compass was invented and it was used on river boats, and by couriers along the land routes of inner Asia; book printing was invented and used for administrative purposes to overcome the slowness of copying in long hand. Gunpowder was invented, also paper, porcelain, silk, alchemy, astronomy (used for astrological purposes of state). Gunpowder was utilized for military purposes probably during the twelfth, certainly during the thirteenth century, in any case, one century before the Florentines are credited with its use in wars. But the Chinese used gunpowder in a very primitive manner. The pacification of the empire simply did not stimulate its perfection. It seems that the guns of the Occident were feared, in the beginning especially because of their presumed magically-determined effect, and the Chinese sought to import them. Concerning the inventions cf. W. A. P. Martin, "Chinese Discoveries in Art and Science," *Journal of the Peking Oriental Society,* vol. IV, p. 19 ff.

10. The term is ambiguous, as we shall see below.

11. They did so with the highly unChristian conclusion that the good in man is an artificial product of culture. This resulted in a still greater affirmative emphasis on the "world" of "culture" and education than had been given to it by the orthodox doctrine.

One may indicate some of its metaphysical assertions (cf. F. Farjenel in the *Journal Asiatique,* vol. XX (1902), p. 113 ff). The eternity of matter is asserted. Its spiritual principle *(ai-chi)* is pantheistically conceived as a principle of goodness and as producing the world. Since the eleventh century it has been represented by an orthodox school of commentators; logically, it seems, it had little consistency. For the rest, it is assumed that even Confucius believed in the astrologically based cosmogony later advocated by Ssu-ma Ch'ien (the five elements succeed one another in the form of the early rulers). Cf. Chavannes in the preface to vol. I of his edition of Ssu-ma Ch'ien (Paris, 1895), p. CXLIII. Of this more below.

12. Allegedly the positional value of numbers was known in Chinese arithmetic during the sixth century. Cf. J. Edkins, "Local Value in Chinese Arithmetical Notation," *Journal of the Peking Oriental Society,* vol. I, No. 4, p. 161 f., who traces this knowledge back to Babylon (?). This alleged knowledge remains questionable. During the nineteenth century, as mentioned above, the *abacus* with balls of local value was used.

13. Until the present, however, mathematics was included among the nine subjects of the elective, additional examination which one could take either to attain preferential promotion or to secure himself against degradation.

14. According to Eitel, *China Review,* vol. XVIII, p. 266. T. de Lacouperie has nevertheless maintained the Babylonian origin of ancient Chinese civilization (*Western Origin of the Ancient Chinese Civilization,* London, 1894).

(*Precession of Equinoxes:* "A slow change in direction of the earth's axis and consequently westward motion of the equinoctial points along the ecliptic caused by the action of the sun, moon, and planets upon the protuberant matter about the earth's equator, in connection with its diurnal rotation;—as is so called because either equinox, owing to its westerly motion, comes to the meridian sooner each day than the point it would have occupied if there were no motion of precession and thus *precedes* that point continually with reference to the time of transit . . ." —*Webster's Dictionary of the English Language*). (Ed.)

15. Cf. the *Shi Luh Kuoh Kiang Yu Tschi,* tr. by Michels, p. XXI of the "Notes" to the commentary.

16. This holds also in relation to the mother. A son in drunkenness had manhandled his scolding mother (in 1882). The mother engaged some men, had the son put in bonds and buried alive, in spite of the heartfelt pleas of all participants. The men were punished because of a formal incorrectness but they were pardoned at once. Sanctions against the mother were entirely out of the question. (Rescript in the *Peking Gazette* of 13 March, 1882.)

17. It also preceded obedience to the prince. During feudal times an official was ordered by a prince to seize his son because of felony. The official refused to do so, and the official who was ordered to seize the father because of his disobedience did likewise. The father then committed suicide and tradition burdened the prince with the sin of this misdemeanor. Tschepe, *loc. cit.,* p. 217.

18. Cf. the request of the son of the commander of Nuichuang re-

ported in the *Peking Gazette* of 6 June, 1896. During the war with Japan, the commander had been accused of cowardice and had been degraded to compulsory labor at the mail routes in the west. The son pleaded permission to take the punishment of his father who had fallen sick under hardships or to pay 4,000 taels for his father's release. The report was passed on to the emperor with a comment pointing up the praiseworthy piety of the petitioner.

19. The memorial underlying the rescript of 2 September, 1905, concerning the abolition of the old "culture"-examinations is rather thin in substance. In essence, it argues merely that the zeal for popular education is inhibited because everybody relies on the examination for entitling him to a prebend.

20. Ssu-ma Ch'ien's biography of Confucius, ed. Chavannes, p. 336.

21. "Sensuality," inimical to all virtue, is viewed as incurable even by the old Annals (Kun Yu, *Discours des Royaumes*, p. 163, takes the form of a doctor's statement concerning a sick prince). The conflict between love and the interest of the state is resolved strictly in favor of the state. The "tragedy" of this situation is poetically treated at least once.

22. Fr. Kuhn, *Abhandlungen der Berliner Akademie* (1914), 4.

23. See Chavannes, preface to his edition, p. XIII.

24. Edkins, "The Place of *Hwang Ti* in Early Taoism," *China Review*, vol. XV, p. 233 f.

25. Against this cf. Pen Piao in Appendix II of Chavannes, *loc. cit.*

26. *Journal Asiatique*, vol. X, Série 14, 1909, ed. Chavannes, pp. 33, 36.

27. Concerning him cf. Chavannes, vol. I, Appendix I, p. CCXXVI f.

28. For the Chinese, castration is an especially terrible misfortune because of the ancestor cult.

29. The belief in immortality would not be classical. Only the belief in spirits is meant.

30. See p. 166 of his biography of Shih Huang Ti, ed. Chavannes.

31. Praised in the inscriptions of the Han period, cited above.

32. *China und die Chinesen* (German by A. Schultze, 1896), p. 222.

33. Confucius is even said to have declared himself incompetent in military matters.

34. *Yu tsiaun tung kian kang mu*, tr. by Delamarre (Paris, 1865), p. 20.

35. Giles, *China and the Chinese* (New York, 1912), p. 105.

36. "Coerced contracts have no force for the spirits do not guard them." This is maintained even in earliest times, cf. E. H. Parker, *Ancient China Simplified* (London, 1908), p. 99.

VII. Orthodoxy and Heterodoxy
(Taoism)

1. Concerning Taoism, consult de Harlez and Legge for sources. In general, see the excellent posthumous work of W. Grube, *Religion und Kultur der Chinesen* and especially de Groot's *Universismus Die Grundlagen der Religion und Ethik, des Staatswesens und der Wissenschaft Chinas* (Berlin, 1918).

2. Besides the previously cited monumental documents we may refer to Chinese literature. Thus, the educational work of *Hsiao Hsüeh*, tr. by de Harlez warns against the swindles of the Buddhist priests who seek to provide otherworldly bliss for the dead. It argues that one can be neither useful nor harmful to the dead for with the decomposition of their bodies their spirits also vanish (*loc. cit.*, Book V, No. 86).

3. Like the Catholic Church the patrimonial institution of grace makes the distinction here that the canonized man enjoyed—in Catholic terms—mere "veneration" and not, like the great spirits of nature, "adoration." In the mind of the masses, to be sure, this distinction was a purely formal one, in this as in similar cases.

4. *Shêng* means Saint; *i*, *yin* mean the segregated ones; *Hsien*, a sign composed of "men" and "mountain," means anchorets.

5. Cf. de Groot's presentation in his *Universismus;* further, A. Conrady, "China," in *Weltgeschichte, die Entwicklung der Menschheit in Staat und Gesellschaft, in Kultur und Geistesleben,* ed. by J. von Pflugk-Hartung (Berlin, Ullstein, 1910), vol. III, pp. 457-567, and the comments in Ssu-ma Ch'ien's *Annals,* ed. by Chavannes.

6. There are paintings which usually portray the Rishis as coarse plebeians.

7. A case in the Annalistics concerns the minister Fan Li of the state of Yüeh. When his king lost a city he declared that according to the old rules he ought to commit suicide, but he did not do so. Apparently the man later built up the enormous fortune which he had collected as a minister through a fortunate war against the Ch'i. Later he actually distributed his wealth among his friends and turned anchoret just as some of the Indian ministers have done up to the present. Cf. Tschepe, "Histoire du Royaume de Ou," *Variétés Sinologiques,* 10 (Shanghai, 1891), p. 157, Appendix I.

8. Tschepe, *loc. cit.* (sixth century B.C.).

9. De Groot argues against this in reference to the early period.

10. De Groot argues for this tradition.

11. Today one may well speak of him as a modish philosopher. We may disregard that Lao-tzu is a semi-mythical figure, that the *Tao*

Teh Ching is strongly suspected of containing interpolations *en masse,* or that its existence is certain only at a late date. Even if Lao-tzu were a fictitious figure the contrast of schools would remain, and that is of exclusive interest to us here.

12. *Ch'ung* means equilibrium (in English: "weak"). It is a basic Confucian concept which in Taoism is interpreted to mean "void."

13. Par. 30. Cf. de Groot, *Religion in China* (London, 1912).

14. For the following see especially de Groot who places the greatest emphasis upon the secondary nature of this schism.

15. De Groot, *loc. cit.*

16. With Wan Fei, third century A.D. Cf. de Groot, *loc. cit.*

17. In reference to this, see the previously cited inscriptions.

18. To be sure, this also holds for Mayana Buddhism with its bonzes as the secular clergy. But with Buddhism the secondary nature of the phenomenon is quite clear; with Taoism that is not the case.

19. To my knowledge the *Tao Tsang* has not been translated; it seems to be rare.

20. Cf. de Groot, who follows Ko Hung's *Hagiography.*

21. De Groot has been used for this and the usual literature. De Groot's lecture in the *Transactions of the Third International Congress of Religions* (Oxford, 1907), vol. I, was not available at the time. The same holds for Imbault-Huart, "La légende du premier pape des Taoistes et l'histoire de la famille pontificale des Tchang," *Journal Asiatique,* Nov.-Dec., 1884, p. 389.

22. Concerning this enmity, see Chavannes about Ssu-ma Ch'ien's treatise, *Rites,* vol. III, p. 210, footnote 1.

23. See Chavannes' preface to Ssu-ma Ch'ien. Ssu-ma Ch'ien, their opponent, laments their ever-renewed ancestry.

24. Thus Jung Lu in 1903.

25. See the official dictionary of prebends of the Chinese state. W. F. Mayer, *The Chinese Government* (Shanghai, 1878), p. 70.

26. This is the case for the above noted inscriptions of the King of Nan Chao, ed. by Chavannes, *Journal Asiatique,* 9th Série, vol. 16 (1900).

27. The developmental course and results of the borrowing of Buddhism from India will be dealt with in the history of Buddhism; here we shall consider only certain formal aspects.

28. We shall discuss this at the proper place. It was not the original Buddhism.

29. See the registration of the cases in Emperor Ch'ien Lung's *Yü chuan t'ung chien kang mu.* For example: in 1451, fifty thousand bonzes were ordered, in spite of the protests of the Confucians (Delamarre, *op. cit.*, p. 288); in 1452, the dominant eunuch was a follower

of Buddha (*ibid.*, p. 292) and hence an enemy of the "officials" (Confucians); in 1481, a bonze became Grand Almonsier (p. 379), who, in 1487 (p. 385), was deposed upon the request of the officials after the fall of an aerolite.

30. Mayer's book of state prebends, *loc. cit.* The local authorities select the *shen lu ssu* (superior), of whom there are two in each district, from the fang chang (elders) of the monasteries. The superiors are responsible for the good conduct of the bonzes.

31. This was often maintained with reference to the former essays on Puritanism. [*The Protestant Ethic and the Spirit of Capitalism*, tr. by Talcott Parsons; "The Protestant Sects and the Spirit of Capitalism," in *From Max Weber: Essays in Sociology* (New York, 1946), Chapter XII, pp. 302-322. Ed.]

32. This held also for orthodoxy, cf. *Se Ma Tsien* (Ssu-ma Ch'ien), ed. Chavannes, vol. I, p. 196: "Heaven does not by itself send premature death. Heaven rather adjusts to Man's behavior." Compare, however, the monumental documents quoted in the beginning of Chapter II.

33. *Universismus*, p. 343; the book has been used here throughout, as every reader will see.

34. De Groot, *loc. cit.* p. 373.

35. In view of de Groot's book the "pan-Babylonian" thesis is no longer likely to be maintained.

36. De Groot, *Religion of China*, p. 64 f. The adoration of living men (mandarins) is declared punishable in a rescript as late as 1883 (*Peking Gazette*, 18 January, 1883).

37. *Peking Gazette*, 24 June, 1878.

38. During religious disputations between Confucians and Buddhists the Buddhist doctrine of Karma usually was declined with special emphasis. It was maintained that the social position of an individual did not result from former deeds but from fate which makes some leaves of a tree swirl upon carpets and others upon dirt.

39. The ease with which this pride in names could turn into the naked craving to live simply in order to live is obvious from the parable of the turtle mentioned above. Its author was not a pure Confucian but quotes Confucius with great reverence. The truly Confucian mentality, however, is not reflected in this but in Ssu-ma Ch'ien's letters and the memorials of the censors to the Empress Tzu Hsi, which are quoted above.

40. At the last moment the rather good doctoral thesis of Wu Chang (Berlin, 1917), comes to my attention, a thesis which is influenced by Herkner, Bortkiewicz, and Eberstadt. The "Chinese Credit Association" represents a type of community bearing the usual club name

huui with appropriate additions which may well serve to illustrate the effects.

The thesis describes the primitive structures of these previously mentioned associations (Chapter I) which are fashioned to serve peasants, small holders at that, and which depend upon the strictly personal acquaintance of the associates.

The contributing members are selected in terms of their purely personal trustworthiness. There are three different types of organizations; in the simplest case, at the first meeting, all members except the first pay to the "first member" their contributions and the current interest on his debts, which meanwhile has perhaps accumulated through capital use. At the "second meeting" all pay for the "second member" and so forth down the line to the "last" member, who thus receives back only his contributions plus interest. The sequence of the members receiving the contributions is mostly determined by lot; if the issue is to rehabilitate a "debtor" he is, of course, the "first member," whereas donators perhaps volunteer to be the "last member." The result is that all members placed before the last one for some time have at their free disposal capital of varying amounts according to their placement.

The individual member makes contributions and pays interest toward the refunding or saving of capital. The credit association required either a certain measure of mutual supervision or precise knowledge of the members' ways of doing business. In its effects the association obviously approximated the *Raiffeisen Darlehenskassen* system. For the small holding peasant population with whom the banks did not do business the credit associations substituted mortgage credit needed to purchase land, but it could serve all conceivable ends.

In contrast to the previously described conditions of the sects (cf. "The Protestant Sects and the Spirit of Capitalism," *From Max Weber: Essays in Sociology*, Chaper XII) aside from the form, the following were characteristic of the Chinese credit association: (1) the concrete economic purpose was primary or rather exclusive; (2) in the absence of the sect's qualifying examination the individual's qualification as a possible credit-recipient had to be determined purely on an individual basis. By the way, these credit associations may indeed serve to illustrate the nature of the Greek "eranos."

41. Piety, to be sure, could also lead to consequences which the political authorities had to reject. In contrast to the mercantilist and status-motivated restriction of luxury-expenditures, especially for festive purposes, the permissible expense for funerals, in accordance with the importance of piety as the ultimate ethical yardstick, was quite horrendous to our mind.

42. In this connection see de Groot's temperamental pamphlet

"Sectarianism and religious persecution in China," *Verh. der. Kon. Ak. van Wetensch. te Amsterdam,* Afd. Letterk. N. Reeks, IV, 1, 2.

43. *Peking Gazette,* 13 January, 1874.

44. *Ibid.,* 13 April and 31 March, 1883.

45. *Ibid.,* 2 October, 1874; for a case of an insane person subjected to exorcism cf. *ibid.,* 20 August, 1878.

46. We wish to emphasize that here we give only a sketch of the relations of Confucianism and the public authorities to the sects. After having presented Buddhism we shall have to return to the sects proper, the most important of which go back to Buddhist influence. Cf. de Groot's presentation in his "Sectarianism and religious persecution in China," *loc. cit.*

47. For a multitude of reasons; see de Groot, *loc. cit.*

48. To maintain that Islamism in China had not undergone any change, as W. Grube occasionally points out, would seem to be something of an overstatement. The peculiar position of the Imams has developed since about the seventeenth century and has certainly emerged under the influence of the example given by Indian and other Far Eastern mystagogues.

49. The name is old; we recall that the Taoist church state used the same name.

50. The official documents of the T'ai P'ing Emperor were first published by the missionary Medhurst in Shanghai with a correspondingly naïve commentary in a missionary magazine. They appeared under the title *Pamphlets in and by the Chinese Insurgents of Nanking* (Shanghai, 1853). They comprised above all the "Book of the Interpretation of the Divine Will"; the "Imperial Declaration of the T'ai P'ing"; the "Book of Religious Precepts"; the "Book of Celestial Decrees"; the so-called "Trimetrical Canon"; the proclamation against the Manchus of 1852; the statutes concerning ceremonial and military organization and the new calendar, which the English man-of-war "Hermes" had brought to Shanghai. The great rebellion was often described, especially in almost all works on China. In German the popular work of C. Spillmann (Halle, 1900) may be mentioned. It is unfortunate that the best expert on the history of Chinese sects, de Groot, has declined discussing more closely the nature of the T'ai P'ing rebellion and disregards the Christian elements. These are certainly not comprehensible in the official documents of the Manchu which are the only ones he cautiously uses. De Groot, however, rates the missionary value low. Hence our presentation claims but hypothetical value.

51. It is impossible for me to check the much disputed facts.

52. Essentially upon this depended the failure at the militarily decisive moment. Without doubt, after the communications had been cut

by the occupation of the Imperial Canal and the conquest of Nanking and the whole Yangtze valley, the destiny of the repeatedly and almost crushingly beaten Peking government would have been sealed, and a completely different course of history for East Asia, at least, might not have been impossible.

53. The name of Jehova for God is found once in the official documents; otherwise, according to the count of the missionaries one finds most frequently (42%) the name of the popular God of Heaven, only half as frequently (21%) the Confucian name of Spirit of Heaven, somewhat oftener the personalist expression of *T'ien fu* or *T'ien* (33%); far less often (4%) *Shên*, which mostly means "spirit."

54. Jesus is conceived as having been married like T'ien Wang. The prophet in a vision had seen his own wife.

55. He rejected for himself the attribute of "holiness" as well as the designation of "father."

56. This was especially offensive to the missionaries. It did indeed represent a concession to tradition although officially any interpretation of the ceremony as a sacrifice to or for the ancestral spirits was rejected. The sacrifice was conceived as a sacrifice to God and, like a Christian death mass, was meant to serve the souls of the ancestors.

57. "When you have money you must make it public and not consider it as belonging to one or another." (The same holds for jewelry.) *Book of Celestial Decrees, loc. cit.*

58. The accessible reports evince strong contradictions about the details. The actual scope of state socialism remains especially obscure. To a large degree it is, of course, to be interpreted as a war economy. In the same way great caution is advisable when accepting the statements of the English missionaries. These have necessarily been used and perhaps de Groot rejects them too sharply. In their zeal the missionaries perhaps noticed more "Christian" elements than actually existed.

59. The commandment of fulfilling one's vocational duty without squinting at success should be followed because in business life, too, success is believed to depend upon fate, not upon man: "Follow your proper avocations and make yourselves easy about the rest." From the *Imperial Declaration of the Tai Ping, loc. cit.* The author refers to Confucius.

60. *Loc. cit.*

61. "In trade principally regard rectitude." "In learning be careful to live by the rule." *Ibid.*

62. The *Book of Religious Precepts* begins with the confession that no man has lived in the world without having sinned against "the commands of Heaven."

63. *Trimetrical Canon, loc. cit.*

64. Cultivation and exports of silk decreased only during the last year of the war. Previously they had increased considerably.

65. At the last moment Palmerston gave orders to support the "Manchu" no longer because of sharp attacks in the House; also because he did not wish to let the Manchus get out of their awkward situation.

66. The T'ien Wang personally and his officers practiced polygamy in the Chinese sense (concubinage).

67. *Peking Gazette,* 2 October, 1874.

68. The T'ien Wang's tent was called "the little Heaven." His rejection of attributes of holiness might very well have been disregarded by possible successors. The ceremonial prescriptions, including titularies of rank, were completely Chinese in character. There was, e.g., among others, a title of "Your Chastity" (!) for high female officials.

69. This holds unless one wishes to classify the festival days, avoidance of ornaments, etc., as asceticism. These, however, remained individual postulates.

70. This sect *(I ho ch'üan)* had emerged even at the beginning of the nineteenth century. De Groot, *Sectarianism,* p. 425.

71. This sect, indeed, believed in this invulnerability. The accessible and examined materials do not suffice for a presentation of the sect. It was constituted as an order, an "ecclesia militans," only against the foreign Barbarians. Concerning the sect see the previously cited memorial to the Empress Tz'u Hsi who, like the princes, believed in the sect's magical charisma. In the same way they believed in the magical qualities of the Krupp cannon. cf. *Peking Gazette,* 13 June, 1878. In view of these Chinese documents one is hardly permitted, in this case, to share de Groot's doubt that heretics such as the "Boxers" had been protected by a "Confucian" government. Cf. *Sectarianism,* p. 430, footnote.

VIII. Conclusions: Confucianism and Puritanism

1. In addition to the aforesaid, compare de Groot, *The Religion of the Chinese* (New York, 1910), p. 130.

2. Reprinted in Chavannes' edition, *op. cit.* vol. III, Chapter XXX.

3. See the earlier discussion of "credit associations" as weak beginnings.

4. It is crystal-clear that defects of technical and inventive genius cannot be attributed to the Chinese. The backwardness of mining (a cause of currency crises), the failure to use coal for the production of

iron (despite the alleged knowledge of the coking process), and the increasing restriction of shipping to river traffic in traditional forms and along traditional routes were not due to lack of inventiveness. *Fêng shui* (magicians) of all sorts, prebend interests—products of magic and the form of state—were the decisive factors.

5. Very good remarks about this are to be found in Ludwig Klages' writings.

GLOSSARY AND INDEX

Abaelard and Héloïse, 168

Achilles, 205

Acosmism: denial of the reality of the world opposite the sole reality and importance of God, hence devaluation of the world, 212

Ad nutum amovibel: removable at will, 32

America, 99, 250, 270

Analects, 124f.

Ancestor worship, 87, 165, 173, 213ff., 229, 230, (ancestral spirits) 143, (ancestral temple) 115

Anchoret: one who retreats from the world to live in seclusion; hermit, 178, 231

Anglican High Church, 221

Animism: belief in spirits presumably standing "behind" and determining the behavior of charismatically qualified natural objects, artifacts, animals, and men. First level of abstraction from pre-animist magical belief in extraordinary, i.e., charismatic forces, 165, 169f., 179, 194, 229

Annals, 36, 38, 41, 110, 112, 130, 140, 204

Anthropolatry: worship of men, 173, 201f., 229

Anti-chresis: a form of mortgage contract by which the mortgagee takes possession of the mortgaged property and has its fruits of profits in lieu of interest, 81

Apotheosis: deification, 173f., 193

Apotropaic: designed to ward off, 135, 196

Archery, 123, 281

Army, 25, 42, 158, 265, 269, 272, (under the Han) 75ff., (morale) 89, (officers) 117

Art, 290, (Buddhist) 8, (Chinese) 97, 151, 198, (magic) 260, (Renaissance) 151

Asceticism: methodical abstention from sleep, food, sexual gratification, etc. Weber distinguishes two main types of asceticism: the "other-worldly" asceticism of the monk and the "inner-worldly" asceticism of the Puritan who lives among the "worldly" without being of them, 186, (and Confucianism) 229, (monachal) 206, 216, (and Protestantism) 237, 247, (of T'ai P'ing) 220, 223

Assignat: inflated note issued during the French Revolution, 7, 10

Astrology, 139, 154, 167, 196f., 207, 261

Astronomy, 196

Ataraxy: peace of mind, calmness, 188

Atharva-Veda, 108

Athens, 14, 80

Augur: an official diviner of ancient Rome, 110

Baal, 23

Babylon, 196, 200, 258

Bachelor house, 24, 271, 275, 281

Beneficia: feudal estates in land, 35

Billet de géminance, 81

Boniface VIII, 26, 258

Bonze: a Buddhist monk, 200, 216, 225, 291

Boxers, 140, 223f., 296

Brahman, 126, 135, (Guru) 108

Buddhism, 152, 155f., 159, 162, 213f., 216, 224, 225, (deities) 174, 177, 205, (function) 230, (Mahayana) 195, 291, (masses for the dead) 195, (membership) 218, (monasteries) 159, 218, (and pacification of Mongols) 71, 217, (persecution of) 7, 159, 195, 216f.

Bureaucracy (under Ch'in and Han) 263f., (and law) 149f., (patrimonial) 48, 136, (and religion) 217

Burning of books, 44, 164, 201, 265

Cadi justice: administration of justice without formal rules of law. The judge considers each case on its merits with regard to persons and circumstances, 102, 149

Calendar, 108, 196, 258f.

Camorra: Italian secret society practicing extortion and violence, 193, 278

Canals, 20, 51f.

Canton, 15, 54, 55, (Cantonese school of officials) 59

Capitalism: refers to different modes of profit making. Weber distinguishes modern industrial capitalism with its rational capital accounting from various universally diffused and ancient types of political capitalism oriented to booty, fiscal, colonial, etc., profit opportunities, 12, 97, 103f., 104, 138, 149, 242, (barriers to) 199, 227, 244, (beginnings of) 231, 238, (booty) 86, 104, (bureaucracy and law) 103, 150, (industrial) 151, (petty capitalism of the Middle Ages) 20, 100, (political) 85f., 238, (rational) 85, 104, 247, (recent) 83

Capping ceremony, 24

Caravan trade, 97

Carlyle, 239

Cartels (of princes) 162, (capitalist) 62

Caste: an Indian status group whose way of life is not only legally and conventionally but also ritually sanctioned, 17, 98

Castration, 168

Casuistry: technology of dealing with moral and/or legal questions from case to case

Catholicism, 128, 212, 214f., 258, 260, 290, (papal Curia) 102

Cattle, 64, 271

Cesaro Papism: defined 30, 110f., 142

Chang Ling, 193

Chang T'ien Shih, 194

Chang Yang, 178

Chariot combat, 24f., 33, 37, 42, 158

Charisma: originally it is conceived to be a magical quality of an extraordinary person, leader, ruler who claim authority and leadership on its basis. Where leadership and group cohesion is based on the belief of the followers in the alleged, presumed, or actual extraordinariness and irreplaceability of the leader, Weber speaks of charismatic leadership, charismatic authority, etc., 30, 190, (and education) 108f., 119f., 135, (virtue of dynasty) 140, 141, 164, (hereditary): the belief in the transfer of extraordinary endowments of a religious, political, or military leader to his descendants. Weber uses also the term "gentile charisma" with reference to such families, 35, 167, 264

Charity, 209

Ch'en She, leader of army revolt, 45

Chi, Spirit of Harvest, 21

Ch'ien Lung, Emperor (1736-1799), 169

Ch'ien-shui-fa system: commutation of taxes in kind and servitudes into money taxes, 76

Ch'in, state of, 38, 42, 70, 280

Ch'in dynasty, 72, 263f.

Chinese traits (acquisitiveness 55, 243, (apolitical masses) 134, 137, (dishonesty) 231f., 234, 237, (distrust) 237, 244, (industry) 231, (internalized bondage of officialdom) 59, (money mindedness) 125, 242, (outer not inner directed personality) 232, 235, (pacifist mentality) 114, 250, (personalism, see below) 209, (thrift) 208, 230, 245

Chou dynasty, 22, 32, 35

Chou Li, 32, 34, 37, 116

Chrematistic: pertaining to the acquisition of wealth, 159

Christendom, 126, 177, 209, (and T'ai P'ing) 219f., 222, 225, (missionary) 219, 229, 295

Christianity (persecution of) 218f.

Chronomantics: magical belief and practice oriented to "fortunate" and "unfortunate" hours and times, 196ff.

Chthonian: in or under the earth, (chthonian mythologies) 26, (chthonian cults) 25, 27

Chuang-tzu, 167, 178, 189, 190, 205

Chu Fu-tzu, atheist materialist, 12th century, 23, 145

Chu-fu-Yen, 46

Chu hou, the princes, 35

Chu Hsi, author of the *Chung Lun*, 166

Chün tzu, gentleman, 24, 25, 46, 131ff., 183f., 228, 244

City: a dense settlement of a large number of households without mutual acquaintance of the inhabitants. Regular exchange of goods in a local market is essential for their economic life, 13ff., 16

Cleisthenes, 14

Club associations (hui) 99, 293

Compagna Communis of Genoa, 14

Competition (among officials) 59, 151, (among philosophical schools) 165, (interstate) 41, 61f., 103

Concubines, 162, see Women and Harem

Confucianism (*ju chiao*) 29, 144, 152ff., 167f., 213, (cardinal virtues of) 190, 228, (equality of men) 146, (ethics) 227, 236, (functions of) 235, (religious indifference) 146, 156, (spirit of) 203, (and traditionalism) 200

Confucians (and magic) 194, 200f., (typical life orientation) 247, (vs. Wang An-shih) 77

Confucius (551-478 B.C.) 28, 46, 25, 112, 113ff., 143, 154ff., 161f., 163, 168, 169, (canonization) 174, (and Lao-tzu) 184, 189f., 207

Coniuratio, 14

Copper, 3ff.

Corporal punishment, see Sanctions

Cortegiano, courtier, 131

Corvée: servitudes, taxes in the form of forced labor (see below) 38, 51ff., 73

Cosmogony: speculation about the origin of the world, 154, 199f.

Cromwell, 147, 221, 222

Dalai Lama: Pontiff of Lamaism, resident in Lhasa, Tibet, since the sixteenth century, 45

De Groot, 165, 189, 197, 213, 217

Deities, 29, 115, 143, 174f., 177, 196, 201, 204, 214, 217, 259

Democracy, 96

D'Este, Renate, 241

Deutero Isaiah, 21

Dharma: legal and moral rules regulating the way of life of Hindu castes in India. Each caste has its special *dharma*, 152

Dies fasti et nefasti: religiously sanctioned days for legal and public business in Rome, 109, ›197

Discipline, 158

Disenchantment of the world, 226
Douceur: tip or bribe, 17

Economic determinism, 25, 61, 196, 203f., 224, 237f.
Ecstasy (apathetic) 181, 206, 233, (emotional) 206
Edicts, 195, (Sacred) 215
Education, 46, (Chinese) 153, 187, 206, 228, 230, 246, (in Germany) 120f., 246, (Hellenic) 122, 246, (types of) 119ff., (Vedic) 108
Egypt, 3, 16, 20ff., 24f., 37, 51, 88, 98, 135, 144, 157, 169, 234, 242
Empathy: to feel as the other does, 186
Emperor, 25, 30ff., 132, 143, 145, 147, 153, 165, 185, 187, 190, 200, 211, 212, 262
Empire (Chinese) 61, 102, 114, 137, (Holy Roman) 26, (Roman) 102, 103, 214f.
England, 51, 63, 137, 211
Ephebe: a Greek youth entering manhood, 122
Equality, 146
Eschatology: teaching of last or final things for individual or world, e.g., judgment day, day of Yahwe, millennium, etc., 145
Esoterics: designed for and understood by select circle of initiates, (Confucian) 206f.
Ethics, 31, 204, 236, (acculturated) 234f., (of capitalist entrepreneur) 247, (Confucian) 229, (Puritan) 247f., (social) 209
Eucharist: a consecrated meal of a religious community, for instance, the Lord's Supper, (tea eucharist) 220
Eunuch, 44, 46, 138f., 140, 194, 203, 266, 285f., 291f., (and Taoism) 195
Euphoria: state of emotional exaltation, 182
Europe (the great historical exception) 61

Examinations, 282, (candidates) 163, (degrees) 129, (economic function of) 86, 117, (finance of) 134, (origin) 116, (popular image of) 128, 135, (privileges) 117, (Taoist) 202f.
Exorcist (from Tibet) 214
Experiment, 150ff.
Exploitation (magical checks upon) 83

Faust, 229
Fêng-shui, 199, 214, 217, 276, 297
Fetishism: belief in objects supposed to have magical power, 174
Feudalism: political structure based upon grants or land or prebends for military and/or administrative services; Weber distinguishes accordingly between two types of feudalism, one primarily based on fiefs, the other on prebends. The latter type is also called "prebendalism," 32, 114, 193
Feudal vassals, 47, 83, (hero) 24f., (hierarchy and fiefs) 37f.
Fiscalism, 88
Francke, Otto, 27, 250
Franklin, Benjamin, 244
Friendship, 162

Gabelle: salt tax, 54, 268
Gentes: sibs, (state of the Gentes) 36
Geomancer: practitioner of geomancy, i.e., divination by means of contours of mountains, shapes of trees, rivers, etc., 195, 198, 199, 214
Gilda mercatoria, merchant guild in England, 14
Gold (i) 4ff., 238
Gracchi, 68
Great Wall, 26, 51, 266
Green sprout measure of 1069, 77
Grube, W., 193, 234
Guild (of artisans) especially 14ff., 17ff., (of bankers) 11, 18, (Co-

hong guild in Canton) 19, 285, (goldbeaters guild of Wenchow) 17, (*hui-kuan* guilds) 18, (*kung so*, local craft and merchant guild) 18, 137, 210, (opium guild) 18

Guru: teacher, spiritual adviser, father confessor, 135

Han dynasty, 208 B.C.-220 A.D., 36, 45, 53, 59, 116, 131, 164, 169, 193, 263f., (inscriptions) 167

Handicraft, 19, 98

Hanlin Yüan (Academy) 117, 140

Hansa: Hanseatic League, a medieval league of German merchant guilds and trading cities, 17f.

Hantgemal, 14

Harem, 138, 162, 195, 203, 222, 259

Hart, Sir Robert, 1835-1911, Administrator in the Chinese service 1863-1907, 54

Heaven, 26, 28f., 153, 166, 174, 193, 259, 276, 292, (god of) 201, (hosts of) 201, (Son of) 31, 128, 212

Hellenic man, 228f., 247

Heresy, 213ff.

Heroism, 168, 207

Herolatric belief, hero worship, 229

Heterodoxy: belief deviating from official standard (Orthodoxy), heretical opinion, 199, 213

Heu tun, Emperor, 70

Hierocracy: priestly rule or influence by means of ministering or withholding grace, 142, 202, 213

Homer, 175, 205

Honor (feudal) 130, 157, 168, 176, (Confucian sense of) 208

Hoplite: heavily armed footsoldier of Greek Antiquity, 122

Hsiao (piety) defined 130, 157

Hsiao Hsüeh schoolbook, 123, 125, 134

Hsiung Nu, the Huns, 7

Hsü Hsing, 166

Hsün-tzu, 166

Hui, religious fraternities, 19, 99

I Li, 191

India, 100, (army) 272, (education) 111, (monasteries) 192, 224, (sib) 34, (unclean occupations) 98

Indoctrination, 214

Intaglio: an incised design on stone or the like, depressed below the surface of the material so that an impression from it yields an image in relief

Intellectuals, 173, 228, 230

Islam, Islamism, 100, 126, 134, 156, 161, 212, 219, 234, 242, (Chinese) 218, 294

Japan, 36, 120, 225

Jen Yen, 168

Jesuits, 139, 154, 221f.

Judaism, 23f., 113f., 121, 126, 155, 221, 281, (in China) 218

K'ang Hsi, Emperor (1662-1722), author of the "Sacred Edict," 23, 145, 195

K'ang Yu-wei (1858-1927), reformer

Kohler, J. F., 101

Kshatriya (India) 111

Kuan Chung, 190

Kuang Wu, Emperor, 117

Kublai Khan, 10

Kuei, evil (harmful) spirits, 28, 131

Labor (apprentice) 98, (class) 98, (forced) 5, 51f., 71, 74, 216, 220, 238, 269, (handicraft) 83, 90, 247, (sib and tribal crafts) 17, 19, (despised skills) 98, 116, (market selection of) 95

Lamaism, 217, 218

Land (distribution) 72ff., 147, (holdings) 71, 74, (landlordism) 64f., 73, 81ff., 86, 272, 274f., (obligatory tillage) 71, (prebends) 36, (reclamation) 52, 269, (registration) 80, 267

Landlordism, 85f., 89

Language, 123ff., (and script) 279, (and speech) 127, 246

Lao-tzu, 155, 162, 177, 178f., 181ff., 191f., 201, 204

Law (*fa*) 16, 17, (and capitalism) 150, (codification) 80, 101, (irrationality of Chinese) 169, (natural) 149, 210, (Roman) 81, (of real property) 80

Legge, James, 124

Leonardo, 151

Levelling tendency, 83

Lex agraria of Antiquity (111 b.c.): Roman agrarian law opening the *ager publicus* for private appropriation and investment, 73

Liberty, 147

Li Chi, 116, 212

Li Hung-chang, 132, 268, 270

Li Pang, founder of Han dynasty, 45

Li Ssu, migrant scholar-statesman, legalist, chief adviser to Shi Huang Ti, 164, 266

Literati, 41, 44, 68, 107ff., 178, 194

Literature, 95, 107f., 114, 123ff., 164, (poetry) 52, 75, 132, 212, (popular drama) 135, 159

Liturgical closure of occupations: barring entrance into occupational groups and holding them responsible for public services and/or financial contributions, 98

Liturgy: public expenditure defrayed by wealthy citizens out of their private fortunes. Weber classifies states according as to whether state finance is based upon tax collection or liturgies, (liturgy state) 74f.

Lung-hua sect, 223

Lu Ssu, 194

Lu, state of, 161

Machiavellism, 41

Macrobiotics: striving for long life by magical means, 181, 191f., 196, 204

Magic, defined, 185, 191f., 204, 260f., (image of the world) 196ff., (and Puritanism) 226f., (reality of)

155, (of script) 135, (and tradition) 240

Manchesterism, *laissez faire* individualism, 188

Manchu (dynasty) 11, 54, 71f., 141, 152, 194, 195, (garrison) 273f., (officials) 267, 281

Mandarin, Chinese official, 49f., 116, 135, 198

Mantic: of or pertaining to divination, 217

Marco Polo, 10

Massa perditionis: the mass of the lost ones (or condemned) 239

Masses (religious needs of) 173, 202, 204, 208, 217, 229, 230, 235

Matriarchy, 24

Ma Tuan-lin, thirteenth century scholar who compiled the *Wen Shien T'ung K'ao*. This work contains a wealth of information on government, population data, etc., 5, 254

Medicine, 197

Meng Tzu, Mencius, social philosopher, 20, 52, 115, 124, 166, 184, 210, 214, 236

Mercantilism: system of economic policies of European despotism especially from the sixteenth to the eighteenth century

Mesopotamia, 20, 25, 88

Middle Realm, 33

Milk consumption, 64, 271

Ming dynasty, 10f., 146, 195, 284

Mir: old Russian village commune based on periodical redistribution of land by apportioning it to each "soul" not to each household as a unit of production, 88

Mjestnitshestvo: Muscovite principle of basing social rank upon the Czar's grant of military or administrative office. The Czar compensated the officeholder with a fief. The nobles thus were made to compete for offices and court favors. They failed to develop into a cohesive status group with common interests in the face of the autocratic ruler, 36, 116

Mobility (of intellectuals) 111, (interstate mobility of nobles) 5, 26, 54, (mental) 112, (of officials) 58f., (residential) 89, 100

Moira, defined, 207, "The Fates, Daughters of Necessity," (Plato, *Republic* X)

Mongols, 7, 10, 26, 52, 68, 114, 217

Montaigne, 207

Moscow, 13

Mo Ti (Mocius) 162, 166, 210

Mou: one *mou* equals 733⅓ square yards; 6.6 *mou* equal 1 acre, 69

Music, 28, 123, 145, 151, 189f., 209, (musicians) 116

Mystagogue: leader of mystery cult, 215, 223

Mysteria: medieval religious dramas based on Bible, 19

Mystery: a secret religious rite (Eleusian) 204, (Hellenic) 225

Mysticism, 179ff., 181, 187, 202, 212, 213, (contemplative) 183, Sufist: a system of Mohammedan mysticism. It originated during the eighth century, its symbolic elaboration inspired poetry; ecstasy and contemplation served the end of gaining union with and insight into the Divine Being, 212

Mythras mysteries, 225

Nadjel: the right of each "soul" to his share in the Russian village land, 71, 272

Narses, 140

Negro Empires, 33

Notables, 83

Officials, officialdom, 47ff., 50, 138, 268, (age of) 37, (charisma of) 32, 101, 128, (cliques within hierarchy) 59, (competition) 59, (and education) 122, (insecurity of individual officials) 58f., 210,

(levelling function of) 83, (low density) 134, 267, (mobility of) 48f., 59, (prestige of) 101, (privileges of) 129, (salary of) 12, 56ff., 158, (unofficial aids) 49f., 101

Oikos: organization of specialized unfree labor in large domestic workshops of Lords. Production for private and/or political needs of Lords, 53, 97

Old age, 135, 178

Orgiasticism: pursuit of ecstasy through intoxicants, dance, music, etc., 27f., 230, 232, (and Confucianism) 209

Orphic: pertaining to Orpheus or the mysteries, or secret rites of the Dionysus cult ascribed to Orpheus, 224, 225, 229

Ossification, 61

Pacifism, Pacification, 25, 61, 103, 114, 169, (of literati) 140

P'an Ku (god of Heaven) 193

Pao Chi, 70

Paradigm: A model or pattern, 113

Paradox of unintended consequences, 238

Patriarchialism: Hereditary domestic authority of the family head who demands personal obedience from the group members in the name of sacred traditions, 32, 37, 264, (and landlordism) 82

Patrimonialism: Type of traditional authority. Patriarchial rule implemented with an administrative staff, 45, 47, 56ff., 61, 133, 136, 137, 138, 164, 176, 213, (and ethics) 234

Peasant, 36, 45, 52, 64f., 83, 162, (and Bolshevism) 94, (tradition in Spain) 234

Pennalism: Student rowdyism at German universities, 129

Pentatonic music: is based on a scale dividing an octave into five tones. The five black keys of the piano, e.g., would represent such a scale. A Chinese tradition ascribes its calculative fixation to the third millennium B.C., 145

Peripety: A change from one state of things within a play to its opposite (Aristotle, *Poetics*); a turning point, 207

Persecution, 214, 223

Personalism: Dealing with others and with affairs in terms of primary group contacts, 209, 223, 236f.

Petty bourgeois mass, 12

Philosophy, 127, 153, 165ff., (Greek) 175f.

Piety, filial: Basic for belief in patriarchical domestic authority internalized during childhood through dependence on primary domestic group. "Paternal authority and filial piety are not primarily based upon actual blood ties, however normal they may be" (Weber, Max, *Wirtschaft und Gesellschaft*, p. 680), 123, 158, 163f., 167, 212, 213, 232, 236, 241

Plato, 122, 160f., 175, 233

Pneuma: (Greek) term of "spirit," especially used in the New Testament, 186

Police, 21, 91, 93f., 214

Polis: City state of Antiquity, 13, 15, 80, 107, 152, 175f.

Pontifex: (Latin) priest, 132, 142, 220

Population, 41, (growth) 54f., (census) 56, 76, (policy) 79f.

Porcelain, 5, 269

Praefecti praetorio: The two commanders of the Imperial guards, 43

Praeter legem-contra legem: Because of the law—against the law, 88

Prayer, 142, 286ff.

Prebend: Right of an officeholder to yields from state or church lands or from other public income. Weber terms such officeholders "prebendaries." A political social system based upon a staff of prebendaries Weber calls "prebendalism," 36, 56, 58, 59, 138, (Buddhist) 195, (goal of apsiration) 126, (for students) 117, (Taoist) 195f.

Priesthood: A special circle of cult leaders officiating at regular recurrent times at fixed places according to definite norms on behalf of religious communities worshipping God or gods, 142, 177, 194f., 201, 204

Property (private) 73f., 80, 147

Prophecy, 23, 110, 142, 202, 209, 219, 223, 229f., 235

Propriety (*Li*) 114, 127, 156f., 162f., 183, 228, 234

Prussian *Kulturkampf:* Bismarck's conflict with the catholic church in the 1870's

Puritanism, 161f., 206, 208, 226, 232, 238, (inner directed personality) 240, 244, 247, (one price system) 99, (trust) 241, 244

Qui trompe t'on? who cheats whom? Adage which according to Bismarck characterized trade, 234

Rational: 1. not magical, 2. logically consistent, 3. systematically ordered, 4. in agreement with scientific rules of evidence, 30, 240

Rationalism (bureaucratic) 95, 142f., 178, 207, (economic) 247f., (limits to) 164, (Protestant and Confucian) 226, 241f.

Rationalization (administrative) 37, 45f., 61f., (barriers to) 236f., (and bureaucracy) 151f., (fiscal) 13, (of law) 149, 150, (of magic) 196f., (of popular belief) 144, (in science) 150f., (economic) 62, (and war) 103f.

Reforms, 60, 68, 134

Regalia: Kingly prerogatives, 5, (mining and minting) 51, 65

Renaissance, 151, 237, 247

Rentier mentality, 61

Repression (Puritan and Confucian) 244

Revolution, rebellion, 60, 61f., (T'ai P'ing) 219ff., (Western) 14, 62, (yellow kerchiefs) 193

Rig-Veda, 108

Ritualism, rites, 107f., 167, 202, 222, 223, 270, 276

River control, 20, 64, (Huang Ho) 206

Rome, Roman (Empire) 5, 214f., (law) 148, 150, (nobility) 36, 146, 181

Ruach: The "spirit"; "breast of life"; in the Old Testament especially in connection with the spirit of God, 22

Salvation (Christian) 210, (and Confucianism) 156, 228, (religions) 224, 227, 229, 233, (and Taoism) 177f., 185

Sanctions, 102, 117, 129, 170, 262, 276, 288f., (caning) 99, 129, 210

Satrap: Governor of a satrapy, a province of ancient Persia, 48, 56

Schools, 117, 126, 129f.

Secret and secret society, 86, 133, 195

Sects, 218f., 223f.

Self-government, 16f., 91, 95

Serfdom, 66f.

Sexagenarios de ponte: Roman elders, rule of elders, 112

Shang Ti, Emperor, 70

Shang Ti, spirit of Heaven, 22

Shang Yang, scholar statesman, 41f., 70, 280

She, spirit of fertile soil, 21

She-chi, dual god of the peasantry, 21f.

Shen, good (useful) spirits, 28, 131

Shen Tsung, Emperor, 70

Shih Ching (hymn book) 81, 113, 163, 220, 231

Shih Huang Ti: Born 259 B.C., Unifier of China, called himself "The First Emperor." He crushed feudalism and established a new model state, 4, 36, 44, 45, 51, 54, 64, 65, 67, 68, 71, 73, 139, 164, 167, 169, 178, 179, 191, 196, 197, 204, 266f.

Shu Ching, 35, 157, 165, 190

Shun, Emperor, 114

Sib, 17, 33, 71, 86ff., 277, (cohesion) 71, 88f., 242, (elders) 89, (emergence of) 272, (and education) 129f., (feuds) 89, (Indian) 34, (holdings) 82, (leadership) 193, (noble) 146, (old age) 135, (property) 89, (sanctions) 88

Silk, 5, 37, 71, 72, 97, 269

Silver, 3ff., 18

Sin, 228f., 235

Slavery, 98, 218

Socialism, 71, 211f., 295

Son of Heaven, see Heaven

Sophrosyne: Good sense resulting from intellectual discipline and self control, 233

Sorcerer, 30, 108, 119, 203

Sordida munera (sordid labor) 129

Soteriology: Religious teaching of salvation and a redeemer, 177, 223, 225

Specialization, 138, 160

Squeeze, 83

Ssu-ma Ch'ien (145-85 B.C.), Confucian historian, 28, 163, 166ff., 194, 237, 285

Status group: Comprises people enjoying the same amount of the same kind of deference, respect, or prestige. This prestige position may rest on differences in political or sacerdotal power, education, wealth, military function, etc., (feudal) 34, (levelling) 44, (religion) 206, (stratification) 99, 117, 119, 129, 137, 146

Stoicism (Chinese) 41, (Confucian) 149, 207, (Roman) 176f.
Successorship, 44, 114, 262
Suicide, 88, 140, 169f., 208, 210, 276
Sultanism: Extreme form of Patrimonialism, maximizing autocratic absolutism of the ruler, backed by bodyguard, aided by upstart favorites (eunuchs) 44, 138, 195
Sung dynasty, 59, 70, 76
Sung K'eng, 166
Su Wen, 198
Synoecism: Process of settling in a city. The Hellenic term refers to the founding of cities by noble families, 3

Tacitus, 176
Tael: A Chinese money of account
T'ai P'ing rebellions, 11, 19, 27, 54, 193, 219ff., 294
Tang dynasty (618 A.D.-904 A.D.), 65, 73, 116, 117
Tao, Taoism, Taoists, defined, 181/2; 8, 27f., 46, 142, 152, 155, 167, 181f., 185, 187, 190, 192, 194ff., 200ff., 217, 228
Tao Mo, 140
Tao-shih, 192f.
Tao Teh Ching, 180, 185, 188, 190, 290f.
Taxes, 47, 51, 64, 269f., (collection of) 234, (joint liability) 68, (and land measurement) 68f., (land tax) 53, 56, 79, 274, (systems of) 69f., (tax farming) 85
Tea, 5, 97, 220
Temples, 22, 92f., 194
Thaumaturgist: A miracle worker, a magician, 195
Theatre, 18, 19, 159
Theocracy: Government of a state by experts in divinity
Theodicy, 206
T'ien Wang, 219
Tolstoy, 96
Totemism, 258, 272
Traders, 196, 234

Traditionalism, 49, 95, 138, (and literature) 164, 205, (and monetary reform) 6, (and money economy) 60f., 83, (and patrimonial state) 61, 100
Tsui shui, 167
Tz'u Hsi, Empress-Dowager, (? - 1908), 132, 140, 194, 203, 261f., 296
Tzu Ssu, 189, 190

Utilitarianism, 187, 241f.

Vanaprastha: Brahmanic hermit, 178
Village, 91, (commons) 65, (elders) 87
Virgin Mother, 222

Wang An-shih, scholar and statesman (1021 A.D.-1085 A.D.), 47, 70, 77, 93, 136f., 138, 154, 266
Wang Ch'ung, scholar (first century A.D.), (conception of god) 22, 144f.
Wang Mang, Regent and Emperor from 1 A.D.-23 A.D., 7, 65, 140
War dance, 27, 123
Warfare, 24f., 37, 40f., 103, 140, (and finance) 68, 136, 138, (and rationalization) 61f., 111, see army
Warring States, 43, 62, 107, 125, 152, 165, 190, 238, 265
Wealth, 53, 147, 158f., 167, 196, 204, 213, 237, 238, 246, (god of) 242
Wei dynasty, 80
Wei, General, 193
Wei Yang, 41
Well system, 72, 272f.
Wen Ti, Emperor, 7, 138
Wesley, John, 245
White Lotos, 195
Women, 89, 162, 203, 224, 296, (magicians) 197, (under T'ai P'ing) 220, 221, (widows) 89
Work discipline, 95
Wrath (ch'i) 168, 233, 240
Wu Ko-tu, 140

Wu Ti, Emperor, 4, 46
Wu Tsung, Emperor, 159
Wu-wei, defined, 180ff.

Yahwe, 23, 27, 155, 260
Yamen: Board, council, committee, 48, 59
Yang Chu, 166
Yao, Emperor, 114

Yin and Yang, 29, 131, 162, 202
Yü, Emperor, 51, 114
Yü min (stupid people) 146
Yuan Ti, 7

Zarlino, Gioseffo (1517-1590) Italian musical theorist, musician and composer, 151
Zeus Erkeios, 14, 22

Law 148-149

Econ — 158

Virtue — 162